ENCYCLOPAEDIA OF
NANO COMPUTERS

ENCYCLOPAEDIA OF
NANO COMPUTERS

Thomas Watts

ANMOL PUBLICATIONS PVT. LTD.
NEW DELHI - 110 002 (INDIA)

ANMOL PUBLICATIONS PVT. LTD.
H.O.: 4374/4B, Ansari Road, Darya Ganj,
New Delhi-110 002 (India)
Ph.: 23278000, 23261597

B.O.: No. 1015, Ist Main Road, BSK IIIrd Stage
IIIrd Phase, IIIrd Block,
Bangalore - 560 085 (India)
Visit us at: www.anmolpublications.com

Encyclopaedia of Nano Computers

First Published, 2006

ISBN 81-261-2979-4

PRINTED IN INDIA

Printed at Mehra Offset Press, Delhi.

Contents

Preface

This book entitled “Encyclopaedia of Nano Computers“ deals with the subject areas of computing, nanotechnology and use of formation processing at the nanoscale. There are so many other applications of nano computers ranging from mundane to incredibly profound. Other applications include energy storage materials, photovoltaic cells, fuel cells, polymer nanocomposites, super-tough nanocoatings, landmine detectors, and thousands more. Although it is a field that has already seen its share of hype, there is a general consensus that over the long term, nano computer is likely to reconfigure everything. Nanostructured materials do not represent a new phenomenon. However, the ability to probe, manipulate, understand and engineer matter at atomic scales has only recently come within our grasp. Developments such as the invention of the Scanning Tunneling Microscope in 1981 have since made nanoscale science a reality. Today, the term nanotechnology is used to describe specific construction and manipulation performed on an atomic and molecular scale. Generally, systems with a maximum size of less than a hundred nanometers are classified as nanotechnology. Nanotechnology is a completely new production process in a molecular world, opening up possibilities far beyond what we have known before.

Experts world over believe nanotechnology will have a more far-reaching impact than the silicon integrated chip with many more applications than electronics. Nanotechnology is expected to revolutionize certain areas, such as semiconductors, pharmaceuticals and materials. The total societal impact of nanotechnology is expected to be much greater than that of the silicon integrated circuit because it is applicable in many more fields than electronics. Nanotechnology experts believe that because of nano chemistry, we would see more changes in the next 30 years than we saw in the entire last century. This book tends to cover the aforementioned subject areas in their broadest possible terms. All useful supplementary research and reference tools have been included for readers' further investigations in the subject area of Nano chemistry. This book mainly focuses on the following areas: Nanotechnology; Nanoparticles, Nanomaterials and Nanostructures. This book seeks to explain this complex field of study. It also seeks to provide an understanding of what is happening now in the field of nano chemistry, as well as what to expect in future by generations to come.

—Editor

1

Advances in Nano Technology & Nano Computers

Even though popular conceptions of nanotechnology are not always clear or well defined, one thing is certain — it will have a significant impact on science and technology in the near future. According to the National Science Foundation, funding available through its nanotechnology initiative will increase to more than $1 billion within five years. Researchers at the URI College of Engineering and beyond are helping drive advances in nanotechnology. Some examples of the nanotechnology research underway at URI include:

Dr. William Euler, professor of chemistry, is working with the Sensors and Surface Technology Partnership to use carbon nanotubes for device applications. In collaboration with scientists from Emitech, Inc., the researchers have fabricated near-infrared photoconductors and electromechanical actuators using carbon nanotubes as the critical, active component. In particular, the actuators rely upon the high-surface area and unique properties of the nanotubes to power devices that work under low voltage and low power conditions. These devices are expected to be used in anti-viion systems or microfluidic applications. Dr. Arun Shukla, professor of mechanical engineering, has recently fabricated polyester/TiO2 nanocomposites and has initiated an investigation to characterize their dynamic fracture constitutive behavior. A relationship between dynamic stress intensity factor, KI, and crack tip velocity has been established. As well, the behavior of the nanocomposites has been compared with that of the virgin polyester matrix. Fractographic analysis has been conducted to correlate fracture surface characteristics to experimental values. Crack propagation velocities in nanocomposites were found to be 50% greater than those in polyester. Crack-arrest toughness in the nanocomposites was 60% greater than in polyester. Dr. Otto Gregory and his research team have developed a nanocomposite coating that has proven to be effective in extending the lifetime and performance of TBCs (thermal barrier coatings). TBCs are used extensively in the aircraft engine and power-generation industry to protect turbine components from the high gas temperatures encountered during operation. TBCs usually employ a bond coat for adhesion and a ceramic overcoat for thermal protection. These coatings are typically applied by thermal spray techniques. However, the difference in thermal expansion between these materials ultimately leads to delamination/decohesion failure at the interface. The metallic bond coat is very rough in the as-sprayed condition, and tends to exaggerate the stresses due to the mismatch in thermal expansion. A nanocomposite coating with an intermediate thermal expansion coefficient was effective in reducing the mismatch between the NiCoCrAlY bond coat and the alumina overcoat. This relatively thin coating effectively reduced the interfacial stresses derived from heating and cooling cycles and substantially increased the thermal fatigue life of TBC's. The nanometer dimensions of the particles comprising the intermediate coating proved effective in-filling the valleys of the rough conformation at the bond coat / topcoat interface. The thermal fatigue life of TBC's using this optimized TCE nanocomposite coating was increased by more than a factor of four.

Dr. Arijit Bose is working on "soap-like" molecules, called surfactants, that have a dual characteristic (a part of the molecule likes a solvent, and the other dislikes it). When added to water, these molecules tend to self-assemble into many interesting aggregate morphologies that balance the molecules' tendency to stay dispersed (entropy) with its penchant for protecting its hydrophobic entities from water (enthalpy). These aggregates are nanometers in dimension, and range from spheres, cylinders, vesicles and liquid crystalline gels. Visualization of these microstructures is essential if they are to be exploited for any applications, yet this is a challenge because of their size (2-100nm), and because any vacuum-based technique will cause solvent evaporation and irreversibly destroy the aggregate. One part of the research is focused on imaging these microstructures using special techniques such cryogenic transmission electron microscopy and freeze fracture direct imaging (URI is the second in the world to develop this), as well as light and small angle neutron scattering. Once the microstructures have been determined, they are used as templates for materials synthesis. In particular, the team has looked at a gel phase formed by adding two surfactants into a mixture of oil and water, and discovered that it contains nanochannels of water dispersed along with oil nanochannels. The nanochannel network of aqueous and organic phases has been exploited for templated synthesis of macroporous silica using hydrolysis of tetraethoxysilane and for the formation of polystyrene and polymethylmethacralate by free radical polymerization. SANS has revealed that the surfactant template is robust, being retained during silica synthesis as well as polymerization. The highly viscous aqueous/organic phase for forming nanocomposites where inorganic nanoparticles are homogeneously distributed without agglomeration within a polymer matrix. These materials have several applications, including multifunctional membranes, high-strength transparent coatings, and as drug delivery vehicles.

Dr. Michael Greenfield is leading a research group that is studying how changes in the molecular architecture impact the structure and arrangements of polymer chains and fluid molecules over nanometer length scales, with a particular interest in the effects of small to moderate molecular weight additives. In a project supported by Ford Motor Company, positions of ultraviolet absorber molecules – protective ingredients that prevent automotive paint photodegradation – within nanoscale free volume holes are calculated using a geometric computational analysis of configurations taken from molecular simulations. Preliminary results suggest that subtle differences in chain-UVA nanopacking could exert large effects on macroscale UV absorption efficiency, with implications for the design and selection of UVA/polymer combinations.

First, where hardware is concerned, natural law sets limits to the possible. Because *assemblers* will open a path to those limits, understanding assemblers is a key to understanding what is possible.

Second, the principles of change and the facts of our present situation set limits to the achievable. Because evolving replicators will play a basic role, the principles of *evolution* are a key to understanding what will be achievable. As for what is desirable or undesirable, our differing dreams spur a quest for a future with room for diversity, while our shared fears spur a quest for a future of safety.

These three questions—of the possible, the achievable, and the desirable—frame an approach to foresight. First, scientific and *engineering* knowledge form a map of the limits of the possible. Though still blurred and incomplete, this map outlines the permanent limits within which the future must move. Second, evolutionary principles determine what paths lie open, and set limits to achievement—including lower limits, because advances that promise to improve life or to further military power will be virtually unstoppable. This allows a limited prediction: If the eons-old evolutionary race does not somehow screech to a halt, then competitive pressures will mold our technological future to the contours of the limits of the possible. Finally, within the broad confines of the possible and the achievable, we can try to reach a future we find desirable.

But how can anyone predict the future? Political and economic trends are notoriously fickle, and sheer chance rolls dice across continents. Even the comparatively steady advance of technology often eludes prediction. Prognosticators often guess at the times and costs required to harness new technologies. When they reach beyond outlining possibilities and attempt accurate predictions, they generally fail. For example, though the space shuttle was clearly possible, predictions of its cost and initial launch date were wrong by several years and billions of dollars. Engineers cannot accurately predict when a technology will be developed, because development always involves uncertainties.

But we have to try to predict and guide development. Will we develop monster technologies before cage technologies, or after? Some monsters, once loosed, cannot be caged. To survive, we must keep control by speeding some developments and slowing others.

Though one technology can sometimes block the dangers of another (defense vs. offense, pollution controls vs. pollution), competing technologies often go in the same direction. On December 29, 1959, *Richard Feynman (now a Nobel laureate) gave a talk* at an annual meeting of the American Physical Society entitled "There's Plenty of Room at the Bottom." He described a non-biochemical approach to nanomachinery (working down, step by step, using larger machines to build smaller machines), and stated that the principles of physics do not speak against the possibility of maneuvering things *atom* by atom. It is not an attempt to violate any laws; it is something, in principle, that can be done; but, in practice, it has not been done because we are too big.... Ultimately, we can do chemical synthesis.... put the atoms down where the chemist says, and so you make the substance." In brief, he sketched another, nonbiochemical path to the assembler. He also stated, even then, that it is "a development which I think cannot be avoided." Assemblers and intelligent machines will simplify many questions regarding the time and cost of technological developments. But questions of time and cost will still muddy our view of the period between the present and these breakthroughs.

Richard Feynman saw in 1959 that nanomachines could direct chemical synthesis, presumably including the synthesis of *DNA*. Yet he could foresee neither the time nor the cost of doing so.

In fact, of course, biochemists developed techniques for making DNA without programmable nanomachines, using shortcuts based on specific chemical tricks. Winning technologies often succeed because of unobvious tricks and details. In the mid-1950s physicists could see that basic semiconductor principles made microcircuits physically possible, but foreseeing how they would be made—foreseeing the details of mask-making, resists, oxide growth, *ion* implantation, etching, and so forth, in all their complexity—would have been impossible. The nuances of detail and competitive advantage that select winning technologies make the technology race complex and its path unpredictable.

But does this make long-term forecasting futile? In a race toward the limits set by natural law, the finish line is predictable even if the path and the pace of the runners are not. Not human whims but the unchanging laws of nature draw the line between what is physically possible and what is not—no political act, no social movement can change the law of gravity one whit. So however futuristic they may seem, sound projections of technological possibilities are quite distinct from predictions. They rest on timeless laws of nature, not on the vagaries of events.

It is unfortunate that this insight remains rare. Without it, we stumble in a daze across the landscape of the possible, confusing mountains with mirages and discounting both. We look ahead with minds and cultures rooted in the ideas of more sluggish times, when both science and technological competition lacked their present strength and speed. We have only recently begun to evolve a tradition of technological foresight.

Drexler-Smalley Debate on Nanotechnology

Many debates about nanotechnology emerge from particular visions of the field. We find, for example, visions of a future dramatically changed by the new technology, with the production of materials and objects with atomic precision in a remarkably short time by self-replicating nanobots (Drexler 1986); but we also find the fear that nanotechnology will quickly run out of control, leaving us powerless behind (Joy 2000). As with most extreme views, it is unlikely that any of these scenarios is completely correct. However, particularly in less radical forms, they may capture something right about certain developments of the field.

In this study, we examine a recent debate in nanotechnology, which was also motivated by different visions of the field. But, in this case, the different visions involved distinct ways of conceptualizing what is (and is not) feasible in the area, and even alternative standards of assessment of such feasibility judgments. In the debate, we find all the interesting features of scientific debates more generally: curious arguments (and often not unproblematic ones), powerful images, unexpected conceptual shifts, the use of diverse standards, and a good bit of rhetoric. What emerges from the exchange examined here is an interesting perspective on how scientific debates can be conducted and interpreted – and why, sometimes, it is so hard to settle them. Nanotechnology, even at the metalevel, never stops to be intriguing. The debate involves two significant characters. On the one hand, we have Eric Drexler, one of the visionaries of nanotechnology. He clearly conceived of a world completely transformed by the developments in the area. A crucial component of his view takes central stage in the exchange below: the notion of a *molecular assembler*. According to Drexler, such an assembler would be able to build virtually anything with atomic precision and no pollution. His vision was first presented in the 1980s, in *Engines of Creation* (Drexler 1986), with the more technical details articulated later in the early 1990s, in *Nanosystems* (Drexler 1992). Drexler is the chairman and cofounder of the Foresight Institute, an institution that aims to help prepare society for advances in technology, with particular emphasis on nanotechnology. Drexler's main background is in engineering, and as we will see, it is from the perspective of an engineer that he approaches nanotechnology. As will become clear below, this explains important features of his vision of the field.

On the other hand, we have Richard Smalley. University Professor of chemistry, physics, and astronomy at Rice University, Smalley was awarded the 1996 Nobel Prize in chemistry for the discovery of fullerenes. His current research is deeply immersed in nanotechnology, focusing, in particular, on the chemistry, physics, and potential applications of carbon nanotubes. With his main background in chemistry and physics, Smalley approaches nanotechnology with an eye for what can actually be implemented and controlled in the laboratory. His approach is not only informed by the relevant chemical and physical theories, but it relies deeply on the actual chemical and physical *practices* to determine the feasibility of proposed views. What is the issue in the debate between Drexler and Smalley? Briefly put, the question is whether *molecular assemblers* are possible. As conceived of by Drexler, molecular assemblers are "devices able to guide chemical reactions by positioning reactive molecules with atomic precision" (Drexler 2003a, p. 38). More specifically, the issue is whether it is *physically* and *chemically* possible to construct such assemblers; *i.e.*, whether the construction of a molecular assembler is *compatible* with accepted physical and chemical principles. Drexler claims it is. In his picture, molecular assemblers are basically *mechanical* devices, controlled by computers to "guide the chemical synthesis of complex structures by mechanically positioning reactive molecules" (Drexler 2003a, p. 38). Smalley disputes the viability of this mechanical picture, challenging the possibility of obtaining the precise control of nanophenomena presupposed by Drexler. According to Smalley, the required control cannot be had – not even in principle.

The debate starts with Smalley questioning Drexler's proposal with two arguments: the so-called *fat fingers* and *sticky fingers* objections. Smalley's point is that it is not possible to pick up and place *individual atoms* with the precision required by Drexler: computer-controlled 'fingers' will be too fat and too sticky for that (Smalley 2001). The talk of fingers in this context may seem strange, given that, literally, there are no at the nanoscale. However, as we will see, this talk plays an important rhetorical role in Smalley's argument, which can be seen as a kind of *reductio* of the mechanical features of Drexler's conception. What Smalley wants to highlight with this language is the difficulty of *actually implementing* Drexler's vision, according to the standards set by Drexler himself. I will consider each argument in turn.

The *fat fingers* objection takes seriously the *mechanical* nature of Drexler's conception of molecular assemblers, and attempts to show that the unfeasibility of the conception is ultimately due to the mechanical assumptions it requires. As we saw, for Drexler, an assembler will "*mechanically* [position] reactive molecules" with "*atomic precision*", and in this way, it will be able to "guide the chemical synthesis of complex structures" (Drexler 2003*a*, p. 38, italics added). What happens if we take literally the idea of *mechanically* locating each atom with atomic *precision*? This would require, according to Smalley, nanobots with *manipulator arms* – this is the point where the mechanical features are taken at face value. But given that the fingers of the nanobot arm must themselves be made of atoms, there would not be enough room at the nanometer scale to allow the control required to *precisely* locate each atom. After all, to have *complete control* of the chemistry, too many fingers in too many arms would be needed. And there is simply not enough room for that. In Smalley's own words: Because the fingers of a manipulator arm must themselves be made out of atoms, they have a certain irreducible size. There just isn't enough room in the nanometer-size reaction region to accommodate all the fingers of all the manipulators necessary to have complete control of the chemistry. [Smalley 2001, p. 77]

According to the *sticky fingers* objection, the precise control over the positioning of atoms required by Drexler cannot be achieved, given that the atoms of the manipulator arms will interact with *other* atoms in unintended ways. Just by positioning an atom in a given place is not enough to guarantee that it will interact *only* with the atoms *we* want it to interact with. As Smalley points out: Manipulator fingers on the hypothetical self-replicating nanobot are [...] too sticky: the atoms of the manipulator hands will adhere to the atom that is being moved. So it will often be impossible to release this minuscule building block in precisely the right spot. [Smally 2001, p. 77] With these two arguments, Smalley thinks that Drexler's mechanical case for molecular assemblers is fundamentally flawed. However, Smalley also raises an additional worry. In his view, Drexler needs *self-replicating* molecular assemblers to implement his vision; otherwise, the rate of production would be too slow. A single *non*-replicating assembler would take a long time to produce only a mole of something: Imagine a single assembler: working furiously, this hypothetical nanorobot would make many new bonds as it went about its assigned task, placing perhaps up to a billion new atoms in the desired structure every second. But as fast as it is, that rate would be virtually useless in running a nanofactory: generating even a tiny amount of a product would take a solitary nanobot millions of years. (Making a mole of something – say, 30 grams, or about one ounce – would require at least 6×10^{23} bonds, one for each atom. At the frenzied rate of 10^9 per second it would take this nanobot 6×10^{14} seconds – that is, 10^{13} minutes, which is 6.9×10^9 days, or 19 million years.) [Smalley 2001, p. 76] In contrast, *self-replicating* nanobots would be much more efficient.

With the ability to self-reproduce, very quickly they could create a whole army of assemblers, which in turn would be able to produce things at a much faster rate. For fun, suppose that each nanobot consisted of a billion atoms (10^9 atoms) in some incredibly elaborate structure. If these nanobots could be assembled at the full billion-atoms-per-second rate imagined earlier, it would take only one second for each nanobot to make a copy of itself. The new nanobot clone would then be 'turned on' so that it could start its own reproduction. After 60 seconds of this furious cloning, there would be 2^{60} nanobots, which is the incredibly large number of 1×10^{18}, or a billion billion. This massive army of nanobots would produce 30 grams of a product in 0.6 millisecond, or 50 kilograms per second. Now we're talking about something very big indeed! [Smalley 2001, p. 76] According to Smalley, the implementation of Drexler's vision requires more than just molecular assemblers; these assemblers need to *self-replicate* as well. How does Drexler respond? First, with regard to the self-replication requirement, even though Drexler himself had an important role in forming the impression that self-replication was necessary for the success of nanotechnology (Drexler 1986), things have changed on this front. Drexler has recently been developing, in collaboration with Chris Phoenix, models that do *not* require self-replication to implement large-scale systems of productive nanomachinery (see Drexler & Phoenix 2004). The details of these models, however, still remain to be seen.

Second, with regard to the fat fingers and the sticky fingers objections, Drexler insists, as noted above, that his assemblers do *not* manipulate individual atoms. They manipulate *reactive molecules* (Drexler 2003a, p. 38). Given that Smalley's two main objections were based on the difficulties associated with manipulating *individual atoms*, they just miss the target. In reply to Drexler's response, Smalley formulates a second version of the fat and sticky fingers objections, extending to reactive molecules the arguments that were initially couched in terms of individual atoms:

The same argument I used to show the infeasibility of tiny fingers placing one atom at a time *applies also to placing larger, more complex building blocks*. Since each incoming 'reactive molecule' building block has multiple atoms to control during the reaction, even more fingers will be needed to make sure they do not go astray. *Computer-controlled fingers will be too fat and too sticky to permit the requisite control*. Fingers just can't do chemistry with the necessary finesse. [Smalley 2003a, p. 39, italics added]

Thus, the original complaint about the unfeasibility of controlling chemical processes with the needed refinement can be easily extended to reactive molecules as well. If anything, in Smalley's view, the second version of the 'fingers' objections is stronger than the first, given that the precise manipulation of a whole *reactive molecule* requires more 'fingers' to control the multitude of atoms involved than what is required by the manipulation of just a *single atom*. Thus, the initial difficulty comes back – now multiplied by each atom involved in the process. In response, Drexler thoroughly rejects the talk of *fingers*. It is not only that this talk cannot be taken literally; there are simply *no* such fingers at the nanometer scale. As he points out: Like enzymes and ribosomes, proposed assemblers neither have nor need these 'Smalley fingers'. The task of positioning reactive molecules simply doesn't require them. [Drexler 2003a, p. 38] In a curious way, both Smalley and Drexler agree on the nonexistence of such 'fingers', albeit for very different reasons. Smalley rejects these 'fingers' as part of his *reductio* of the *mechanical* approach to assemblers, which he correctly takes to be Drexler's view. Drexler, in turn, denies commitment to these (obviously nonexistent) objects as part of his attempt to defuse Smalley's objection. But once this is clear, we can see the significance of Smalley's 'fingers' objection: it challenges Drexler to spell out *not* the mechanical, but the *chemical processes* underlying Drexler's conception of molecular assemblers. The objection ultimately disputes the feasibility of controlling the *chemical* reactions that would inevitably take place if a mechanical molecular assembler were ever produced. In this way, by skillfully shifting the issue from the mechanical to the chemical domain, the objection defies the viability of Drexler's proposal.

However, once it is agreed that there are no fingers at all at the nanoscale, Smalley raises a *new* challenge. If the process of placing reactive molecules does not involve fingers, and if molecular assemblers are to use enzymes and ribosomes in this process – as Drexler himself acknowledges (Drexler 2003*a*, p. 38) – further difficulties emerge. After all, we should now take seriously the need for describing the *chemical* processes involved in the implementation of a molecular assembler; in other words, the chemical details have to be articulated. In particular, several points need to be spelled out. For example: How is it that the nanobot picks just the enzyme molecule it needs out of this cell, and how does it know just how to hold it and make sure it joins with the local region where the assembly is being done, in just the right fashion? How does the nanobot know when the enzyme is damaged and needs to be replaced? How does the nanobot do error detection and error correction? [Smalley 2003a, p. 39]

Without answering questions of this sort, it is unclear how a molecular assembler – with the particular type of control and precision required by Drexler's proposal – could actually be constructed, even in principle. The outcome of these considerations is what can be called *Smalley's dilemma*. Supposing that Drexler's molecular assembler will use something like enzymes and ribosomes, then either the assembler is a water-based entity, or it is not. If it is a water-based entity, then it is limited in what it can achieve; for instance, it *cannot* produce anything that is chemically unstable in water. (And how will it then produce steel, cooper, aluminum, or titanium?) If the assembler is *not* water based, then the chemistry that underlies it eludes us. In Smalley's own words:

The central problem I see with the nanobot self-assembler then is primarily chemistry. If the nanobot is restricted to be a water-based life-form, since this is the only way its molecular assembly tools will work, then there is a long list of vulnerabilities and limitations to what it can do. If it is a non-water-based life-form, then there is a vast area of chemistry that has eluded us for centuries. [Smalley 2003a, p. 40] In either case, according to Smalley, there is trouble. The first horn seems to bring major limitations to what could be achieved by a water-based assembler (*e.g.* nothing that is unstable in water could then be produced). The second horn, with a non-water-based assembler, requires a chemistry whose details we may not have completely mastered yet. Interestingly enough, Drexler's response to the dilemma does not address any of the two horns. Instead, he returns from *chemistry* to *mechanics*. Talking about Feynman's famous 1959 talk (Feynman 1960), Drexler insists: Although inspired by biology (where nanomachines regularly build more nanomachines despite quantum uncertainty and thermal motion), Feynman's vision of nanotechnology is *fundamentally mechanical, not biological*. Molecular manufacturing concepts [that is, Drexler's own approach] follow this lead. [Drexler 2003b, p. 40, italics added] With the acknowledgment of Feynman, Drexler then rejects the need for accommodating the details of chemical processes that, *prima facie*, seem to be required for the implementation of his own vision. By emphatically putting himself back into a purely mechanical world, he denies any role for biological or strictly chemical processes in his proposal:

Nanofactories contain *no enzymes*, *no living cells*, no swarms of roaming, replicating *nanobots*. Instead, they use *computers* for digitally *precise control*, *conveyors* for *parts transport*, and *positioning devices* of assorted sizes to *assemble small parts into larger parts*, building macroscopic products. The smallest devices *position molecular parts* to assemble structures through *mechanosynthesis* – 'machine-phase' chemistry. [Drexler 2003b, p. 41, italics added]

Without a doubt, Drexler emphasizes here the mechanical features of his conception of assemblers, invoking conveyors, computers, and positioning devices to assemble structures. We are now miles away from any chemical understanding of a molecular assembler. This is perhaps the position Drexler wants to be in. Presumably, he sees it as a safe place from which to disarm Smalley's dilemma, given that the latter does not arise for a nonchemical conception of assemblers. This may be so, but the move has its cost too. And as Smalley does not fail to point out in his final reply, instead of exploring the chemical details that need to the articulated for Drexler's conception to get off the ground, Drexler simply returned to his mechanical view, bringing back the same difficulties along the way. For Smalley, a purely mechanical conception of molecular assemblers is miles away from anything that could actually be implemented – even in principle – due to the unfeasibility of the required control. With noticeable disappointment, Smalley notes: "I see you have now walked out of the room where I had led you to talk about *real chemistry*, and you are now back in your *mechanical world*. [...] Much like you can't make a boy and a girl fall in love with each other simply by pushing them together, you cannot make *precise chemistry* occur as desired between two molecular objects with *simple mechanical motion* along a few degrees of freedom in the assembler-fixed frame of reference. Chemistry, like love, is more subtle than that. You need to *guide the reactants* down a particular reaction coordinate, and this coordinate treads through a many-dimensional hyperspace. I agree you will get a reaction when a robot arm pushes the molecules together, *but most of the time it won't be the reaction you want.*" [Smalley 2003b, p. 41, italics added]

However, with Drexler's return to the mechanical view, we are back to the main trouble: the level of control over reactive molecules that is presupposed by this view simply cannot be obtained. In the passage that follows, Smalley emphasizes just this point: "Chemistry of the complexity, richness, and precision needed to come anywhere close to making a molecular assembler – let alone a self-replicating assembler – cannot be done simply by *mushing two molecular objects together*. *You need more control*. There are *too many atoms involved* to handle in such a clumsy way." [Smalley 2003b, p. 41, italics added]

However, if a purely mechanical approach to assemblers does not quite work, what is the alternative? Not surprisingly perhaps, Smalley's final conclusion insists on the need for returning to a *chemical* conception of assemblers, as a way to try to obtain, at least in part, some of the required control. As he insists: "To control these atoms you need some sort of molecular chaperone that can also serve as a *catalyst*. You need a fairly large group of other atoms arranged in a complex, articulated, three-dimensional way to *activate the substrate and bring in the reactant*, and massage the two until they react in just the desired way. You need something very much like an *enzyme*." [Smalley 2003b, p. 41, italics added]

In other words, to get the control Drexler needs, it is crucial to appeal to a *chemical* understanding of the phenomena: instead of conveyors, computers, and positioning devices, we have catalysts, reactants, and enzymes. Even then, it is not entirely obvious that one can fully implement Drexler's overall vision. After all, chemical processes are often capricious, subtle, and delicate – in ways that repeatedly elude us.

After reviewing the main features of the debate, it is hard to resist the temptation of giving at least a partial diagnosis. Although I do not intend to be comprehensive, I want to highlight significant features that should help us understand some of the moves made above.

First, we clearly have here two *radically different* approaches to molecular assemblers. On the one hand, there is Drexler's *mechanical* conception, which is developed as an *engineer's* (conceptual) prototype. It examines, from a mechanical point of view and purely theoretically, in what way molecular assemblers are possible, by essentially formulating a theoretical model in which the relevant physical principles are not violated. The irony is that, as an engineer, Drexler only provides *theoretical* artifacts, rather than *physical* ones. For Drexler, however, this is not at all a problem. It is simply part of his *theoretical applied science* project, which does not aim at providing experimental results, but develops instead only a "theoretical analysis demonstrating the *possibility* of a class of as-yet *unrealizable* devices" (Drexler 1992, p. 489, the first italic is mine). Instead of producing physical devices, the aim is to generate theoretical results. In much the same way, the aim of interpreting a physical theory (say, quantum mechanics) typically is the formulation of *theoretical results* regarding the *possibility* of certain aspects of the world (on the assumption that the theory in question is true), rather than the generation of new experimental results. The activity of interpretation may not be the most typical activity in scientific practice, but it is a significant part of it nonetheless. On the other hand, there is Smalley's *chemical* approach to molecular assemblers, which challenges the *feasibility* of Drexler's *mechanical* conception. As a chemist, Smalley insists on the production of *detectable* and *controllable* effects, emphasizing the need for accommodating the *actual*, *chemical* details that are part of the phenomena. (This is precisely what Drexler is unwilling to do.) However, as we saw, Smalley's challenge goes deeper, given that it disputes even the feasibility *in principle* of actually implementing anything like a mechanical molecular assembler, due to the difficulty of having the required control. As a result, and very briefly put, we are faced here with a *disciplinary* clash (between chemistry and engineering), with different *conceptions* of the *nature* of molecular assemblers (chemical versus mechanical), and with distinct *practices* that may lead to their construction (effective implementation versus conceptual exploration). It is perhaps not surprising that we have hardly any agreement in the debate!

Given the significant differences between the two approaches, the picture that emerges is one of *incommensurability* (see, *e.g.*, Kuhn 1970, Feyerabend 1981, Siegel 1980, Hoyningen-Huene 1993, and Sankey 1994). After all, there are no *common standards* to assess the adequacy of each conception. According to the standards that Drexler set out to himself – namely, to articulate theoretical artifacts – his approach is perfectly adequate. His criteria of adequacy require only the *mechanical feasibility* of molecular assemblers, in the sense that the phenomena in question are not incompatible with any known physical (and perhaps chemical) principles – even though we may *not* have the slightest idea of how to *actually implement* and construct the devices under consideration. For Drexler, the process of actual construction will come later. But we also saw that, in response to Smalley's challenge, Drexler's own conception seems to shift, back and forth, between mechanical and chemical representations of molecular assemblers. Due to the nature of these shifts, we clearly have here incommensurability of a *conceptual* nature. Drexler's considered view, however, seems to favor the *mechanical* conception, which makes his proposal undoubtedly open to Smalley's criticisms. Smalley challenges, in fact, even the *feasibility in principle* of such assemblers. Why? Because Smalley criticizes the core of Drexler's approach: the requirement of positioning reactive molecules with *atomic precision*. That is, Drexler demands (a) a perfect control of the *position* where each reactive molecule will be placed, and (b) a perfect control of the *way* in which a given reactive molecule will interact with other molecules. Smalley challenges both assumptions. If we were to implement anything like Drexler's proposal in the lab, we would face insurmountable difficulties. Given the huge number of atoms present in the phenomena, we would not have the precise control to determine in which way a given reactive molecule would interact (against (b)). Thus, it would not be possible to position precisely the reactive molecule (against (a)).

Smalley, in turn, adopts a radically different *conception* of the nature of molecular assemblers. With his *chemical* conception, assemblers are subject to all the vagaries of chemical processes. And it is this conception that grounds Smalley's criticism of Drexler's idea of *atomic precision*. If the *chemical factors* involved in the interactions between reactive molecules are taken into account, it becomes clear that we cannot simply have the required control envisaged by the mechanical approach.

Smalley also challenges the *methods* used by Drexler to implement his proposal. The construction of theoretical artifacts – as the outcome of Drexler's theoretical applied science – is not enough to establish the feasibility of molecular assemblers as Drexler conceives of them. After all, any attempt to actually implement such assemblers (for example, by trying to construct them in the lab) will immediately face trouble, given the relatively limited control that we can actually have over chemical reactions at the nanoscale.

The points just made indicate that there are at least three levels of incommensurability here: cognitive, conceptual, and methodological (see, *e.g.*, Kuhn 1970, Laudan 1984, and Sankey 1994). (i) *Cognitive* incommensurability emerges when there are no *common standards* to assess the *adequacy of certain theories* about the phenomena under examination. (ii) *Conceptual* incommensurability is the outcome of the lack of common standards to *adjudicate concepts* used to describe the phenomena. (iii) And finally, *methodological* incommensurability arises from the lack of common standards of *assessment of the reliability of the different methods used*. How do these levels of incommensurability bear on the present discussion?

The debate here involves *cognitive* incommensurability in that each side adopts different theories to articulate the corresponding conception of assembler: mechanical theories in Drexler's case and chemical theories in Smalley's. Each of these theories is, of course, adequate *in its respective domain*, but given the dramatically different ways in which Drexler and Smalley conceptualize the domains (one mechanically, the other chemically), it is unclear how one could assess the *overall* adequacy of the theories without simply begging the question against the rival proposal.

(ii) The debate also involves *conceptual* incommensurability, given the radically different ways in which molecular assemblers have been conceptualized: Drexler conceives of them in basically mechanical terms, whereas Smalley is highly sensitive to the chemical features involved in the phenomena. But how could we assess the adequacy of such concepts without simply prejudging the nature of the assemblers themselves? Depending on the view of assemblers we adopt (a chemical or a mechanical view), we obtain very different answers regarding the adequacy of the concepts in question.

(iii) Finally, the debate includes *methodological* incommensurability as well, given that each view has a different method of articulation of molecular assemblers. Drexler's theoretical applied science approach insists that we should first develop theoretical artifacts, establishing the theoretical possibility of such assemblers. Smalley, in turn, with a chemically grounded view, highlights the need for controllable and detectable results before we could even talk *realistically* about the possibility of such objects. Unless we could, in principle, develop techniques of implementation of molecular assemblers – identifying the relevant operations to be performed in the lab – it is hard to judge how such assemblers are *technologically* possible. The fact that a device is *theoretically* possible (that is, its existence does not violate any laws of physics or chemistry) is not sufficient to guarantee that we can *construct that device*, and hence establish that it is possible in the *actual* world, given *our technology*. Drexler agrees, of course, with the distinction between *theoretical* and *technological* possibility, and in fact, theoretical applied science often moves ahead of technology (Drexler 1992). But for Smalley, without accommodating the *practical details of what actually goes on in the lab*, without taking into account the *technological* aspects of current chemistry, we cannot claim to have established even the *theoretical* possibility of the devices in question. We need more than lack of inconsistency with physical and chemical principles. The technology that goes on in the lab is as much part of science as the theories that are articulated there. Given that the production of a molecular assembler crucially relies on that technology, we need to consider the latter as well.

Note that the fact that Drexler and Smalley's views are incommensurable does *not* entail that they are incomparable. The absence of common standards of assessment only entails that evaluative judgments cannot be made without begging some questions, such as assuming the set of standards of one view to judge the adequacy of the other. Concepts, theories, and methods can, of course, be compared. We have been doing this all along. What may not happen is that we will be in a position to decide – without circularity – the adequacy of these concepts, theories, and methods, given the lack of a common standard of adequacy.

Why is it significant to identify the various kinds of incommensurability found in the debate between Drexler and Smalley? Because this helps to explain in which ways the debate has been inconclusive, and why it is inevitable to end up with the impression that Drexler and Smalley are simply talking past each other. With different conceptions of assemblers and with different methodological strategies to articulate such assemblers (*i.e.*, strategies that aim to show the feasibility of such assemblers and to sketch how the latter could, in principle, be constructed), it is not surprising that there is no agreement as to how the debate could be settled. Without common standards of evaluation, or common methods of assessment and construction of assemblers, it is hard to see how to resolve this debate without simply begging the question against one side or the other.

By highlighting the incommensurability involved in the discussion, we can also understand another feature of the debate: the many layers in which it takes place. As noted above, we find not only different *conceptions* of molecular assemblers (chemical versus mechanical), different *methods* of construction or implementation of such assemblers (actual implementation versus conceptual exploration), but also, more generally, different *goals* for nanotechnology research – given the different *visions* underlying Drexler's and Smalley's projects. As we saw, Drexler's vision for nanotechnology is one of atomic precision and perfect and complete control over molecular reactions. It is essentially an *engineer's* vision. Smalley's vision, in turn, insists on the production of detectable and controllable phenomena, and takes as a crucial part of scientific activity the manipulation and stabilization of the phenomena. This vision challenges the viability of a notion of *control* that is not grounded on what can *actually be performed* in the lab. It is essentially a *chemist's* vision. And, as was pointed out, in each of these levels, we have incommensurability.

The considerations just made implicitly suggest an alternative strategy to analyze the debate between Drexler and Smalley. Perhaps with some adjustments, this alternative could provide a way to 'settle' the dispute without (hopefully) begging any questions.

As is well known, Larry Laudan developed a very interesting framework to assess scientific debates: the reticulated model (Laudan 1984). The idea is that scientific practice is articulated in terms of three interrelated levels: goals, methods, and theories. The level of *goals* involves the aims and values shared by a particular scientific community. These goals include certain ways of assessing and structuring scientific research, for example, searching for and valuing empirically testable and informative theories over mere conceptual sketches of possible experiments. The level of *methods* deals with methods of theory construction and theory evaluation, as well as the particular experimental strategies used to implement, control, and stabilize the phenomena. Finally, the level of *theories* includes the various theories and theoretical assumptions adopted by a particular community to explain and predict the phenomena.

According to this picture, scientific change involves change on at least one of the three levels, but *never* changes in all of them at once. Thus, we could use the 'shared' level (say, the level of theories) to assess the adequacy of the remaining levels (say, goals and methods), and in this way, try to settle the debate. For instance, suppose that a given community has as one of its goals to construct a machine that accelerates objects with a speed faster than that of light. But if the community also accepts a theory that states that no object could travel faster than light, this would establish the unfeasibility of the goal. Thus, the community could invoke that theory to revise the goal.

Of course, this simple model does not cover all of the crucial elements of scientific practice. We also have, at least, the level of *scientific instruments* (for a fascinating and sophisticated account, see Baird 2004); and instruments cannot be identified with any of the three previous levels. (i) Although *theories* are often invoked in the construction and manipulation of instruments (including the *interpretation* of the results), instruments are, of course, much more than theories, and play a significantly different role in scientific practice. For instance, instruments provide the tools in terms of which experiments are possible, allowing scientists to probe details of the physical world that would otherwise be unavailable to them. (ii) Although the use of instruments require, of course, ingenuity and technique, the skills demanded go well beyond whatever *methodological rules* that may be adopted in scientific practice. Learning such skills involves special requirements and abilities, such as to be able to calibrate the instrument and to distinguish artifacts of the instrument from genuine information it provides. (iii) Finally, the *goals* and *values* of instrumental practice need not be the same as those of theoretical practice, given that the former is concerned with details of the instrumental apparatus that need not be the primary concern of the latter. Thus, instruments are a crucial *additional* level of consideration in scientific practice.

For simplicity's sake, let us consider scientific practice as involving certain *aims*, *methods*, *theories*, and *instruments*. Bearing this in mind, we can now return to the Drexler-Smalley debate and identify the levels in which it has been conducted. As noted above, there are differences in all of the first three levels. We have distinct *aims*: Drexler's theoretical applied science project is ultimately concerned with the production of *theoretical artifacts*, whereas Smalley insists on the need for the construction of *detectable and controllable phenomena*. There are different *methods*: Drexler invokes *theoretical exploration* to establish the possibility of certain devices, whereas Smalley insists on the *actual implementation* of the relevant phenomena in the lab. Finally, there are different *theories*: Drexler's *mechanical* approach to molecular assemblers emphasizes the *mechanical* features of the phenomena, whereas Smalley insists on the need for accommodating the relevant *chemistry*.

Despite the disagreements at these three levels, the picture changes if we consider the fourth level, that of *instruments*. Here, at last, we find *agreement* between our authors. Both agree that the use of appropriate microscopy devices is crucial for the implementation of the phenomena in question, and *necessary* for the *actual* construction of a molecular assembler (assuming that it can be done). After all, it is through these instruments that the scientific community has the control it has over nanoscale phenomena. And it is *only* in terms of appropriate *instruments* that the community might be able to build an assembler. After all, given the size of such assemblers, the mediation of appropriate instruments is indispensable to control them.

With this minimal agreement, we can now work our way upward, and assess the debate from the point of view of instruments. Given that instruments are *indispensable* to the construction, stabilization, and control of phenomena at the nanoscale – and both sides of the debate agree on that – a *purely theoretical* approach to molecular assemblers that does *not* take into account the need for such instruments misses a *crucial point* of what needs to be accommodated. And Smalley's insistence on the need for the production of controllable and detectable devices can be seen as an emphasis on just the need for appropriate instruments.

In this way, we see how Smalley is ultimately justified in making the requirement he makes, without begging the question against Drexler. After all, *both parties share their commitment to the indispensability of appropriate instruments to control nanophenomena*. Smalley, however, articulates this commitment further, introducing the requirement that detectable results should be produced as part of the determination of the possibility of molecular assemblers. After all, given that instruments are indispensable for the construction of such assemblers, to determine whether the latter are possible, it is crucial to be able, *at least in principle*, to produce detectable results. In this way, the overall proposal Smalley advocates seems more adequate.

Of course, this does not establish the adequacy of Smalley's *criticism* of Drexler. This is a separate issue, and is open to the incommensurability charge discussed above. For, as was noted, the criticism relies on concepts, methods, and theories that are *not* shared by Drexler. However, the emphasis on *instruments* indicates one way in which the debate could be decided. After all, there is a common perspective – the commitment to the indispensability of instruments – that is shared by both sides, and from which the overall adequacy of the two proposals can be determined, without assuming points that are contentious in the debate.

As we saw, the debate between Drexler and Smalley has many levels and involves a variety of moves. Given the dramatic differences in concepts, aims, theories, and methods, and the difficulty of finding common standards of assessment of them, it is understandable that we are faced with many levels of incommensurability.

However, by exploring the shared commitment to instruments – as the basic source of stable information about the phenomena under consideration – it is possible to overcome, in part, the incommensurability and decide the debate. Not in the sense of conclusively settling the issue, which is not to be had in any case. But at least in the sense of appreciating what needs to be done to carry out the visions that underlie each proposal. By identifying the crucial role that instruments play in the articulation of these visions, we also see the role these visions can play in shaping nanotechnology.

Assessment of Nanotechnology

On March 27, 1981, CBS radio news quoted *a NASA scientist* as saying that engineers will be able to build self-replicating robots within twenty years, for use in space or on Earth. These machines would build copies of themselves, and the copies would be directed to make useful products. He had no doubt of their possibility, only of when they will be built. He was quite right. Since 1951, when John von Neumann outlined the principles of self-replicating machines, scientists have generally acknowledged their possibility. In 1953 *Watson* and *Crick* described the structure of *DNA*, which showed how living things pass on the instructions that guide their construction. Biologists have since learned in increasing detail how the self-replicating molecular machinery of the *cell* works. They find that it follows the principles von Neumann had outlined. As birds prove the possibility of flight, so life in general proves the possibility of self-replication, at least by systems of molecular machines. The NASA scientist, however, had something else in mind.

Biological replicators, such as viruses, bacteria, plants, and people, use molecular machines. Artificial replicators can use *bulk technology* instead. Since we have bulk technology today, engineers may use it to build replicators before *molecular technology* arrives. The ancient myth of a magical life-force (coupled with the misconception that the increase of *entropy* means that everything in the universe must constantly run down) has spawned a *meme* saying that replicators must violate some natural law. This simply isn't so. Biochemists understand how cells replicate and they find no magic in them. Instead, they find machines supplied with all the materials, energy, and instructions needed to do the job. Cells *do* replicate; robots could replicate. Advances in automation will lead naturally toward mechanical replicators, whether or not anyone makes them a specific goal. As competitive pressures force increased automation, the need for human labor in factories will shrink. *Fujitsu Fanuc* already runs the machining section in a manufacturing plant twenty-four hours a day with only nineteen workers on the floor during the day shift, and *none* on the floor during the night shift. This factory produces 250 machines a month, of which 100 are robots.

Eventually, robots could do all the robot-assembly work, assemble other equipment, make the needed parts, run the mines and generators that supply the various factories with materials and power, and so forth. Though such a network of factories spread across the landscape wouldn't resemble a pregnant robot, it would form a self-expanding, self-replicating system. The *assembler* breakthrough will surely arrive before the complete automation of industry, yet modern moves in this direction are moves toward a sort of gigantic, clanking *replicator*.

But how can such a system be maintained and repaired without human labor? Imagine an automatic factory able to both test parts and assemble equipment. Bad parts fail the tests and are thrown out or recycled. If the factory can also take machines apart, repairs are easy: simply disassemble the faulty machines, test all their parts, replace any worn or broken parts, and reassemble them. A more efficient system would diagnose problems without testing every part, but this isn't strictly necessary. A sprawling system of factories staffed by robots would be workable but cumbersome. Using clever design and a minimum of different parts and materials, engineers could fit a replicating system into a single box—but the box might still be huge, because it must contain equipment able to make and assemble many different parts. How many different parts? As many as it itself contains. How many different parts and materials would be needed to build a machine able to make and assemble so many different materials and parts? This is hard to estimate, but systems based on today's technology would use *electronic chips*. Making these alone would require too much equipment to stuff into the belly of a small replicator.

Rabbits replicate, but they require prefabricated parts such as vitamin molecules. Getting these from food lets them survive with less molecular machinery than they would need to make everything from scratch. Similarly, a mechanical replicator using prefabricated chips could be made somewhat simpler than one that made everything it needed. Its peculiar "dietary" requirements would also tie it to a wider "ecology" of machines, helping to keep it on a firm leash. Engineers in NASA-sponsored studies have proposed using such semireplicators in space, allowing space industry to expand with only a small input of sophisticated parts from Earth. Still, since bulk-technology replicators must make and assemble their parts, they must contain both part-making and part-assembling machines. This highlights an advantage of molecular replicators: their parts are *atoms*, and atoms come ready-made.

It is often asserted that the starting point of nanotechnology was the classic talk given by *Feynman (1959)*, in which he said: "The principles of physics, as far as I can see, do not speak against the possibility of maneuvering things atom by atom...It would be, in principle, possible (I think) for a physicist to synthesize any chemical substance that the chemist writes down. Give the orders and the physicist synthesizes it. How? Put the atoms down where the chemist says, and so you make the substance." Today's champions of nanotech add: "We need to apply at the molecular scale the concept that has demonstrated its effectiveness at the macroscopic scale: making parts go where we want by putting them where we want!" (*Merke 2003*) This cannot be the whole story. If the essence of nanotechnology were that it manipulates matter on the atomic scale, no new philosophical attitude different from the one to other scientific disciplines would be necessary. Indeed, chemistry has been manipulating matter on the atomic scale for at least the past two centuries. We believe there is indeed some kind of unity behind the nanotech enterprise and the NBIC convergence (*Roco et al. 2002*); but that this unity lies at the level of the 'metaphysical research program' that underpins such convergence. It is at this level that nanoethics must address novel issues. Let us recall that Karl Popper, following the lead of *Emile Meyerson (1927)*, defined the notion of metaphysical research program as a set of ideas and worldviews that underlie any particular scientific research agenda. The positivist philosophy that drives most of modern science (and much of contemporary philosophy) takes 'metaphysics' to be a meaningless quest for answers to unanswerable questions. However, Popper showed that there is no scientific (or, for that matter, technological) research program that would not rest on a set of general presuppositions about the structure of the world. To be sure, those metaphysical views are not empirically testable and they are not amenable to 'falsification.' However, this does not imply that they are not of less importance or that they do not play a fundamental role in the advancement of science. Those who deny metaphysics simply render it invisible, and it is very likely that their hidden metaphysics is bad or inconsistent. To the amazement of those who mistook him for a positivist, Karl Popper claimed that the philosopher or historian of science's task was twofold: first, unearth and make visible the metaphysical ideas that lie underneath scientific programs in crder to make them amenable to criticism; second, to proceed to a critical examination of those metaphysical theories, in a way that is different from the criticism of scientific theories, since no empirical testing is here possible, but nevertheless rational. Our claim is that the major ethical issues raised by the nanotech enterprise and the NBIC convergence are novel and that they originate in the metaphysical research program on which such convergence rests. In order to substantiate this claim, we submit that the origin of the NBIC convergence is to be sought in another classic conference, the one *John von Neumann* gave at Caltech (*1948*) on complexity and self-reproducing automata.

Turing's and Church's theses were very influential at the time, and they had been supplemented by cyberneticians Warren McCulloch and Walter Pitts' major finding on the properties of neural networks (*Dupuy 2000b*, pp. 68-69). Cybernetics' credo was then: every behavior that is unambiguously describable in a finite number of words is computable by a network of formal neurons—a remarkable statement, as von Neumann recognized. However, he put forward the following objection: is it reasonable to assume as a practical matter that our most complex behaviors are describable in their totality, without ambiguity, using a finite number of words? In specific cases it is always possible: our capacity, for example, to recognize the same triangular form in two empirical triangles displaying differences in line, size, and position can be so described. But would this be possible if it were a matter of globally characterizing our capacity for establishing 'visual analogies'? In that case, von

Neumann conjectured, it may be that the simplest way to describe a behavior is to describe the structure that generates it. It is meaningless, under these circumstances, to 'discover' that such a behavior can be embodied in a neural network since it is not possible to define the behavior other than by describing the network itself. To take an illustration: The unpredictable behaviour of nanoscale objects means that engineers will not know how to make nanomachines until they actually start building them (The Economist, March 2003). Von Neumann thus posed the question of complexity, foreseeing that it would become the great question for science in the future. Complexity implied for him, in this case, the futility of the constructive approach of McCulloch and Pitts, which reduced a function to a structure, thus leaving unanswered the question of what a complex structure is capable. It was in the course of his work on automata theory that von Neumann was to refine this notion of complexity. Assuming a magnitude of a thermodynamic type, he conjectured that below a certain threshold it would be degenerative, meaning that the degree of organization could only decrease, but that above this threshold an increase in complexity became possible. Now this threshold of complexity, he supposed, is also the point at which the structure of an object becomes simpler than the description of its properties. Soon, von Neumann prophesied, the builder of automata would find himself as helpless before his creation as we feel ourselves to be in the presence of complex natural phenomena (*Dupuy 2000b*).

At any rate, von Neumann was thus founding the so-called bottom-up approach. In keeping with that philosophy, the engineers will not be any more the ones who devise and design a structure capable of fulfilling a function that has been assigned to them. The engineers of the future will be the ones who know they are successful when they are surprised by their own creations. If one of your goals is to reproduce life, to fabricate life, you have to be able to simulate one of its most essential properties, namely the capacity to complexify.

Admittedly, not all of nanotech falls under the category of complexity. Most of today's realizations are in the field of nanomaterials and the problems they pose have to do with toxicity. However, as a recent report by the European Commission says, "the powerful heuristic of Converging Technologies will prove productive even if it is or should be realized to a small extent only" (*Nordmann 2004*). The effects that pose ethical problems are not only the effects of technology per se, but also the effects of the metaphysical ideas that drive technology, whether technological realizations see the light of day or not. We are here mainly interested in these. Among them the novel kind of uncertainty associated with an ambition or a dream to set off complex phenomena looms large.

In her masterly study of the frailties of human action, Hannah Arendt brought out the fundamental paradox of our time: as human powers increase through technological progress, we are less and less equipped to control the consequences of our actions. From the start, a long excerpt is worth quoting, as its relevance for our topic cannot be overstated—and we should keep in mind that this was written in 1958:

> ...the attempt to eliminate action because of its uncertainty and to save human affairs from their frailty by dealing with them as though they were or could become the planned products of human making has first of all resulted in channeling the human capacity for action, for beginning new and spontaneous processes which without men never would come into existence, into an attitude toward nature which up to the latest stage of the modern age had been one of exploring natural laws and fabricating objects out of natural material. To what extent we have begun to act into nature, in the literal sense of the word, is perhaps best illustrated by a recent casual remark of a scientist who quite seriously suggested that "basic research is when I am doing what I don't know what I am doing."
>
> This started harmlessly enough with the experiment in which men were no longer content to observe, to register, and contemplate whatever nature was willing to yield in her own appearance, but began to prescribe conditions and to provoke natural processes.
>
> What then developed into an ever-increasing skill in unchaining elemental processes, which, without the interference of men, would have lain dormant and perhaps never have come to pass, has finally ended in a veritable art of 'making' nature, that is, of creating 'natural' processes which without men would never exist and which earthly nature by herself seems incapable of accomplishing...
>
> The very fact that natural sciences have become exclusively sciences of process and, in their last stage, sciences of potentially irreversible irremediable 'processes, of no return' is a clear indication that, whatever the brain power necessary to start them, the actual underlying human capacity which alone could bring about this development is no 'theoretical' capacity, neither contemplation nor reason, but the human ability to act—to start new unprecedented processes whose outcome remains uncertain and unpredictable whether they are let loose in the human or the natural realm.
>
> In this aspect of action...processes are started whose outcome is unpredictable, so that uncertainty rather than frailty becomes the decisive character of human affairs (Arendt 1958, 230-232; our emphasis).

No doubt that with an incredible prescience this analysis applies perfectly well to the NBIC convergence, in particular on two scores. Firstly, the ambition to (re-)make nature is an important dimension of the metaphysical underpinnings of the field. If the NBIC converging technologies purport to take over Nature's and Life's job and become the engineers of evolution, it is because they have redefined Nature and Life in terms that belong to the realm of artifacts. See how one of their most vocal champions, Damien Broderick, rewrites the history of life, or, as he puts it, of "living replicators":

> Genetic algorithms in planetary numbers lurched about on the surface of the earth and under the sea, and indeed as we now know deep within it, for billions of years, replicating and mutating and being winnowed via the success of their expressions—that is, the bodies they manufactured, competing for survival in the macro world. At last, the entire living ecology of the planet has accumulated, and represents a colossal quantity of compressed, schematic information (2001, p. 116).

Once life has thus been transmogrified into an artifact, the next step is to ask oneself whether the human mind couldn't do better. The same author asks rhetorically, "Is it likely that nanosystems, designed by human minds, will bypass all this Darwinian wandering, and leap straight to design success?" (p. 118) Secondly, as predicted by von Neumann, it will be an inevitable temptation, not to say a task or a duty, for the nanotechnologists of the future to set off processes upon which they have no control. The sorcerer's apprentice myth must be updated: it is neither by error nor by terror that Man will be dispossessed of his own creations but by design. There is no need for Drexlerian self-assemblers to come into existence for this to happen. The paradigm of complex, self-organizing systems envisioned by von Neumann is stepping ahead at an accelerated pace, both in science and in technology. It is in the process of shoving away and replacing the old metaphors inherited from the cybernetic paradigm, like the ones that treat the mind or the genome as computer programs. In science, the central dogmas of molecular biology received a severe blow on two occasions recently. First, with the discovery that the genome of an adult, differentiated cell can be 'reprogrammed' with the cooperation of maternal cytoplasm—hence the technologies of nucleus transfer, including therapeutic and reproductive cloning. Secondly, with the discovery of prions, which showed that self-replication does not require DNA. As a result, the sequencing of the human genome appears to be not the end of the road but its timid beginning. Proteinomics and complexity are becoming the catchwords in biology, relegating genomics to the realm of passé ideas.

In technology, new feats are being flaunted every passing week. Again, the time has not come—and may never come—when we manufacture self-replicating machinery that mimics the self-replication of living materials. However, we are taking more and more control of living materials and their capacity for self-organization and we use them to perform mechanical functions.

Examples are plenty. To give just one: In November 2003, scientists in Israel built transistors out of carbon nanotubes using DNA as a template. A Technion-

Israel scientist said, "What we've done is to bring biology to self-assemble an electronic device in a test tube...The DNA serves as a scaffold, a template that will determine where the carbon nanotubes will sit. That's the beauty of using biology" (*Chang 2003*). From a philosophical point of view the key issue is to develop new concepts of prudence that are suited to this novel situation. A long time ago Aristotle's phronesis was dislodged from its prominent place and replaced with the modern tools of the probability calculus, decision theory, the theory of expected utility, etc. More qualitative methods, such as futures studies, 'Prospective', and the scenario method were then developed to assist decision-making. More recently, the precautionary principle emerged on the international scene with an ambition to rule those cases in which uncertainty is mainly due to the insufficient state of our scientific knowledge. We believe that none of these tools is appropriate for tackling the situation that we are facing now.

From the outset we make it explicit that our approach is inherently normative. German philosopher Hans Jonas cogently explains why we need a radically new ethics to rule our relation to the future in the "technological age" (*Jonas 1985*). This "Ethics of the Future" (Ethik für die Zukunft)—meaning not a future ethics, but an ethics for the future, for the sake of the future, i.e. the future must become the major object of our concern—starts from a philosophical aporia. Given the magnitude of the possible consequences of our technological choices, it is an absolute obligation for us to try and anticipate those consequences, assess them, and ground our choices on this assessment. Couched in philosophical parlance, this is tantamount to saying that when the stakes are high, as in predicting the future, none of the normative ethics that are available is up to the challenge. Virtue ethics is manifestly insufficient since the problems ahead have very little to do with the fact that scientists or engineers are beyond moral reproach or not. Deontological doctrines do not fare much better since they evaluate the rightness of an action in terms of its conformity to a norm or a rule, for example to the Kantian categorical imperative: we are now well acquainted with the possibility that 'good' (e.g. democratic) procedures lead one into an abyss. As for consequentialism—i.e. the set of doctrines that evaluate an action based on its consequences for all agents concerned—it treats uncertainty as does the theory of expected utility, namely by ascribing probabilities to uncertain outcomes. Hans Jonas argues that doing so has become morally irresponsible. The stakes are so high that we must set our eyes on the worst-case scenario and see to it that it never sees the light of day.

However, the very same reasons that make our obligation to anticipate the future compelling, make it impossible for us to do so. Unleashing complex processes is a very perilous activity that both demands certain foreknowledge and prohibits it. Indeed, one of the very few unassailable ethical principles is that ought implies can. There is no obligation to do that which one cannot do. However, we do have here an ardent obligation that we cannot fulfil: anticipating the future. We cannot but violate one of the foundations of ethics. What is needed is a novel approach to the future, neither scenario nor forecast. We submit that what we call ongoing normative assessment is a step in that direction. In order to introduce this new concept we need to take a long detour into the classic approaches to the problems raised by uncertainty. The precautionary principle triumphantly entered the arena of methods to ensure prudence. All the fears of our age seem to have found shelter in the word 'precaution'. Yet, in fact, the conceptual underpinnings of the notion of precaution are extremely fragile.

Let us recall the definition of the precautionary principle formulated in the French Barnier law: "The absence of certainties, given the current state of scientific and technological knowledge, must not delay the adoption of effective and proportionate preventive measures aimed at forestalling a risk of grave and irreversible damage to the environment at an economically acceptable cost" (1995). This text is torn between the logic of economic calculation and the awareness that the context of decision-making has radically changed. On one side, the familiar and reassuring notions of effectiveness, commensurability and reasonable cost; on the other, the emphasis on the uncertain state of knowledge and the gravity and irreversibility of damage. It would be all too easy to point out that if uncertainty prevails, no one can say what would be a measure proportionate (by what coefficient?) to a damage that is unknown, and of which one therefore cannot say if it will be grave or irreversible; nor can anyone evaluate what adequate prevention would cost; nor say, supposing that this cost turns out to be 'unacceptable,' how one should go about choosing between the health of the economy and the prevention of the catastrophe.

One serious deficiency, which hamstrings the notion of precaution, is that it does not properly gauge the type of uncertainty with which we are confronted at present. The report on the precautionary principle prepared for the French Prime Minister (*Kourilsky& Viney 2000*) introduces what initially appears to be an interesting distinction between two types of risks: 'known' risks and 'potential' risks. It is on this distinction that the difference between prevention and precaution is said to rest: precaution would be to potential risks what prevention is to known risks. A closer look at the report in question reveals 1) that the expression 'potential risk' is poorly chosen, and that what it designates is not a risk waiting to be realized, but a hypothetical risk, one that is only a matter of conjecture; 2) that the distinction between known risks and, call them this way, hypothetical risks corresponds to an old standby of economic thought, the distinction that John Maynard Keynes and Frank Knight independently proposed in 1921 between risk and uncertainty. A risk can in principle be quantified in terms of objective probabilities based on observable frequencies; when such quantification is not possible, one enters the realm of uncertainty.

The problem is that economic thought and decision theory underlying it were destined to abandon the distinction between risk and uncertainty as of the 1950s in the wake of the exploit successfully performed by Leonard Savage with the introduction of the concept of subjective probability and the corresponding philosophy of choice under conditions of uncertainty: Bayesianism. In Savage's approach, probabilities no longer correspond to any sort of objective regularity present in nature, but simply to the coherent sequence of a given agent's choices. In philosophical language, every uncertainty is treated as epistemic uncertainty, meaning an uncertainty associated with the agent's state of knowledge. It is easy to see that introduction of subjective probabilities erases Knight's distinction between uncertainty and risk, between risk and the risk of risk, between precaution and prevention. If a probability is unknown, all that happens is that a probability distribution is assigned to it subjectively. Then further probabilities are calculated following the Bayes rule. No difference remains compared to the case where objective probabilities are available from the outset. Uncertainty owing to lack of knowledge is brought down to the same plane as intrinsic uncertainty due to the random nature of the event under consideration. A risk economist and an insurance theorist do not see and cannot see any essential difference between prevention and precaution and, indeed, reduce the latter to the former. In truth, one observes that applications of the 'precautionary principle' generally boil down to little more than a glorified version of 'cost-benefit' analysis.

Our situation with respect to new threats is different from the above-discussed context. The novel feature this time is that although uncertainty is objective, we are not dealing with a random occurrence either. This is because each of the future great discoveries or of the future catastrophes must be treated as a singular event. Neither random, nor uncertain in the usual epistemic sense, the type of 'future risk' that we are confronting is a monster from the standpoint of classic distinctions. Indeed, it merits a special treatment, which the precautionary principle is incapable of giving. When the precautionary principle states that the "absence of certainties, given the current state of scientific and technical knowledge, must not delay etc.," it is clear that it places itself from the outset within the framework of epistemic uncertainty. The assumption is that we know we are in a situation of uncertainty. It is an axiom of epistemic logic that if I do not know P, then I know that I do not know P. Yet, as soon as we depart from this framework, we must entertain the possibility that we do not know that we do not know something. In cases where uncertainty is such that it entails that uncertainty itself is uncertain, it is impossible to know whether or not the conditions for application of the precautionary principle have been met. If we apply the principle to itself, it will invalidate itself before our eyes.

Moreover, "given the current state of scientific and technical knowledge" implies that a scientific research effort could overcome the uncertainty in question, whose existence is viewed as purely contingent. It is a safe bet that a 'precautionary policy' will inevitably include the edict that research efforts must be pursued—as if the gap between what is known and what needs to be known could be filled by a supplementary effort on the part of the knowing subject. But it is not uncommon to encounter cases in which the progress of knowledge comports an increase in uncertainty for the decision-maker, a thing inconceivable within the framework of epistemic uncertainty. Sometimes, to learn more is to discover hidden complexities that make us realize that the mastery we thought we had over phenomena was in part illusory.

From the point of view of mathematics of complex systems one can distinguish several different sources of uncertainty. Some of them appear in almost any analysis of uncertainties; others are taken into account quite rarely. Presence of tipping points, i.e. such points on the system's landscape of trajectories that trigger an abrupt fall of the system into states completely different from the states that the system had previously occupied, is one of the reasons why uncertainty is not amenable to the concept of probability. As long as the system remains far from the threshold of the catastrophe, it may be handled with impunity. Here cost-benefit analysis of risks is bound to produce a banal result, because the trajectory is predictable and no surprises can be expected. To give an example, this is the reason why humanity was able to blithely ignore, for centuries, the impact of its mode of development on the environment. But as the critical thresholds grow near, cost-benefit analysis, previously a banality, becomes meaningless. At that point it is imperative not to enter the area of critical change at any cost, if one, of course, wants to avoid the crisis and sustain the smooth development. We see that for reasons having to do, not with a temporary insufficiency of our knowledge, but with the structural properties of complex systems, economic calculation is of little help.

We now turn to another source of uncertainty that appears in the case of systems in whose development participates the human society. Technology here is just one example. To these systems the usual techniques for anticipating the future, as discussed in the next section, are inapplicable. The difficulty comes from the fact that, in general, any system where the society plays an active role is characterized by the impossibility to dissociate the observed part of the system ('the sphere of technology') from the observer ('society at large'), who himself is influenced by the system and must be viewed as one of its components. In a usual setting, the observer looks at the system that he studies from an external point, and both the observer and the system evolve in linear physical time. The observer can then treat the system as independent from the act of observation and can create scenarios in which this system will evolve in linear time. Not so if the observer can influence the system and, in turn, be influenced by it. What evolves as a whole in linear time is now a conglomerate, a composite system consisting of both the complex system and the observer. However, the evolution of the composite system in the linear time becomes of no interest for us, for the act of observation is performed by the observer who is a part of the composite system; the observer himself is now inside the big whole, and his point of view is no more an external one. The essential difference is that the observer and the complex system enter into a network of complex relations with each other, due to mutual influence. In science such composite systems are referred to as self referential systems. They were first studied by von Neumann in his famous book on the theory of self-reproducing automata, which consequently gave rise to a whole new direction of mathematical research.

According to Breuer's theorem, the observer involved in a self-referential system can never have full information on the state of the system. This is a fundamental source of uncertainty in the analysis of complex systems that involve human action. We should take very seriously the idea that there is a "co-evolution of technology and society" (*Rip et al. 1995*). The dynamics of technological development is embedded in society. The consequences of the development of nanotechnology will concern society as well as technology itself. Technology and society shape one another. One can then prove mathematically that the society cannot know with certainty where the technological progress will take it nor make any certain predictions about its own future state.

It is a gross simplification to treat the sphere of technology as if it developed only according to its internal logic. Political decision-making and the opinion of the society influence research. The decisions that will be made or not, such as various moratoria and bans, will have a major impact on the evolution of research. Scientific ethics committees would have no raison d'être otherwise. If many scientists and experts ponder over the strategic and philosophical questions, it is not only out of curiosity; rather, it is because they wish to exert an influence on the actions that will be taken by the politicians and, beyond, the peoples themselves. These observations may sound trivial. It is all the more striking that they are not taken into account, most of the time, when it comes to anticipating the evolution of research. When they are, it is in the manner of control theory: human decision is treated as a parameter, an independent or exogenous variable, and not as an endogenous variable. Then, a crucial causal link is missing: the motivational link. It is obvious that human decisions that will be made will depend, at least in part, on the kind of anticipation of the future of the system, this anticipation being made public. And this future will depend, in turn, on the decisions that will be made. A causal loop appears here, that prohibits us from treating human action as an independent variable. Thus, research and technology are systems in which society is a participant. By and large there are three ways of anticipating the future of a human system, whether purely social or a hybrid of society and the physical world. The first one we call Forecasting. It treats the system as if it were a purely physical system. This method is legitimate whenever it is obvious that anticipating the future of the system has no effect whatsoever on the future of the system.

The second method we call, in French, 'Prospective'. Its most common form is the scenario method. Ever since its beginnings the scenario approach has gone to great lengths to distinguish itself from mere forecast or foresight, held to be an extension into the future of trends observed in the past. We can forecast the future state of a physical system, it is said, but not what we shall decide to do. It all started in the 1950s when a Frenchman, Gaston Berger, coined the term 'Prospective'—a substantive formed in analogy with 'Retrospective'—to designate a new way to relate to the future. That this new way had nothing to do with the project or the ambition of anticipating, that is, knowing the future, was clearly expressed in the following excerpt from a lecture given by French philosopher Bertrand de Jouvenel. In "Of Prospective" he said:

> It is unscholarly perforce because there are no facts on the future. Cicero quite rightly contrasted past occurrences and occurrences to come with the contrasted expressions facta and futura: facta, what is accomplished and can be taken as solid; futura, what shall come into being, and is as yet 'undone,' or fluid. This contrast leads me to assert vigorously: 'there can be no science of the future.' The future is not the realm of the 'true or false' but the realm of 'possibles.' (*de Jouvenel 1964*)

Another term coined by Jouvenel that was promised to a bright future was 'Futuribles,' meaning precisely the open diversity of possible futures. The exploration of that diversity was to become the scenario approach. A confusion spoils much of what is being offered as the justification of the scenario approach. On the one hand, the alleged irreducible multiplicity of the 'futuribles' is explained as above by the ontological indeterminacy of the future: since we 'build,' 'invent' the future, there is nothing to know about it. On the other hand, the same multiplicity is interpreted as the inevitable reflection of our inability to know the future with certainty. The confusion of ontological indeterminacy with epistemic uncertainty is a very serious one. From what we read in the literature on nanotechnology, we got the clear impression that the emphasis is put on epistemic uncertainty, but only up to the point where human action is introduced: then the scenario method is used to explore the sensitivity of technological development to human action. The temporality that corresponds to Prospective or the scenario approach is the familiar decision tree. We call it occurring time. It embodies the familiar notions that the future is open and the past is fixed. In short, time in this model is the usual linear one directional time arrow. It immediately comes to mind that, as we have stated above, linear time does not lead to the correct type of observation and prediction if the observer is an observer-participant. This is precisely the case with the society at large and its technology, and, consequently, one must not expect a successful predictive theory of the latter to operate in the linear occurring time.

We submit that occurring time is not the only temporal structure we are familiar with. Another temporal experience is ours on a daily basis. It is facilitated, encouraged, organized, not to say imposed by numerous features of our social institutions. All around us, more or less authoritative voices are heard that proclaim what the more or less near future will be: the next day's traffic on the freeway, the result of the upcoming elections, the rates of inflation and growth for the coming year, the changing levels of greenhouse gases, etc. The futurists and sundry other prognosticators know full well, as do we, that this future they announce to us as if it were written in the stars is, in fact, a future of our own making. We do not rebel against what could pass for a metaphysical scandal (except, on occasion, in the voting booth). It is the coherence of this mode of coordination with regard to the future that we have endeavored to bring out, under the name of projected time.

To return to the three ways of anticipating the future, the foresight method can be said to be a view of an independent observer from outside the physical system. Counter-argument to it is that in reality the observer is not independent and has a capacity to act as to produce causal effects on the system. The second way of anticipation, 'Prospective,' or its version such as the scenario approach, is a view on the system where the observer is not independent any more, but the view itself is still taken from outside the system. Thus, the one who analyzes and predicts is the same agent as the one who acts causally on the system. As explained in the previous section, this fact entails a fundamental limit on the capacities of the anticipator. What is needed, therefore, is a replacement of the linear occurring time with a different point of view. This means taking seriously the fact that the system involves human action and requiring that predictive theory accounts for this. It is only such a theory that will be capable of providing a sound ground for non-selfcontradictory, coherent anticipation. A sine qua non must be respected for that coherence to be the case: a closure condition, as shown on the graph. Projected time takes the form of a loop, in which past and future reciprocally determine each other. It appears that the metaphysics of projected time differs radically from the one that underlies occurring time, as counterfactual relations run counter causal ones: the future is fixed and the past depends counterfactually upon the future. To foretell the future in projected time, it is necessary to seek the loop's fixed point, where an expectation (on the part of the past with regard to the future) and a causal production (of the future by the past) coincide. The predictor, knowing that his prediction is going to produce causal effects in the world, must take account of this fact if he wants the future to confirm what he foretold. Therefore the point of view of the predictor has more to it than a view of the human agent who merely produces causal effects. By contrast, in the scenario ('prospective') approach the self-realizing prophecy aspect of predictive activity is not taken into account.

We will call prophecy the determination of the future in projected time, by reference to the logic of self-fulfilling prophecy. Although the term has religious connotations, let us stress that we are speaking of prophecy here in a purely secular and technical sense. The prophet is the one who, prosaically, seeks out the fixed point of the problem, the point where voluntarism achieves the very thing that fatality dictates. The prophecy includes itself in its own discourse; it sees itself realizing what it announces as destiny. In this sense, as we said before, prophets are legion in our modern democratic societies, founded on science and technology. What is missing is the realization that this way of relating to the future, which is neither building, inventing or creating it, nor abiding by its necessity, requires a special metaphysics, which is precisely provided by what we call projected time (*Dupuy 1989*; *1992*; *1998*; *2000a*).

If the future depends on the way it is anticipated and this anticipation being made public, every determination of the future must take into account the causal consequences of the language that is being used to describe the future and how this language is being received by the general public, how it contributes to shaping public opinion, and how it influences the decision-makers. In other terms, the very description of the future is part and parcel of the determinants of the future. This self-referential loop between two distinct levels, the epistemic and the ontological, is the signature of human affairs. Let us observe that this condition provides us with a criterion for determining which kinds of description are acceptable and which are not: the future under that description must be a fixed point of the self-referential loop that characterizes projected time.

Any inquiry on the kind of uncertainty proper to the future states of the co-evolution between technology and society must therefore include a study of the linguistic and cognitive channels through which descriptions of the future are made, transmitted, conveyed, received, and made sense of. This is a huge task, and we will limit ourselves here to two dimensions that seem to us of special relevance for the study of the impact of the new technology: the aversion to not knowing, and the impossibility to believe. A third such dimension that we do not discuss here is the certainty effect studied by Tversky and Kahneman. This effect consists in a practical observation that certainty exaggerates the aversiveness of losses that are certain relative to losses that are merely probable.

In 1950s, soon after Savage's work, a debate on the subjective probabilities was initiated by Maurice Allais. Allais intended to show that Savage's axioms are very far from what one observes, in economics, in practical decision-making contexts. Soon an example was proposed, a version of which is known under the name of Ellsberg paradox (*Ellsberg 1961*). The key idea of Allais and, later on, of Ellsberg is that there exists aversion to not knowing. Not knowing must be understood as the opposite of knowing, negation of a certain ascribed property, and must be differentiated from the unknown or ignorance. Ignorance presupposes that something can possibly be known, while here we are concerned with a situation of not knowing and not being able to know, because of the game conditions or because of some real-life factors. Aversion to not knowing can take the form of aversion to uncertainty in situations where uncertainty means epistemic uncertainty according to Frank Knight's distinction between risk and uncertainty. However, as a general principle aversion to not knowing exceeds the conceptual limits of Savage's theory.

The Ellsberg paradox is an example of a situation where agents would irrationally prefer the situation with some information to a situation without any information, although it is rational to prefer to avert from information. Consider two urns, A and B. It is known that in urn A there are exactly ten red balls and ten black balls. About urn B it is only said that it contains twenty balls, some red and some black. A ball from each urn is to be drawn at random. Free of charge, a person can choose one of the two urns and then place a bet on the colour of the ball that is drawn. According to Savage's theory of decision-making, urn B should be chosen even though the fraction of balls is not known. Probabilities can be formed subjectively, and a bet shall be placed on the subjectively most likely ball colour. If subjective probabilities are not fifty-fifty, a bet on urn B will be strictly preferred to one on urn A. If the subjective probabilities are precisely fifty-fifty then the decision-maker will be indifferent. Contrary to the conclusions of Savage's theory, Ellsberg argued that a strict preference for urn A is plausible because the probability of drawing a red or black ball is known in advance. He surveyed the preferences of an elite group of economists to lend support to this position and found that his view was right and that there was evidence against applicability of Savage's axioms. Thus, the Ellsberg paradox challenges the appropriateness of the theory of subjective probability. We shall also say that the Ellsberg paradox challenges the usual assumption that human decision-makers are probability calculators. Indeed, had one given himself the task of assessing the problem with urns from the point of view of probabilities, it would be inevitable to make use of the Bayes rule and thus conclude that urn B is the preferred choice. But, as shown by Ellsberg, aversion to not knowing is a stronger force than the tendency to calculate probabilities. Aversion to not knowing therefore erects a cognitive barrier that separates human decision-maker from the field of rational choice theory.

Let us again return to the precautionary principle. By placing the emphasis on scientific uncertainty, it misconstrues the nature of the obstacle that keeps us from acting in the face of catastrophe. The obstacle is not just uncertainty, scientific or otherwise; it is equally, if not a more important component, the impossibility of believing that the worst is going to occur. Contrary to many the basic assumption of epistemic logic, one can know that P but still not believe in P.

Pose the simple question as to what the practice of those who govern us was before the idea of precaution arose. Did they institute policies of prevention, the kind of prevention with respect to which precaution is supposed to innovate? Not at all. They simply waited for the catastrophe to occur before taking action—as if its coming into existence constituted the sole factual basis on which it could be legitimately foreseen, too late of course. We submit that there exists a deep cognitive basis for such a behaviour, which is exhibited by human decision makers in a situation when they know that a singular event, like a catastrophe, stands right behind the door. In these circumstances arises a cognitive barrier of the impossibility to believe in the catastrophe.

To be sure, there are cases where people do see a catastrophe coming and do adjust. That just means that the cognitive barrier in question is not absolute and can be overcome. We will introduce further a method that makes such overcoming more likely. However, by and large, even when it is known that it is going to take place, a catastrophe is not credible. On the basis of numerous examples, an English researcher David Fleming identified what he called the "inverse principle of risk evaluation": the propensity of a community to recognize the existence of a risk seems to be determined by the extent to which it thinks that solutions exist (*Fleming 1996*). There is no subjective or objective probability calculus here; knowing that P but not believing in P has a different origin.

What could this origin be? Observe first that the aversion to not knowing and the impossibility to believe do not go unconnected. Both are due to the fact that human action as cognitive decision-making process vitally depends on having information. Cognitive agents cannot act without having information that they rely upon, and the experience from which they build analogies with a current situation. Consequently, a fundamental cognitive barrier arises, which is that if an agent does not have information or experience, then he does not take action, a situation that for an outsider appears as paralysis in decision-making. Aversion to not knowing is caused by the cognitive barrier but the agent, like in the Ellsberg paradox, is forced to act. He then chooses an action which is not rational but which escapes to the largest degree the situation of not having information. Were the agent allowed not to act at all, as in real life situations, the most probable outcome becomes the one of paralysis. When the choice is between the relatively bad, the unknown, and doing nothing, the last option happens to be the most attractive one. If it is dropped and the choice is just between the relatively bad and the unknown, relatively bad may turn out to be the winner. To summarize, we argue that a consequence of the cognitive barrier is that if in a situation of absence of information and of the singular character of the coming event there is a possibility not to act, this will be the agent's preference. Standing face to face with a catastrophe or a dramatic change in life, most people become paralyzed. As cognitive agents, they have no information, no experience, and no practical know-how concerning the singular event, and the cognitive barrier precludes the human decision-maker from action. Another consequence of the cognitive barrier is that if an agent is forced to act, then he will do his best to acquire information. Even though it may later be found out that he had made wrong decisions or his action had not been optimal, in the process of decision-making itself the cognitive barrier dictates that the agent collects as much information as he can get and acts upon it. Reluctance to bring in available information or, yet more graphically, refusal to look for information are by themselves special decisions and require that the agent consciously chooses to tackle the problem of the quality and quantity of information that he wants to act upon. If the agent does so, i.e. if he gives himself the task to analyze the problem of necessary vs. superficial information, then it is comprehensible that the agent would refuse to acquire some information, as does the rational agent in the Ellsberg paradox. But if the meta-analysis of the preconditions of decision-making is not undertaken, then the agent will naturally tend to collect at least some information that is available on the spot. Such is the case in most real life situations. Consequently, the cognitive barrier entails that the directly available information is viewed as relevant to decision-making; if there is no such information, then the first thing-to-do is to look for one.

Cognitive barrier in its clear-cut form applies to situations where one faces a choice between total absence of information and availability of at least some knowledge. The reason why agents have no information on an event and its consequences is usually that this event is a singular event. Singular events, by definition, mean that the agent cannot use his previous experience for analyzing the range of possible outcomes and for evaluating particular outcomes in this range. To enter into Savage's rational decision-making process, agents require previous information or experience that allow them to form priors. If information is absent or is such that no previous experiential data is available, the process is easily paralyzed. Contrary to the prescription of the theory of subjective probabilities, in a situation of absence of information real cognitive agents do not choose to set priors arbitrarily. To them, selecting probabilities and even starting to think probabilistically without any reason to do so appears as purely irrational and untrustworthy. Independently of the projected positive or negative outcome of a future event, if it is a singular event, then cognitive agents stay away from the realm of subjective probabilistic reasoning and are led to paralysis. Now, our immediate concern becomes to offer a way of functioning, which is capable of bringing the agents back to operational mode from the dead end of cognitive paralysis.

The methodology that we propose is different from a one-time probabilistic analysis that is devoted to constructing a range of scenarios, all developing in the linear time which forks into a multitude of branches, and choosing 'the best', whatever the criterion. Our method does not rest on the application of an a priori principle, such as the Precautionary Principle. We submit that no principle can do the job of dealing with the kind of uncertainty that the new technological wave generates. What we propose can be viewed as a practice, rather than a principle, as a way of life or a procedural prescription for all kinds of agents: from a particular scientist and a research group to the whole of the informed society, telling them how to proceed with questions regarding the future, on a regular basis in course of their usual work. Our methodology is a methodology of ongoing normative assessment. It is a matter of obtaining through research, public deliberation, and all other means, an image of the future sufficiently optimistic to be desirable and sufficiently credible to trigger the actions that will bring about its own realization. The sheer phrasing of the methodology suggests that it rests on the metaphysics of projected time, of which it reproduces the characteristic loop between past and future. Importantly, one must note that these two goals, for an image to be both optimistic and credible, are seen as entering in a contradiction. Yet another contradiction arises from the requirement of anticipating a future state early enough, when its features cannot yet be seen clearly, and not waiting until it is too late, when the future is so close to us that it is unchangeable. Both contradictions hint at a necessary balance between the extremes. It is not credible to be too optimistic about the future, but cognitive paralysis arises when the anticipated future is irreparably catastrophic. It is not credible to announce a prediction too early, but it becomes, not a prediction but a matter of fact, if waited for too long. The methodology of ongoing normative assessment prescribes to live with the uncertain future and to follow a certain procedure in continuously evaluating the state of the analyzed system.

The methodology of ongoing normative assessment can also be viewed as a conjunction of inverse prescriptions. This time, instead of an optimistic but credible image of the future, one should wish to obtain at every moment of time an image of the future sufficiently catastrophic to be repulsive and sufficiently credible to trigger the actions that would block its realization. As shown in the discussion of projected time, a closure condition must be met, which takes here the following form: a catastrophe must necessarily be inscribed in the future with some vanishing, but non-zero weight, this being the condition for this catastrophe not to occur. The future, on its part, is held as real. This means that a human agent is told to live with an inscribed catastrophe. Only so will he avoid the occurrence of this catastrophe. Importantly, the vanishing non-zero weight of the catastrophic real future is not the objective probability of the catastrophe and has nothing to do with an assessment of its frequency of occurrence. The catastrophe is altogether inevitable, since it is inscribed in the future: however, if the methodology of ongoing normative assessment is correctly applied, the catastrophe will not occur. A damage that will not occur must be lived with and treated as if inevitable: this is the aporia of our human condition in times of impending major threats.

To give an example of how ongoing normative assessment is applied in actual cases, we cite the Metropolitan Police commissioner Sir John Stevens, who, speaking about terrorist attacks in London as reflected in his everyday work, said in March

2004, "We do know that we have actually stopped terrorist attacks happening in London but... there is an inevitablity that some sort of attack will get through but my job is to make sure that does not happen" (*Stevens 2004*).

Each term in the formulation of the methodology of ongoing normative assessment requires clarification. We start with the word ongoing. The assessment that we are speaking about implies systems where the role of the human observer (individual or collective) is the one of observer-participant. As discussed in Section 3.2, the observer-participant does not analyze the system that he interacts with in terms of linear time; instead, he is constantly involved in an interplay of mutual constraints and interrelations between the system being analyzed and himself. The temporality of this relation is the circular temporality of projected time: if viewed from an external, Archimedes' point, influences go both ways, from the system to the observer and from the observer to the system. The observer, who preserves his identity throughout the whole development and whose point of view is 'from the inside', is bound to reason in a closed loop temporality, the only one that takes into account the mutual character of the constraints. Now, if one is to transpose the observer's circular vision back into the linearly developing, occurring time, he finds that the observer cannot do all his predictive work at one and only one point of occurring time. Circularity of relations within a complex system requires that the observer constantly revise his prediction. To make sure that the loop of interrelations between the system and himself is updated consistently and does not lead to a catastrophic elimination of any major component of either the system in question or of the observer himself, the latter must not stop addressing the question of the future at all times. No fixed-time prediction conserves its validity due to the circularity and self-referentiality of the complex system.

We now address the next term in the formulation of our methodology, normative assessment. A serious deficiency of the precautionary principle is that, unable to depart from the normativity proper to the calculus of probabilities, it fails to capture what constitutes the essence of ethical normativity concerning choice in a situation of uncertainty. We argue that judgements are normative but that this normativity, applied to the problem of the future, takes on a special form.

We refer to the concept of 'moral luck' in moral philosophy. Let us first illustrate with an example why probabilistic reasoning does not lead to any satisfactory account of judgement. Imagine that one must reach into an urn containing an indefinite number of balls and pull one out at random. Two thirds of the balls are black and only one third are white. The idea is to bet on the color of the ball before seeing it. Obviously, one should bet on black. And if one pulls out another ball, one should bet on black again. In fact, one should always bet on black, even though one foresees that one out of three times on average this will be an incorrect guess. Suppose that a white ball comes out, so that one discovers that the guess was incorrect. Does this a posteriori discovery justify a retrospective change of mind about the rationality of the bet that one made? No, of course not; one was right to choose black, even if the next ball to come out happened to be white. Where probabilities are concerned, the information as it becomes available can have no conceivable retroactive impact on one's judgement regarding the rationality of a past decision made in the face of an uncertain or risky future. This is a limitation of probabilistic judgement that has no equivalent in the case of moral judgement.

Take another example. A man spends the evening at a cocktail party. Fully aware that he has drunk more than is wise, he nevertheless decides to drive his car home. It is raining, the road is wet, the light turns red, and he slams on the brakes, but a little too late: after briefly skidding, the car comes to a halt just past the pedestrian crosswalk. Two scenarios are possible: either there was nobody in the crosswalk, and the man has escaped with no more than a retrospective fright. Or else the man ran over and killed a child. The judgement of the law, of course, but above all that of morality, will not be the same in both cases. Here is a variant: the man was sober when he drove his car. He has nothing to reproach himself for. But there is a child whom he runs over and kills, or else there is not. Once more, the unpredictable outcome will have a retroactive impact on the way the man's conduct is judged by others and also by the man himself. Therefore, moral luck becomes an argument proving that ethics is necessarily a future ethics, in Jonas's sense as described earlier, when it comes to judgement about a future event. However, the implementation of that future ethics is impeded in practice by the very inevitability of the uncertainty of the future. This is the ethical aporia we started with.

Is there a way out? Hans Jonas's credo is that there is no ethics without metaphysics. Only a radical change in metaphysics can allow us to escape from the ethical aporia. The major stumbling block of our current, implicit metaphysics of temporality turns out to be our common conception of the future as unreal. From the human belief in free will—'we may act otherwise'—is derived the conclusion that the future is not real, in the philosophical sense: 'future contingents', i.e. propositions about actions taken by a free agent in the future, e.g. 'John will pay back his debt tomorrow', are held to have no truth value. They are neither true nor false. If the future is not real, then it is not something that we can have cognizance of. If the future is not real, then it is not something that projects its shadow onto the present. Even when we know that a catastrophe is about to happen, we do not believe it: we do not believe what we know. If the future is not real, there is nothing in it that we should fear, or hope for. From our point of view, the derivation from free will to the unreality of the future is a sheer logical fallacy.

Like the car driver, but on an entirely different scale, human society taken as a collective subject has made a choice in the development of its potential capabilities that brings it under the jurisdiction of moral luck. It may be that its choice will lead to great and irreversible catastrophes; it may be that it will find the means to avert them, to get around them, or to get past them. No one can tell which way it will go. Judgement can only be retrospective. However, it is possible to anticipate, not the judgement itself, but the fact that it must depend on what will be known once the 'veil of ignorance' covering the future is lifted. Thus, there is still time to insure that our descendants will never be able to say 'too late!' — a too late that would mean that they find themselves in a situation where no human life worthy of the name is possible. Retrospective character of judgement means that, on the one hand, application of the existing norms for judging facts and, on the other hand, evaluation of new facts for updating the existing norms and creating new ones, are two complementary processes. While the first one is present in almost any sphere of human activity, the second process prevails over the first and acquires an all-important role in the anticipation of the future. What is a norm is being revised continuously, and at the same time this ever-changing normativity is applied to new facts. It is for this reason that the methodology of ongoing assessment requires that the assessment be normative and that the norms themselves be addressed in a continuous way.

Nanotechnology: Limitations and Gaps

The discussions of potential economic, medical, and environmental benefits may have given the false impression that nanotechnology will create a wondrous utopia in which all human problems are solved and we all live happily ever after. This is even more mistaken than the idea that new technologies always cause more problems than they solve. Many of the main constraints and difficulties faced by people are based not on technology or its lack, but instead by the very nature of the world we live in and the essence of our humanness. Increasing affluence based on molecular manufacturing won't end economic problems any more than past increases in affluence have. Wilderness can still be destroyed; people can be oppressed; financial markets can be unstable; trade wars can be waged; inflation can soar; individuals, companies, and nations can go into debt; bureaucracy can stifle innovation; tax levels can become crippling; wars and terrorism can rage. None of these will automatically be stopped by advanced technology. What is more, the potential benefits of new technologies aren't automatic. Nanotechnology could be used to restore the environment, to spread wealth, and to cure most illness. But will it? This depends on human action, working within the limits set by the real world. This chapter first describes some of the limits to what nanotechnology can accomplish, and then some of the adverse side effects of its basically good applications. The next will discuss the problem of accidents, which seems manageable, and then the far greater problem of potential abuse of new capabilities. The world imposes limits on what we can do. Technology in general (and nanotechnology in particular) can provide padding for us as we throw ourselves against these hard, sharp limitations, and can sometimes help us slip past old limits through previously unknown gaps. Eventually, though, we will encounter new limits. In the end, solid constraints will limit human action no matter how much we juggle atoms and molecules, or the bits and bytes of information. Let's look at some of these, starting with the most abstract and long term—the most definite and hardest to avoid—and moving toward the more personal and near term. Many problems differ fundamentally from the material problems of limited matter and energy: they involve information. Some of the most precious stores of information in the world today are the genetic codes of the biosphere. This information, different for virtually every individual organism, is the product of millions of events that we are incapable of modeling or recreating. When this information is lost, it is lost forever. When the atoms encoding this information are thoroughly scattered, there seems to be no way to retrieve it. With any species, most genetic information is shared in common, found in all members of that species. But the variations in genetic code between individuals are important, both to the individuals themselves and to the health and prospects of the species as a whole. Consider the northern white rhino, whose numbers have dropped to an estimated thirty-two animals, or the California condor, of which only forty remain, all in captivity. Even if biologists succeed in reestablishing these species—eight condors were hatched in 1989—much of the diversity of their genetic information has been lost. Worse yet are extinctions of species for which no tissue samples were saved. The future may see some amazing recoveries: dry skin and bones may yield a complete set of genes when sifted by molecular machinery, and even current techniques have been used to recover genes from an ancient leaf, almost 20 million years old. Our eyes and instruments cannot yet tell us how much information from the past remains, but we do know that genetic information is being lost every day, and once lost, it is irretrievable.

People have often been wrong about physical limits, confusing the limits of their technology with the limits of the possible. As a result, learned men first dismissed the idea of heavier-than-air flight, and then dismissed the idea of flying to the Moon. Yet physical limits are real, and all technology—past, present, and future—will stay within those limits. There is even reason to suspect that some of those limits are where the learned now believe them to be. Nanotechnology will make it possible to push closer to the real limits set by natural law, but it will not change those laws or the limits they set. It will not affect the law of gravity, the gravitational constant, the speed of light, the charge of the electron, the radius of the hydrogen atom, the value of Planck's constant, the effects of the uncertainty principle, the principle of least action, the mass of the proton, the laws of thermodynamics, or the boiling point of water. Nanotechnology won't make energy or matter from nothing. It seems a good bet that no one will build a faster than light spacecraft, or an antigravity machine, or a cable twice as strong as diamond. There are limits. Science today may be wrong about some limits, but scientific knowledge is practically defined to be our best information about how the world works, so it isn't wise to bet against it. There will be claims that nanotechnology will be able to do things that it can't, or that capabilities are around the corner when they aren't. Sometimes these will be innocent errors, sometimes they will be culpably stupid errors, and sometimes they will be what amounts to fraud. Among the problems that nanotechnology cannot solve is that of misguided claims, by people calling themselves "scientists," "engineers," or "businesspeople," that they have a big technical breakthrough worth a fortune. Every interesting new technology, particularly in its early days, is a chaotic mix of competent workers and charlatans. For every Thomas Edison inventing useful products such as light bulbs or the precursor of movie projectors, there were people promoting electric hairbrushes to cure baldness, and electric shoes, electric belts, electric hats—the list goes on—that authoritatively claimed cures for infertility, overweight, underweight, and all the ills and discomforts of mankind. Today, we laugh at the credulity of our forefathers who bought these gadgets; we shouldn't, unless we laugh at our own times as well.

Natural law imposes limits, but so does the nature of human beings. These will continue as long as people do. Reproduction is a deeply ingrained instinct enforced by the march of time, which ruthlessly discards the genetic material of all who neglect it. Many would argue that the Earth is already overpopulated. While nanotechnology could enable the current population, and even a greatly increased one, to live more lightly on the Earth, there will still be limits to Earth's capacity. The norms of human life are shaped by ancient patterns: high rates of infant or childhood mortality have been facts of life for millennia, and having many, many children has been a way to ensure that one or two will survive to work on the farm, and to care for you in your old age. Large families naturally become traditional. When modern medicine and reliable food supplies change those conditions—as they have, in cultural terms, virtually overnight—behavior does not shift as quickly. The result is the Third World population boom. In Western countries, where there has been time for behavior to adapt, a huge family is the exception. It might seem that our problem is solved. Molecular manufacturing can make everyone wealthy, and wealthy populations today have stable or shrinking populations. The Earth can support more people with advanced technologies, and these will also open up the vast room and resources of the world beyond Earth. Would that this were true. If 99 per cent of the people in a population respond to wealth by reducing childbearing, the population will indeed stabilize or shrink, for a while. But populations are not uniform. What of the 1 per cent, say, who are members of a minority with different values? If that minority has a growth rate of 5 per cent per year, then in ninety-five years they will be the majority, and in one thousand years their population will have grown by a factor of 1,500,000,000,000,000,000,000, if resource limits or genocide haven't intervened. Note that the Hutterites of North America, a reasonably wealthy religious group viewing fertility control as a sin and high fertility as a blessing, have managed an average of ten children per woman. Given enough time, exponential growth of even the smallest population can consume all the resources in reach. The right to reproduce is often regarded as basic, as illustrated by the outrage at reports of forced abortion in the People's Republic of China. The Hutterites and many others regard it as part of their freedom of religion. But what happens when parents have more children than they can support—does redistribution solve the problem? If reproduction is not forcibly suppressed, and if resources are forcibly and repeatedly redistributed so that each human being has a roughly equal share, then each person's share will steadily shrink. Even given the most optimistic assumptions regarding available resources, with a policy of resource redistribution and unlimited reproduction, the amount per person would eventually be insufficient to sustain life. This policy must be avoided, because if it is followed, it will kill everyone. As soon as we grant that any entity is entitled to certain rights—whether that entity be a human child, an animal, or some future artificial intelligence—the question arises of who is responsible for providing resources to support it when it can't do so for itself. The above argument indicates that a policy of coercion by some central power to compel the entire population to support an exponentially exploding population of these individuals would lead directly to disaster. Ultimately, this responsibility must rest with the entities' initiator: the designer of the artificial intelligence, the owner of the pet, the parents of the child. No new technology can magically remove the limits imposed by natural law, and thereby lift the burden of human responsibility.

Every time a technology solves a problem, it creates new problems. This doesn't mean that the change is neutral, or for the worse, of course. The Salk and Sabin vaccines for polio virtually destroyed the iron-lung industry, and the pocket calculator virtually destroyed the slide-rule industry, but these advances were worth the price of some economic adjustment. Molecular manufacturing and nanotechnology will bring far greater changes, placing far greater strains on our ability to adapt. We shouldn't be surprised when basically beneficial applications make someone miserable. Our lives are largely centered around problems. If we can solve many of these problems, the centers of our lives will shift, creating fresh problems. This section sketches some of the issues of change and adaptation more to raise questions than to offer solutions.

Molecular manufacturing offers the possibility of drastic change, a change in the means of production more fundamental than the introduction of industry, or of agriculture. Our economic and social structures have evolved around assumptions that will no longer be valid. How will we handle the changes in the way we work and live? Nanotechnology will have wide-ranging impact in many areas, including economic, industrial, and social patterns. What do historical patterns in similar circumstances tell us about the future? Any powerful technology with broad applications revolutionizes lives, and nanotechnology will be no exception. Depending on one's point of view, this may sound exciting or it may sound disturbing, but it most certainly does not sound comfortable. In comparison to many projections of the twenty-first century, though, nanotechnology may lead to comparatively comfortable change. The changes most often projected—for a future not including nanotechnology—have been ecological disaster, resource shortages, economic collapse, and a slide back into misery. The rise of nanotechnology will offer an alternative—green wealth—but that alternative will bring great changes from the patterns of recent decades. Times of rapid technological change are disconcerting. For most of humanity's existence, people lived in a stable pattern. They learned to live as their parents had lived—by hunting and gathering, later by farming—and changes were small and gradual. A knowledge of the past was a reliable guide to the future. Sudden changes, when they did occur, were apt to be ruinous: invasions or natural disasters. These sudden changes were fought or repaired or survived as best one could. Making major changes by choice was rare, and radical innovations were generally for the worse: the old ways at least ensured the ancestors' survival, the new might not. This made cultures conservative. It is only natural that there be efforts to resist change, but before undertaking such an effort, it makes sense to examine the record of what works and what doesn't. The only examples of successful change fighters have been communities that have created and maintained barricades to isolate themselves from the outside world socially, culturally, and technologically.

For the two centuries before 1854, Japan turned its back on the outside world, following a deliberate policy of seclusion. The leaders of Albania restricted contacts for many years; only recently have they started to open up. Isolation attempts have worked better on a smaller scale, when participation is voluntary rather than decreed by government. Today, within the Hawaiian island chain, the tiny, privately owned island of Niihau, sixteen miles long and six miles wide, is deliberately kept as a preserve of the nineteenth-century Hawaiian lifestyle. Over two hundred full-blooded Hawaiians there speak the Hawaiian language and use no telephones, plumbing, television, and no electricity (except in the school). The Amish of Pennsylvania have no surrounding ocean to help maintain their isolation, but rely instead on tight social, religious, and technological rules aimed at keeping external technology and culture out, and themselves grouped in; those who leave the fold are excluded. On a national scale, attempts to take only one part of the package—whether social or technological—haven't done well at all. For decades, the Soviet Union and the Eastern bloc nations welcomed Western technology but attempted tight restrictions on the passage of people, ideas, and goods. Yet illegal music, thoughts, literature, and other knowledge still crept in—as they do into the Islamic countries. Fighting technological change in society at large has had little success, where that change gave some large group what it wanted. The most famous fighters of technological change—the Luddites—were unsuccessful. They smashed "automated" textile machinery that was replacing old hand looms during the early industrial revolution in England, but people wanted affordable clothing, and smashing equipment in one place just moved the business elsewhere. Change has sometimes been postponed, as when a later group, under the banner of "Captain Swing," smashed hundreds of threshing machines in a wide area of southern England in 1830. They succeeded in keeping the old, labor-intensive ways of harvesting for over a generation.

In previous centuries, when the world was less tightly connected by international trade, communications, and transportation, delays of years and even decades could be enforced through violence or legal maneuvers such as tariffs, trade barriers, regulations, or outright banning. Attempting to stop or postpone change is less successful today, when technology moves internationally almost as easily as people do—and human travel is so easy that 25 million people cross the Atlantic each year. Change fighters find that the problems they create mount with time. Products made using the old, high-cost techniques are uncompetitive. There is no way to bring back the "old jobs": they no longer make sense. But old habits die hard, and these same responses to the prospect of technological change continue today—ignoring it, denying it, and opposing it. Societies that have fought change, as Britain did, have fallen behind in a cloud of coal smoke. Why did the Luddites respond violently? Perhaps their response can be attributed to three factors: First, the change in their lives was sudden and radical; second, it affected a large group of people at one time, in one area; and third, in a world unprepared for rapid technological change, there was no safety net to catch the unemployed. While local economies might have been able to absorb a trickle of hungry laid-off workers, they lacked the size and diversity needed to offer other employment options quickly to large numbers of unemployed. In the twentieth century, however, societies have of necessity become somewhat better adapted to change. This has been a matter of necessity, because sluggish communities soon fall behind. In the ancient days of peasant stability, there was no need for institutions like Consumer Reports to study and rate new products, or regulators like the Environmental Protection Agency to watch over new hazards. We developed the needs, and we developed the institutions. These mechanisms represent important adaptions, not so much to the technologies of the twentieth century, but to the increasing change in technology during the twentieth century. There is great room for improvement, but they can perhaps provide a basis for adapting to the next century as well. Even with the best of institutions to cushion shocks and discourage abuse, there will be problems. The very act of solving problems of production—of increasing wealth—will create problems of economic change.

Over centuries, the trend has seemed to be toward centralization, beginning with the rise of factories and industrial towns. What drove these developments was the high cost of machinery and plant operations, the need to be near power sources, the impracticality of transportation among many small, dispersed sites, and the need for face-to-face communication. Beginning with the first industrial revolution, factories employed large numbers of people in one place, leading to overcrowding and making local economies dependent on one industry and sometimes on a single company.

Costly equipment necessitated central locations for textile production, rather than the cottage industries where a lone woman could earn a livelihood carding wool and creating thread on a spinning wheel (providing the origin of the term *spinster*). By the 1930s, the belief in the virtues of centralization and central planning—the supposed efficiencies and economies of scale—led to nationwide or continentwide experiments in centralization. But over the last decade, these large-scale experiments have been dismantled, from Britain's privatization of nationalized utilities to the beginning of a return to the market system in Eastern European countries. Because the old limits on transportation, energy sources, and communication have fallen, business is now decentralizing. Between 1981 and 1986, the Forbes 500 companies cut their employees by 1.8 million. But during those same years, total civilian jobs went up by 9.2 million. Start-up companies created 14 million jobs; small companies created another 4.5 million. Telecommuting is booming, as are new businesses, independent professionals, and cottage industries. We've also seen the resurgence of small, but highly diverse stores: gourmet food shops, specialty ethnic shops, tea and coffee purveyors, organic and health food stores, bakeries, yogurt shops, gourmet ice-cream stores, convenience stores offering twenty-four-hour access, shops selling packaged food plus snacks. These stores epitomize something fundamental: At some point, what we want is not a standard good at an ever cheaper price, but special things customized to meet our own individual tastes or needs. The trend for advanced technologies seems to be leading away from centralization. Will nanotechnology counter or accelerate this trend? By reducing the cost of equipment, by reducing the need for large numbers of people to work on one product, and bringing greater ability to produce the customized goods that people want, nanotechnology will probably continue the twentieth-century trend toward decentralization. The results, though, will be disruptive to existing businesses. The computer industry perhaps provides a clue to what might happen as costs are lowered by nanotechnology. The computer-software industry is characterized by the garage-shop start-up. When your equipment is cheap—inexpensive PCs built around low-cost chips—and you can make a product by throwing in some ingenuity and human labor, it's possible to start a new industry on a shoestring. In 1900, when cars were simple, there were many car manufacturers. By the 1980s, if you weren't an industrial giant like General Motors or Ford, Honda or Nissan, you had to be John De Lorean to even get a shot at acquiring the capital to play in the business. If molecular manufacturing can slash the capital costs for producing cars or other plant-intensive equipment, we will see the equivalent of garage-shop businesses springing up to offer new products, and hiring workers away from the industrial giants of today just as the personal computer has destroyed the dominance of the mainframe.

The U.S.A. dream is to be an entrepreneur, and the technological trends of the twentieth century point in that direction. Nanotechnology probably continues it. In one area, however, the late twentieth-century trend has been toward uniformity. The nations of Western Europe are in the process of uniting under one set of economic rules, and parts of Eastern Europe are anxious to join them. More and more supranational and transnational organizations knit the world together. The growth of trade has motivated economic integration. Molecular manufacturing will work against this trend as well, permitting radical decentralization in economic terms. This will help groups that wish to step aside from the stream of change, enabling them to be more independent of the turbulent outside world, picking and choosing what technologies they use. But it will also help groups that wish to free themselves from the constraints of the international community. Economic sanctions will have little force against countries that need no imports or exports to maintain a high standard of living. And export restrictions will likewise do little to hamper a military buildup. By weakening the ties of trade, molecular manufacturing threatens to weaken the glue that holds nations together. We need that glue, though, to deal with the arms control issues raised by molecular manufacturing itself. This problem, caused by the potential for decentralization, may loom large in the coming years.

Lester Milbrath, professor of sociology and political science, observes, "Nanotechnologies will create the problem of how to meaningfully and sustainably occupy the time of people who need not perform much work in order to have a sufficiency of life's goods. Our society has never faced this problem before, and it is not clear what social restructuring will be required to have a good society in those circumstances. We face much deep social learning." The world has had little experience with what anthropologists call "abundance economies." The native American tribes of the Pacific Northwest were one of those rarities. Ruth Benedict, in her classic book *Patterns of Culture*, wrote, "Their civilization was built upon an ample supply of goods, inexhaustible, and obtained without excessive expenditure of labor." The Kwakiutls became famous for their "potlatches": contests in which they sought to shame their rivals by heaping more gifts upon them than they could ever return. The potlatches would often be a year in preparation, last for days, and occasionally involve destruction of entire buildings. It was certainly a colorful form of keeping up with the Joneses. What will motivate us, once we have achieved an abundance economy? What will we regard as worthwhile goals to pursue? Increased knowledge, new art, improved philosophy, eliminating human and planetary ills? Will we find ourselves creating a better, wiser world, or sunk in boredom and jaded now that we have all and want nothing? If boredom gets out of hand, the lively spectacle of wealthy donors seeking to outdo each other to endow the arts, aid the poor, and do other good deeds for the sake of prestige would be welcome. What will happen as life spans continue to lengthen and the time needed to make a living decreases? Even today, there are people who, when confronted with the prospect of a significantly longer life span, exclaim that they couldn't imagine what they would do with all that time. This response can be hard to understand, when it would take a thousand years to walk all the world's roads, more thousands of years to read all the world's books, and another ten thousand years to have a dinner conversation with each of the world's people—but tastes differ, and even a few decades of bad television might make anyone long for the peace of the grave.

A major concern, and certainly the single area of greatest upheaval, is employment (which may become hard to distinguish from leisure). Once, people had little choice of employment. To keep a full belly, most had to work at the only job available: peasant farming. Eventually, people will have a complete choice of employment: they will be able to keep a full belly and a wealthy lifestyle while doing whatever they please. Today, we are about halfway between those extremes. In advanced economies, many different jobs are deemed useful enough that other people will offer an adequate income in exchange for the result. Some people can make a living doing something they enjoy—is this work, or leisure? The impact of nanotechnology on patterns of employment will depend on when it arrives. Current demographics show a shrinking supply of young people entering the work force. Agriculture, the assembly line, and entry level service jobs are experiencing a labor shortage, and no relief is in sight. If these trends continue, nanotechnology may show up in the midst of a shortage of labor. If it arrives late enough, it may compete with industries that are already nearing full automation; "job displacement" may mean replacing an industrial robot with a nanomachine. Employment patterns have shifted radically in the past. One hundred and fifty years ago, the United States was an agricultural nation—69 per cent of all people worked the land and a growing percentage worked in industry doing things like building steam locomotives for Baldwin Locomotives Works or tanning leather for the giant Central Leather monopoly. By the early twentieth century, agriculture was waning in numbers but increasing in productivity; most people worked in industry, and the tiny information and service sector was beginning to grow. Today, the picture has reversed: 69 per cent of employed Americans work in information or service jobs, only 28 per cent work in industrial production, and 3 per cent in agriculture. This tiny fraction feeds the other 97 per cent of Americans, exports hugely to other countries, and receives subsidies and price support payments to stop them from growing even more food. Manufacturing, even without nanotechnology, seems to be heading toward a similar condition. With an ever-declining percentage of our population working in manufacturing, we have as everyday products things that were once available only to kings and the high nobility. Yet owning multiple suits of clothes, having personal portraits of ourselves and family members, having music upon our command, having a personal bedroom, and having a coach awaiting our need—these are now regarded as being among the bare necessities of life. It may be possible to adjust to even greater wealth with even less required labor, but the adjustment will surely cause problems. In a world in which nanotechnology reduces the need for workers in agriculture and manufacturing still further, the question will be asked, "What jobs are left for people to do once food, clothing, and shelter are very inexpensive?" Again, the twentieth century provides some guidelines. As technology has reduced costs by efficiently producing many units of an identical item, people have begun to demand customization to meet individual needs or preferences. As a result, there are ever more jobs in producing custom goods. Today, semi-custom goods that try to help us meet our needs or express our taste abound: designer linens, ready-to-wear fashions, cosmetics, cars, trucks, recreational vehicles, furniture, carpeting, shoes, televisions, toys, sports equipment, washing machines, microwave ovens, food processors, bread bakers, pasta makers, home computers, telephones, answering machines—are all available in large and ever-changing variety.

Just as varied is the fabulous wealth and diversity of information produced in the twentieth century. Information products are a large factor in the economy: Americans buy 2.5 billion books, 6 billion magazines, and 20 billion newspapers each year. In recent years, new magazines have been invented and launched at the rate of one every business day of the year. A visit to a well-stocked magazine rack shows only a hint of the wealth of highly specialized publications, each one focused on a specialized interest or attitude: hotdog skiing, low-fat gourmet cooking, travel in Arizona, a magazine for people with a home office and a computer, and finely tuned magazines on health, leisure, psychology, science, politics, movie stars and rock stars, music, hunting, fishing, games, art, fashion, beauty, antiques, computers, cars, guns, wrestling. Motion pictures, which started as a flock of independent production companies and then consolidated into the great studios of the 1930s, have since followed the decentralization and diversification trends of recent years. Now an expanding range of film entertainment comes via network TV, cable channels, private networks, videotapes, music videos. Independent producers are aided by the technology innovations of cable, direct broadcast satellites, videotape technology, laser disks, videocameras.

The arts have burgeoned, with the general public as the new patron of the arts. Any artist or art form that could find and satisfy a market boomed in the twentieth century. Not just the traditional arts of actors, writers, musicians, and painters, but all forms of "domestic" artistry have grown to unprecedented levels: landscape and interior design, fashion design, cosmetics, hairstyling, architecture, bridal consulting. Providing for these demands are some of the "service and information" jobs created in the late twentieth century. "Service" jobs include many ways of helping other people: from nursing to computer repairs to sales. In "information" jobs, projected to have the fastest percentage growth over the next decade, people find, evaluate, analyze, and create information. A magazine columnist or TV news producer obviously has an "information" job. But so do programmers, paralegals, lawyers, accountants, financial analysts, credit counselors, psychologists, librarians, managers, engineers, biologists, travel agents, and teachers. "Increasingly," states *Forbes* magazine, "people are no longer laborers; they are educated professionals who carry their most important work tools in their heads. Dismissing them from their jobs, cutting them off from their places of employment may hurt them emotionally and financially. But it doesn't separate them from their vocation in the same way that pushing a farmer off his freshly seeded land does. For centuries workers were more dependent on a particular physical setting than they are now. Modern occupations generally give their practitioners more independence—and greater mobility—than did those of yesteryear." These human skills that people carry with them will continue to be valued: managing complexity, providing creativity, customizing things for other people, helping people deal with problems, providing old services in new contexts, teaching, entertaining, and making decisions. A reasonable guess would be that many of the service and information industries of the twentieth century will continue to evolve and exist in a world with nanotechnology. What is harder to imagine would be what new industries will come into being once we have new capabilities and lower costs. Along with the old economic law of supply and demand is another governing factor: price elasticity effects. People's desire for something is "elastic": it expands or contracts when the cost of something valuable goes down or up. If the price of a flight to Europe is five hundred dollars, more people will take a European vacation than if the price is five thousand dollars. When you had to hire a highly trained mathematician to do equations, calculation was slow and expensive. People didn't do much of it unless they absolutely had to. Today, computers make calculation cheap and automatic. So now businesses do sophisticated financial modeling, chemists design protein molecules, students calculate orbital trajectories for spaceships, children play video games, moviemakers do ever more amazing special effects, and the cartoon—virtually extinct because of high labor costs—has returned to movie theaters, all because computers permit cheap calculation. Nanotechnology will offer new, affordable capabilities to these and other people. Today, it's as hard to predict what new industries will be invented as it would have been for the creators of the ENIAC computer to have predicted cheap, handheld game computers for children.

So rather than producing drastic unemployment, nanotechnology seems likely to continue the trend already seen today, away from jobs that can be automated and into jobs where the human perspective is vital. But the true possibilities are, as always in the modern world, beyond predicting.

Major shifts in demographics always cause disruptions. Even when we know they are coming, we never prepare for them. Our plans are based on expectations of what will happen. If things don't go as expected, we find that we have "malinvested." Houston real estate was valuable and looked to become even more so when times were good for the oil business there; when the fortunes of the oil business changed, Houston real estate was found to have been overbuilt, overpriced, and many millions of dollars were lost. Lengthening life spans push people toward taking a longer-term perspective, but rapid rates of change force a shorter-term perspective in investments. Turbulence in technology and in governmental monetary policy have already shortened time horizons. Businesspeople once routinely built plants with a thirty-year useful life. Today, the rate of change is too fast, and uncertainty regarding inflation and potential changes in tax laws is too great for such investments to make sense. Faster change will shrink time horizons further. Governments have taken on themselves the burden of looking a lifetime ahead, and the Social Security Administration is in for some rough times. When Otto von Bismarck, Germany's Iron Chancellor, came up with the notion of a guaranteed old age pension, it was a cynically clever and low-cost way to gain popular goodwill. So few people lived to age sixty-five that the amounts paid out in pensions were a pittance. After watching the German experiment for a handful of years, other governments began following suit. None of them expected a world like ours where a baby girl born in the United States today has an average life expectancy of 78.4 years—double that of Bismarck's time—and even this estimate is based on the faulty assumption that her medical care will be no better than her great-grandmother's was. At present, the Social Security Administration has two models: one they call "positive" and one they call "negative." In the "positive" model, people work like dogs until old age, retire, and promptly die—presumably before they've had a chance to collect substantial social security or medical benefits. In the "negative" model, people retire early, develop illnesses that require medical intervention, and then live a long time making doctor visits and hospital stays during those years. Plans based on these models deserve to be disrupted. A better, more realistic scenario would have people living and able to support themselves for a long time, with illnesses that can be handled easily and inexpensively. Present social security benefits are enough to provide a certain standard of living—food, housing, transportation, and so forth. In a future of great material wealth, these benefits will be easy to provide, and present projections of economic woe resulting from an aging population will seem quaint. Back in the seventies, author Alvin Toffler brought out a book called *Future Shock*, describing how disturbing rapid change is for people. The book was a best-seller, but how much actual future shock has been seen in the past decade? Most people seem to have come through the last two decades pretty much all right, not in a state of shock at all. Rather than being shocked by technology, they are instead annoyed about pollution and traffic. Does this mean Toffler was wrong in predicting future shock? It's true that technology has been advancing rapidly in many areas over the past twenty years. But consider the average person's home life: How much of this rapid technological advance has shown up there? A great deal, yet most of it is hidden, unlike the earlier part of the century, where obvious change was the norm. Electric lights and appliances, automobiles, telephones, airplanes, radio, and television affected almost everyone's private life. One person's life could span the time from horse-and-buggy travel to watching the Moon landings on television. In contrast, the past twenty years have seen new technologies move more quietly into the home. The VCR and microwave oven don't seem nearly as revolutionary as earlier inventions. Telephone answering machines are useful but haven't caused major changes in lifestyles. Fax machines are handy, but they're much like having very fast mail, and as this is written, fax machines aren't yet in most homes. So it's not surprising that the average person has felt little future shock lately. New medicines taken as pills—which may be radically improved—look just like the earlier pills. The computerized bills that come in the mail aren't any more exciting to pay than the old human-prepared bills. This situation is unlikely to last. How much longer can technology advance so rapidly in so many fields without major effects on our lifestyles? There's been a respite from future shock in the last three decades; people have had a chance to catch their breath. When nanotechnology arrives, will future shock arrive with it? Some segments of society today are already getting practice in dealing with rapid technological advance. Those getting the most vigorous workout are in the computer field, where a machine two years old is regarded as obsolete, and software must be updated every few months to keep abreast of the new developments. But has this terrific rate of progress been dizzying or overwhelming? Not for the consumer—on the contrary, computers have become easier to use. In the 1960s, the New Math that was introduced into American grade schools and junior high schools included extensive study of arithmetic using numbers written in something other than the familiar base 10. This was to prepare the "Adults of Tomorrow" for "The Computer Age" in which we would all be writing assembly language computer programs in binary (base 2) code. But customers now purchase software rather than write it themselves—they need never deal with computer languages at all, much less a primitive assembly language. The rapid increase of computer speed has helped make computers easier to use. This progression has occurred many times before: Cars started off with external hand cranks, then advanced to starters you could yank from the comfort of the driver's seat; now starters perform invisibly when you turn the key in the ignition.

This pattern will surely continue. First, some people will adapt to the technology, but in the long run the technology will adapt to us. The more flexible and powerful the technology, the more easily it will adapt. Seen from a distance, seemingly trivial patterns of adaptation form part of a larger process that has marked the last century: the Western world has begun to invent mechanisms to handle a world of persistent change. Our mechanisms are by no means perfect or painless, as any unemployed person can testify. Employment agencies and headhunters for job seekers; unemployment and severance packages to ease job transitions; on-the-job training, continuing education, retraining, specialized seminars to update professional skills, professional associations, networking, community resources centers, government training programs, and volunteer agencies are just a few of the inventions dealing with change and transition. Consumer information services, regulatory agencies, and environmental organizations are others. The most effective will endure. More options will continue to be invented.

REFERENCES

Averback, R.S., J. Bernholc, and D.L. Nelson. 1991. *MRS Symposium Proceedings* Vol. 206.

Baird, D. & Shew, A.: 2004, 'Probing the History of Scanning Tunneling Microscopy', in: D. Baird, A. Nordmann & J. Schummer (eds.), *Discovering the Nanoscale*, Amsterdam: IOS Press, pp. 145-156.

Baird, D.; Nordmann, A. & Schummer, J. (eds.): 2004, *Discovering the Nanoscale*, Amsterdam: IOS Press.

Baker, R.T.K. Synthesis, properties and applications of graphite nanofibers. In *R&D status and trends*, ed. Siegel et al.

Bate, R., Frazier, G., Frensley, W., Reed., M., "An Overview of Nanoelectronics," *Texas Instruments Technical Journal*, July-August 1989, pp. 13-20.

Beck, J.S., J.C. Vartuli, W.J. Roth, M.E. Leonowicz, C.T. Kresge, K.D. Schmitt, C.T.-W. Chu, D.H. Olsen, E.W. Shepard, S.B. McCullen, J.B. Higgins, and J.L. Schlenker. 1992. *J. Am. Chem. Soc.* 114:10834.

Bensaude-Vincent, B.: 2001, 'The Construction of a Discipline: Materials Science in the United States', *Historical Studies in the Physical and Biological Sciences*, 31, 223-248.

Bensaude-Vincent, B.: 2004, 'Two Cultures of Nanotechnology?', *Hyle: International Journal for Philosophy of Chemistry*, 10(2), 65-82.

Berube, D.M.: 2004, 'The Rhetoric of Nanotechnology', in: D. Baird, A. Nordmann & J. Schummer (eds.), *Discovering the Nanoscale*, Amsterdam: IOS Press, pp. 173-192.

Bowes, C.L., A. Malek, and G.A. Ozin. 1996. *Chem. Vap. Deposition* 2:97.

Braun, P.V., P. Osenar, and S.I. Stupp. 1996. *Nature*. 368: 2.

Braun, T.; Schubert, A. & Zsindely, S.: 1997, 'Nanoscience and nanotechnology on the balance', *Scientometrics*, 38, 321-325.

Brinker, C.J. 1996. *Curr. Opin. Solid State Mater. Sci.* 1:798.

Brown, N.: 2004, 'Needle on the Real: Technoscience and Poetry at the Limits of Fabrication', in: N.K. Hayles (ed.), *Nanoculture: Implications of the New Technoscience*, Bristol, UK: Intellect Books, pp. 173-190.

Bueno, O.: 2004, 'The Drexler-Smalley Debated on Nanotechnology: Incommensurability at Work?', *Hyle: International Journal for Philosophy of Chemistry*, 10(2), 83-98.

Bueno, O.: 2004, 'Von Neumann, Self-Reproduction and the Constitution of Nanophenomena', in: D. Baird, A. Nordmann & J. Schummer (eds.), *Discovering the Nanoscale*, Amsterdam: IOS Press, pp. 101-115.

Carroll, J.S.: 2001, 'Social Science Research Methods for Assessing Societal Implications of Nanotechnology', in: M.C. Roco and W.S. Bainbridge (eds.), *Societal Implications of Nanoscience and Nanotechnology*, Dordrecht: Kluwer, pp. 188-192.

Chen, C-Y., S.L. Burkett, H.-X. Li, and M.E. Davis. 1993. *Microporous Mater.* 2:27.

Chianelli, R.R. 1998. Synthesis, fundamental properties and applications of nanocrystals, sheets, and fullerenes based on layered transition metal chalcogenides. In *R&D status and trends*, ed. Siegel et al.

Chianelli, R.R., M. Daage, and M.J. Ledoux. 1994. *Advances in Catalysis* 40:177.

Claeson, T., and Likharev, K.," Single Electronics," *Scientific American,* June 1992, pp. 80-85.

Coenen, C.: 2004, 'Nanofuturismus: Anmerkungen zu seiner Relevanz, Analyse und Bewertung', *Technikfolgenabschätzung ' Theorie und Praxis*, 13 (2), 78-85.

Crandall, B.C. and Lewis, J., *Nanotechnology: Research and Perspectives*, MIT Press, Cambridge, 1992.

Crow, M. & Sarewitz, D.: 2001, 'Nanotechnology and Societal Transformation', in: M.C. Roco and W.S. Bainbridge (eds.), *Societal Implications of Nanoscience and Nanotechnology*, Dordrecht: Kluwer, pp. 45-54.

de Souza e Silva, A.: 2004, 'The Invisible Imaginary: Museum Spaces, Hybrid Reality and Nanotechnology', in: N.K. Hayles (ed.), *Nanoculture: Implications of the New Technoscience*, Bristol, UK: Intellect Books, pp. 27-82.

Decker, M.; Fiedeler, U.; Fleischer, Th.: 2004, 'Ich sehe was, was Du nicht siehst... zur Definition von Nanotechnologie', *Technikfolgenabschätzung ' Theorie und Praxis*, 13 (2), 10-16.

Dresselhaus, M., and G. Dresselhaus. 1995. *Ann. Rev. Mat. Sci*. 25:487.

Dresselhaus, M.S. 1998. Carbon-based nanostructures. In *R&D status and trends*, ed. Siegel et al.

Dresselhaus, M.S., G. Dresselhaus, and P. Eklund. 1996. *Science of fullerenes and carbon nanotubes*. San Diego: Academic Press.

Drexler, K.E.: 2004, 'Nanotechnology: From Feynman to Funding', *Bulletin of Science, Technology & Society*, 24, 21-27.

Dupuy, J.-P.: 2004, 'Complexity and Uncertainty: A Prudential Approach To Nanotechnology', in: European Commission (Community Health and Consumer Protection): *Nanotechnologies: A Preliminary Risk Analysis on the Basis of a Workshop, Brussels, 1-2 March 2004*, pp. 71-93 (www.europa.eu.int/comm/health/ ph_risk/documents/ev_20040301_en.pdf).

Dupuy, J.-P.: 2004, 'Pour une évaluation normative du programme nanotechnologique', *Annales des Mines*, (February 2004), 27-32.

Einsiedel, E.F.; Goldenberg, L.: 2004, 'Dwarfing the Social? Nanotechnology Lessons from the Biotechnology Front', *Bulletin of Science, Technology & Society*, 24, 28-33.

ETC: 2003a, *The Big Down: Atom Tech ' Technologies Converging at the Atomic Scale*. Winnipeg, Canada: Action Group on Erosion, Technology and Concentration [www.etcgroup.org/ documents/TheBigDown.pdf].

ETC: 2003b, 'No Small Matter II: The Case for a Global Moratorium ' Size Matters!' *Occasional Paper Series* 7(1) [www.etcgroup.org/documents/Occ.Paper_Nanosafety.pdf].

Etzkowitz, H., 2001, 'Nano-Science and Society: Finding a Social Basis for Science Policy', in: M.C. Roco and W.S. Bainbridge (eds.), *Societal Implications of Nanoscience and Nanotechnology*, Dordrecht: Kluwer, pp. 121-128.

European Comission: *European Workshop on Social and Economic Research on Nanotechnologies and Nanosciences, Brussels, 14-15 April 2004* [www.stage-research.net/STAGE/PAGES/ Nano.html].

European Commission (Community Health and Consumer Protection): 2004, *Nanotechnologies: A Preliminary Risk Analysis on theBasis of a Workshop, Brussels, 1-2 March 2004* [www.europa.eu.int/comm/health/ ph_risk/documents/ev_20040301_en.pdf].

European Commission: 2004, *Converging Technologies: Shaping the Future of European Societies (Report of the High Level Expert Group "Foresighting the New Technology Wave")*, Brussels:

European Commission Research [http://europa.eu.int/comm/research/conferences/2004/ntw/index_en.html].

F. Buot, "Mesoscopic Physics and Nanoelectronics: Nanoscience and Nanotechnology," *Physics Reports*, pp.73-174, 1993.

F. Capasso and S. Datta, "Quantum Electron Devices," *Physics Today*, pp.74-82, February 1990.

Feynman, R., "There's Plenty of Room at the Bottom: An invitation to Enter a New Field of Physics," Talk at the Annual Meeting of the American Physical Society, 29 December 1959. Reprinted in Appendix B of Crandall and Lewis. See citation above.

Fielder, F.A.; Reynolds, G.H.: 1994, 'Legal Problems of Nanotechnology: An Overview', *Southern California Interdisciplinary Law Journal*, 3, 593-629.

Fleischer, Th.; Decker, M. & Fiedeler, U. (eds.): 2004, *Große Aufmerksamkeit für kleine Welten ' Nanotechnologie und ihre Folgen*, special issue of *Technikfolgenabschätzung ' Theorie und Praxis*, 13 (2), 5-85 [www.itas.fzk.de/tatup/042/inhalt.htm].

Fogelberg, H. & Glimell, H.: 2003, 'Molecular Matters: In Search of the Real Stuff', in: H. Fogelberg & H. Glimell, *Bringing Visibility to the Invisible: Towards A Social Understanding of Nanotechnology*, Göteborg: Göteborg University, pp. 5-32 [www.sts.gu.se/publications/STS_report_6.pdf].

Fogelberg, H. & Glimell, H.: 2003, *Bringing Visibility to the Invisible: Towards A Social Understanding of Nanotechnology*, Göteborg: Göteborg University [www.sts.gu.se/publications/STS_report_6.pdf].

Fogelberg, H.: 2003, 'The Grand Politics of Technoscience: Contextualizing Nanotechnology', in: H. Fogelberg & H. Glimell, *Bringing Visibility to the Invisible: Towards A Social Understanding of Nanotechnology*, Göteborg: Göteborg University, pp. 33-54 [www.sts.gu.se/publications/STS_report_6.pdf].

Fogelberg, H.: 2003, 'The Material Culture of Nanotechnology', in: H. Fogelberg & H. Glimell, *Bringing Visibility to the Invisible: Towards A Social Understanding of Nanotechnology*, Göteborg: Göteborg University, pp. 99-114.

Frazier, G., "An Ideology For Nanoelectronics," in *Concurrent Computations: Algorithms, Architecture, and Technology*, Plenum Press, New York, 1988.

Glimell, H.: 2001, 'Challenging Limits ' Excerpts from an Emerging Ethnography of Nano Physicists', in: H. Glimell & O. Johlin (eds.), *The Social Production of Technology: On the Everyday Life with Things*, Göteburg, SE: BAS Publisher, chapter 7, pp. 111-131 (reprinted in: H. Fogelberg & H. Glimell, *Bringing Visibility to the Invisible: Towards A Social Understanding of Nanotechnology*, Göteborg: Göteborg University, pp. 115-139.

Glimell, H.: 2001, 'Dynamics of the Emerging Field of Nanoscience', in: M.C. Roco and W.S. Bainbridge (eds.), *Societal Implications of Nanoscience and Nanotechnology*, Dordrecht: Kluwer, pp. 156-160.

Glimell, H.: 2003, 'A Nano Narrative: The Mircopolitics of a New Generic Enabling Technology', in: H. Fogelberg & H. Glimell, *Bringing Visibility to the Invisible: Towards A Social Understanding of Nanotechnology*, Göteborg: Göteborg University, pp. 55-77 [www.sts.gu.se/publications/STS_report_6.pdf].

Glimell, H.: 2003, 'Dynamics of the Emerging Field of Nanoscience', in: H. Fogelberg & H. Glimell, *Bringing Visibility to the Invisible: Towards A Social Understanding of Nanotechnology*, Göteborg: Göteborg University, pp. 79-85 [www.sts.gu.se/publications/STS_report_6.pdf].

Glimell, H.: 2004, 'Grand Visions and Lilliput Politics: Staging the Exploration of the 'Endless Frontier", in: D. Baird, A. Nordmann & J. Schummer (eds.), *Discovering the Nanoscale*, Amsterdam: IOS Press, pp. 231-246.

Goldhaber-Gordon, D., Montemerlo, M.S., Love, J.C., Opiteck, G.J., and Ellenbogen, J.C., "Overview of Nanoelectronic Devices," submitted to the *Proceedings of the IEEE*, February 1997. For more information, please send e-mail to nanotech@mitre.org.

Gorman, M.E.; Groves, J.F. & Shrager, J.: 2004, 'Societal Dimensions of Nanotechnology as a Trading Zone: Results from a Pilot Project', in: D. Baird, A. Nordmann & J. Schummer (eds.), *Discovering the Nanoscale*, Amsterdam: IOS Press, pp. 63-73.

Grinbaum, A. & Dupuy, J.-P.: 2004, 'Living with Uncertainty: Toward the Ongoing Normative Assessment of Nanotechnology', *Techne: Research in Philosophy and Technology*, 8(3) (forthcoming).

Grinbaum, A.: 2004, 'La condition de l'homme moderne et les nanotechnologies', in: G. Nivat (ed.), *Les limites de l´humain. 39èmes Rencontres Internationales de Genève*, L´Age d´Homme, Genève, p. 141.

Grunwald, A.: 2004, 'Ethische Aspekte der Nanotechnologie. Eine Felderkundung', *Technikfolgenabschätzung ' Theorie und Praxis*, 13 (2), 71-78.

Gupta, V.K. & Pangannaya, N.B.: 2000, 'Carbon nanotubes: bibliometric analysis of patents', *World Patent Information*, 22, 185-189.

Hansson, S.O.: 2004, 'Great Uncertainty about Small Things', *Techne: Research in Philosophy and Technology*, 8(3) (forthcoming).

Haruta, M. 1997. *Catalyst surveys of Japan* 1:61 and references therein.

Hennig, J.: 2004, 'Changes in the Design of Scanning Tunneling Microscopic Images from 1980 to 1990', *Techne: Research in Philosophy and Technology*, 8(3) (forthcoming).

Hessenbruch, A.: 2004, 'Nanotechnology and the Negotiation of Novelty', in: D. Baird, A. Nordmann & J. Schummer (eds.), *Discovering the Nanoscale*, Amsterdam: IOS Press, pp. 135-144.

Hullmann, A. & Meyer, M.: 2003, 'Publications and Patents in Nanotechnology. An overview of previous studies and the state of the art', *Scientometrics*, 58 (3) 507-527.

Huo, Q., D.I. Margolese, U. Ciesla, P. Feng, T.E. Gier, P. Sieger, R. Leon, P.M. Petroff, F. Schuth, and G.D. Stucky. 1994. *Nature* 368:317.

Jena, P., S.N. Khanna, and B.K. Rao. 1996. In *Science and technology of atomically engineered materials*, ed. P. Jena. River Edge, NJ: World Scientific.

Johansson, M.: 2003, 'Plenty of room at the bottom: Towards an anthropology of nanoscience', *Anthropology Today*, 19 (No. 6), 3-6.

Johnson, A.: 2004, 'The End of Pure Science: Science Policy from Bayh-Dole to the NNI', in: D. Baird, A. Nordmann,& J. Schummer (eds.), *Discovering the Nanoscale*, Amsterdam: IOS Press, pp. 217-230.

Jounet, C., W.K. Maser, P. Bernier, A. Loiseau, M. Lamy de la Chapelle, S. Lefrant, P. Deniard, R. Lee, and J.E. Fischer. 1997. *Nature* 388:756.

K.E. Drexler, *Nanosystems: Molecular Machinery, Manufacturing, and Computation,* Wiley, New York, 1992.

Karger, J., and D.M. Ruthven. 1992. *Diffusion in zeolites*. New York: J. Wiley.

Keiper, A.: 2003, 'The Nanotechnology Revolution', *The New Atlantis*, 2, 17-34.

Khushf, G.: 2004, 'A Hierarchical Architecture for Nano-scale Science and Technology: Taking Stock of the Claims About Science Made By Advocates of NBIC Convergence', in: D. Baird, A. Nordmann & J. Schummer (eds.), *Discovering the Nanoscale*, Amsterdam: IOS Press, pp. 21-33.

Khushf, G.: 2004, 'Systems Theory and the Ethics of Human Enhancement: A Framework for NBIC Convergence', *Annals of the New York Academy of Sciences*, 1013, 124-149.

Krätschmer, W., L.D. Lamb, K. Fostiropoulos, and D.R. Huffman. 1990. *Nature* 347:354.

Kresge, C.T., M.E. Leonowicz, W.J. Roth, J.C. Vartuli, and J.S. Beck. 1992. *Nature* 359:710.

Kupperman, A., S. Nadimi, S. Oliver, G. Ozin, J. Garcés, and M. Olken. 1993. *Nature* 365:239.

Kuusi, O.; Meyer, M.: 2002, 'Technological generalizations and leitbilder ' the anticipation of technological opportunities', *Technological Forecasting & Social Change*, 69, 625-639.

Landon, B.: 2004, 'Less is More: Much Less is Much More: The Insistent Allure of Nanotechnology Narratives in Science Fiction', in: N.K. Hayles (ed.), *Nanoculture: Implications of the New Technoscience*, Bristol, UK: Intellect Books, pp. 131-146.

Laszlo, P.: 2004, 'Is There Life After Partington?', *Hyle: International Journal for Philosophy of Chemistry*, 10(2), 169-178.

Lenhard, J.: 2004, 'Nanoscience and the Janus-Faced Character of Simulations', in: D. Baird, A. Nordmann & J. Schummer (eds.), *Discovering the Nanoscale*, Amsterdam: IOS Press, pp. 93-100.

Lent, C.S., Tougaw, P.D., Porod, W., Bernstein, G.H., "Quantum Cellular Automata," *Nanotechnology*, Vol. 4, p. 49, 1993.

Lewak, S.E.: 2004, 'What's the Buzz? Tell Me What's A-Happening: Wonder, Nanotechnology, and Alice's Adventures in Wonderland', in: N.K. Hayles (ed.), *Nanoculture: Implications of the New Technoscience*, Bristol, UK: Intellect Books, pp. 201-.

Lide, D.R., ed. 1993-1994. *CRC Handbook of Chemistry and Physics*, 74th ed.

Lin-Easton, P.C.: 2001, 'It's Time for Environmentalists to Think Small ' Real Small: A Call for the Involvement of Environmental Lawyers in Developing Precautionary Policies Molecular Nanotechnology', *Georgetown International Law Review*, 14, 106-134.

López, J.: 2004, 'Bridging the Gaps: Science Fiction in Nanotechnology', *Hyle: International Journal for Philosophy of Chemistry*, 10(2), 129-152.

Lösch, A.: 2004, 'Nanomedicine and Space: Discursive Orders of Mediating Innovations', in: D. Baird, A. Nordmann & J. Schummer (eds.), *Discovering the Nanoscale*, Amsterdam: IOS Press, pp. 193-202.

Marshall, K.: 2004, 'Atomizing the Risk Technology', in: N.K. Hayles (ed.), *Nanoculture: Implications of the New Technoscience*, Bristol, UK: Intellect Books, pp. 147-160.

Martin, T.P., N. Malinowski, U. Zimmerman, U. Naher, and H. Schaber. 1993. *J. Chem. Phys.* 99:4210.

Martin, T.P., U. Naher, H. Schaber, U. Zimmerman. 1993. *Phys. Rev. Lett.* 70:3079.

Mayer, S.: 2002, 'From genetic modification to nanotechnology: the dangers of 'sound science'', in: T. Gilland (ed.), *Science: Can We Trust the Experts?*, London: Hodder and Stoughton, pp. 1-15.

Mehta, M.D.: 2002, 'Nanoscience and Nanotechnology: Assessing the Nature of Innovation in These Fields', *Bulletin of Science, Technology & Society*, 22(4), 269-273.

Mehta, M.D.: 2004, 'From Biotechnology to Nanotechnology: What Can We Learn from Earlier Technologies?, *Bulletin of Science, Technology & Society*, 24, 34-39.

Meyer, M. & Kuusi, O.: 2004, 'Nanotechnology: Generalizations in an Interdisciplinary Field of Science and Technology', *Hyle: International Journal for Philosophy of Chemistry*, 10(2), 153-168.

Meyer, M.: 2000a, 'Does science push technology? Patents citing scientific literature', *Research Policy*, 29, 409-434.

Meyer, M.: 2000b, 'Patent citations in a novel field of technology: What can they tell about interactions of emerging communities of science and technology?', *Scientometrics*, 48, 151-178.

Meyer, M.: 2001a, 'Patent citations in a novel field of technology: An exploration of nano-science and nano-technology', *Scientometrics*, 51, 163-183.

Meyer, M.: 2001b, 'Socio-economic Research on Nanoscale Science and Technology: A European Overview and Illustration', in: M.C. Roco and W.S. Bainbridge (eds.), *Societal Implications of Nanoscience and Nanotechnology*, Dordrecht: Kluwer, pp. 217-241.

Meyer, M.; Persson, O.: 1998, 'Nanotechnology ' interdisciplinarity, patterns of collaboration and differences in application', *Scientometrics*, 47, 195'205.

Milburn, C.: 2002, 'Nanotechnology in the age of post-human engineering: science fiction as science', *Configurations*, 10, 261-295 [reprinted in: N.K. Hayles (ed.), *Nanoculture: Implications of the New Technoscience*, Bristol, UK: Intellect Books, 2004, pp. 109-130].

Milburn, C.: 2004, 'Nano/Splatter: Disintegrating the Postbiological Body', *New Literary History*, 35 (in print).

Mnyusiwalla, A.; Abdallah, S.D.; Singer, P.A.: 2003, 'Mind the gap: science and ethics in nanotechnology', *Nanotechnology*, 14, R9-R13.

Mody, C.C.M.: 2004, 'How Probe Microscopists Became Nanotechnologists', in: D. Baird, A. Nordmann & J. Schummer (eds.), *Discovering the Nanoscale*, Amsterdam: IOS Press, pp. 119-133.

Mody, C.C.M.: 2004, 'Instruments in Training: The Growth of American Probe Microscopy in the 1980s', in: D. Kaiser (ed.), *Pedagogy and the Practice of Science: Producing Physical Scientists, 1800-2000*, Cambridge, MA: MIT Press (forthcoming).

Mody, C.C.M.: 2004, 'Small, but Determined: Technological Determinism in Nanoscience', *Hyle: International Journal for Philosophy of Chemistry*, 10(2), 99-128.

Mody, C.C.M.: 2004, *Crafting the Tools of Knowledge: The Invention, Spread, and Commercialization of Probe Microscopy, 1960-2000*, Ph.D. dissertation, Cornell University.

Montemerlo, M.S., Love, J.C., Opiteck, G.J., Goldhaber, D. J., and Ellenbogen, J.C., "Technologies and Designs for Electronic Nanocomputers," MITRE Technical Report 96W0000044, The MITRE Corporation, McLean, VA, July 1996. For more information, send e-mail to nanotech@mitre.org.

Moor, J.H. & Weckert, J.: 2004, 'Nanoethics: Assessing the Nanoscale From an Ethical Point of View', in: D. Baird, A. Nordmann & J. Schummer (eds.), *Discovering the Nanoscale*, Amsterdam: IOS Press, pp. 301-310.

Munn Sanchez, E.: 2004, 'The Expert's Role in Nanoscience and Technology', in: D. Baird, A. Nordmann & J. Schummer (eds.), *Discovering the Nanoscale*, Amsterdam: IOS Press, pp. 257-266.

Nordmann, A.: 2003, 'Shaping the World Atom by Atom: Eine nanowissenschaftliche WeltBildanalyse', in: A. Grunwald (ed.), *Technikgestaltung zwischen Wunsch und Wirklichkeit*, Berlin: Springer, pp. 191-199.

Nordmann, A.: 2004, 'Molecular Disjunctions: Staking Claims at the Nanoscale', in: D. Baird, A. Nordmann & J. Schummer (eds.), *Discovering the Nanoscale*, Amsterdam: IOS Press, pp. 51-62.

Nordmann, A.: 2004, 'Nanotechnology: Convergence and Integration', Presentation at *EuroNanoForum, Trieste, December 10, 2003* (Proceedings in preparation).

Nordmann, A.: 2004, 'Nanotechnology's WorldView: New Space for Old Cosmologies', *IEEE Technology and Society Magazine*, 23.

Nordmann, A.: 2004, 'Social Imagination for Nanotechnology', in: European Commission (Community Health and Consumer Protection): *Nanotechnologies: A Preliminary Risk Analysis on the Basis of a Workshop, Brussels, 1-2 March 2004*, pp. 111-113 [www.europa.eu.int/comm/health/ph_risk/documents/ev_20040301_en.pdf].

Nordmann, A.: 2004, 'Was ist TechnoWissenschaft? ' Zum Wandel der Wissenschaftskultur am Beispiel von Nanoforschung und Bionik', in: T. Rossmann & C. Tropea (eds.), *Bionik ' Neue Forschungsergebnisse aus Natur-, Ingenieur- und Geisteswissenschaften*, Berlin: Springer, 2004 (forthcoming)

Paschen, H.; Coenen, C.; Fleischer, T.; Grünwald, R.; Oertel, D. & Revermann, C.: 2004, *Nanotechnologie: Forschung, Entwicklung, Anwendung*, Berlin: Springer (*Nanotechnologie, TAB-Arbeitsbericht 92*, Berlin: Büro für Technikfolgen-Abschätzung beim Deutschen Bundestag).

Pitt, J.C.: 2004, 'The Epistemology of the Very Small', in: D. Baird, A. Nordmann & J. Schummer (eds.), *Discovering the Nanoscale*, Amsterdam: IOS Press, pp. 157-163.

Pressman, J.: 2004, 'Nano Narrative: A Parable from Electronic Literature', in: N.K. Hayles (ed.), *Nanoculture: Implications of the New Technoscience*, Bristol, UK: Intellect Books, pp. 191-200.

Prigogine, I., and S. Rice. 1988. *Advances in chemical physics*, Vol. 70, Parts 1 & 2. New York: J. Wiley.

Rao, M.B., and S. Sircar. 1993. *Gas Separation and Purification* 7:279.

Reed, M.A., "Quantum Dots," *Scientific American,* January 1993, pp. 118-123.

Roberts, J.A.: 2004, 'Deciding the Future of Nanotechnologies: Legal Perspectives on Issues of Democracy and Technology', in: D. Baird, A. Nordmann & J. Schummer (eds.), *Discovering the Nanoscale*, Amsterdam: IOS Press, pp. 247-255.

Robinson, C.: 2004, 'Images in NanoScience/Technology', in: D. Baird, A. Nordmann & J. Schummer (eds.), *Discovering the Nanoscale*, Amsterdam: IOS Press, pp. 165-169.

Robison, W.L.: 2004, 'Nano-Ethics', in: D. Baird, A. Nordmann & J. Schummer (eds.), *Discovering the Nanoscale*, Amsterdam: IOS Press, pp. 285-300.

Roco, M.C. & Bainbridge, W.S. (eds.): 2001, *Societal implications of nanoscience and nanotechnology*, (Proceedings of a workshop organized by the National Science Foundation, September 28-

29, 2000), Kluwer: Dordrecht [available online at http://itri.loyola.edu/nano/societalimpact/nanosi.pdf]

Roco, M.C. & Tomellini, R. (eds.): 2002, *Nanotechnology: Revolutionary Opportunities and Societal Implications, Workshop, Lecce (Italy), 31 January - 1 February 2002*, Luxemburg: Office for Official Publications of the European Communities, [200 pp.]

Roco, M.C.; Bainbridge, W.S. (eds.): 2002, *Converging Technologies for Improving Human Performance: Nanotechnology, Biotechnology, Information Technology and the Cognitive Science*, Arlington, VA: National Science Foundation.

Roher, H. 1993. *Jpn. J. Appl. Phys.* 32:1335.

Rohlfing, E.A., D.M. Cox, and A. Kaldor. 1984. *J. Chem. Phys.* 81:3846.

Rosen, A. 1998. A periodic table in three dimensions: A sightseeing tour in the nanometer world. In *Advances in quantum chemistry*. In press.

Ruthven, D.M., S. Farooq, K.S. Knaebel. 1994. *Pressure swing adsorption*. New York: VCH Publishers.

Sarewitz, D.; Woodhouse, E.: 2003, 'Small is Powerful', in: A. Lightman, D. Sarewitz & Chr. Desser, (eds.), *Living with the Genie: Essays on Technology and the Quest for Human Mastery*, Washington, DC: Island Press, pp. 63-83.

Schiemann, G.: 2004, 'Dissolution of the Nature-Technology Dichotomy? Perspectives on Nanotechnology from an Everyday Understanding of Nature', in: D. Baird, A. Nordmann & J. Schummer (eds.), *Discovering the Nanoscale*, Amsterdam: IOS Press, pp. 209-213.

Schmidt, J.C.: 2004, 'Unbounded Technologies: Working Through Technological Reductionism of Nanotechnology', in: D. Baird, A. Nordmann & J. Schummer (eds.), *Discovering the Nanoscale*, Amsterdam: IOS Press, pp. 35-50.

Schuler, E.: 2004, 'Perception of Risks and Nanotechnology', in: D. Baird, A. Nordmann & J. Schummer (eds.), *Discovering the Nanoscale*, Amsterdam: IOS Press, pp. 279-284.

Schummer, J.: 2001, 'Ethics of Chemical Synthesis', *Hyle: International Journal for Philosophy of Chemistry*, 7, 103-124 [online: www.hyle.org/journal/issues/7/schummer.htm].

Schummer, J.: 2003, 'Aesthetics of Chemical Products: Materials, Molecules, and Molecular Models', *Hyle: International Journal for Philosophy of Chemistry*, 9, 73-104 [online: www.hyle.org/journal/issues/9-1/schummer.htm].

Schummer, J.: 2003, 'The Notion of Nature in Chemistry', *Studies in History and Philosophy of Science*, 34 (2003), 705-736.

Schummer, J.: 2004, 'Interdisciplinary Issues in Nanoscale Research', in: D. Baird, A. Nordmann & J. Schummer (eds.), *Discovering the Nanoscale*, Amsterdam: IOS Press, pp. 9-20.

Schummer, J.: 2004, 'Multidisciplinarity, Interdisciplinarity, and Patterns of Research Collaboration in Nanoscience and Nanotechnology', *Scientometrics*, 59, 425-465.

Schummer, J.: 2004, 'Naturverhältnisse in der modernen Wirkstoff-Forschung', in: K. Kornwachs (ed.), *Technik ' System ' Verantwortung*, Münster: LIT, pp. 629-638.

Schummer, J.: 2004, 'Why do Chemists Perform Experiments?', in: D. Sobczynska, P. Zeidler, E. Zielonacka-Lis (eds.), *Chemistry in the Philosophical Melting Pot*, Peter Lang (Frankfurt/M.), 2004, pp. 395-410.

Schummer, J.: 2005, 'Reading Nano: The Public Interest in Nanotechnology as Reflected in Book Purchase Patterns", *Public Understanding of Science*, 14 (2) (forthcoming).

Schummer, J.; Baird, D. (eds.): 2004-5, *Nanotech Challenges*, joint special issue of *Hyle: International Journal for Philosophy of Chemistry & Techne: Research in Philosophy and Technology* (forthcoming).

Schwarz, A.E.: 2004, 'Shrinking the 'Ecological Footprint' with NanoTechnoScience?', in: D. Baird, A. Nordmann & J. Schummer (eds.), *Discovering the Nanoscale*, Amsterdam: IOS Press, pp. 203-208.

Schwarz, R.B. 1998. Storage of hydrogen in powders with nanosized crystalline domains. In *R&D status and trends*, ed. Siegel et al.

Siegel, R.W., E. Hu, and M.C. Roco, eds. 1998. *R&D status and trends in nanoparticles, nanostructured materials, and nanodevices in the United States*. Baltimore: Loyola College, International Technology Research Institute. NTIS #PB98-117914.

Stix Gary., "Toward 'Point One'," *Scientific American*, February 1995, pp. 90-95.

Stuckless, J.T, D.E. Starr, D.J. Bald, C.T. Campbell. 1997. *J. Chem. Phys.* 107:5547.

Suchman, M.: 2001, 'Envisioning Life on the Nano-Frontier', in: M.C. Roco and W.S. Bainbridge (eds.), *Societal Implications of Nanoscience and Nanotechnology*, Dordrecht: Kluwer, pp. 211-216.

Suchman, M.: 2002, 'Social Science and Nanotechnologies', M. Roco & R. Tomellini (eds.), *Nanotechnology ' Revolutionary Opportunities and Societal Implications*, Luxembourg: European Communities, pp. 95-99.

Sweeney, A.E.; Seal, S. & Vaidyanathan, P.: 2003, 'The promises and perils of nanoscience and nanotechnology: Exploring emerging social and ethical issues', *Bulletin of Science, Technology & Society*, 23 (4), 236-245.

Swiss Re: 2004, *Nanotechnology: Small Matter, Many Unknowns*, Zurich: Swiss Re [www.swissre.com].

Tanev, P.T., M. Chibwe, and T.J. Pinnavaia. 1994. *Nature* 368:321.

Taylor, K.J., C.L. Pettiette-Hall, O. Cheshnovsky, and R.J. Smalley. 1992. *J. Chem. Phys.* 96:3319.

Tenner, E.: 2001, 'Nanotechnology and Unintended Consequences', in: M.C. Roco and W.S. Bainbridge (eds.), *Societal Implications of Nanoscience and Nanotechnology*, Dordrecht: Kluwer, pp. 241-246.

The Royal Society & The Royal Academy of Engineering: 2004, *Nanoscience and nanotechnologies: opportunities and uncertainties*, London [www.nanotec.org.uk/finalReport.htm].

2

Nano Computers and Nano Robotics

Introduction

A nanorobot is a tiny machine designed to perform a specific task or tasks repeatedly and with precision at nanoscale dimensions, that is, dimensions of a few nanometers (nm) or less, where 1 nm = 10^{-9} meter. Nanorobots have potential applications in the assembly and maintenance of sophisticated systems. Nanorobots might function at the atomic or molecular level to build devices, machines, or circuits, a process known as molecular manufacturing. Nanorobots might also produce copies of themselves to replace worn-out units, a process called self-replication. Nanorobots are of special interest to researchers in the medical industry. This has given rise to the field of nanomedicine. It has been suggested that a fleet of nanorobots might serve as antibodies or antiviral agents in patients with compromised immune systems, or in diseases that do not respond to more conventional measures. There are numerous other potential medical applications, including repair of damaged tissue, unblocking of arteries affected by plaques, and perhaps the construction of complete replacement body organs. A major advantage of nanorobots is thought to be their durability. In theory, they can remain operational for years, decades, or centuries. Nanoscale systems can also operate much faster than their larger counterparts because displacements are smaller; this allows mechanical and electrical events to occur in less time at a given speed.

Nanorobotics is an emerging field that deals with the controlled manipulation of objects with nanometer-scale dimensions. Typically, an atom has a diameter of a few Ångstroms (1 Å = 0.1 nm = 10^{-10} m), a molecule's size is a few nm, and clusters or nanoparticles formed by hundreds or thousands of atoms have sizes of tens of nm. Therefore, Nanorobotics is concerned with interactions with atomic and molecular-sized objects and is sometimes called Molecular Robotics. Molecular Robotics falls within the purview of nanotechnology, which is the study of phenomena and structures with characteristic dimensions in the nanometer range. The birth of Nanotechnology is usually associated with a talk by Nobel Prize winner Richard Feynman entitled

"There is plenty of room at the bottom. Nanotechnology has the potential for major scientific and practical breakthroughs. Future applications ranging from very fast computers to self-replicating robots are described in Drexler's seminal book. In a less futuristic vein, the following potential applications were suggested by well-known experimental scientists at the Nano4 conference held in Palo Alto in November 1995:

- Cell probes with dimensions ~ 1/1000 of the cell's size.
- Space applications, e.g. hardware to fly on satellites.
- Computer memory.
- Near field optics, with characteristic dimensions ~ 20 nm.
- X-ray fabrication, systems that use X-ray photons.
- Genome applications, reading and manipulating DNA.
- Nanodevices capable of running on very small batteries.
- Optical antennas.

Nanotechnology is being pursued along two converging directions. From the top down, semiconductor fabrication techniques are producing smaller and smaller structures. For example, the line width of the original pentium chip is 350 nm. Current optical lithography techniques have obvious resolution limitations because of the wavelength of visible light, which is in the order of 500 nm. X-ray and electron-beam lithography will push sizes further down, but with a great increase in complexity and cost of fabrication. These top-down techniques do not seem promising for building nanomachines that require precise positioning of atoms or molecules. Alternatively, one can proceed from the bottom up, by assembling atoms and molecules into functional components and systems. There are two main approaches for building useful devices from nanoscale components. The first is based on self-assembly, and is a natural evolution of traditional chemistry and bulk processing see e.g. [Gómez-López *et al*. 1996]. The other is based on controlled positioning of nanoscale objects, direct application of forces, electric fields, and so on. The self-assembly approach is being pursued at many laboratories. Despite all the current activity, self-assembly has severe limitations because the structures produced tend to be highly symmetric, and the most versatile self-assembled systems are organic and therefore generally lack robustness. The second approach involves Nanomanipulation, and is being studied by a small number of researchers, who are focusing on techniques based on scanning probe microscopy. A top-down technique that is closely related to Nanomanipulation involves removing or depositing small amounts of material by using an SPM. This approach falls within what is usually called Nanolithography. SPM-based Nanolithography is akin to machining or to rapid prototyping techniques such as stereolithography. For example, one can remove a row or two of hydrogen atoms on a silicon substrate that has been passivated with hydrogen by moving the tip of an SPM in a straight line over the substrate and applying a suitable voltage. The removed atoms are "lost" to the environment, much like metal chips in a machining operation. Lines with widths in the order of 10 to 100 nm have been written by these techniques.

Nanorobotics research has proceeded along two lines. The first is devoted to the design and computational simulation of robots with nanoscale dimensions. Drexler's nanorobot uses various mechanical components such as nanogears built primarily with carbon atoms in a diamondoid structure. A major issue is how to build these devices, and little experimental progress has been made towards their construction. The second area of Nanorobotics research involves manipulation of nanoscale objects with macroscopic instruments. Experimental work has been focused on this area, especially through the use of SPMs as robots. To begin with we focus on the state of the art in the field of nano-robotics by describing various molecular level systems and associated design and control issues. Nanorobots are controllable machines at the nano (10^{-9}) meter or molecular scale that are composed of nanoscale components. With the modern scientific capabilities, it has become possible to attempt the creation of nanorobotic devices and interface them with the macro world for control. There are countless such machines that exist in nature and there is an opportunity to build more of them by mimicking nature. Even if the field of nanorobotics is fundamentally different than that of macro robots due to the differences in scale and material, there are many similarities in design and control techniques that eventually could be projected and applied. There are many applications for nanorobotic systems and its biggest impact would be in the area of medicine.

Nanotechnology can best be defined as a description of activities at the level of atoms and molecules that have applications in the real world. A nanometer is a billionth of a meter, that is, about 1/80,000 of the diameter of a human hair, or 10 times the diameter of a hydrogen atom. The size-related challenge is the ability to measure, manipulate, and assemble matter with features on the scale of 1-100nm. In order to achieve cost-effectiveness in nanotechnology it will be necessary to automate molecular manufacturing. The engineering of molecular products needs to be carried out by robotic devices, which have been termed nanorobots. A nanorobot is essentially a controllable machine at the nano meter or molecular scale that is composed of nanoscale components. The field of nanorobotics studies the design, manufacturing, programing and control of the nanoscale robots. We talk about the state of the art in the emerging field of nanorobotics, its applications and discusses in brief some of the essential properties and dynamical laws which make this field more challenging and unique than its macroscale counterpart.

Nanorobots would constitute any passive or active structure (nanoscale) capable of actuation, sensing, signaling, information processing, intelligence, swarm behavior at nanoscale. These functionalities could be illustrated individually or in combinations by a nanorobot (swarm intelligence and co-operative behavior). So, there could be a whole genre of actuation and sensing or information processing nanorobots having ability to interact and influence matter at the nanoscale. Some of the characteristic abilities that are desirable for a nanorobot to function are:

- Swarm Intelligence—decentralization and distributive intelligence.
- Cooperative behavior—emergent and evolutionary behavior.
- Self assembly and replication—assemblage at nanoscale and 'nano maintenance'.
- Nano Information processing and programmability—for programing and controlling nanorobots (autonomous nanorobots).
- Nano to macroworld interface architecture—an architecture enabling instant access to the nanorobots and its control and maintenance.

There are many differences between macro and nanoscale robots. However, they occur mainly in the basic laws that govern their dynamics. Macroscaled robots are essentially in the Newtonian mechanics domain whereas the laws governing nanorobots are in the molecular quantum mechanics domain. Furthermore, uncertainty plays a crucial role in nanorobotic systems. The fundamental barrier for dealing with uncertainty at the nanoscale is imposed by the quantum and the statistical mechanics and thermal excitations. For a certain nanosystem at some particular temperature, there are positional uncertainties, which can not be modified or further reduced. The nanorobots are invisible to naked eye, which makes them hard to manipulate and work with. Techniques like Scanning Electron Microscopy (SEM) and Atomic Force Microscopy (AFM) are being employed to establish a visual and haptic interface to enable us to sense the molecular structure of these nanoscaled devices. Virtual Reality (VR) techniques are currently being explored in nanoscience and biotechnology research as a way to enhance the operator's perception (vision and haptics) by approaching more or less a state of 'full immersion' or 'telepresence'. The development of nanorobots or nanomachine components presents difficult fabrication and control challenges. Such devices will operate in microenvironments whose physical properties differ from those encountered by conventional parts. Since these nanoscale devices have not yet been fabricated, evaluating possible designs and control algorithms requires using theoretical estimates and virtual interfaces/environments. Such interfaces/simulations can operate at various levels of detail to trade-off physical accuracy, computational cost, number of components and the time over which the simulation follows the nanoobject behaviors. They can enable nanoscientists to extend their eyes and hands into the nanoworld and also enable new types of exploration and whole new classes of experiments in the biological and physical sciences. VR simulations can also be used to develop virtual assemblies of nano and bio-nano components into mobile linkages and predict their performance. Nanorobots with completely artificial components have not been realized yet. The active area of research in this field is focused more on molecular robots, which are thoroughly inspired by nature's way of doing things at nano scale. Mother nature has her own set of molecular machines that have been working for centuries, and have been optimized for performance and design over the ages. As our knowledge and understanding of these numerous machines continues to increase, we now see a possibility of using the natural machines, or creating synthetic ones from scratch, using nature's components. This chapter focuses more on molecular machines and explores various designs and research prevalent in this field. The main goal in the field of molecular machines is to use various biological elements—whose function at the cellular level creates motion, force or a signal—as machine components. These components perform their preprogramed biological function in response to the specific physiochemical stimuli but in an artificial setting. In this way proteins and DNA could act as motors, mechanical joints, transmission elements, or sensors. If all these different components were assembled together in the proper proportion and orientation they would form nano devices with multiple degrees of freedom, able to apply forces and manipulate objects in the nanoscale world. The advantage of using nature's machine components is that they are highly efficient and reliable.

Nanorobotics is a field which calls for collaborative efforts between physicists, chemists, biologists, computer scientists, engineers and other specialists to work towards this common objective. The various fields which come under the field of bionanorobotics (this is just a representative figure and not exhaustive in nature). Currently this field is still evolving, but several substantial steps have been taken by great researchers all over the world and are contributing to this ever challenging and exciting field. The ability to manipulate matter at the nano scale is one core application for which nanorobots could be the technological solution. A lot has been written in the literature about the significance and motivation behind constructing a nanorobot. The applications range from medical to environmental sensing to space and military applications. Molecular construction of complex devices could be possible by nanorobots of the future. From precise drug delivery to repairing cells and fighting tumor cells; nanorobots are expected to revolutionize the medical industry in the future. These applications come under the field of nanomedicine which is a very active area of research in nanotechnology. These molecular machines hence form the basic enablers of future applications. In the next section, we shall try to understand the principles, theory and utility of the known molecular machines and look into the design and control issues for their creation and modification. A majority of natural molecular machines are protein-based, while the DNA-based molecular machines are mostly synthetic. Nature deploys proteins to perform various cellular tasks—from moving cargo, to catalyzing reactions, while it has kept DNA as an information carrier. It is hence understandable that most of the natural machinery is built from proteins. With the powerful crystallographic techniques available in the modern world, the protein structures are clearer than ever. The ever increasing computing power makes it possible to dynamically model protein folding processes and predict the conformations and structure of lesser known proteins. All this helps unravel the mysteries associated with the molecular machinery and paves the way for the production and application of these miniature machines in various fields including medicine, space exploration, electronics and military.

Self replicating molecular machine systems will revolutionize manufacturing at some point in the not too distant future. While there are many architectures for such systems, a frequently mentioned approach is the molecular assembler. Assemblers as proposed would be sized on the order of a few hundred nanometers, would be constrained to replicate only in a carefully controlled environment, and could be programmed to build a wide range of useful and highly desirable products. In a recent article in *Scientific American* George Whitesides said "Fabrication based on the assembler is not, in my opinion, a workable strategy and thus not a concern." As the key technical issues have been published for some time (certainly since the publication of *Nanosystems* in 1992), and as yet no fundamental barriers have withstood review in any technical forum, the claim by Whitesides that such fundamental barriers exist deserves thoughtful scrutiny. Here, we review Whitesides' stated objections to determine if any of them constitute fundamental issues that might make the eventual design and construction of a molecular assembler "unworkable", or render the paths to a nonbiological assembler unproductive. Whitesides' claims are interspersed with appropriate references, analysis and commentary.

Whitesides expresses concern about moving parts, friction and stiction:

> Many interesting problems plague the fabrication of nanodevices with moving parts. A crucial one is friction and sticking (sometimes combined in talking about small devices in the term "stiction"). Because small devices have very large ratios of surface to volume, surface effects—both good and bad—become much more important for them than for large devices. Some of these types of problems will eventually be resolved if it is worthwhile to do so, but they provide difficult technical challenges now. We will undoubtedly progress toward more complex micromachines and nanomachines modeled on human-scale machines, but we have a long path to travel before we can produce nanomechanical devices in quantity for any practical purpose. Nor is there any reason to assume that nanomachines must resemble human-scale machines.

Analysis of the "stiction" issue dates back to at least 1959 when Feynman suggested running bearings dry. It was subsequently analyzed in more detail by Drexler in 1987 when he examined the symmetry considerations involved in making bearings that exhibit low static friction. The issue was again analyzed in *Nanosystems*, including the more general case of two surfaces sliding over each other. Merkle analyzed bearings in greater depth, again concluding that bearings with very low static friction should be feasible. Experimental evidence that molecules can rotate freely in an appropriate environment is overwhelming, including, for instance, the work of Gimzewski showing that the rotation of individual molecules on a surface can be stopped or started by changes in the local molecular environment, the work of Cumings and Zettl demonstrating near-frictionless sliding of nested carbon nanotubes, and the common observation that molecules can rotate freely around a single bond and that even fairly large molecules often move freely on a surface.

While bearings and sliding surfaces are often of very low quality when made using existing lithographic methods, these involve surfaces that are imperfectly characterized and which are, at the molecular scale, very rough. Properly designed molecularly precise surfaces will be able to slide over each with little friction or wear for long periods of time (years or longer). Whitesides is correct that "we have a long path to travel before we can produce nanomechanical devices in quantity", but this is an assessment of the current primitive state of molecular systems engineering, not a description of a fundamental barrier presented by physical laws.

> Could these systems self-replicate? At present, we do not know how to build self-replicating machines of any size or type.

This statement is factually incorrect. Numerous proof-of-concept mechanical devices physically capable of self-replication from simple substrates have been known since the 1950s, including most notably the early working models of Jacobson and Penrose, and the simple demonstration design of Morowitz.

> We know, from recent biological studies, something about the minimum level of complexity in a living cell that will sustain self-replication: a system of some 300 genes is sufficient for self-replication. We have little sense for how to translate this number into mechanical machines of the types more familiar to us, and no sense of how to design a self-sustaining, self-replicating system of machines. We have barely taken the first steps toward self-replication in nonbiological systems [see "Go Forth and Replicate," by Moshe Sipper and James A. Reggia; Scientific American, August].

We agree that there is much work to do, and much that can be learned from nature. In the biotechnology arena Arcady Mushegian of Akkadix Corp. has looked at the genes present in the genomes of fully sequenced microbes to see which ones are always conserved in nature. He concludes that as few as 300 genes are all that may be required for life, constituting the minimum possible genome for a functional microbe. An organism containing this minimal gene set would be able to perform the dozen or so functions required for life — manufacturing cellular biomolecules, generating energy, repairing damage, transporting salts and other molecules, responding to environmental chemical cues, and replicating. Thus the minimal microbe — a basic cellular chassis — could be specified by an artificial genome about only 150,000 nucleotides bases in length. Glen Evans, now at Egea BioSciences, can currently produce made-to-order DNA strands that are 10,000 nucleotide bases in length and is striving to increase this length by at least a factor of ten. The engineered full-genome DNA, once synthesized, could then be placed inside an empty cell membrane — most likely a living cell from which the nuclear material had been removed. Used in medicine, these artificial biobots could be designed to produce useful vitamins, hormones, enzymes or cytokines in which a patient's body was deficient, or to selectively absorb and metabolize into harmless endproducts harmful substances such as poisons, toxins, or indigestible intracellular detritis, or even to perform useful mechanical tasks.

At least one private company has already been formed to pursue the construction of these artificial biological devices. Mushegian's results suggest that the minimal autonomous artificial biological replicator consists of at least 300 different (protein) "nanoparts", multiple copies of each being assembled into a working biological robot. However, nonbiological engineered replicators: (1) need not be designed for operation on diverse organic substrates, (2) need not be capable of self-assembly but may employ positional assembly techniques, (3) need not be capable of surviving mutation or evolution, and (4) need not contain (and by necessity maintain to high fidelity) their own description within their own onboard structure. Hence, it is likely that a positionally-assembled mechanical replicator can be as simple, and designed using no more different kinds of parts than are found in the biological proof-of-concept.

The study and design of mechanical kinematic replicators is yet in its infancy, but it is incorrect to assert that we have "no sense of how to design a self-sustaining, self-replicating system of machines." A 1980 NASA Summer Study examined this very question at the insistence of Robert Frosch, the NASA Administrator at the time. This technical study produced two distinct conceptual system designs for a macroscale self-replicating system of machines (both functionally scalable to smaller sizes). The final report, published in 1982, offered the following technical conclusions: "The theoretical concept of machine duplication is well developed. There are several alternative strategies by which machine self-replication can be carried out in a practical engineering setting. There is also available a body of theoretical automation concepts in the realm of machine construction by machine, in machine inspection of machines, and machine repair of machines, which can be drawn upon to engineer practical machine systems capable of replication. An engineering demonstration project can be initiated immediately, to begin with simple replication of robot assembler by robot assembler from supplied parts, and proceeding in phased steps to full reproduction of a complete machine processing or factory system by another machine processing system, supplied, ultimately, only with raw materials." If there were a vital economic need, there is little doubt that a fully teleoperated self-replicating macroscale machine shop could be built today.

Compelling examples of artificial replicators exist in the robotics world. For example, the Japanese manufacturing company Fujitsu Fanuc Ltd. briefly operated the first "unmanned" robot factory in the early 1980s, then reopened an improved automated robot-building factory in April 1998 that uses larger two-armed robots to manufacture smaller robots with a minimum of human intervention, starting from inputs of robot parts, at the rate of 1000 daughter copies (of individual robots) per year; apparently a different part of the factory uses a distributive warehouse system for automatically assembling the larger robots. Other robotic manufacturers such as Yasukawa Electric also use robots to make robot parts. The existence of extensive theoretical work on self-replication and nanoscale manufacturing strongly support the claim — as yet unproven experimentally — that submicron mechanical self-replicating systems are feasible, amenable to human design, and will eventually be developed to support molecular nanotechnology

> And other problems cast long shadows. Where is the power to come from for an autonomous nanomachine? There are no electric sockets at the nanoscale. The cell uses chemical reactions of specific compounds to enable it to go about its business; a corresponding strategy for nanoscale machines remains to be developed.

The fact that cells can use chemical reactions to power internal nanomechanical operations such as kinesin locomotion along microtubules and positional assembly of amino acids into linear peptide chains by ribosomes constitutes an existence proof that chemically powered mechanical operations by autonomous biological nanomachines are feasible. Corresponding strategies for powering autonomous nonbiological nanomachines have been proposed, studied, and in a few cases even demonstrated experimentally, casting some light into the "long shadows" that may have existed in the past.

Chemical power is most accessible to current experimental techniques. For example, Mao *et al.* have constructed a mechanical device using DNA as structural scaffolding that might serve as the basis for a nanoscale robotic actuator. The mechanism has two rigid double-stranded arms a few nanometers long that can be made to rotate between fixed positions by introducing a positively charged cobalt compound into the solution surrounding the molecules, causing the bridge region to be converted from the normal B-DNA structure to the unusual Z-DNA structure. The free ends of the arms shift position by 2-6 nanometers during this fully reversible structural conversion, like a hinge opening and closing. The actuator can be powered indefinitely by this means. Yurke and Turberfield have synthesized another actuator using three single strands of artificial DNA which, when placed together, find their complementary partners and self-assemble to form a V-shaped structure. The open mouth of this nanotweezer can be made to close by adding a special "fuel" strand which binds to the single-stranded DNA dangling from the ends of the arms of the tweezers and zips them closed. A special "removal" strand, when added, binds to the fuel strand and pulls it away, opening the nanotweezers again. The cycle may then be repeated. These are examples that follow Whitesides' suggestion of using biological parts and mechanisms to achieve new nanotechnology mechanisms. Numerous similar examples of chemical power delivered to working artificial nanomotors have been reported in the experimental literature. For example, a 78-atom chemically-powered inorganic rotating nanomotor was synthesized in 1999 as a proof of principle by chemist T. Ross Kelly at Boston College. Ben Feringa at the University of Groningen in the Netherlands has built an artificial 58-atom motor molecule that spins when illuminated by solar energy.

Montemagno's group has created an artificial nanomotor comprised of organic and inorganic components that is powered by ATP. The group's first integrated molecular motor ran for 40 minutes at 3-4 revolutions per second. Subsequent motors have been operated for hours continuously by feeding them plenty of ATP. Such motors potentially may be very useful for powering autonomous nanorobots operating in the intracellular regime, as they could borrow their fuel source directly from the living cell. Montemagno reportedly is also trying to build a solar-powered, biomolecular motor-driven autonomous nanodevice, wherein light energy is converted into ATP which then serves as a fuel source for the motor, and has been quoted as saying: "We think we'll be able to make autonomous devices that are powered by light on a scale of 1 micron or less, smaller than bacteria."

Other modes of chemical power for future autonomous nanomachines have been proposed and discussed at length in the theoretical literature, but have not yet been subjected to rigorous experimental scrutiny and verification. For instance, hydrogen-oxygen, methane-oxygen, and ethanol-oxygen fuel cells are well-known and in wide commercial use; a medical nanodevice might prefer a glucose-oxygen fuel cell because of the greater availability of glucose in a typical biological system, as considered by Freitas. Fuel cells appear attractive because the fundamental principles readily scale to the molecular size. To date, the closest laboratory demonstrations are microbial fuel cells containing captive bacteria or immobilized enzymes which, when fed organic material, convert chemical energy into electricity that could be used to power tiny motors. Other possible strategies for chemically powered nanoscale machines have been proposed by Freitas by analogy to demonstrated macroscale techniques, which theory suggests should be scalable to submicron dimensions. Powering nanoscale machines using acoustic energy has been proposed and analyzed by Drexler, Merkle, and Freitas. The analysis and design is straightforward. One approach is to use pistons (which have sliding surfaces). Maximum energy output can be readily determined by computing the change in Gibbs free energy between the extended and contracted piston configurations, given by the excess pressure times the change in volume. Small devices (a few thousand cubic nanometers) with modest pressure changes (one atmosphere) can readily produce sufficient energy (~300 zJ/cycle, or ~100 kT at room temperature) to power ratchets able to drive step motions in which individual steps are about a nanometer. The low-friction character of carefully chosen sliding surfaces in a pistonlike configuration of nested carbon nanotubes has been verified experimentally by Cumings and Zettl.

Drexler has described nanoscale electrostatic motors that could be externally driven by electrical energy. Other strategies for powering autonomous nanoscale machines have been reviewed or proposed by Freitas, including heat engines, Brownian motors, mechanoelectric transducers, piezoelectric actuators, electrochemical transducers, light-driven proton pumps and photoelectric cells, rf antennas, radionuclide batteries, and various alternate strategies for transmitting power to tethered nanoscale machines from macroscale electrical, electromagnetic, hydraulic, acoustic, mechanical, and chemical energy sources. In fact, there appear to be many theoretically feasible organic and inorganic methods of delivering power to nanoscale assemblers or to nanorobots. The problem is not the theoretic feasibility of powering assemblers, but rather the fact that the experimental engineering is in its infancy. This should be a reason to move forward with the engineering work of building assemblers, rather than interpreted as a fundamental barrier.

> How would a self-replicating nanomachine store and use information? Biology has demonstrated a strategy based on DNA, so it can be done, but if one wanted a different strategy, it is not clear where to start.

If onboard storage is deemed necessary, the biological strategy of storing information in polymers can readily be adopted — there is no fundamental need to adopt a different approach. It would also be possible to employ any one of numerous different classes of molecular memory. Excellent proposals for molecular data storage and, more recently, experimental results can be found in. However, for the "foreseeable future" it is likely that onboard storage of information will not be required by nanomechanical replicators. One example of an inherently safer and more flexible approach is the broadcast architecture. In this approach, information is broadcast by any of several means to the replicating component. The replicator can be built with an internal "dead man switch" that is automatically off unless activated by an encrypted broadcast signal. The physical replicator becomes, in essence, a remote-controlled manipulator receiving instructions from the outside that guide it, step by step, in assembling a second remote-controlled manipulator. After some number of repeat cycles, the result is a large number of identical remote-controlled manipulators. These manipulators can then be used to assemble large numbers of useful product objects by altering the stream of instructions sent to the population of replicated manipulator devices. Acoustic broadcast (mentioned earlier) can be used to combine both power and information transmission in one convenient mechanism.

> The assembler, with its pick-and-place pincers, eliminates the many difficulties of fabricating nanomachines and of self-replication by ignoring them: positing a machine that can make any composition and any structure by simply placing atoms one at a time dismisses the most vexing aspects of fabrication. The assembler seems, however, from the vantage of a chemist, to be unworkable. Consider just two of the constraints.
>
> First is the pincers, or jaws, of the assembler. If they are to pick up atoms with any dexterity, they should be smaller than the atoms. But the jaws must be built of atoms and are thus larger than the atom they must pick and place. (Imagine trying to build a fine watch with your fingers, unaided by tools.) Second is the nature of atoms. Atoms, especially carbon atoms, bond strongly to their neighbors. Substantial energy would be needed to pull an atom from its place (a problem for the energy supply) and substantial energy released when it is put in place (a problem of cooling). More important, a carbon atom forms bonds with almost everything. It is difficult to imagine how the jaws of the assembler would be built so that, in pulling the atoms away from their starting material, they would not stick. (Imagine trying to build your watch with parts salvaged from another watch in which all the parts were coated with a particularly sticky glue: if you could separate the pieces at all, they would stick to your fingers.) Problems with the assembler are also discussed by Richard E. Smalley in his essay on page 76.

We have critiqued Smalley's essay elsewhere, and found the "problems" he raised concerning the infeasibility of the assembler to be without merit. "Pincers" or "jaws" are imprecise and misleading metaphors for an assembler manipulator end-effector, because the assembler designs proposed by Drexler or Merkle have contained no such pincers or jaws. The active tip of a mechanosynthetic manipulator tool need be no larger than a single atom, covalently attached to a progressively larger inverted conical handle structure. Hence the active site of the proposed tool need be no larger than the atom it must pick and place. A wide range of possible mechanosynthetic reactions and mechanisms has been proposed and analyzed theoretically by Drexler, Merkle, and others. Significant modeling work has been done on mechanosynthetic reactions that should be useful in the controlled synthesis of diamondoid structures.

For example, the ability to selectively remove (or abstract) a hydrogen from a hydrogenated diamond surface appears to be a fundamental reaction in the controlled synthesis of diamond and related structures. The theoretical analysis of the hydrogen abstraction tool has involved the work of many people, including: Donald W. Brenner, Richard J. Colton, K. Eric Drexler, William A. Goddard III, J.A. Harrison, Jason K. Perry, Ralph C. Merkle, Charles B. Musgrave, Michael Page, O.A. Shenderova,

Susan B. Sinnott, and Carter T. White. The institutions involved include the Materials and Process Simulation Center at Caltech; the Department of Materials Science and Engineering at North Carolina State University; the Institute for Molecular Manufacturing; the Department of Chemicals and Materials Engineering at the University of Kentucky; the Chemistry Department of the United States Naval Academy; the U.S. Naval Research Laboratories, Surface Chemistry Branch; and the Xerox Palo Alto Research Center. Related work on hydrogen abstraction has progressed on the experimental front as well. For instance, Lyding *et al.* have demonstrated the ability to abstract an individual hydrogen atom from a specific atomic position in a covalently-bound hydrogen monolayer on a flat Si(100) surface, using an STM tip in ultrahigh vacuum. Depositional covalent mechanosynthesis with atomic positional precision has also been demonstrated experimentally. For example, Ho and Lee used an STM tip first to locate two carbon monoxide (CO) molecules and one iron (Fe) atom adsorbed on a silver surface in vacuum at 13 K. Next, they lowered the tip over one CO molecule and increased the voltage and current flow of the instrument to pick up the molecule; then they moved the tip-bound molecule over the surface-bound Fe atom and reversed the current flow, causing the CO molecule to covalently bond to the Fe atom, forming an iron carbonyl Fe(CO) molecule on the surface. Finally, the researchers repeated the procedure, returning to the exact site of the first Fe(CO) and adding a second CO molecule to the Fe(CO), forming a molecule of $Fe(CO)_2$, which in subsequent images of the surface appeared as a tiny "rabbit ears" structure, covalently bound to the silver surface. Ho's group has also demonstrated single-atom hydrogen abstraction experimentally, using an STM.

If steric constraints near the tool tip make it unexpectedly difficult to manipulate particular individual atoms or small molecules experimentally with sufficient reliability, a simple alternative is to rely upon conventional solution or gas phase chemistry for the bulk synthesis of nanoparts consisting of 10-100 atoms.

> Would a nanosubmarine work if it could be built? A human-scale submarine moves easily in water by a combination of a rotating propeller—which, in spinning, forces the water backward and the submarine forward—and movable planes that guide its direction.

The term "nanosubmarine" implies the necessity for purposeful powered locomotion by molecular nanorobots. Many proposed molecular machines do not require active locomotion or navigation. Such machines would include assemblers replicating in a vat of liquid, respirocytes flowing in the blood, or the like. Even for devices requiring powered locomotion, the term "nanosubmarine" is another instance of an imprecise and misleading metaphor for a medical nanorobot that is commonly employed by the popular media to connote a nanomachine swimming through a liquid sea. Nanotechnology researchers recognize that "nanosubmarine" is not a technically precise description, and hence avoid its use in scientific discourse. This is because they realize, for example, that the Reynolds number (the dimensionless ratio of inertial to viscous forces) may be ~10^8 for a military submarine, ~10^5 for a human swimmer in water, ~10^{-2} for a 1-micron nanorobot locomoting at 1 cm/sec through the bloodstream, and ~10^{-5} for the even slower-moving typical flagellar bacterial swimmer. Since the onset of turbulent flow occurs at a Reynolds number above ~10^3, this implies that real submarines and human swimmers move through a fluid in which turbulence is commonplace and Newtonian forces are paramount. In contrast, nanorobots (and bacteria) inhabit a remarkably different environment in which all flow is laminar and viscous forces are paramount. Purcell once observed that for a man to be swimming at the same Reynolds number as his own sperm, he would have to be placed in a swimming pool full of molasses and then be forbidden to move any part of his body faster than 1 cm/min, roughly the speed of the minute-hand of a large wall clock. These facts will not prevent the development of medical nanorobots, even though the design and function of such nanorobots must necessarily differ significantly from those of macroscale submarines.

> Bacteria that swim actually use structures—flagella—that look more like flexible spirals or whips but serve a function similar to a propeller. They typically do not steer a very purposeful path but rather dash about, with motion that, if all goes well, tends in the general direction of a source of food.

It is well-known that micron-size bacteria "do not steer a very purposeful path but rather dash about" because the purpose of their motions is to overcome the diffusion limit to absorption of essential nutrients from the local environment. In general, outswimming diffusion requires semirandomized burst movements (most usefully along rising concentration gradients) over a characteristic distance $L_s \sim D/v_{swim}$. For bacteria moving at $v_{swim} \sim 30$ micron/sec and absorbing small nutrient molecules with diffusion coefficient $D \sim 10^{-11}$ m^2/sec, then $L_s \sim 30$ microns, roughly the sprint distance exhibited by flagellar microbes such as *E. coli*. Interestingly, there seems to be a sharp minimum size limit of ~0.6 microns for free-swimming foraging microbes, below which size locomotion confers no apparent benefit to microbes. In contrast, the theoretical power and materials import requirements for medical nanorobots are usually held to 10% or less of available diffusion currents, as a conservative design practice, so that materials diffusion currents are usually not a significant operational consideration. Nanorobots which locomote through fluids will therefore have markedly different performance objectives (e.g. purposeful directional travel) than outswimming diffusion (as exemplified by bacteria), and so nanorobot design, performance, and limitations will likewise be markedly different from bacteria as well. Freitas has reviewed or proposed numerous alternative methods for purposeful directional fluidic locomotion, including the flexible oar, the invaginating torus, the rolling bispheroids, the viscous helicopter, the use of surface traveling waves, propulsive cilia, the counterrotating dual screw drive, volume displacement, and viscous anchoring. The dual screw drive appears to provide the best combination of speed, safety, directional control, and energy efficiency of the proposed designs.

> For nanoscale objects, even if one could fabricate a propeller, a new and serious problem would emerge: random battering by water molecules. These water molecules would be smaller than a nanosubmarine but not much smaller, and their thermal motion is rapid on the nanoscale. Collisions with them make a nanoscale object bounce about rapidly (a process called Brownian motion) but in random directions: any effort to steer a purposeful course would be frustrated by the relentless collisions with rapidly moving water molecules. Navigators on the nanoscale would have to accommodate to the Brownian storms that would crash against their hulls. For ships of approximately 100 nanometers in scale, the destination of most voyages would be left to chance, because the tiny craft would probably be impossible to steer, at least in a sense familiar to a submariner. Cells in the bloodstream—objects 10 or 100 times more massive than a nanosubmarine—do not guide themselves in it: they simply tumble along with it. At best, a nanosubmarine might hope to select a general direction but not a specific destination. Regardless of whether one could make or steer devices at the nanoscale, they would not work for the sophisticated tasks required to detect disease if one could make them.

All extant technical designs for medical nanorobots describe them as ~1 micron in size and constructed of thousands to millions of nanoscale "parts." This is approximately the same size as a typical bacterium or mitochondrion and ~1000 times the volume of the 0.1-micron "nanosubmarines" that Whitesides imagines. Medical nanorobots with complex nanoscale parts will be ~1-3 microns in size or larger, but may require mobility in fluid. These devices are distinct from molecular assemblers, which may be as small as 100 nm in size, but do not require mobility in fluid. The statement that "water molecules would be smaller than a nanosubmarine but not much smaller" is grossly in error, since a water molecule is only ~0.00015 microns in diameter, or ~10,000 times smaller than proposed medical nanorobots. This is an important distinction in the "bombardment" argument. According to Einstein's approximation for Brownian motion, after 1 second has elapsed at room temperature a fluidic water molecule has, on average, diffused a distance of ~50 microns (~400,000 molecular diameters) whereas a 1-micron nanorobot immersed in that same fluid has displaced by only ~0.7 microns (only ~0.7 device diameter) during the same time period. Thus Brownian motion is at most a minor source of navigational error for motile medical nanorobots.

Freitas notes that motile nanorobots should be able to safely traverse *in vivo* fluid volumes at speeds up to ~1 cm/sec, up to 100 times faster than the 100-200 micron/sec velocity achieved during the purposeful locomotion of swimming sperm and more than fast enough to negotiate capillaries and small blood vessels with ease. Vascular wall ambulation has also been proposed and described. The fact that biological cells in the bloodstream do not locomote their way through human fluid volumes at high speed reflects the rather obvious truth that doing so would confer no significant evolutionary advantage — not that doing so is impossible for any fundamental physical reason, as Whitesides implies. Methods for steering fluid-borne motile medical nanorobots have been described by Freitas.

> Parts of the "little submarine" strategy for detecting and destroying diseased cells in the body, such as cancer cells, would have to focus on finding their prey. In doing so, they would probably have to mimic aspects of the immune system now functioning in us.

While it is true that immunochemical molecular recognition is often the quickest and most reliable technique for detecting specific cell types, and one could do worse than mimic biological immune systems, many other techniques are potentially available to medical nanorobots to detect cancer cells and malignant neoplasms. For exâmple, specific thermographic dermal patterns may signal the presence of osteoid osteomas, breast cancers, or melanomas. The exact spatial coordinates of these patterns could be recorded in the nanorobot computer memory prior to injection, or could be transmitted to *in vivo* medical nanorobots during a therapeutic procedure.

In *Nanomedicine*, Freitas points out that *in vivo* thermal mapping nanorobots or "thermographicytes" could detect subtle internal thermal anomalies reflecting the presence of interior hematomas, lipomas, myomas, edemas and hydromas, and slowly growing tumors could be found by searching for localized, shallow, but monotonic thermal gradients in the ~microkelvin/sec range in the historical data. Mobile nanorobots passing near any thermographicyte would interrogate the device's thermographic data library and thus may examine all or part of the current whole-body coarse thermal map. Similarly, historical and current data can be transmitted to medical personnel who interrogate the *in vivo* nanorobotic communications network. In principle, an expanding (warm) tumor could be detected after growing to a volume encompassing a maximum pathological cell count of ~100. For continuous surveillance of an entire organ to microkelvin accuracy, Freitas estimates that up to ~16 million monitoring units are required, dissipating at most ~0.3 watts which must also be taken into account. (The liver, for example, typically generates ~10 watts metabolically.) Of course, tumors which are metabolically less active are harder to detect by this means. Also, measuring heat from tumors located in organs having high metabolic activity (e.g. liver, kidney) is even more difficult, especially given the large caloric variations after consuming food or drink, or during normal hormonal responses, and given the relatively high normal rate of cell division in some organs (e.g. liver, gut) that must be distinguished from abnormal tumor growth. Another approach to cancer detection by medical nanorobots proposed by Freitas is the deployment of chemical demarcation markers to direct the nanorobots to particular locations. Such markers may include injected chemical plumes, time release implants, remote-triggered releasers (e.g. pressure-release multi-chemical-bearing labels), and tissue-coded markers (analogous to radiolabeled iodine concentrating in the thyroid gland, alkali metal ions seeking out bone, or cancer-cell-targeted light-sensitive drug molecules in photodynamic therapy) — all of which may establish useful localized chemical gradients. The use of such chemical beacons for chemonavigational triangulation is not efficient over large distances, since the required volume of signal chemical rises as the cube of the range. However, chemical localization may be moderately useful in close quarters. For instance, a micron-size nanorobot constructed of nanoscale parts, could be equipped with two antipodal chemical sensors that angularly resolve two periodic sources of dissimilar signal molecules to the limit of nanodevice rotation during a Brownian motion-limited measurement time. This means that a pair of 10-probe sensors taking measurements every ~1 millisec (concentration differential Dc/c ~ 20% over the full nanomedically-relevant range of $K_d = 10^{-4}$ to 10^{-13} molecules/nm^3) could resolve ~ 3° of arc, equivalent to two chemical point-emitters separated by ~1 micron at a range of ~20 microns (~1 cell width) from the nanorobot.

Detailed chemomapping of individual patients may allow customization of standardized human chemographic profiles, e.g. to identify problem areas. Chemographicytes (surveyor-class medical nanorobots) may assist in the mapping process at up to ~KHz sampling frequencies. For example, regions of hypoxia develop in all solid tumors where rapidly dividing cells are supplied by inadequate or poorly developed vasculature. A continuously updated whole-body tissue oxygenation map would allow recognition of growing hypoxic regions, permitting prompt detection of nascent tumors.

> The recognition of a cell as "normal" or "pathogen" or "cancer" is an extraordinarily complex process—one that requires the full panoply of our immune system, including the many billions of specialized cells that constitute it. No simple markers on the outside of most cancer cells flag them as dangerous. In many of their characteristics, they are not enormously different from normal cells.

This statement is factually incorrect. The full complexity of our immune system is not necessary to recognize a cell as normal or pathogenic. It is also not true that cancer cells bear no easily detectable extracellular plasma membrane markers. For instance, GM2 ganglioside is a well-known glycolipid present on the surface of ~95% of melanoma cells, with the carbohydrate portion of the molecule conveniently jutting out on the extracellular side of the melanoma cell membrane. GM2 and another ganglioside, GD2, are expressed in several types of cancer cells including small-cell lung, colon, and gastric cancer, sarcoma, lymphoma, and neuroblastoma. This is not to minimize the complexity and variety of cancer cells, but the point is that while we should learn what we can from our immunological mechanisms, we should also not be limited by them. We have already extended their range in the macroworld by MRI, genetic marker screening, and enzyme concentration testing.

Properly-designed medical nanorobots used for surveillance should find it relatively straightforward and safe to extract a quick cytoplasmic sample from all tissue cells that are even slightly suspicious. For example, a whole-body map of the concentration of intracellularly sampled telomerase (or associated proteins such as TRF1/TRF2, Ku, and tankyrase, or even telomerase mRNA levels) may provide a good first-cut toward a whole-body late-stage cancer map, since 85%-90% of all primary tumors display this biochemical marker. (However, ~10% of human cancer cells maintain their telomeres without telomerase and telomerase expression per se is not oncogenic.) Cancer cells also display above-normal concentrations of b1 integrins, survivin, sialidase-sensitive cancer mucins and leptin receptors such as galectin-3, and below-normal concentrations of b4 integrins. Numerous specific markers of disease (an emerging field known as molecular epidemiolo) are available for detection and mapping by nanorobots.

> A little submarine that was to be a hunter-killer for cancer cells would have to carry on board a little diagnostic laboratory, and because that laboratory would require sampling devices and reagents and reaction chambers and analytical devices, it would cease to be little. Operating this device would also require energy. The cells of the immune system use the same nutrients as do other cells; a little submarine would probably have to do the same.

Bloodborne phagocytic biological cells such as neutrophils, lymphocytes, and monocytes manage to detect, engulf and digest pathogenic cells without elaborate onboard chemical laboratories, and phagocytes have evolved by trial and error, not through efficient and rational design. As Whitesides points out, human engineers have the advantage of being able to learn from nature. They may extend natural methods, or innovate new ones, as they have in the macroworld. Again, this is a medical and engineering problem, not a fundamental problem with physical limits.

Like natural hunter-killer cells, the simplest artificial nanorobotic phagocytes could employ chemical recognition sensors at their outermost surface of sufficient number and diversity to guarantee selectivity for a specific type of cancerous or pathogenic cell. Chemotactic sensor pads can in principle be quite small, on the order of ~100 nm^2 each and perhaps 10^5-10^7 nm^2 for complete cell detection arrays. The use of dedicated molecular binding sites permits the direct detection of target molecular species, largely eliminating the need for the antiquated (in this context) paraphernalia of bulk chemistry such as reagents and reaction chambers.

Chemotactic sensor pads that detect an adhesion force of ~100 pN through a mechanical sensor movement of ~10 nm require an energy input of ~1000 zJ per detection. Hence a 100 pW medical nanorobot that devotes just 1% of its onboard power supply to chemotactic sensing could afford to measure up to 10^6 adhesion contact events per second and still remain within the stated power budget constraints.

Medical nanorobots may indeed make use of a few of the same nutrients as immune system cells — in particular, as noted earlier, glucose and oxygen. A trillion (10^{12}) therapeutic nanorobots each consuming 100 pW of power would produce a total whole-body waste heat of 100 watts — roughly equivalent to the human basal metabolic rate and representing an insufficient thermal load to trigger any significant response by the human thermoregulatory system.

> *Small machines will eventually be made, but the strategy used to make them, and the purposes they will serve, remain to be devised.*

We agree with Whitesides that small machines will eventually be made. Strategies to make them have been discussed in the technical literature. The purposes they will serve, for instance in the medical arena, have also been discussed in the technical literature. As the strategies become more complete and more fully verified by experimental results, the purposes these machines may serve will become clearer and the need to confront their social, financial and ethical implications will become increasingly urgent.

> *Biology provides one brilliantly developed set of examples: in living systems, nanomachines do exist, and they do perform extraordinarily sophisticated functions. What is striking is how different the strategies used in these nanometer-scale machines are from those used in human-scale machines. In thinking about how best to make nanomachines, we come up against two limiting strategies. The first is to take existing nanomachines—those present in the cell—and learn from them. We will undoubtedly be able to extract from these systems concepts and principles that will enable us to make variants of them that will serve our purposes, and others that will have entirely new functions. Genetic engineering is already proceeding down this path, and the development of new types of chemistry may enable us to use biological principles in molecular systems that are not proteins and nucleic acids. The second is to start from scratch and independently to develop fundamental new types of nanosystems. Biology has produced one practical means for fabrication and synthesis of functional nanomachines, and there is no reason to believe that there cannot be others. But this path will be arduous.*

It is true that there is much to be learned from biological examples of nanomachines. It is also true that nonbiological nanomachines need to be designed so as to not interfere with biological systems. However, it is not clear why the task of reverse engineering the entire baroque molecular structure and function of living cells involving potentially hundreds of thousands of distinct parts is inherently less difficult than the task of converting inherently scalable macroscale machine systems to nanoscale implementations involving potentially orders of magnitude fewer distinct parts. Our scientific knowledge of biological molecular machines spans mere decades whereas our direct experience with macroscale machines spans millennia.

> *Looking at the machines that surround us and expecting to be able to build nanoscale versions of them using processes analogous to those employed on a large scale will usually not be practical and in many cases impossible. Machining and welding do not have counterparts at nanometer sizes. Nor do processes such as moving in a straight line through a fluid or generating magnetic fields with electromagnets.*

Nanosystems provides a useful overview of scaling laws. For instance, magnetic force scales adversely with size. Magnetic forces between nanoscale current elements are usually negligible in comparison with typical intermolecular forces. On the other hand, electrostatic forces scale more favorably, leading to the design for an electrostatic motor measuring 100-400 nm in diameter.

Some macroscopic machines scale to smaller sizes quite readily. Others scale well in general, but require some modifications. Other approaches do not scale well. Specific proposals need to be examined, and specific conclusions need to be reached based on their merits. In general, macroscopic machines that rely on simple mechanical interactions (gears, belts, pulleys, levers, wheels, bearings, shafts, struts, ratchets, and many others) can be scaled to molecular sizes without undue difficulty. To our knowledge, there have been no proposals for machining or welding parts at the nanoscale. This form of argumentation is simply knocking a strawman.

> *Techniques devised to manufacture electronic devices will certainly be able to make some simple types of mechanical nanodevices, but they will be limited in what they can do.*

The limitations depends upon what those techniques are. If they involve the positional assembly of nanoscale components synthesized via conventional bulk chemistry or other means, then they may have more general applicability.

> *The dream of the assembler holds seductive charm in that it appears to circumvent these myriad difficulties. This charm is illusory: it is more appealing as metaphor than as reality, and less the solution of a problem than the hope for a miracle. Considering the many constraints on the construction and operation of nanomachines, it seems that new systems for building them might ultimately look much like the ancient systems of biology. It will be a marvelous challenge to see if we can outdesign evolution. It would be a staggering accomplishment to mimic the simplest living cell.*

Molecular nanotechnology researchers who accept the proposition that molecular assemblers are physically possible are neither "seduced" nor "charmed." Rather, they have become convinced of the accuracy of this proposition only after studying the technical literature. These researchers are the least likely people to find "hoping for a miracle". Rather, they are striving to create the theoretical underpinnings, and to achieve the experimental results that will bring the full potential of molecular assemblers to fruition. There are many constraints on the construction and operation of nanomachines, just as there are many constraints on the construction and operation of biological cells. The mere existence of such constraints does not imply impossibility or even implausibility, as demonstrated by biology.

Mimicking the simplest living cell would indeed be a staggering accomplishment. Fortunately it is not necessary to mimic all of the functions of the living cell in every nanomachine. For example, virtually all medical nanomachines will lack the ability of the biological cell to reproduce and to evolve new structures and functions on their own, *making artificial nanomachines inherently safer than biological cells in terms of the potential for a loss of control*. Most medical nanomachines will not require the capacity for complex onboard organic synthesis, and many nanorobots will not require the abilities of locomotion, manipulation, or various forms of global navigation or communication as are possessed by different types of biological cells.

Among those biological functions that must be mimicked by the mechanical nanodevice, more compact and efficient implementations can sometimes be found by rational design. A straight line drawn between two points is always a shorter path than a random walk. In some cases, evolution may have produced optimal designs. In other cases, designs survived because they were good enough to do the job, and the primary biological selection pressure was on other parts of the organism. We regularly build macroscale artificial systems that outperform biological systems in some dimensions. Examples include: numerical calculating chips, x-ray imaging systems, and subsonic jets for high-speed locomotion. There is no reason to assume that we will not be able to accomplish unique nonbiological designs at the nanoscale.

> Biological structures work in water, and most work only in a narrow range of temperatures and concentrations of salts. They do not, in general, conduct electricity well (although some, such as the chloroplast and the mitochondrion, move electrons around with great sophistication). They do not carry out binary computation and communications. They are not particularly robust mechanically.

This is a useful summary of some of the major limitations of existing biological approaches, and some of the major motivations for considering alternative approaches.

> Thus, a great many types of function must be invented if nanomachines are to succeed in nonbiological environments.

This is a useful recognition of the exciting engineering challenges ahead and the likelihood that mechanical nanomachines, once designed and built, may have greater functionality than biological-based systems, when placed in nonbiological environments.

> And what have we learned from all this about the doomsday scenario of gray goo? If a hazard were to arise from nanomachines, it would lie in a capability for self-replication. To be self-replicating, a system must contain all the information it needs to make itself ...

This assertion is likely to mislead scientists who are not familiar with the extensive literature on self-replication. Replicative architectures exist which do not require a system to explicitly contain all the information needed to make itself. For example, Laing has described a process of machine replication without self-description, also known as "replication by inspection". Another example is "exponential assembly" as recently proposed by researchers at Zyvex Corp.

> ...and must be able to collect from its environment all the materials necessary both for energy and for fabrication. It must also be able to manufacture and assemble (or allow to assemble) all the pieces needed to make a copy of itself. Biology has solved all these problems,...

Given that biology has had over 3 billion years to solve all of these problems, whereas a small number of human scientists and engineers have been trying to design and build kinematic replicators for only a few decades, we think progress has been remarkably rapid on this front. As Whitesides points out, it is always instructive to examine the solutions in nature's 10^8-fold headstart, but this an opportunity, not a fundamental problem.

> ...and self-replicating biological systems—from pathogenic bacteria to cancer cells—are a danger to us. In computer systems, self-replicating strings of bits (computer viruses), although not material objects, are also at least a great nuisance, but only indirectly a danger, to us. If a new system—any system—were able to replicate itself using materials present in the environment, it would be cause for concern. So biology and chemistry, not a mechanical engineering textbook, point in the direction we should look for answers—and it is also where our fears about organisms or devices that multiply uncontrollably are most justified. In thinking about self-replication, and about the characteristics of systems that make them "alive," one should start with biology, which offers a cornucopia of designs and strategies that have been successful at the highest levels of sophistication.

We agree that biological machines such as viruses and bacteria that have been selected to be robust in the natural environment are a greater danger than artificial nanomachines that have been designed with multiple safeguards and specifically engineered to not operate in the natural environment. However, we should all be seriously concerned about the potential for danger from microbial agents engineered from scratch, from accidentally engineered microbial agents, from accidental or malicious releases of modified or natural (archived) microbial agents, from the acquisition of multidrug resistance by existing microbial strains, or from the natural emergence or evolution of new and deadly natural pathogens against which we currently have no defenses. Nonbiological nanomachines could be designed to greatly reduce every one of these risks, and they should be developed as rapidly as possible for this purpose. This includes their potential use in detecting and defending against malicious or accidental misuse of biological or nonbiological systems.

> But we now know enough to realize how far we are from reproducing self-replication in a nonbiological system. Fabrication based on the assembler is not, in my opinion, a workable strategy and thus not a concern. For the foreseeable future, we have nothing to fear from gray goo. If robust self-replicating micro (or perhaps nano) structures were ultimately to emerge, they would probably be chemical systems as complex as primitive bacteria. Any such system would be both an incredible accomplishment and a cause for careful assessment. Any threat will not be from assemblers gone amok but from currently unimaginable systems of self-catalyzing reactions.

As we have seen, Whitesides did not demonstrate that there is anything inherently "unworkable" about molecular assemblers or nanorobots. We believe that the medical, environmental, and industrial benefits are well worth the engineering challenges. However, we also believe that all powerful technologies are double-edge swords, and molecular nanotechnology is no exception to this rule It is not clear what time frame Whitesides regards as the "foreseeable future." Estimates of the time frame needed to develop assemblers vary, but they are typically measured in decades. Thus, if the "foreseeable future" is the next five to ten years, then perhaps gray goo is not an immediate concern. On the other hand, scientific and engineering knowledge are on a growth curve that is accelerating exponentially, and international progress in molecular nanotechnology may surprise us. If the "foreseeable future" encompasses our lifetimes and the lifetimes of our children, then we certainly need to address these issues forthrightly.

Flexures for High Precision Robotics

High precision robots are often used for complex assembly or positioning tasks. One way to achieve high motion precision is to design mechanical systems based on flexure joints. Flexure joints (or flexures) utilize the elastic properties of matter, which brings avoidance of dry friction. Nanometer scale motions are then possible, without wear, mechanical play or particle emission. Leading to high performance systems in terms of dynamics, parallel kinematics are useful for high precision robot design. Two research projects are presented in this paper. The first one has already led to the realization of a micro electro-discharge machine (i-EDM), and the second one's goal is to generate a family of compact ultra-high precision manipulators.

Today, developments in micro-technologies are essentially based on photolithographic techniques. The fabrication and assembly of advanced systems such as optical fiber connectors, pacemakers or insulin pumps require high precision, flexibility and reliability. In addition to wafer-based manufacturing techniques, there is still a need for high precision robots, especially for positioning and assembly. There are many ways to improve the precision of a required task. In the case of assembly, it is possible to change the process, the environment or the shape of the parts (self-alignment). Another possibility is to increase the manipulator's precision. The present paper and the related work focus on this possibility and, further more, on the mechanical structure of the robotic system. An innovative approach permits us to overcome the limitations due to dry friction by the use of flexure joints.

Flexures (or flexure joints) are widely used in fields such as astronautics (spacecraft, aeronautical structures), measurement devices (for example weight measurement) but yet seldom used in the design of multi-degrees of freedom (multi-DOF) robotic systems. Flexures have many advantages that may be helpful for the design of high precision robots. A flexure joint links two solids (permitting relative motion in some directions while constraining motion in others), using the elastic properties of matter, which brings numerous advantages:

- *Avoidance of dry friction*: almost all of the advantages listed below are consequences of the fact that there is no dry friction or rolling phenomenon in flexures. In other terms, the motion permitted by a flexure joint is smooth, even at the nanometer scale.
- *Absence of mechanical play*: this is essential if high precision motions are targeted. The important fact is that flexures do not need to be pre-loaded.
- *No wear*: as a consequence of the absence of dry friction, no wear appears during the lifetime of the structure. This lifetime is limited by the eventual fatigue of the material. A good design maintains the stresses below the fatigue limit, allowing almost infinite lifetime.
- *Immunity to contamination*: the working of a flexure joint is not affected by the presence of dust and flexures can be used in severe environments. In contrast, flexures may also be used in clean environments, with an extremely low rate of particle emission.
- *High stiffness*: if the targeted tasks are demanding in terms of stiffness, flexures should appear as a valuable design choice. Two types of stiffness have to be considered: on one hand, the stiffness of the constrained degrees of freedom (which depends on the design of the structure and the choice of the material; can be very high), on the other hand, the stiffness of the controlled degrees of freedom (which depends on the control loop and is a function of the force disturbance frequency).

- *Compact and monolithic structures*: the basic idea when talking about monolithic structures is to avoid problems and costs related to assembly. Several fabrication processes can lead to monolithic mechanisms with flexure joints. Besides traditional machining, we may mention electro-discharge machining (EDM) for conductive materials or lithographic etching for silicon wafers or copper sheets.

The design of a flexures based mechanism begins with the study of elementary flexures. There are several types of elementary flexures, among them: the cantilever beam, the notch hinge and the torsion rod spring. These elementary flexures permit us to design almost all the classical joints (revolute joint, U-joint, slider, cylindrical, ball joint, etc.). With these joints, it is possible to design sub-assemblies and finally, complete robots. Of course there are some limitations in the use of flexure joints. Perhaps the most constraining limit is the stroke. The need for long strokes (up to 10mm) requires flexures with thin cross-sections (typically about 100ìm) whereas the need for high stiffness requires thick cross-sections. Manufacturing high aspect ratio sections can solve this contradiction. Wire electro-discharge machining (EDM) has been shown to be one of the most suited manufacturing processes for this purpose. It allows, for example, the manufacturing of flexure hinges of thickness of less than 50ìm and cross-sections with typical aspect ratio of 200. EDM machining also produces a low surface roughness, which is very important to ensure a long lifetime. Another limit for the use of flexures might be the quite complex design procedure, but these aspects have been intensively studied in several books (Smith, 2000; Henein, 2001). Requirements of a high precision system are not only precision, but also bandwidth, trajectory tracking, low sensitivity to perturbations, etc. All these characteristics are related to dynamics. In robotics, a particular family of robots called "parallel robots" presents advantages of special interest for high precision robots. They are especially known for the low weight of their moving parts, high bandwidth or high accelerations. They can achieve these performances because all the drives are located on the fixed base and because more than one kinematic chain link the end-effector to the base, increasing the structural stiffness.

Obviously, the mechanical structure is not sufficient to ensure the performances of the whole system. The choice of sensors and actuators must be consistent with the use of flexures, which means that contact-free sensors and actuators have to be selected (for example: optical encoders and direct drive electromagnetic motors).

The basic idea of our work is to benefit from the advantages of both flexures and parallel kinematics to obtain high performance multi-DOF systems. Two research projects exploring this approach are currently running at the Institut de Production et Robotique (IPR). The first one's objective is the realization of an ultra-high precision electro-discharge machine (EDM) of small size, the Delta^3 (Delta cube) robot. The second one, more generic, leads to the creation an ultra-high precision parallel manipulator family with three to six degrees of freedom.

Electro discharge machining (EDM) is a manufacturing process based on controlled electric discharges (sparks). The material removal takes place without any mechanical interaction between the electrode (the tool) and work-piece. Every spark melts and evaporates a tiny amount of the work-piece (and also of the electrode). A dielectric liquid cools and cleans the working zone. The notion of ì-EDM is related to the typical energy brought by a spark (one refers to ì-EDM when this energy is about 1ìJ). When the discharge energy of the sparks decreases, the volume of the material removed diminishes and the geometry and the surface roughness can be improved. If the pulse parameters (energy, polarity ...) have the main influence on the result, the flushing conditions also strongly affect the geometrical accuracy as well as the surface roughness. In fact, the process stability in ì-EDM depends on the cleanness of the discharge gap (distance between electrode and work-piece during the sparks). The particles melted and evaporated during the process have to be evacuated by flushing. The flushing consists of evacuating the dirty dielectric of the gap and bringing some clean dielectric for the next sparks. For micro-holes with diameters below 100ìm, tube shaped electrodes (commonly used because the dielectric liquid can be injected through the tube) are impossible to use. In this case, the currently used flushing method is a high-speed (1,600 rpm) electrode rotation. This flushing strategy provides little particle transport out of the discharge gap (5ìm) and limits the aspect ratio at about ten for a diameter of 50ìm (Koch *et al.*, 2001). Thanks to its high dynamic and high precision it is possible to generate a controlled 500Hz vibration with 2ìm of amplitude and an accuracy of 20nm. This kind of vibration can be generated independently on the three axes of the robot. The small amplitude of the vibrations allows us to work with typical gap of 5ìm. Furthermore, it is possible to combine the vibrations with fast and precise timer movements (cleaning cycles), which evacuate the dirty particles from the gap and bring fresh dielectric. The electromagnetic linear motors of the Delta^3 are able to manage high accelerations. This reduces the duration of the cleaning cycles in order to optimize the time of machining.

Although EDM has been in use for 40 years, ì-EDM is at the beginning of its potential. Today, only a few companies propose small EDM machines. In fact, most of them propose big machines adapted for miniature parts machining. The collaboration with the EDM-machine manufacturer AGIE has led to the present new concept of ì-EDM machines. ì-EDM is not yet a common manufacturing process in the semiconductor industry, even if it is known (Heeren *et al.*, 1997) that machining silicon with ì-EDM has several advantages compared to the traditional techniques:

- ì-EDM requires low installation costs compared to etching techniques.
- ì-EDM requires little overhead job, such as designing masks, etc.

- ì-EDM is very flexible; it is well adapted for prototypes or small batches of products with a high added value.
- ì-EDM can easily machine complex (even 3D) shapes. Shapes that are difficult to realize with etching techniques, might be quite easy to manufacture by ì-EDM.

The goal of this project is to generate a whole family of compact ultra-high precision manipulators based on the use of flexures, parallel kinematics with three, four, five and six DOF and contact-free sensors and actuators. Expected travel ranges are 10mm for linear motions and 10? for rotations. The total volume of the manipulators should not exceed a few dm^3. Resolutions as low as 5nm for translations and 100nrad for rotational movements are targeted for displacements over the entire workspace. The identified technology and control allows a high usable bandwidth of more than 100Hz, merging the usual two-stage coarse/fine architecture into one single actuation stage. The generally added piezoelectric stage for fine resolutions and high dynamics over small strokes of less than 100ìm is therefore unnecessary in this new approach. An industrial application in the domain of micro-assembly of submillimetric optical components guides the ongoing project. The main effort in this project is the mechanical design of manipulators fulfilling the high requirements in terms of resolution, repeatability, workspace, stiffness, dynamics, number of DOF and total volume. The work will lead to the synthesis of a design methodology guiding the engineering process of this kind of robots.

An inherent limitation in the use of elementary metallic flexures as rotational articulations is the maximum usable angle of about 10? above which the lateral stiffness of the pivot becomes critically low and motion errors become non-negligible. This limitation strongly influences the design and makes it possible to optimally use parallel kinematics by placing the workspace in a singularity-free region. The coupling of the different axes can also be held low. A first one DOF linear prototype has been designed, simulated and optimized by the finite element method, and then realized and characterize. The results meet the expected specifications. The implemented controller allows us to maintain any desired position at (I1 encoder increment of 5nm. The next step was the design and realization of a six DOF prototype using the same technology. This prototype is currently being mounted and characterization will soon be undertaken. Through this paper, the advantages and limits of flexures in high precision robotics have been pointed out. The use of flexure joints allows us to reach nanometer resolution and repeatability thanks to the absence of dry friction. Two research projects have been presented, and the first results shown. It is relevant to notice that these projects are part of an innovative concept called "Micro/nano factory". The "micro/nano factory" concept is based on the idea of concentrating as many production steps as possible into a very compact space. It refers to a set of cooperating machines in a tabletop containment to produce, process and manipulate complex micro and nano devices, letting the human operator remain outside the production space. Many tasks have to be done in this factory, among them: manipulation, vision, transfer, bonding, machining, environment control. The ı-EDM machine would be suited to machining in this nano factory, and as the nano-family of robots would be well suited to object manipulation or positioning.

Future Applications

Nanorobots as already explained are nanodevices that will be used for the purpose of maintaining and protecting the human body against pathogens. They will have a diameter of about 0.5 to 3 microns and will be constructed out of parts with dimensions in the range of 1 to 100 nanometers. The main element used will be carbon in the form of diamond/fullerene nanocomposites because of the strength and chemical inertness of these forms. Many other light elements such as oxygen and nitrogen can be used for special purposes. To avoid being attacked by the host's immune system, the best choice for the exterior coating is a passive diamond coating. The smoother and more flawless the coating, the less the reaction from the body's immune system. Such devices have been designed in recent years but no working model has been built so far. The powering of the nanorobots can be done by metabolising local glucose and oxygen for energy. In a clinical environment, another option would be externally supplied acoustic energy. Other sources of energy within the body can also be used to supply the necessary energy for the devices. They will have simple onboard computers capable of performing around 1000 or fewer computations per second. This is because their computing needs are simple. Communication with the device can be achieved by *broadcast-type acoustic signaling*. A navigational network may be installed in the body, with stationkeeping navigational elements providing high positional accuracy to all passing nanorobots that interrogate them, wanting to know their location. This will enable the physician to keep track of the various devices in the body. These nanorobots will be able to distinguish between different cell types by checking their surface antigens (they are different for each type of cell). This is accomplished by the use of chemotactic sensors keyed to the specific antigens on the target cells. When the task of the nanorobots is completed, they can be retrieved by allowing them to exfuse themselves via the usual human excretory channels. They can also be removed by active scavenger systems. This feature is design-dependent. Some possible applications using nanorobots are as follows:

1. To cure skin diseases, a cream containing nanorobots may be used. It could remove the right amount of dead skin, remove excess oils, add missing oils, apply the right amounts of natural moisturising compounds, and even achieve the elusive goal of 'deep pore cleaning' by actually reaching down into pores and cleaning them out. The cream could be a smart material with smooth-on, peel-off convenience.

2. A mouthwash full of smart nanomachines could identify and destroy pathogenic bacteria while allowing the harmless flora of the mouth to flourish in a healthy ecosystem. Further, the devices would identify particles of food, plaque, or tartar, and lift them from teeth to be rinsed away. Being suspended in liquid and able to swim about, devices would be able to reach surfaces beyond reach of toothbrush bristles or the fibres of floss. As short-lifetime medical nanodevices, they could be built to last only a few minutes in the body before falling apart into materials of the sort found in foods (such as fibre).
3. Medical nanodevices could augment the immune system by finding and disabling unwanted bacteria and viruses. When an invader is identified, it can be punctured, letting its contents spill out and ending its effectiveness. If the contents were known to be hazardous by themselves, then the immune machine could hold on to it long enough to dismantle it more completely.
4. Devices working in the bloodstream could nibble away at arteriosclerotic deposits, widening the affected blood vessels. Cell herding devices could restore artery walls and artery linings to health, by ensuring that the right cells and supporting structures are in the right places. This would prevent most heart attacks.

The typical medical nanodevice will probably be a micron-scale robot assembled from nanoscale parts. These parts could range in size from 1-100 nm (1 nm = 10^{-9} meter), and might be fitted together to make a working machine measuring perhaps 0.5-3 microns (1 micron = 10^{-6} meter) in diameter. Three microns is about the maximum size for bloodborne medical nanorobots, due to the capillary passage requirement. Carbon will likely be the principal element comprising the bulk of a medical nanorobot, probably in the form of diamond or diamondoid/fullerene nanocomposites—largely because of the tremendous strength and chemical inertness of diamond. Many other light elements such as hydrogen, sulfur, oxygen, nitrogen, fluorine, silicon, etc. will be used for special purposes in nanoscale gears and other components. From a medical standpoint, it makes sense to regard the nanorobot as having two spaces which should be considered separately—its interior and its exterior. It is true that the nanorobot exterior will be exposed to the diverse chemical brew that makes up our human biochemistry. But the interior of the nanorobot may be a highly controlled environment, possibly a vacuum, into which external liquids cannot normally intrude. Of course it may often be necessary for a nanorobot to import external fluids in a controlled manner for chemical analysis or other purposes. But the important thing is that the device will be watertight and airtight. Body fluids cannot get into the interior of the device, unless these fluids are purposely pumped in for some specific reason. In most cases a human patient who is is undergoing a nanomedical treatment is going to look just like anyone else who is sick. The typical nanomedical treatment (e.g. to combat a bacterial or viral infection) will consist of an injection of perhaps a few cubic centimeters of micron-sized nanorobots suspended in fluid (probably a water/saline suspension). The typical therapeutic dose may include up to 1-10 trillion (1 trillion = 10^{12}) individual nanorobots, although in some cases treatment may only require a few million or a few billion individual devices to be injected. Each nanorobot will be on the order of perhaps 0.5 micron up to perhaps 3 microns in diameter. (The exact size depends on the design, and on exactly what the nanorobots are intended to do.) The adult human body has a volume of perhaps 100,000 cm^3 and a blood volume of ~5400 cm^3, so adding a mere ~3 cm^3 dose of nanorobots is not particularly invasive. The nanorobots are going to be doing exactly what the doctor tells them to do, and nothing more (barring malfunctions). So the only physical change you will see in the patient is that he or she will very rapidly become well again. Most symptoms such as fever and itching have specific biochemical causes which can also be managed, reduced, and eliminated using the appropriate injected nanorobots. Major rashes or lesions such as those that occur when you have the measles will take a bit longer to reverse, because in this case the broken skin must also be repaired.

It is impossible to say exactly what a generic nanorobot would look like. Nanorobots intended to travel through the bloodstream to their target will probably be 500-3000 nanometers (1 nanometer = 10^{-9} meter) in characteristic dimension. Nonbloodborne tissue-traversing nanorobots might be as large as 50-100 microns, and alimentary or bronchial-traveling nanorobots may be even larger still. Each species of medical nanorobot will be designed to accomplish a specific task, and many shapes and sizes are possible. Finally, and perhaps most importantly, no actual working nanorobot has yet been built. Many theoretical designs have been proposed that look good on paper, but these preliminary designs could change significantly after the necessary research, development and testing has been completed.

One very simple nanorobot that I designed a few years ago is the artificial mechanical red cell, which I call a *"respirocyte."* The respirocyte measures about 1 micron in diameter and just floats along in the bloodstream. It is a spherical nanorobot made of 18 billion atoms. These atoms are mostly carbon atoms arranged as diamond in a porous lattice structure inside the spherical shell. The respirocyte is essentially a tiny pressure tank that can be pumped full of up to 9 billion oxygen (O_2) and carbon dioxide (CO_2) molecules. Later on, these gases can be released from the tiny tank in a controlled manner. The gases are stored onboard at pressures up to about 1000 atmospheres. (Respirocytes can be rendered completely nonflammable by constructing the device internally of sapphire, a flameproof material with chemical and mechanical properties otherwise similar to diamond.) The surface of each respirocyte is 37 per cent covered with 29,160 molecular sorting rotors (Nanosystems) that can load and unload gases into the tanks. There are also gas concentration sensors on the outside of each device. When the nanorobot passes through the lung capillaries, O_2 partial pressure is high and CO_2 partial pressure is low, so the onboard computer tells the sorting rotors to load the tanks with oxygen and to dump the CO_2. When the device later finds itself in the oxygen-starved peripheral tissues, the sensor readings are reversed. That is, CO_2 partial pressure is relatively high and O_2 partial pressure relatively low, so the onboard computer commands the sorting rotors to release O_2 and to absorb CO_2. Respirocytes mimic the action of the natural hemoglobin-filled red blood cells. But a respirocyte can deliver 236 times more oxygen per unit volume than a natural red cell. This nanorobot is far more efficient than biology, mainly because its diamondoid construction permits a much higher operating pressure. (The operating pressure of the natural red blood cell is the equivalent of only about 0.51 atm, of which only about 0.13 atm is deliverable to tissues.) So the injection of a 5 cm^3 dose of 50 per cent respirocyte aqueous suspension into the bloodstream can exactly replace the entire O_2 and CO_2 carrying capacity of the patient's entire 5,400 cm^3 of blood! Respirocytes will have pressure sensors to receive acoustic signals from the doctor, who will use an ultrasound-like transmitter device to give the respirocytes commands to modify their behavior while they are still inside the patient's body. For example, the doctor might order all the respirocytes to just stop pumping, and become dormant. Later, the doctor might order them all to turn on again.

What if you added 1 liter of respirocytes into your bloodstream, the maximum that could possibly be safe? You could then hold your breath for nearly 4 hours if sitting quietly at the bottom of a swimming pool. Or if you were sprinting at top speed, you could run for at least 15 minutes before you had to take a breath! It is clear that very "simple" medical nanodevices can have extremely useful abilities, even when applied in relatively small doses. Other more complex devices will have a broader range of capabilities. Some devices may have mobility—the ability to swim through the blood, or crawl through body tissue or along the walls of arteries. Others will have different shapes, colors, and surface textures, depending on the functions they must perform. They will have different types of robotic manipulators, different sensor arrays, and so forth. Each medical nanorobot will be designed to do a particular job extremely well, and will have a unique shape and behaviour. Following most simple treatments, nanodoctors of the 21st century will want to remove their therapeutic nanorobots from the patient's body as soon as the nanodevices have finished the job. So there will be little danger of "old nanorobots" breaking down or malfunctioning, or causing something unpleasant to happen to the patient after the original disease or traumatic condition has been treated. Additionally, nanorobots will be designed with a high level of redundancy to ensure fail-operational and fail-safe performance, further reducing the medical risk. Some nanodevices will be able to exfuse themselves from the body via the usual human excretory channels; others will be designed to allow ready exfusion by medical personnel using apheresis-like processes (commonly called nanapheresis) or active scavenger systems. It is very design dependent. In the case of the respirocytes, the removal procedure is fairly simple: "Once a therapeutic purpose is completed, it may be desirable to extract artificial devices from circulation. Onboard water ballast control is extremely useful during respirocyte exfusion from the blood. Blood to be cleared may be passed from the patient to a specialized centrifugation apparatus where acoustic transmitters command respirocytes to establish neutral buoyancy. No other solid blood component can maintain exact neutral buoyancy, hence those other components precipitate outward during gentle centrifugation and are drawn off and added back to filtered plasma on the other side of the apparatus. Meanwhile, after a period of centrifugation, the plasma, containing mostly suspended respirocytes but few other solids, is drawn off through a 1-micron filter, removing the respirocytes. Filtered plasma is recombined with centrifuged solid components and returned undamaged to the patient's body. The rate of separation is further enhanced either by commanding respirocytes to empty all tanks, lowering net density to 66 per cent of blood plasma density, or by commanding respirocytes to blow a 5-micron O_2 gas bubble to which the device may adhere via surface tension, allowing it to rise at 45 mm/hour under normal gravitational acceleration."

Immune system response is primarily a reaction to a "foreign" surface. Nanorobot size is also an important variable, along with device mobility, surface roughness, surface mobility, and other factors. Yet the problem of nanodevice biocompatibility is in principle no more difficult than the biocompatibility of medical implants generally. In some ways it may even be an easier problem, because many medical nanorobots will have only temporary residence in the body. Even today, application of immunosuppressive agents during the treatment period would allow poorly-engineered non-bioinactive nanorobots to perform their repair work without trouble. Passive diamond exteriors may turn out to be ideal. Several experimental studies hint that the smoother and more flawless the diamond surface, the less leukocyte activity and the less fibrinogen adsorption you will get. So it seems reasonable to hope that when diamond coatings can be laid down with almost flawless atomic precision, making nanorobot exterior surfaces with near-nanometer smoothness, that these surfaces may have very low bioactivity. Due to the extremely high surface energy of the passivated diamond surface and the strong hydrophobicity of the diamond surface, the diamond exterior is almost completely chemically inert and so opsonization should be minimized. However, even if flawless diamond surfaces alone do not prove fully bioinactive as hoped, active surface management of the nanorobot exterior can be used to ensure complete nanodevice biocompatibility. Allergic and shock reactions are similarly easily avoided.

This is a very common error. Medical nanorobots need not EVER replicate. In fact, it is unlikely that the FDA (or its future equivalent) would ever approve for general use a medical nanodevice that was capable of *in vivo* replication. Except in the most unusual of circumstances, you would never want anything that could replicate itself to be turned loose inside your body. Replicating bacteria are trouble enough! Replication is a crucial basic capability for molecular manufacturing. But aside from the most aggressive applications, there is simply no good reason to risk manufacturing "fertile" nanorobots inside the human body, when "mule" nanorobots can be manufactured so cheaply, conveniently, and in such vast numbers outside of the human body. Replicators will almost certainly be very tightly regulated by governments everywhere. This is another common error. Many medical nanorobots will have very simple computers on board each device. Respirocytes, for example, have only a ~1,000 operations/sec computer on board each device—far less computing power than an old Apple II. Most cellular repair nanorobots will not need more than 10^6-10^9 operations/sec of onboard computing capacity to do their work. This is a full 4-7 orders of magnitude below (even the potential for) true human-equivalent computing at 10 teraflops (~10^{13} operations/sec). Faster computing capacity is simply not required for most medical nanorobots. One of the earliest proposals by Drexler in *Engines of Creation* was that an *in vivo* medical nanodevice could metabolize local glucose and oxygen for energy. Another possibility is externally supplied acoustic power, which is probably most appropriate in a clinical setting. There are literally dozens of useful power sources that are potentially available in the human body.

There are many different ways to do this. One of the simplest ways to send broadcast-type messages into the body, to be received by *in vivo* nanorobots, is acoustic messaging. A device similar to an ultrasound probe would encode messages on acoustic carrier waves at frequencies between 1-10 MHz. Thus, the supervising physician can easily send new commands or parameters to nanorobots already at work inside the body. Each nanorobot has its own power supply, computer, and sensorium, thus can receive the physician's messages via acoustic sensors, then compute and implement the appropriate response. The other half of the process is getting messages back out of the body, from the working nanodevices out to the physician. This can also be done acoustically. However, onboard power requirements for micronscale acoustic wave generators in water dictate a maximum practical transmission range of at most a few hundred microns for each individual nanorobot. Therefore, it is convenient to establish an internal communications network that can collect local messages and pass them along to a central location, which the physician can then monitor using sensitive ultrasound detectors to receive the messages. Such a network can probably be deployed inside a patient in less than an hour, may involve up to 100 billion mobile nanorobotic network nodes, and may release at most 60 watts of waste heat (less than the 100-watt human body basal rate) assuming a (worst case) full 100 per cent network duty cycle. There are many other techniques that may be used as well—this one is just the easiest to describe.

A navigational network may be installed in the body, with stationkeeping navigational elements providing high positional accuracy to all passing nanorobots that interrogate them, wanting to know their location. Physical positions can be reported continuously using an *in vivo* communications network. Since the typical therapeutic dose may involve billions or trillions of nanorobots (e.g. up to a few cm^3 of injection), it will usually be impractical to address nanorobots individually, though this is in principle possible for treatments involving only a few million devices, or fewer. Each cell type has its own unique set of surface antigens. Other cell surface antigens indicate the health status of the cell, the parent organ type, the species of the animal, and even the identity of the individual—a kind of biochemical Social Security Number. So the short answer to this question is: use chemotactic sensors (crudely analogous to chemical force microscopy), keyed to the specific known antigens on the target cells you are looking for.

Once you've identified a group of cells that needs some chemical substance delivered to it, you can simply release the agent from onboard tanks after the nanorobot arrives on the scene. A 1 cm^3 injection of 1-micron nanodevices could probably hold at least 0.5 cm^3 of chemical agent. Virtually all of these billions of nanites (in the 1 cm^3) will be smart enough to show up at the correct group of cells that are targeted for destruction, so delivery efficiency is virtually 100 per cent. Onboard sensors can test for ambient levels of the chemical agent, to prevent overdose. However, this question is a good example of an "anachronistic" application—one that could be done using medical nanorobots, but in fact would probably never be done that way, because in an era of advanced nanotechnology much more efficient and much less destructive ways would exist to get the same job done. In the above example, bulk delivery of cytotoxins to tissue cells is completely unnecessary if the means exists to reverse the carcinomatous process at the cellular and genetic level.

Yes, nanodevices could probably be observed at work inside the body using MRI, especially if their diamond components were manufactured using mostly ^{13}C atoms rather than the more common natural ^{12}C isotope of carbon, since ^{13}C has a nonzero nuclear magnetic moment. But in the nanomedical era, such an approach may again be somewhat anachronistic. Here's why. Applying the classical medical model to a typical nanomedical treatment, the medical nanodevices would first be injected into a human body, and would then go to work—say, in a specific organ or tissue mass. The physician wants to be able to monitor their progress, and make certain that the nanodevices have gotten to the correct target treatment region. So the first instinct of the contemporary physician who is contemplating a prospective nanomedical treatment will be to insist on the ability to directly image the nanorobots. In other words, the doctor wants to be able to scan a section of the body, and actually see the nanodevices congregated neatly around their target, say, a tumor mass, so that he can be absolutely certain that the therapy is proceeding as (and where) planned.

However, if the technology exists to fabricate nanorobots to molecular precision, then this same technology will allow communication and navigational mechanisms to be designed and built into each and every nanorobot, and will also allow communications and navigational networks to be deployed inside the body. Therapeutic nanodevices may be programed to home in on a very precisely-specified set of surface antigens populating the surface of the target tumor mass. As an additional guide, internal reference frame navigation with millimeter (or better) accuracy may be used to direct the nanorobots to the close vicinity of the target treatment volume.

So the correct medical treatment model in the nanomedical era is as follows: Injected and circulating nanorobots would remain absolutely inactive outside of the target volume. Even once inside the target treatment volume, nanorobots would still remain inactive until the precise antigenic signature of the target tissue was chemotactically detected by nanorobot sensors. The nanorobots could further be programed to remain inactive until they received an acoustic command from the physician telling them that they were free to begin the active treatment, perhaps after the physician receives confirmation through the navigational grid that most of the devices have reached their proper destinations. The physician retains complete control throughout the course of the treatment process; a signal ordering all nanorobots to halt may be sent at any time. Equally important, nanorobots can communicate their positions, operational statuses, and the success or failure of the treatment as the treatment progresses. Bandwidth limitations will require considerable information pooling, but this should not present a problem. In this treatment model, the physician receives continuous reports from the active nanorobots. They tell you their physical coordinates in the body, so you know where they are. They tell you how many cancer cells they have encountered and inactivated (or whatever is the appropriate metric to establish progress for the particular treatment). They will have multiple-redundant systems (like the five consensus computers onboard the space shuttle), establishing a fail-operational or a fail-safe design—upon detecting a critical component failure, the device places itself in shutdown mode in preparation for exfusion. So in this kind of scenario, it may be quite unnecessary to image the nanodevices directly, because the feedback available to the supervising physician from other means will be far more sophisticated, reliable, useful, and complete.

Yes, it would be possible to biopsy tissue and then image the embedded nanomachines using transmission electron microscopy. However, the normal presumption will be that your medical nanorobots are working properly. Because of fail-safe design, the nanodevices should only rarely be a part of the problem. On the contrary, they will likely be a major part of the solution. In the usual biopsy situation, your primary interest is in the condition of the tissue, not the condition of the nanodevices embedded in it. But nanodevices can be used to rapidly examine a given piece of tissue, surveying its biochemistry, biomechanics, and histometric characteristics in great detail. Indeed, in an era of proficient nanomedicine, it should rarely be necessary to remove tissue samples from patients for testing at all. Most testing should be possible *in situ*, with the added benefits of reduced intrusiveness, increased patient comfort, and greater fidelity of results since the target tissue can be examined in its active state in the actual host environment.

The incompetence or negligence of medical personnel is always a potential concern. However, in the nanomedical era, as today, such occurrences should be infrequent and notorious. A true glitch will come from some direction that nobody anticipated. Biocompatibility problems are well anticipated, and multiple-redundant onboard computers should ensure safe operation, correct operation, and reprogramability of operational parameters even after the devices have been launched on their mission—especially to permit deactivation if anything goes wrong. Fail-stop protocols may be particularly appropriate in high-risk missions where large numbers of replacement nanorobots are readily available. Therefore, the most serious problems may devolve from the inherent complexity of a trillion machines independently trying to cooperatively work on a very complex repair problem in a short period of time. One class of malfunction might involve some unexpected emergent machine-machine interaction—the kind of subtle interaction that is unlikely to have been exhaustively tested in full-up systems, in advance. As a simple example, consider two nanorobot species that are jointly repairing a given block of tissue. If the nanorobot programing allows species A to interpret the repair work of species B as a new tissue flaw that lies within species A's original repair mission parameters, and vice versa, then it would be possible for the two species to become locked in an endless recursive cycle, as each species attempted repeatedly to undo the other's work. But even in such cases, control over the devices is not lost. The supervising physician, upon observing the fault, would simply shut down one or the other species to allow the work to proceed, or would shut down both species and reprogram them both (while they are still inside the body) to avoid the unwanted emergent behavior. The doctor must always be able to "pull the plug" on the nanomachines. This is one of the most important design constraints, one that will probably become a strict and universal regulatory requirement for all medical nanodevices.

Nanomedicine will eliminate virtually all common diseases of the 20th century, virtually all medical pain and suffering, and allow the extension of human capabilities—most especially our mental abilities. Consider that a nanostructured data storage device measuring ~8,000 micron^3, a cubic volume about the size of a single human liver cell and smaller than a typical neuron, could store an amount of information equivalent to the entire Library of Congress. If implanted somewhere in the human brain, together with the appropriate interface mechanisms, such a device could allow extremely rapid access to this information. A single nanocomputer CPU, also having the volume of just one tiny human cell, could compute at the rate of 10 teraflops (10^{13} floating-point operations per second), approximately equalling (by many estimates) the computational output of the entire human brain. Such a nanocomputer might produce only about 0.001 watt of waste heat, as compared to the ~25 watts of waste heat for the biological brain in which the nanocomputer might be embedded. But perhaps the most important long-term benefit to human society as a whole could be the dawning of a new era of peace. We could hope that people who are independently well-fed, well-clothed, well-housed, smart, well-educated, healthy and happy will have little motivation to make war. Human beings who have a reasonable prospect of living many "normal" lifetimes will learn patience from experience, and will be extremely unlikely to risk those "many lifetimes" for any but the most compelling of reasons.

REFERENCES

Adleman, L., "Molecular Computation of Solutions to Combinatorial Problems," Science, Vol. 266, 11 November 1994, pp. 1021-1023. *This is THE landmark paper that started the new field of DNA computing.*

Albus, J.S.: 2003, 'Engineering of Mind for Enhancing Human Productivity', in: M.C. Roco, W.S. Bainbridge (eds.), *Converging Technologies for Improving Human Performance*, Kluwer, Dordrecht, pp. 281-293.

Albus, J.S.; Bainbridge, W.S.; Banfield, M.; Dastoor, C.A.; Murray, K.; Carley,M.; Hirshbein, T.; Masciangioli, T.; Miller, R.; Norwood, R.; Price, P.; Rubin, J.; Sargent,G.; Wallace, W.A.: 2003, 'Enhancing Group and Societal Outcomes: Theme D Summary', in M.C. Roco, W.S. Bainbridge (eds.), *Converging Technologies for Improving Human Performance*, Kluwer, Dordrecht, pp. 275-277.

Alexandra Goho, "Protein Power: Solar cell produces electricity from spinach and bacterial proteins," Science News Online, week of June 5, 2004: Vol. 165, No. 2, p. 355.

Alibek, K. A., Testimony of Dr. Kenneth Alibek, Chief Scientist at Hadron, Inc., before the House Armed Services Committee, October 20, 1999. Ref: http://www.house.gov/hasc/testimony/106thcongress/99-10-20alibek.htm.

Allara, D. L. 1995. "Critical Issues in Applications of Self-Assembled Monolayers", *Biosensors & Bioelectronics*, 10, 771-783.

Anne Eisberg, "Benign Viruses Shine on the Silicon Assembly Line," New York Times, February 12, 2004.

Antonio Regalado, "Nanotechnology Patents Surge as Companies Vie to Stake Claim," Wall Street Journal, June 18, 2004, p. 1.

Arap W., R. Pasqualini, E. Ruoslahti. 1998. "Cancer Treatment by Targeted Drug Delivery to Tumor Vasculature in a Mouse Model", *Science*, Jan 16; 279 (5349): pp. 377-380.

Arias, T.A. and Sohrab Ismail-Beigi. 2000. Novel algebraic formulation of density-functional calculation. *Computer Physics Communications*. In press.

Asimov, I., *A Choice of Catastrophes*, Simon and Schuster, NY (1979).

Atkins, P.: 2003 'The Future of Matter', in: J. Brockman (ed.), *The Next Fifty Years: Science in the First Half of the Twenty-First Century*, Vintage Books, New York, pp.194-205.

Babbie, E. *The Practice of Social Research*, 5th ed. Belmont, CA: Wadsworth, 1989. Bachand, G. and C.D. Montemagno. 2000. Constructing organic/inorganic NEMS devices powered by biomolecular motors. *Journal of Biomedical Microdevices.* 2, No.3, 179-184.

Bai, Q., K.D. Wise, and D.J. Anderson. 2000. A high-yield microassembly structure for three-dimensional microelectrode arrays. *IEEE Trans. Biomed Eng*. 47(3): p. 281-9.

Bainbridge, W.S.: 2002, 'Public Attitudes Toward Nanotechnology', *Journal of Nanoparticle Research*, 4, 561-570.

Barber, Benjamin. 1996. *Jihad vs. McWorld: How Globalism and Tribalism are Reshaping the World* (New York: Ballantine Books).

Baschnagel, J., K. Binder, K. Kremer et al. 2000. Bridging the gap between atomistic and coarse-grained models of polymers: status and perspectives. *Advances in Polymer Science*. Volume 152. Springer- Verlag.

Bass, T.A., "Gene Genie," Wired Magazine, August 1995, p. 114. *Well-informed and well-written survey of the technical developments and people in the new field of DNA computing.*

Ben-David, Joseph and Randall Collins, 1966. "Social Factors in the Origins of a New Science: the Case of Psychology." *American Sociological Review.* Vol. 31 pp 451-465.

Bijker, W. E. *Of Bicycles, Bakelites, and Bulbs: Toward a Theory of Sociotechnical Change*. Cambridge, MA: MIT Press, 1995.

Billings P.R., M.A. Kohn, M. de Cuevas, J. Beckwith, J.S. Alper, M.R. Natowicz. 1992. "Discrimination as a Consequence of Genetic Testing," *American Journal of Human Genetics*, Mar; 50 (3): pp. 476-82. Drews, J. 1996. "Genomic Sciences and the Medicine of Tomorrow," *Nature Biotechnology*, Nov., 14 (11), pp. 1516-1518.

Bimber, B., and Guston, D., eds., *Technology Assessment: The End of OTA*, special issue of *Technology Forecasting and Social Change*, Vol. 54, No. 2 and 3, 1997

Black, C.T.; Murray, C.B.; Sandstrom, R.L.; Sun, S.H. 2000 "Spin-dependent tunneling in self-assembled cobalt-nanocrystal superlattices", *Science*, 290, 1131-1134.

Blumenthal, D. 1992. "Academic-Industry Relationships: Extent, Consequences, and Management," *The Journal of the American Medical Association*, 268:3, December, pp. 3344 -3349.

Blumenthal, D.M., M. Gluck, K.S. Louis, M. Stoto, and D. Wise. 1986. "University-Industry Research Relationships in Biotechnology: Implications for the University," *Science* 232: pp. 1361-1366 (June 13).

BMBF. 1996. "Delphi-Bericht 1995 zur Entwicklung von Wissenschaft und Technik – Mini-Delphi." Bonn, author's translation.

Bockrath, M., D.H. Cobden, P.L. McEuen, N.G. Chopra, A. Zettl, A. Thess, and R.E. Smalley. 1997. "Single-Electron Transport in Ropes of Carbon Nanotubes." *Science*, 275.

Bonnemain, B. 1998. "Superparamagnetic agents in magnetic resonance imaging: Physicochemical characteristics and clinical applications - A review", *Journal of Drug Targeting*, 6, 167-174.

Brandt, A. 2000. *Multiscale Scientific Computation: 2000*. Weizmann Institute preprint. October.

Brave, Ralph. 2000. "Genome Hell is Revealed in Many Forms." *Baltimore Sun*, July 2, p. 1C.

Brown, J. S. and Duguid, P. Don't Count Society Out: A Response to Bill Joy. Paper prepared for the Societal Implications of Nanotechnology Conference, 2000.

Brown, J.S. , and Paul Duguid. 2001. Don't count society out. *Societal Implications of Nanoscience and Nanotechnology.* National Science Foundation. Arlington, VA. March.

Brown, J.S. and P. Daguid. 2001. "Don't Count Society Out: A Response to Bill Joy" in this volume: *Societal Implications of Nanoscience and Nanotechnology*. National Science Foundation, Arlington, VA.

Brown, Lawrence A. 1981. *Innovation Diffusion: A New Perspective*. New York: Methuen.

Brown, N.: 2003, 'Hope Against Hype – Accountability in Biopasts, Presents and Futures', *Science Studies*, 16(2), 3-21.

Bruchez, M.; Moronne, M.; Gin, P.; Weiss, S.; Alivisatos, A.P. 1998. "Semiconductor nanocrystals as fluorescent biological labels", *Science*, 281, 2013-2016.

Bush, Vannevar. 1945. *Science, the Endless Frontier*. Washington D.C. U.S. Government Printing Office.

Byl, J., Physica D 34,295-299 (1989). *Self-Reproduction in Small Cellular Automata*.

Caflisch, R.E., W. E, M.F. Gyure, B. Merriman, and C. Ratsch. 1999. Kinetic model for a step edge in epitaxial growth. *Phys. Rev. E*. Vol 59. 6879.

Callon, M.: 1986, 'Some Elements of a Sociology of Translation', in J. Law (ed.), *Power, Action and Belief: A New Sociology of Knowledge?*, Routledge, London, pp. 196-223.

Carroll, J.S.: 2001, 'Social Science Research Methods for Assessing Societal Implications of Nanotechnology', in: M.C. Roco, W.S. Bainbridge (eds.), *Societal Implications of Nanoscience and Nanotechnology*, National Science Foundation, pp. 188-192.

Casey, Jr., H.C., and M.B. Panish. 1978. *Heterostructure Lasers, Part A: Fundamental Principles*. (Academic Press. New York). pp. 1-9.

Cerf, Christopher, and Victor Navasky. 1984. *The Experts Speak*. New York: Pantheon Books.

Cetron, M., and Davies, O. 1997. *Probable Tomorrows: How Science and Technology Will Transform Our Lives in the Next Twenty Years* (New York: St. Martin's Press).

Chan, W.C.W. and S. Nie. 1998. Quantum dot bioconjugates for ultrasensitive nonisotopic detection. *Science*. 281, 2016 (25 September).

Chen, C.-Y., K. Ishihara, N. Nakabayashi, E. Tamiya, and I. Karube. 1999. Multifunctional biocompatible membrane and its application to fabricate a miniaturized glucose sensor with potential for use *in vivo. Journal of Biomedical Microdevices*. 1, No.2, 155-166.

Chondroudis, K. and D.B. Mitzi. 1999. Electroluminescence from an organic-inorganic perovskite incorporating a quaterthiophene dye within lead halide perovskite layers. *Chemistry of Materials*. Vol 11. p. 3028.

Christensen, Clayton M. *The Innovator's Dilemma: When New Technologies Cause Great Firms to Fail*. New York: Harperbusiness, 2000.

Cipra, Barry A. 2000. The best of the 20th century: editors name top 10 algorithms. *SIAM News*. vol. 33(4).

Clifford Lau of the US Defense Department to Barnaby Feder, "Frontier of Military Technology is the Size of a Molecule," New York Times, April 8, 2003, p. C2.

Collier, C.P., E.W. Wong, M. Belohradsky, F.M. Raymo, J.F. Stoddart, P.J. Kuekes, R.S. Williams, and J.R. Heath. 1999. "Electronically Configurable Molecular-Based Logic Gates." *Science*, 285.

Cook, T. K. and Campbell, D. T. *Quasi-Experimentation*. Rand-McNally, 1979 Fischer, C. S. *America Calling: A Social History of the Telephone to 1940*. Berkeley: U. of California, 1992.

Crommie, M.F.; Lutz, C.P.; Eigler, D.M.; Heller, E.J. 1996. "Quantum interference in 2D atomic-scale structures," *Surface Science*, 362, 864-869.

Crow, M. & Sarewitz, D.: 2001, 'Nanotechnology and Societal Transformation', in: M.C. Roco, W.S. Bainbridge (eds.), *Societal Implications of Nanoscience and Nanotechnology*, National Science Foundation, pp. 45-54.

Crowe, W. J., Statement of Admiral William J. Crowe, Jr., before the House Committee on Government Reform, October 12, 1999. Ref: http://www.house.gov/reform/hearings/healthcare/ 99.10.12/ crowe.htm.

Csicsery-Ronay, I. Jr.: 1991, 'The SF of Theory: Baudrillard and Haraway', *Science Fiction Studies*, 18, 387-404.

Csicsery-Ronay, I. Jr.: 1996, 'The Seven Beauties of Science Fiction', *Science Fiction Studies*, 23, 385-392.

Darden, T., L. Perera, L. Li, L. Pedersen, 1999, New tricks for modelers from the crystallization toolkit: The particle mesh Ewald algorithm and its use in nucleic acid simulations, *Structure*. Vol. 7, R55-R60.

David, Paul. 1991. "Computer and Dynamo: The Modern Productivity Paradox in a Not-too-Distant Mirror," *Technology and Productivity: The Challenge for Economic Policy* (Paris: OECD).

de Gennes, P.G. 1974. *The Physics of Liquid Crystals*. Oxford University Press.

Delaney, S.R.: 1984, *Starboard Wine: More Notes on the Language of Science Fiction*, Dragon Press, New York.

Delaney, S.R.: 1994, *Silent Interviews*, Univ. Press of New England, Hanover, NH.

DeSimone, J.M., E.T. Samulski, et al. 2000. Critical micelle density for the self-assembly of block copolymer surfactants in supercritical carbon dioxide. *Langmuir*. Vol.16. 416-421.

Di Paolo, E. A., *Artificial Life Bibliography of On-line Publications*, June 28, 2000.

Dimitrakopoulos, C.D., S. Purushothaman, J. Kymissis, A. Callegari, and J.M. Shaw. 1999. Low-voltage organic transistors on plastic comprising high dielectric constant gate insulators. *Science*. Vol. 283, 5 February. pp. 822 - 824.

DiVincenzo, D. P., "Quantum Computation," Science, vol. 270, 13 October 1995, pp. 255-261

Doering, R.R. and P.K. Chatterjee. 1998. "The Future of Microelectronics." *Proceedings of the IEEE*, 86, 1.

Doering, Robert and Yoshio Nishi. 2000. "Limits of Integrated-Circuit Manufacturing." *Proceedings of the IEEE*. September.

Doi, M. and S.F. Edwards. 1986. *The Theory of Polymer Dynamics*. Oxford University Press (Clarendon), London-New York.

Donald, A.M. and A.H. Windle. 1992. Liquid crystalline polymers. *Cambridge Solid State Science Series*. Cambridge University Press.

Drell, S. D., A. D. Sofaaer, and G. D. Wilson, Hoover Digest 2000, No. 1, *The Present Threat*.

Drell, S. D., A. D. Sofaaer, and G. D. Wilson, *The New Terror, Facing the Threat of Biological and Chemical Weapons*, Hoover Institution Press, Stanford University (1999).

Drexler, E.: 1990 [1986], *Engines of Creation*, Anchor Books, New York.

Drexler, E.; Smalley, R.E.: 2003, 'Point-Counterpoint: Nanotechnology', *Chemical and Engineering News*, 81(48), 37-42.

Drexler, K. Eric. 1986. *Engines of Creation*. Garden City, N.Y.: Anchor Press/Doubleday.

Ehrlich, Paul R., Anne H. Ehrlich, and John P. Holdren. 1977. *Ecoscience: Population, Resources, Environment*. San Francisco: W.H. Freeman.

Elkins, C.: 1979, 'Science Fiction versus Futurology: Dramatic Versus Rational Models', *Science Fiction Studies*, 6, 20-31.

Ellul, J. 1964. *The Technological Society*. New York: Alfred Knopf. (First published 1954).

Empedocles, S.; Bawendi, M. 1999. "Spectroscopy of single CdSe nanocrystallites," *Accounts of Chemical Research*, 32, 389-396.

Esant. 1999. "Economic and Social Aspects of Nanotechnology." First draft report of working group 6 of the Euroconferences on Nanoscience for Nanotechnology. Also at http://www.nano.org.uk/ESANT99.htm.

Etzkowitz, H., M. Gulbrandsen and J. Levitt. 2000. *Public Venture Capital: Government Funding Sources for Technology Entrepreneurs*. New York: Harcourt.

Etzkowitz, Henry 2001. "The Endless Transition: Finding a Social Basis for Science Policy." *Scipolicy: The Journal of Science and Health Policy*. Vol. 1. No.2, Spring 2001.

Etzkowitz, Henry, Carol Kemelgor and Brian Uzzi. 2000. *Athena Unbound: The Advancement of Women in Science and Technology*. Cambridge: Cambridge University Press.

Evans, J.H.: 2002, *Playing God? Human Genetic Engineering and the Rationalization of Public Bioethical Debate*, Chicago University Press, Chicago.

Fantel, Hans. 1987. "Portable CD Players Advance." *New York Times*, May 17, Section 2, p. 33, col. 1.

Fermi, E., J. Pasta, and S. Ulam. 1974. Studies of nonlinear problems, I. *Los Alamos Report*. LA1940. 1955.

Feynman, R.P. 1961. "There is plenty of room at the bottom." In *Miniaturization*. New York: Reinhold.

Fisher, D. E. and Fisher, M. J. *Tube: The Invention of Television*. Harcourt Brace, 1997.

FitzGerald, Frances. 2000. *Way Out There in the Blue: Reagan, Star Wars, and the End of the Cold War*. New York: Simon & Schuster.

Fogelberg, H.: 2003, '"Science" and "Technology" as Knowledge Cultures', in: H. Fogelberg, H. Glimell, *Bringing Visibility to the Invisible: Towards a Social Understanding of Nanotechnology*, Göteborg University, Göteborg, pp. 77-85.

Fogelberg, H.; Glimell, H.: 2003, *Bringing Visibility to the Invisible: Towards a Social Understanding of Nanotechnology*, Göteborg University, Göteborg.

Forest, G. 2000. Comment at Conference on Societal Implications of Nanoscience and Nanotechnology, September 29, 2000, NSF, Arlington, VA.

Forest, M.G., Q. Wang, and H. Zhou. 2000a. Exact banded patterns from a Doi-Marrucci-Greco model of nematic liquid crystal polymers. *Physical Review E*. Vol. 61(6). 6665-6672.

Forest, M.G., Q. Wang, and H. Zhou. 2000b. Homogeneous pattern selection and director instabilities of nematic liquid crystal polymers induced by elongational flows. *Physics of Fluids*. Vol. 12(3). 490-498.

Forum Proceedings of Sigma Xi, the Scientific Research Society, *Ethics, Values, and the Promise of Science*, Feb. 25-26, 1993.

Foucault, M. 1977. *Power/Knowledge: Selected Interviews and Other Writings 1972-1977.* New York, Pantheon Books.

Fourier, J. 1878. *The Analytical Theory of Heat.* translated by A. Freeman. Cambridge University Press. London and New York.

Frankel, M. 1996. "Perception, Reality, and the Political Context of Conflict of Interest in University-Industry Relationships," *Academic Medicine*, 71:12, December, pp. 1297-1304.

Franklin, N.R.; Dai, H.J. 2000. "An enhanced CVD approach to extensive nanotube networks with directionality", *Advanced Materials*, 12, 890-894.

Freitas, L. *Nanomedicine*. Bioscience, 1999.

Frenken, J.W.M. 1998. "Scanning Tunneling Microscopy", section 5.2, A. ten Wolde (ed.), *Nanotechnology: Towards a molecular construction kit*. STT Report #60, The Hague, 289-299.

Gates, B.; Park, S.H.; Xia, Y.N. 2000. "Tuning the photonic bandgap properties of crystalline arrays of polystyrene beads by annealing at elevated temperatures", *Advanced Materials*, 12, 653-656.

Geneva Convention, *Protocol for the Prohibition of the Use in War of Asphyxiating, Poisonous or Other Gases, and of Bacteriological Methods of Warfare*, signed at Geneva on June 17,1925.

Gergen, K. J. Social psychology as history. *Journal of Personality and Social Psychology*, 1973, 26, 309- 20.

Gerlach, N.; Hamilton, S.: 2000, 'Telling the Future, Managing the Present: Business Restructuring Literature as SF', *Science Fiction Studies*, 27, 461-477.

Goldbeck-Wood, G. and A.H. Windle. 1999. Lattice modeling of nematodynamics. *Rheol. Acta*. Vol. 38. 548-561.

Graham, P.: 2002, 'Hypercapitalism: Language, New Media and Social Perceptions of Value', *Discourse and Society*, 13(2), 227-249.

Gref, Ruxandra, Yoshiharu Minamitake, Maria Teresa Peracchia, Vladimir Trubetskoy, Vladimir Torchilin, Robert Langer. 1994. "Biodegradable Long Circulating Polymeric Nanospheres", *Science*, Vol. 263, 18 Mar, pp 1600-1603.

Griliches, Zvi. 1957. "Hybrid Corn: An Exploration in the Economics of Technological Change," *Econometrica*, 25 (4), pp 501-522.

Griliches, Zvi. 1960. "Hybrid Corn and the Economics of Innovation," *Science*, 132, pp 275-280. Mass, William. 1989. "Mechanical and Organizational Innovation: The Case of the Draper Loom," *Business History Review*, 63 (Winter).

Gröndahl B., W. Puppe, A. Hoppe, I. Kühne, J.A. Weigl, H.J. Schmitt. 1999. "Rapid Identification of Nine Microorganisms Causing Acute Respiratory Tract Infections by Single-Tube Multiplex Reverse Transcription-PCR: Feasibility Study." *Journal of Clinical Microbiology*, Jan; 37 (1): pp. 1-7.

Grosberg, A.Y. and A.R. Khokhlov. 1994. *Statistical Physics of Macromolecules*, AIP Series in Polymers and Complex Materials, AIP Press, New York.

Gubrud, M. A., *Nanotechnology and International Security*, Fifth Foresight Conference on Molecular

Nanotechnology, November 5-8, 1997. Ref: http://www.foresight.org/Conferences/MNT05/Papers/Gubrud/.

Gurley, Bill. 2000. Digital music: the real law is Moore's law. *Fortune.* 2 October. page 268. Joy, Bill. 2000. Why the future doesn't need us. *Wired*. April. pp. 238 - 262.

Hadjiconstantinou, N.G. 1999. Combining atomistic and continuum simulations of contact-line motion. *Physical Review E.* Vol. 59(2).2, 2475-2478.

Hamilton, S.: 2003, 'Biotechnology, SF and the Media', *Science Fiction Studies*, 30, 267-282.

Haraway, D.J.: 1997, *Modest Witness@Second Millenium.FemaleManã Meets OncoMouseä*, Routledge, London and New York.

Hayes, B., "The Square Root of NOT," *American Scientist*, July-August 1995, pp. 304-308.

Hayward, R.C.; Saville, D. A.; Aksay, I.A. 2000. "Electrophoretic assembly of colloidal crystals with optically tunable micropatterns", *Nature*, 404, 56-59.

Hendrickson, C.T., A. Horvath, S. Joshi, and L.B. Lave. 1998. Economic input-output models for environmental life-cycle assessment. *Environmental Science & Technology*. p. 32.

Hughes, P. M., *Global Threats and Challenges: The Decades Ahead*, Lt. Gen. Patrick M. Hughes, Director of the Defense Intelligence Agency, in Statement for the Senate Committee on Intelligence, January 28, 1998. Ref:http://www.fas.org/irp/congress/1998_hr/s980128h.htm.

Huijer, M.: 2003, 'Reconsidering Democracy: History of the Human Genome Project', *Science Communication*, 24(4), 479-502.

Huntington, Samuel P. 1996. *The Clash of Civilizations and the Remaking of the World Order* (New York: Simon and Schuster).

Jacobs, K.M., et al. 2000. Postlesional epilepsy: the ultimate brain plasticity. *Epilepsia*. 41(Suppl 6): p. S153-61.

James, E.: 1994, *Science Fiction in the 20th Century*, Oxford University Press, Oxford.

Jameson, F.: 1982, 'Progress Versus Utopia; or, Can We Imagine the Future', *Science Fiction Studies*, 9, 147-158.

Janet Raloff, "Nano Hazards: Exposure to minute particles harms lungs, circulatory system," Science News Online, Week of March 19, 2005; Vol. 167, No. 12.

Johnson, D.G. and H. Nissenbaum (eds). 1995. *Computers, Ethics and Social Values*. Prentice Hall:Englewood Cliffs, NJ. pp. 262-393.

Johnson, P.C.: 2003, 'Implications of the Continuum of Bioinformatics', in: M.C. Roco; W.S. Bainbridge (eds.), *Converging Technologies for Improving Human Performance*, Kluwer, Dordrecht, pp. 207-212.

Joy, Bill. "Why the Future Doesn't Need Us." *Wired*, April 8, 2000.

Joy, W. 2000. Why the Future Doesn't Need Us. *Wired*, April.

Judd, C., Smith, E. and Kidder, L. *Research Methods in Social Relations*, (6th Edition). Holt, Rinehart, Winston, 1991.

Kalman B., F.D. Lublin. 1999. "The Genetics of Multiple Sclerosis. A Review." *Biomedicine and Pharmacotherapy*, Sep; 53 (8): pp. 358-370.

Kay, L.: 2000, *Who Wrote the Book of Life? A History of the Genetic Code*, Stanford University Press, Stanford.

Kennedy, P., *The Rise and Fall of the Great Powers, Economic Change and Military Conflict from 1500 to 2000*,Random House (1987).

Kennedy, Paul. *The Rise and Fall of the Great Powers, Economic Change and Military Conflict from 1500 to 2000*. New York: Random House,1987.

Keyssar, Alexander. 1986. *Out of Work: The First Century of Unemployment in Massachusetts* (Cambridge: Cambridge University Press).

Kolata, G., "A Vat of DNA May Become a Vast Computer of the Future," N.Y. Times, 11 April 1995, p. C1. *Large, much cited spread at the top of the front page of the Tuesday "Science Times" Section that first brought the Adelman discovery to wide public attention. Beautiful illustrations that explain how it works.*

Kruskal, M., and N. Zabusky. 1965. Interaction of solitons in a collisionless plasma and the recurrence of initial states, *Phys. Rev. Lett.* Vol. 15. 240-243.

Kupferman, R., M. Kawaguchi, and M.M. Denn. 2000. Emergence of structure in models of liquid crystalline polymers with elastic coupling. *J. Non-Newtonian Fluid Mech.* Vol. 91. 255-271.

Kurzweil, R. 1999. *The Age of Spiritual Machines*. Penguin Books.

Kuusi, O. 1999b. *Expertise in the future use of generic technologies*. VATT Research Reports #59, Helsinki.

Kuusi, O. and M. Meyer. 2001. "Technology Generalizations and Leitbilds – The Anticipation of Technological Opportunities." Manuscript submitted to *Technological Forecasting and Social Change*.

Kuusi, O., 1999. "Epistemic value analysis – a tool to evaluate technological options." Personal communication.

Laibinis, P.E.; Hickman, J.J.; Wrighton, M.S.; Whitesides, G.M. 1989. "Orthogonal Self-Assembled Monolayers - Alkanethiols On Gold and Alkane Carboxylic-Acids On Alumina", *Science*, 245, 845- 847.

Lambright, W. Henry. 1995. *Powering Apollo: James E. Webb of NASA*. Baltimore: Johns Hopkins University Press.

Landon, B.: 2004, 'Less is More: Much Less is Much More: The Insistent Allure of Nanotechnology Narratives in Science Fiction', in: K. Hayles (ed.), *NanoCulture*, Intellect Books, Bristol, pp. 59-78.

Lapham, E.V., C. Kozma, J.O. Weiss. 1996. "Genetic Discrimination: Perspectives of Consumers." *Science*, Oct 25; 274 (5287): pp. 621-624.

Larson, R.G. 1999. *The Structure and Rheology of Complex Fluids*. Oxford University Press.

Latour, B. & Woolgar, S.: 1986, *Laboratory Life: The Social Construction of Scientific Facts*, 2nd edn., Princeton University Press, Princeton.

Latour, B.: 1986, 'Visualisation and Cognition: Thinking With Eyes and Hands', *Knowledge and Society*, 6, 1-40.

Latour, B.: 2002, 'Morality and Technology: The End of the Means', *Theory, Culture and Society*, 19(5/6), 247-260.

Lave, L.B. & H.L. MacLean. 2000. *An Environmental-Economic Evaluation of Hybrid Electric Vehicles: Toyota's Prius vs. Its Conventional Internal Combustion Engine Corolla*. working paper. August.

Lave, L.B., A. Russell, F.C. McMichael, and C.T. Hendrickson. 1996. Environmental implications of battery powered vehicles as a transitional technology: ozone vs. lead. *Environmental Science & Technology*. p. 30.

Lave, L.B., C.T. Hendrickson, and F. C. McMichael. 1995b. Environmental implications of electric cars. *Science*. vol. 268: 992-5. May 19.

Lave, L.B., E. Cobas-Flores, C.T. Hendrickson, and F.C. McMichael. 1995a. Using input-output analysis to estimate economy wide discharges. *Environmental Science & Technology*, 29(9).

Lax, Peter D. 1989. The flowering of applied mathematics in America. in *A Century of Mathematics in America-Part II*. edited by Peter Duren et al. American Mathematical Society. 455-466.

Leah Eisenberg, "Medicating Death Row Inmates So They Qualify for Execution," AMA Case in Health Law, Vol. 6, No. 9, September 2004.

Ledley, Fred D. 1995. "Nonviral Gene Therapy: The promise of Genes as Pharmaceutical Products," *Human Gene Therapy*, Vol. 6, Sep, pp 1129-1144.

Lee, M.S. and M. Head-Gordon. 2000. Absolute and relative energies from polarized atomic orbital selfconsistent field calculations and a second order convergence with size and composition of the secondary basis. *Computers and Chemistry*. Vol. 24(3,4). 295-301.

Lee, S.C. 1998. The nanobiological strategy for construction of nanodevices. *Biological molecules in nanotechnology: the convergence of biotechnology, polymer chemistry and materials science*. edited by S.C. Lee and L. Savage (IBC Press, Southborough, MA).

Lemann, Nicholas. 1991. *The Promised Land: The Great Black Migration and How it Changed America* (New York: Random House).

Lipson, H. and J. B. Pollack, Nature, 406, 974-978, (2000). *Automatic design and manufacture of robotic life forms*. See, also, several additional articles on this subject in contemporary issues of Nature.

Lloyd, S., "A Potentially Realizable Quantum Computer," *Science*, 17 September 1993, pp. 1569-1571.

López, J.: 2003, *Society and Its Metaphors: Language Social Theory and Social Structure*, Continuum, New York and London.

López, J.: 2004, 'How Sociology Can Save Bioethics...Maybe', *Sociology of Health and Illness*, 26(7), 1-22.

Lu, H.P.; Xun, L.Y.; Xie, X.S. 1998. "Single-molecule enzymatic dynamics", *Science*, 282, 1877-1882.

Lynn, David M., Robert Langer. 2000. "Degradable Poly(b-amino esters): Synthesis, Characterization, and Self-Assembly with Plasmid DNA," *Journal of the American Chemical Society*, Vol. 122.

M.C. Roco, "National Nanotechnology Initiative: Overview," September 20, 2004.

Mahmood U., C.H. Tung, A. Bogdanov Jr., R. Weissleder. 1999. "Near-Infrared Optical Imaging of Protease Activity for Tumor Detection." *Radiology*, Dec; 213 (3): pp. 866-870.

Malinow, R., Z.F. Mainen, and Y. Hayashi. 2000. LTP mechanisms: from silence to four-lane traffic. *Curr. Opin. Neurobiol*. 10(3): p. 352-7.

Mark, H., Statement of The Honorable Hans Mark, Director, Defense Research and Engineering, before the House Armed Service Committee, October 20, 1999. Ref: http://www.house.gov/hasc/testimony/ 106thcongress/99-10-20mark.htm.

Marshall, K.: 2004, 'Atomizing Risk Technology', in: K. Hayles (ed.), *NanoCulture*, Intellect Books, Bristol, pp. 79-102.

Matsuki, H., K. Ofuji, N. Chubachi, and S. Nitta. 1996. Signal transmission for implantable medical devices using figure-of-eight coils. *IEEE Trans. on Magnetics.*, vol. 32. No.5, 5121. September.

Matsuki, H., Y. Yamakata, N. Chubachi, S. Nitta, and H. Hashimoto. 1996. Transcutaneous DC-DC converter for totally implantable artificial heart using synchronous rectifier. *IEEE Trans. On Magnetics*. 32, No.5, 5118 (Sept.).

McCain, L.: 2002, 'Informing Technology Policy Decisions: the US Human Genome Project's Ethical, Legal and Social Implications Programs as a Critical Case', *Technology and Society*, 24, 111-132.

McConnell, S.A., ed. 1998. *Pharmaceuticals*. Dun and Bradstreet Industry Reference Handbooks, Gale, Detroit, pp. 30-34.

McHale, B.: 1987, *Postmodern Fiction*, Methuen, New York & London.

Merz, J.L. 1986. "The Optoelectronics Joint Research Laboratory: Light Shed on Cooperative Research in Japan." *Scientific Bulletin* (ONR Far East Office). 11 (4), 1-30 (Oct.-Dec.).

Meyer, M. 2000. "Patent citations in a novel field of technology: What can they tell about interactions of emerging communities of science and technology?" *Scientometrics*, XXXXIIX (2), 151-178.

Meyer, M. 2000b. "Hurdles on the way to growth. Commercializing novel technologies." Institute of Strategy and International Business, Working Papers Series 2000/1, Helsinki University of Technology, Espoo.

Meyer, M. and O. Persson. 1998. "Nanotechnology - interdisciplinarity, patterns of collaboration and differences in application," *Scientometrics*, XXXXII (2), 195-205.

Michalet, X. and D. Bensimon. 1988. Vesicles of toroidal topology: observed morphology and shape transformations. *J. Phys. II*. France. Vol. 5. 598.

Mihail Roco and William Sims Bainbridge, eds., Converging Technologies for Improving Human Performance, NSF/DOC Report, June 2002.

Miksanek, T.: 2001, 'Microscopic Doctors and Molecular Black Bag: Science Fiction's Prescription for Nanotechnology and Medicine', *Literature and Medicine*, 21(1), 55-70.

Milburn, C.: 2002 'Nanotechnology in the Age of Posthuman Engineering: Science Fiction as Science', *Configurations*, 10, 261-295.

Mirsky, Steve. 2000. "Tantalizing Tubes." *Scientific American*. June.

Mizrach, S., *Should there be a limit placed on the integration of humans and computers and electronic technology?* Ref: http://www.limmat.ch/koni/texte/cyborg-ethics.html.

Mnyusiwalla, A.; Daar, A.S.; Singer, P.A.: 2003, '"Mind the Gap": Science and Ethics in Nanotechnology, *Nanotechnology*, 14, R9-R13.

Moronne, M.M.; Ben Dahan, M.; Bruchez, M.; Hamamoto, D.J.; Weiss, S.; Alivisatos, A.P. 1999. "Nanocrystal phosphors as biological probes for fluorescence microscopy", *Biophysical Journal*, 76, A450-A450.

Mumford, Lewis. 1934. *Technics and Civilization* (New York: Harcourt Brace Jovanovich, Inc.). National Science and Technology Council (NSTC). 1999. *Nanotechnology: Shaping the World Atom by Atom* (Washington, DC: September; available at http://www.nano.gov).

Murray, C.B.; Kagan, C.R.; Bawendi, M.G. 2000. "Synthesis and characterization of monodisperse nanocrystals and close-packed nanocrystal assemblies", *Annual Review of Materials Science*, 30. 545- 610.

Nardi, B. 2001. "Cultural Ecology of Nanotechnology" in this volume: *Societal Implications of Nanoscience and Nanotechnology*. National Science Foundation, Arlington, VA.

Nardi, B., O'Day, V. 1999. *Information Ecologies: Using Technology with Heart*. MIT Press.

National Coordination Office for Information Technology, *Ethical, Legal, and Societal Implications of Information Technology Research and Development*. Available at: http://www.itrd.gov, October 1999.

National Human Genome Research Institute, *Ethical, Legal, and Social Implications of Human Genetics Research of the National Institutes of Health*. Available at:

National Science and Technology Council (NSTC). 2000. *National Nanotechnology Initiative: Leading to the Next Industrial Revolution* (Supplement to the President's FY 2001 Budget) (Washington, DC: February; available at http://www.nano.gov).

National Science and Technology Council (NSTC). 2000. *National Nanotechnology Initiative: Leading to the Next Industrial Revolution*. February. (http://www.nano.gov/nni.pdf).

Naughton, G. 1999. The Advanced Tissue Sciences story. *Sci. Am.* 280(4): p. 84-5.

Nauta, K. and R.E. Miller. 1999. Non-equilibrium self-assembly of long chains of polar molecules in superfluid helium. *Science*. Vol. 283. 1895-1897.

Nicholas Wade, "A DNA Success Raises Bioterror Concern," New York Times, January 12, 2005.

Nowotny, H.; Scott, P.; Gibbons, M.: 2001, *Re-thinking Science*, Polity, Cambridge.

NSET. 2000. *National Nanotechnology Initiative: Leading to the Next Industrial Revolution*. 2000. A report by the Interagency Working Group on Nanoscience, Engineering and Technology (NSET), of the National Science and Technology Council's Committee on Technology. Washington, D.C., February.

NSTC (National Science and Technology Council): 1999, *Nanotechnology: Shaping the World Atom by Atom* [www.wtec.org/loyola/nano/IWGN.Public.Brochure/IWGN.Nanotechnology.Brochure.pdf, accessed: 15 Nov. 2003].

Parikh, A.N.; Schivley, M.A.; Koo, E.; Seshadri, K.; Aurentz, D.; Mueller, K.; Allara, D.L. 1997. "nalkylsiloxanes: From single monolayers to layered crystals. The formation of crystalline polymers from the hydrolysis of n- octadecyltrichlorosilane", *Journal of the American Chemical Society*, 119, 3135-3143.

Parr, R.G. and W. Yang. 1989. *Density-Functional Theory of Atoms and Molecules*. Oxford University Press. Oxford.

Peng, X.G.; Manna, L.; Yang, W.D.; Wickham, J.; Scher, E.; Kadavanich, A.; Alivisatos, A.P. 2000. "Shape control of CdSe nanocrystals", *Nature*, 404, 59-61.

Perkal M., C. Marks, M.I. Lorber, W.H. Marks. 1992. "A three-year experience with serum anodal trypsinogen as a biochemical marker for rejection in pancreatic allografts. False positives, tissue biopsy, comparison with other markers, and diagnostic strategies." *Transplantation*, Feb; 53 (2): pp. 415-419.

Philip Ball, "Synthetic Biology: Starting from Scratch," Nature, 431, pp. 624-626, 7 October 2004.

Philipse, A.P. 1998. "Colloidal Dispersions," section 3.4, A. ten Wolde (ed.), *Nanotechnology: Towards a molecular construction kit*. STT Report #60, The Hague, 171-178.

Phoenix, C.; Drexler, E.: 2004, 'Safe Exponential Manufacturing', *Nanotechnology*, 15, 869-872.

Pierce, N.A. and M.B. Giles. 2000. Adjoint reconstruction of superconvergent functionals from PDE approximations. *SIAM Rev.* Vol. 42(2). 247-264.

Piveteau, Laurent-Dominique, Anthe S. Zandvliet and Robert Langer. 2001. "Nitroxide and Galactose Grafted Dendrimer: A Specifically Targeted Contrast Agent for MRI and EPR Imaging of the Liver," *in preparation.*

Polanyi, Karl. 1944. *The Great Transformation: The Political and Economic Origins of Our Time* (Boston: Beacon Press, 1957; orig. ed. 1944).

Poldrack, R.A. 2000. Imaging brain plasticity: conceptual and methodological issues — a theoretical review. *Neuroimage.* 12(1): p. 1-13.

Pollock, C.R. 1995. *Fundamentals of Optoelectronics*. Irwin, Inc. pp. 3-5.

Porod, W., C.S. Lent, G.H. Bernstein, A.O. Orlov, I. Amlani, G.L. Snider, and J.L. Merz. 1999. Quantumdot cellular automata: computing with coupled quantum dots. *Int. Journal of Electronics* 86, No.5, 549-590.

Pritchard, M.S. 1996. "Conflicts of Interest: Conceptual and Normative Issues," *Academic Medicine*, 71:12, December, pp. 1305-1313.

Putnam, D., Gentry, C.A., Pack, D.W., Langer, R. 2001. "Polymer-based Gene Delivery with Low Cytotoxicity by a Unique Balance of Side-chain Termini." *Proceedings of the National Academy of Sciences*, U.S.A., Volume 98, Number 3, pages 1200-1205.

Ramos, L.; Lubensky, T.C.; Dan, N.; Nelson, P.; Weitz, D.A. 1999. "Surfactant-mediated two-dimensional crystallization of colloidal crystals", *Science*, 286, 2325-2328.

RAND Corporation. *The Potential of Nanotechnology for Molecular Manufacturing*. 1995.

Reed, Mark A. and James M. Tour. 2000. "Computing with Molecules." *Scientific American*. June.. SIA (Semiconductor Industry Association). 1999. "1999 International Technology Roadmap for Semiconductors."

Rinzler, A.G.; Liu, J.; Dai, H.; Nikolaev, P.; Huffman, C.B.; Rodriguez-Macias, F.J.; Boul, P.J.; Lu, A.H.; Heymann, D.; Colbert, D.T.; Lee, R.S.; Fischer, J.E.; Rao, A.M.; Eklund, P.C.; Smalley, R.E. 1998.

Roco, M. C., R. S. Williams, and P. Alivisatos, *Nanotechnology Research Directions: Vision for Nanotechnology in the Next Decade*, Kluwer Academic Publishers (2000).

Roco, M.C. & Bainbridge, W.S., (eds.): 2001, *Societal Implications of Nanoscience and Nanotechnology*, National Science Foundation [online: www.wtec.org/loyola/nano/societalimpact/nanosi.pdf , accessed: 15 November 2003].

Roco, M.C. & Bainbridge, W.S., (eds.): 2003, *Converging Technologies for Improving Human Performance: Nanotechnology, Biotechnology, Information Technology and Cognitive Science*, Kluwer, Dordrecht.

Roco, M.C., R.S. Williams, and P. Alivisatos (eds). 1999. *Nanotechnology Research Directions: IWGN Workshop Report, Vision for Nanotechnology R&D in the Next Decade*. (Kluwer Academic Publishers.

Roco, M.C.: 2003a, 'Broader Societal Issues of Nanotechnology', *Journal of Nanoparticle Research*, 5, 181-189.

Roco, M.C.: 2003b, 'Coherence and Divergence in Megatrends in Science and Engineering', in: M.C.

Roco, W.S. Bainbridge (eds.), *Converging Technologies for Improving Human Performance*, Kluwer, Dordrecht, pp. 79-96.

Roco, M.C.: 2003c, 'Fundamentally New Manufacturing Processes and Products', in: Roco, M.C. & Bainbridge, W.S., (eds.), *Converging Technologies for Improving Human Performance*, Kluwer, Dordrecht, pp. 300-302.

Roco, M.C.: 2004, 'The Emergence and Policy Implications of Converging Technologies' [www.nsf.gov/home/crssprgm/nano/nbic_roco_04_0422_@aaas_57sl.pdf, accessed May 2004].

Rodney Brooks, "The Merger of Flesh and Machines," The Next Fifty Years: Science in the First Half of the Twenty-First Century, ed. by John Brockman, 2002, p. 191.

Rosenberg, Nathan. 1994. *Exploring the Black Box: Technology, Economics, and History*. New York: Cambridge University Press.

Rothman, B.K.: 1998, *Genetic Maps and Human Imagination*, W.W. Norton, New York & London,

San Francisco Chronicle, *Scientist Is Fearful of Computer Mutiny; Sun Micro co-founder says replicating robots could replace humans*, March 13, 2000.

Santini, John T., Jr., Michael J. Cima and Robert Langer. 1999. "A Controlled-release Microchip" *Nature*, Vol 397, 28 Jan, p 335-338.

Schummer, J.: 2004, 'Interdisciplinary Issues in Nanoscale Research', in: D. Baird, A. Nordmann, J. Schummer (eds.), *Discovering the Nanoscale*, IOS Press, Amsterdam, pp. 9-20.

Schumpeter, Joseph Alois. 1942. *Capitalism, Socialism, and Democracy*. New York: Harper.

Senturia, S., N. Aluru, and J. White. 1997. Simulating the behavior of MEMS devices: computational methods and needs. *IEEE Computational Science and Engineering*. Vol. 4(1). 30-43.

Shor, P., *Proc. 35th Ann. Symp. Foundations of Computer Science*, 1994.

Shultz, W.: 2000, 'Nanotechnology: The Next Big Thing', *Chemical and Engineering News*, 78(18), 41-47.

Simon, Julian L. (ed). 1995. *The State of Humanity*, Oxford: Blackwell.

Simos, P.G., et al. 2000. Insights into brain function and neural plasticity using magnetic source imaging. *J.*

Smalley, R.E. 2000. Hearing of the Senate Science and Technology Caucus on Nanotechnology. April 5, (unpublished).

Smalley, R.E.: 2001, 'Of Chemistry, Love and Nanobots', *Scientific American*, 285(3), September, 76-77.

Smith, A., *The Wealth of Nations: An Inquiry into the Nature and Causes*, Random House, New York, 1994.

Smith, D., H. Babcock, and S. Chu. 1999. Single-polymer dynamics in steady shear flow. *Science*. Vol. 283. 1724-1727. March.

Snider, G.L.; Orlov, A.O.; Amlani, I.; Zuo, X.; Bernstein, G.H.; Lent, C.S.; Merz, J.L.; Porod, W. 1999. "Quantum-dot cellular automata: Review and recent experiments (invited)", *Journal of Applied Physics*, 85, 4283-4285.

Soong, R.K.; Bachand, G.D.; Neves, H.P.; Olkhovets, A.G.; Craighead, H.G.; Montemagno, C.D. 2000. "Powering an inorganic nanodevice with a biomolecular motor", *Science*, 290, 1555-1558.

Steelman, John R. 1947. *Science and Public Policy* (Washington, DC: US Government Printing Office). Stephenson, Neal. 1995. *The Diamond Age, or, Young Lady's Illustrated Primer* (New York: Bantam Books).

Sterling, B., *When Robots Act Like Rabbits*, The Wall Street Journal, September 6, 2000.

Sterman, J. D. (1989b). Modeling Managerial Behavior: Misperceptions of Feedback in a Dynamic Decision Making Experiment. *Management Science*, 35(3), 321-339.

Steve, Jurvetson, "Transcending Moore's Law with Molecular Electronics," Nanotechnology Law & Business Journal, Vol. 1, No. 1, article 9, p. 9.

Stipe, B.C.; Rezaei, M.A.; Ho, W. 1998. "Single-molecule vibrational spectroscopy and microscopy", *Science*, 280, 1732-1735.

Stix, G.: 1996, 'Trends in Nanotechnology: Waiting for Breakthroughs', *Scientific American*, 274(4), 94-99.

Stokes, Donald E. 1997. *Pasteur's Quadrant: Basic Science and Technological Innovation*. Washington, D.C.: Brookings Institution Press.

Storrs, J., Hall, *Flying Saucers?* http://www.nanocentral.com/NanoWorld/Perspectives/JoshHall/askjosh_aug96.html.

Stranick, S.J.; Atre, S.V.; Parikh, A.N.; Wood, M.C.; Allara, D.L.; Winograd, N.; Weiss, P.S. 1996. "Nanometer-scale phase separation in mixed composition self-assembled monolayers", *Nanotechnology*, 7, 438-442.

Sun, S., C.B. Murray, D. Weller, L. Folks, and A. Moser. 2000. Monodisperse fept nanoparticles and ferromagnetic fept nanocrystal superlattices. *Science.* Vol. 287, 17 March. pp. 1989 - 1992.

Sun, S.H.; Murray, C.B. 1999. "Synthesis of monodisperse cobalt nanocrystals and their assembly into magnetic superlattices", *Journal of Applied Physics*, 85, 4325-4330.

Sun, S.H.; Murray, C.B.; Weller, D.; Folks, L.; Moser, A. 2000. "Monodisperse FePt nanoparticles and ferromagnetic FePt nanocrystal superlattices", *Science*, 287, 1989-1992.

Suvin, D.: 1979, *Metamorphoses of Science Fiction*, Yale University Press, New Haven.

Tadmor, E., R. Phillips, and M. Ortiz. 2000. Hierarchical modeling in the mechanics of materials. *Int. J. Solids Struct*. Vol. 37. 379.

Thacker, E.: 2000, 'SF, Technoscience, Net.art: The Politics of Extrapolation (science fiction)', *Art Journal*, 59(3), 64-73.

Theis, T.: 2001, 'Information Technology Based on a Mature Nanotechnology', in: M.C. Roco, W.S. Bainbridge (eds.), *Societal Implications of Nanoscience and Nanotechnology*, National Science Foundation, pp. 60-67.

Thomas, E.L., D.M. Anderson, C.S. Henkee, and D. Hoffman. 1988. Periodic area-minimizing surfaces in block copolymers. *Nature.* Vol. 334. 598.

Thompson, P.B.: 2001, 'Social Acceptance of Nanotechnology', in: M.C. Roco, W.S. Bainbridge (eds.), *Societal Implications of Nanoscience and Nanotechnology*, online: National Science Foundation, pp. 198-202.

Tilton, John E. (ed). 1991. *World Metal Demand*, Washington, DC: Resources for the Future.

Tobio, M., R. Gref, A. Sanchez, R. Langer and M.J. Alonso. 1998. "Stealth PLA-PEG Nanoparticles as Protein Carriers for Nasal Administration", *Pharmaceutical Research*, Vol. 15, No 2, pp 270-275.

Tramontin, A.D. and E.A. Brenowitz. 2000. Seasonal plasticity in the adult brain. *Trends Neurosci*. 23(6): p. 251-8.

Tsuji, T. and A. Rey. 1998. Orientation mode selection mechanisms for sheared nematic liquid crystalline materials. *Phys. Rev. E*. Vol. 57(5). 5609-5625.

Turnbull, D.: 2000, *Masons, Tricksters and Cartographers*, Harwood, Amsterdam.

Tushman, Michael and Philip Anderson (1996), Managing Strategic Innovation and Change: A Collection of Readings. London: Oxford University Press.

Vaia, R., D. Tomlin, M. Schulte, and T. Bunning. 2000. Two-phase nanoscale morphology of polymer/LC composites. *Polymer*. In press.

Vale, R.D.; Milligan, R.A. 2000. "The way things move: Looking under the hood of molecular motor proteins", *Science*, 288, 88-95.

Valenti. Plaza y Valdes, S.A. de C.V. Instituto de Investigaciones Sociales. Universidad Nacional Autonoma de Mexico. Universidad Autonoma Metropolitana, pp.81-93.

Van Maanen, J. *Tales of the Field*. Chicago: U. Chicago, 1988.

Vettiger, P.; Brugger, J.; Despont, M.; Drechsler, U.; Durig, U.; Haberle, W.; Lutwyche, M.; Rothuizen, H.; Stutz, R.; Widmer, R.; Binnig, G. 1999. "Ultrahigh density, high-data-rate NEMS-based AFM data storage system", *Microelectronic Engineering*, 46, 11-17.

Vettiger, P.; Despont, M.; Drechsler, U.; Durig, U.; Haberle, W.; Lutwyche, M.I.; Rothuizen, H.E.; Stutz, R.; Widmer, R.; Binnig, G.K. 2000. "The "Millipede" - More than one thousand tips for future AFM data storage", *IBM Journal of Research and Development*, 44, 323-340.

Voter, A.F. 1997. Hyperdynamics: accelerated molecular dynamics of infrequent events. *Phys. Rev. Lett.* Vol. 78. 3908.

Warner, M. and E. M. Terentjev. 1996. Nematic elastomers: a new state of matter? *Progress in Polymer Science*. Vol. 21(5). 853.

Warner, M., E. M. Terentjev, R. B. Meyer, and Y. Mao. 2000. Untwisting of a cholesteric elastomer by a mechanical field. *Phys. Rev. Lett.* Vol. 85(11). 2320.

Washington, London, and Moscow Convention, Convention on the prohibition of the development, production and stockpiling of bacteriological (biological) and toxin weapons and on their destruction, signed Washington, London, and Moscow April 10,1972, entered into force March 26, 1975.

Webb, E. J., Campbell, D. T., Schwartz, R. D., Sechrest, L., and Grove, J. B. *Unobtrusive Measures: Nonreactive Research in the social Sciences* (2nd ed.). Boston: Houghton Mifflin, 1981.

Webster, A. and H. Etzkowitz. 1991. "Academic-industry Relations: The Second Academic Revolution?" Science Policy Support Group, London, 1991.

Weil, V. 1988. "Afterword," *Biotechnology: Professional Issues and Social Concerns*. (AAAS Publication) co-edited with Paul DeForest, Mark Frankel, and Jeanne Poindexter.

Weil, V. 1996. "Biotechnology: Societal Impact and Quandaries," in *Biotechnology and Ethics: A Blueprint for the Future, Report of NSF Workshop*, Northwestern University, Center for Biotechnology.

Weil, V. 2000. "Como Pueden Convivir Los Valores Universitarios Y Las Normes Empresariales?" in *Dos Ejes en La Vinculacion de Las Universidades a la Produccion*. ed. by Rosalba Casas and Giovanna

Weiss, S. 1999. "Fluorescence spectroscopy of single biomolecules", *Science*, 283, 1676-1683.

White, Lynn Jr. 1974. Technology assessment from the stance of a medieval historian. *The American Historical Review*. 79(1): 1-13.

White, Lynn T. 1962. *Medieval Technology and Social Change* (London: Oxford University Press).

Whitesides, G.M.; Mathias, J.P.; Seto, C.T. 1991. "Molecular Self-Assembly and Nanochemistry - a Chemical Strategy For the Synthesis of Nanostructures", *Science*, 254, 1312-1319.

Wilbur, J.L.; Whitesides, G.M. 1999. *Self-Assembly and Self-Assembled Monolayers in Micro- and Nanofabrication*; Timp, G., Ed.; Springer-Verlag New York, Inc.: New York, pp 331-370.

William-Jones, B.; Corrigan, O.: 2003, 'Rhetoric and Hype: Where's the Ethics in Pharmacogenomics?', *American Journal of Pharmacogenomics*, 3(6), 375-383.

Winner, Langdon, ed., *Democracy in a Technological Society, in Philosophy and Technology*, Vol. 9, Kluwer Academic Publishers, Dordrecht, The Netherlands, 1992.

Wong, H.-S.P., D.J. Frank, and P.M. Solomon. 1998. "Device Design Considerations for Double-Gate, Ground-Plane, and Single-Gated Ultra-Thin SOI MOSFETs at the 25-nm Channel-Length Generation." *Technical Digest of the 1998 International Electron Devices Meeting*.

Wood, S., Jones, R.; Geldart, A.: 2003, *The Social and Economic Challenges of Nanotechnology*, UK Economic and Social Research Council [www.esrc.ac.uk/esrccontent/DownloadDocs/Nanotechnology.pdf, accessed: 3 Feb. 2004].

Wynne, B. 1991. "Knowledges in Context." *Science, Technology, and Human Values*, 16:1, Winter 1991, pp. 111-121.

Zachary, G. Pascal. 1997. *Endless Frontier: Vannevar Bush, Engineer of the American Century*. New York: Free Press.

Zinchenko, V. 1996. Developing Activity Theory. In B. Nardi, Ed. *Context and Consciousness: Activity Theory and Human-Computer Interaction*. MIT Press.*

3

Nano Computers and Nano Electronics

Nano Computers: An Introduction

The concept of a Universal Computer, a device able to compute anything computable, dates back to Babbage in the early part of the 19th century, and to Turing, Church, and von Neumann in the 20th century. The concept of a "Universal Constructor" is perhaps more recent. The concept was well understood by von Neumann in the 1940's, who defined a "Universal Constructor" in a two-dimensional cellular automata world. Such a model is a mathematical abstraction something like an infinite checkerboard, with several different types of "checkers" that might be on each square. The different pieces spontanesouly change and move about depending on what pieces occupy neighboring squares, in accordance with a pre-defined set of rules. Von Neumann used the concept of a Universal Constructor in conjunction with a Universal Computer as the core components in a self-replicating system. The possibility of fabricating structures by putting "...the atoms down where the chemist says..." was recognized by Feynman in 1959. Drexler recognized the value of the "assembler" in 1977. (Note: Drexler said "Though assemblers will be powerful ... they will not be able to build everything that could exist.") The assembler is analogous to von Neumann's Universal Constructor, but operates in the normal three dimensional world and can build a large, atomically precise structures by manipulating atoms and small clusters of atoms. He published the concept in 1981 and in subsequent work [6] has proposed increasingly detailed designs for such devices. The basic design of Drexler's assembler consists of (1) a molecular computer, (2) one or more molecular positioning devices (which might resemble very small robotic arms), and (3) a well defined set of chemical reactions (perhaps one or two dozen) that take place at the tip of the arm and are able to fabricate a wide range of structures using site-specific chemical reactions. It is now common for forecasts of future technical abilities to include the ability to fabricate molecular devices and molecular machines with atomic precision.

While there continues to be debate about the exact time frame, it is becoming increasingly accepted that we will, eventually, develop the ability to economically fabricate a truly wide range of structures with atomic precision. This will be of major economic value. Most obviously a molecular manufacturing capability will be a prerequisite to the construction of molecular logic devices. The continuation of present trends in computer hardware depends on the ability to fabricate ever smaller and ever more precise logic devices at ever decreasing costs. The limit of this trend is the ability to fabricate molecular logic devices and to connect them in complex patterns at the molecular level. The manufacturing technology needed will, almost of necessity, be able to economically manufacture large structures (computers) with atomic precision (molecular logic elements). This capability will also permit the economical manufacture of materials with properties that border on the limits imposed by natural law. The strength of materials, in particular, will approach or even exceed that of diamond. Given the broad range of manufactured products that devote substantial mass to load-bearing members, such a development by itself will have a significant impact. A broad range of other manufactured products will also benefit from a manufacturing process that offers atomic precision at low cost.

Given the promise of such remarkably high payoffs it is natural to ask exactly what such systems will look like, exactly how they will work, and exactly how we will go about building them. One might also enquire as to the reasons for confidence that such an enterprise is feasible, and why one should further expect that our current understanding of chemistry and physics (embodied in a number of computational chemistry packages) should be sufficient to explain the operating principles of such systems.

It is here that the value of computational nanotechnology can be most clearly seen. Molecular machine proposals, provided that they are specified in atomic detail (and are of a size that can be dealt with by current software and hardware), can be modeled using the tools of computational chemistry.

There are two modeling techniques of particular utility. The first is molecular mechanics, which utilizes empirical force fields to model the forces acting between nuclei. The second is higher order ab initio calculations, which will be discussed in a few paragraphs.

A few links to internet computational chemistry resources are provided here to provide those new to the area with some feel for what's available.

Nanoelectronics: Molecular Mechanics

Molecular mechanics allows computational modeling of the positions and trajectories of the nuclei of individual atoms without an undue computational load. Current packages available on personal computers can readily do energy minimizations on systems with thousands of atoms, while supercomputers can handle systems with hundreds of thousands of atoms or more. More complex analyses, particularly analyses that involve searching through large configuration spaces, can limit the size of system that can be effectively handled. As will be discussed later the need to search through large configuration spaces (as when determining the native folded structure of an arbitrary protein) can be avoided by the use of relatively rigid structures (which differ from relatively floppy proteins and have few possible configurations). The modeling of machine components in vacuum reduces the need to model solvation effects, which can also involve significant computational effort.

In molecular mechanics the individual nuclei are usually treated as point masses. While quantum mechanics dictates that there must be a certain degree of positional uncertainty associated with each nucleus, this positional uncertainty is normally significantly smaller than the typical internuclear distance. Bowen and Allinger provide a good recent overview of the subject.

While the nuclei can reasonably be approximated as point masses, the electron cloud must be dealt with in quantum mechanical terms. However, if we are content to know only the positions of the nuclei and are willing to forego a detailed understanding of the electronic structure, then we can effectively eliminate the quantum mechanics. For example, the H_2 molecule involves two nuclei. While it would be possible to solve Schrodinger's equation to determine the wave function for the electrons, if we are content simply to know the potential energy contributed by the electrons (and do not enquire about the electron distribution) then we need only know the electronic energy as a function of the distance between the nuclei. That is, in many systems the only significant impact that the electrons have on nuclear position is to make a contribution to the potential energy E of the system. In the case of H_2, E is a simple function of the internuclear distance r. The function E(r) summarizes and replaces the more complex and more difficult to determine wave function for the electrons, as well as taking into account the inter-nuclear repulsion and the interactions between the electrons and the nuclei. The two hydrogen nuclei will adopt a position that minimizes E(r). As r becomes larger, the potential energy of the system increases and the nuclei experience a restoring force that returns them to their original distance. Similarly, as r becomes smaller and the two nuclei are pushed closer together, we also find that a restoring force pushes them farther apart, again restoring them to an equilibrium distance.

More generally, if we know the positions r_1, r_2, ... r_N of N nuclei, then $E(r_1, r_2, ... r_N)$ gives the potential energy of the system. Knowing the potential energy as a function of the nuclear positions, we can readily determine the forces acting on the individual nuclei and therefore can compute the evolution of their position over time. The function E is a newtonian potential energy function (not quantum mechanical), despite the fact that the particular value of E at a particular point could be computed from Schrodinger's equation. That is, the potential energy E is a newtonian concept, but the particular values of E at particular points are determined by Schrodinger's equation.

Often called the Born-Oppenheimer approximation, this approach allows a great conceptual and practical simplification in the modeling of molecular systems. While it would in principle be possible to determine E by solving Schrodinger's equation, in practice it is usual to use available experimental data and to infer the nature and shape of E by interpolation. This approach, in which empirically derived potential energy functions are created by interpolation from experimental data, has spawned a wide range of potential energy functions, many of which are sold commercially. Because the gradient of the potential energy function E defines a conservative force field F, molecular mechanics methods are also called "force field" methods. While it is common to refer to "empirical force field" methods, the more recent use of ab initio methods to provide data points to aid in the design of the force fields makes this term somewhat inaccurate, though still widely used.

The utility of molecular mechanics depends crucially on the development of accurate force fields. Good quality force fields have been developed for a fairly broad range of compounds including many compounds of interest in biochemistry. While we will not attempt to survey the wide range of force fields that are available, one particular subset of compounds for which good quality force fields are available involve H, C, N, O, F, Si, P, S, Cl (and perhaps a few others) when they are restricted to form chemically uncomplicated structures (e.g., bond strain is not too great, dangling bonds are few or absent, etc). Many atomically precise structures which should be useful in nanotechnology fall in this class and can be modeled with an accuracy adequate to determine the behavior of molecular machines.

A potential energy function of particular utility in modeling diamondoid structures was described by Brenner (*Empirical potential for hydrocarbons for use in simulating the chemical vapor deposition of diamond films*, Donald W. Brenner, Phys Rev B, Vol. 42, No. 15, November 15 1990, pages 9458-9471). Brenner's potential energy function, though limited to the elements carbon and hydrogen, has the great advantage that it will handle transition states, unstable structures, and the like. Thus, given essentially arbitrary coordinates of the carbon and hydrogen atoms in a system, Brenner's potential will return the energy of the system. This permits molecular dynamical modeling of arbitrary hydrocarbon systems, including systems which use synthetic reactions involved in the synthesis of diamond. A particular reaction of interest. See *Surface patterning by atomically-controlled chemical forces: molecular dynamics simulations* by Sinnott et al., Surface Science 316 (1994), L1055-L1060; see also the work of for an illustration of the use of Brenner's potential in modeling the behavior of graphitic gears, including failure modes). Brenner has commented on the utility of this potential for modeling proposed molecular machine systems.

Of course, the "accuracy" of the force fields depends on the application. A force field which was accurate to (say) 10 kcal/ mole would be unable to correctly predict many properties of interest in biochemistry. For example, such a force field would lead to serious errors in predicting the correct three-dimensional structure of a protein. Given the linear sequence of amino acids in a protein, the protein folding problem is to determine how it will fold in three dimensions when put in solution. Often, the correct configuration will have an energy that differs from other (incorrect) configurations by a relatively modest amount, and so a force field of high accuracy is required.

Unlike the protein folding problem, where an astronomical range of configurations of similar energy are feasible, the bearing basically has only one configuration: a bearing. While the protein has many unconstrained torsions, there are no unconstrained torsions in the bearing. To significantly change any torsion angle in the bearing would involve ripping apart bonds. Thus, the same force field which is of marginal utility in dealing with strands of floppy protein is quite adequate for solid blocks of stiff diamondoid material. Not only will small errors in the force field still result in an accurate prediction of the global minima, (which in this case will be a single large basin in the potential energy surface) but also the range of possible structures is so sharply limited that little or no computational effort need be spent comparing the energies of different configurations. Long computational runs to evaluate the statistical properties of ensembles of configurations are thus eliminated.

This style of design has been called, only half in jest, "molecular bridge building" because bridges are also designed with large safety margins.

This observation, that the same force field that is inadequate for one class of structures is quite adequate for the design and modeling of a different class of structures, leads to a more general principle. Computational experiments generally provide an answer with-some error distribution. If the errors produced by the model are of a similar size to the errors that would result in incorrect device function, then the model is unreliable. On the other hand, if the errors in the model are small compared with the errors that will produce incorrect device function, then the results of the model are likely to be reliable. If a device design falls in the former category, i.e., small errors in the model will produce conflicting forecasts about device function, then the conservative course of action is to reject the proposed design and keep looking. That is, *we can deliberately design structures which are indeed adequately handled by our computational tools*. As illustrated by the bearing, there are a wide range of basically mechanical structures whose stability is sufficiently clear and whose interactions with other structures is sufficiently simple that their behavior can be adequately modeled with currently available force fields.

An even stronger (although somewhat more subtle) statement is possible. The strain in the axle and the sleeve is proportional to the diameter of the bearing. By increasing the diameter, we can reduce the strain. Thus, we can design bearings in this broad class in which the strain can be reduced to whatever level we desire. Because we are dealing with what amounts to a strained block of diamond, the fact that we can reduce strain arbitrarily means that we can design a bearing whose local structure bears as close a resemblance to an unstrained block of diamond as might be wished. We can therefore be very confident indeed that some member of this class will perform the desired function (that of a bearing) and will work in accordance with our expectations. Given that we have developed software tools that are capable of creating and modeling most of the members of a broad class of devices, then we can investigate many individual class members. This investigation then lets us make rather confident statements about the functionality that members of this class can provide, even if there might be residual doubts about individual class members.

A moments reflection will show that the class of objects which are chemically reasonably inert, relatively stiff (no free torsions), and which interact via simple repulsive forces that occur on contact; can describe a truly vast class of machines. Indeed, it is possible to design computers, robotic arms and a wide range of other devices using molecular parts drawn from this class.

Ab Initio Methods

While empirical force fields are sufficiently accurate to model the behavior of chemically stable stiff structures interacting with other chemically stable stiff structures, they do not (at present) provide sufficient accuracy to deal with chemical transitions. Thus, if we wish to model the manufacture of a molecular part then we must use higher order ab initio techniques (another paper in this issue illustrates what is meant by this in detail). These techniques impose severe constraints on the number of atoms that can be modeled (perhaps one or two dozen heavy atoms, depending on the hardware, software, and specific type of modeling being attempted), but can provide an accuracy sufficient to analyze the chemical reactions that must necessarily take place during the synthesis of large, atomically precise structures. More generally, higher order ab initio techniques are sufficient to analyze the addition or removal of a small number of atoms from a specific site on a work piece. Synthesis of a large object would then consist of repeated site specific applications of a small number of basic operations, where each basic operation changed the chemical structure of only a small number of atoms at a time. Provided that we reject reaction mechanisms where the result predicted depends on errors that are smaller than can reasonably be modeled, the analysis of these basic operations can be satisfactorily carried out with current methods and hardware.

Several reactions mechanisms have been discussed, and a great many more are feasible.

Sufficiency of Current Modeling Methods

In summary, it is quite possible to adequately model the behavior of molecular machines that satisfy two constraints: (1) they are built from parts that are sufficiently stable that small errors in the empirical force fields do not raise significant questions about the shape or stability of the parts, and (2) the synthesis of the parts is done by using positionally controlled reactions, where the actual chemical reactions involve a relatively small number of atoms whose behavior can be adequately modeled with higher order ab initio methods.

Clearly, not all molecular machines satisfy these constraints. Is the range of molecular machines which do satisfy these constraints sufficiently large to justify the effort of designing and modeling them? And in particular, can we satisfactorily model Drexler's assembler within these constraints?

The fundamental purpose of an assembler is to position atoms. To this end, it is imperative that we have models that let us determine atomic positions, and this is precisely what molecular mechanics provides. Robotic arms or other positioning devices are basically mechanical in nature, and will allow us to position molecular parts during the assembly process. Molecular mechanics provides us with an excellent tool for modeling the behavior of such devices.

The second fundamental requirement is the ability to make and break bonds at specific sites. While molecular mechanics provides an excellent tool for telling us where the tip of the assembler arm is located, current force fields are not adequate to model the specific chemical reactions that must then take place at the tip/work-piece interface involved in building an atomically precise part (though this statement must be modified in light of the work done with Brenner's potential, discussed above). For this, higher order ab initio calculations are sufficient.

The glaring omission in this discussion is the modeling of the kind of electronic behavior that occurs in switching devices. Clearly, it is possible to model electronic behavior with some degree of accuracy, and equally clearly molecular machines that are basically electronic in nature will be extremely useful. It will therefore be desirable to extend the range of computational models discussed here to include such devices. For the moment, however, the relatively modest inclusion of electrostatic motors as a power source is probably sufficient to provide us with adequate "design space" to design and model an assembler. While it might at first glance appear that electronics will be required for the computational element in the assembler, in fact molecular mechanical logic elements will be sufficient. Babbage's proposal from the 1800's clearly demonstrates the feasibility of mechanical computation (it is interesting to note that a working model of 's difference engine has been built and is on display at the British Museum of Science. They were careful to use parts machined no more accurately than the parts available to Babbage, in order to demonstrate that his ideas could have been implemented in the 1800's). Drexler's analysis of a specific molecular mechanical logic element and further analysis of system design issues also make it clear that molecular mechanical computation is sufficient for the molecular computer required in an assembler.

Molecular electronic proposals for computation have not been worked out as clearly at the system level as the molecular mechanical concepts. Thus, at the moment, molecular mechanical proposals are better understood, at least in this particular context. This situation is likely to change, and when it does the electronic designs could be incorporated (where appropriate) into the design and modeling of an assembler. However, it is not entirely obvious that electronic designs will prove superior to molecular mechanical designs, particularly when device parameters such as size and energy dissipation are considered. While it seems virtually certain that electronic devices will prove faster than molecular mechanical devices, it is less obvious that electronic devices must necessarily be either smaller or dissipate less energy (though confer more recent work on *reversible logic*). Indeed, given the difficulty of localizing individual electrons, it seems possible that electronic devices will prove to be inherently larger than molecular mechanical devices. This might provide a long term role for molecular mechanical devices as high density memory elements, or as logic elements when space (or atom count) is particularly constrained.

Whether the assembler is designed and built with an electronic or mechanical computer is less significant than designing and building it. By way of example, a stored program computer can be built in many different ways. Vacuum tubes, transistors, moving mechanical parts, fluidics, and other methods are all entirely feasible. Delaying the development of the Eniac because transistors are better than vacuum tubes would have been a most unwise course of action. Similarly, as we consider the design, modeling, and construction of an assembler, we should not hesitate to use simpler methods that we can understand in favor of better methods that are not yet fully in hand.

The methods of computational chemistry available today allow us to model a wide range of molecular machines with an accuracy sufficient in many cases to determine how well they will work. We can deliberately confine ourselves to the subset of devices where our modeling tools are good enough to give us confidence that the proposals should work. This range includes bearings, computers, robotic arms, site-specific chemical reactions utilized in the synthesis of complex structures, and more complex systems built up from these and related components. Drexler's assembler and related devices can be modeled using our current approaches and methods.

Molecular Compilers

(Much of this section has been superceded by work on molecular CAD tools with graphical user interfaces: in particular, work by *Geoff Leach on Crystal Clear.*) Computational nanotechnology includes not only the tools and techniques required to model proposed molecular machines, it must also include the tools required to specify such machines. Molecular machine proposals that would require millions or even billions of atoms have been made. The total atom count of an assember might be roughly a billion atoms. While commerically available molecular modeling packages provide facilities to specify arbitrary structures, it is usually necessary to "point and click" for each atom involved. This is obviously unattractive for a device as complex as an assembler with its roughly one billion atoms. It should be clear that molecular CAD tools will be required if we are to specify such complex structures in atomic detail with a reasonable amount of effort. An essential development is that of "molecular compilers" which accept, as input, a high level description of an object and produce, as output, the atomic coordinates, atom types, and bonding structure of the object. The first line, "scale 0.9," is simply an instruction to shrink the size of the axle by 10% compared with the normal size. This allows the axle to be positioned inside the sleeve before joint minimization of the axle and sleeve is done (using MSI's PolyGraf, a commercially available molecular mechanics package that implements both MM2 and the Dreiding II force field). If the axle w were not done, then the atoms in the axle and the sleeve would be comingled, and minimization would produce meaningless results.

The second line begins with the "tube" specifier. This tells the program to produce a tubular structure, rather than a "block" or a "ring." the "ring" specifier is used to produce toroidal structures, e.g., tubes that have been further bent into donuts. The first triplet of numbers following "tube," "0 0.75 0.75," specifies the offset to be used for the crystal lattice. The second triplet, "1.75 0 0" specifies that the surface of the tube is (100), and that the thickness of the tube wall is 1.75 lattice spacings. The third triplet, "0 17 -17," specifies the direction and length of the circumference of the tube. The direction (or [0 1 -1]) is at right angles to [1 0 0], the direction of the tube surface. The circumference of the tube is simply the length of the [0 17 -17] vector. Finally, "0 5.25 5.25" gives the direction of the axis and the length of the tube.

This does not fully specify the axle of the bearing, for the 100 surface has been cut circumferentially to produce grooves. The next command, "grid 0 0.5 -0.5 0 1 1" specifies that a grid is to be laid down on the surface. The grid is specified by two vectors, "0 0.5 -0.5" and "0 1 1,"" which give the directions and lengths of the edges of the unit parallelogram from which the grid is composed. The next command, "delete 1.25 0 0"" specifies that the point at coordinates "1.25 0 0" is to be deleted, and further, that all points in the same location with respect to any unit parallelogram of the grid are also to be deleted. Thus, this "grid .... delete ...." cuts out the grooves that are visible on the outer surface of the axle.

A similar set of commands was used to specify the sleeve of the bearing. It is easy to specify bearings with different surfaces, surface orientations, circumferences, lengths, etc. To select a (111), (110), (312), or any other surface, it is sufficient to change the vector that specifies the surface, and the vectors that specify the tangent to the surface and the axis of the tube (which must be at right angles to the surface vector). Thus, complex structures involving many atoms can be generated quickly and easily with a few lines of input specification.

The C source code is available at URL ftp://ftp.parc.xerox.com/pub/nano/tube.c. The program will generate output in either PolyGraf format or in Brookhaven format, so the output should be readable by most computational chemistry packages.

The software required to design and model complex molecular machines is either already available, or can be readily developed over the next few years. Many of the modeling issues can be dealt with by existing commercially available computational chemistry packages. The molecular compilers and other molecular CAD tools needed for this work can be implemented using generally understood techniques and methods from computer science. Using this approach, it will be possible to substantially reduce the development time for complex molecular machines, including Drexler's assembler. This approach is similar in spirit to the computer aided design and modeling used to speed the development of many products today. The author was part of a general purpose computer start up which successfully designed and built a new computer from scratch. This included the hardware, software, compilers, operating system, etc. During this process, extensive use was made of computational models to verify each level of the design. The operating system was written in Pascal, and checked out on another computer. The compilers were written in Pascal, and also checked out on another computer. The code produced by the compilers was checked out on an instruction set simulator. The microcode was checked out on a micro-instruction simulator. The logic design was checked out with logic level simulation tools, and circuit simulation packages were used to verify the detailed electronic design. All this work was done at the same time. The software was written and debugged even though the machine on which it would eventually be executed didn't exist. The microcode was written and debugged before the hardware was available. When the hardware was finally made available, system integration went relatively rapidly.

Imagine, for a moment, how long it would have taken to develop this system had we carried out the development in the obvious sequential fashion. First, we would have implemented the hardware and only then begun work on the microengine. Later, with the hardware and microengine fully checked out and working, we could have developed and debugged the microcode. With this firmly in hand, we could then have written the compilers and verified the code they produced. Finally, we could have implemented and checked out the operating system. Needless to say, such a strategy would have been very slow and tedious.

Doing things in the simple and most obvious way often takes a lot longer than is needed. If we were to approach the design and construction of an assembler using the simple serial method, it would take a great deal longer than if we systematically attacked and simultanesouly solved the problems that arise at all levels of the design at one and the same time. That is, by using methods similar to those used to design a modern computer, including intensive computational modeling of individual components and sub- systems, we can greatly shorten the time required to design and build complex molecular machines.

This can be further illustrated by considering the traditional manner of growth of our synthetic capability over time. Today, we find we are able to synthesize a certain range of compounds and structures. As time goes by, we will be able to synthesize an ever larger range of structures. This growth in our ability will proceed on a broad front, and reflects the efforts of a broad range of researchers who are each pursuing individual goals without concern about the larger picture into which they might fit. Sufficient time we will eventually be able to synthesize complex molecular machines simply because we will eventually develop the ability to synthesize just about anything.

However, if we wish to develop a particular kind of device, e.g., an assembler, then we can speed the process up by conducting computational experiments designed to clarify the objective and to specify more precisely the path from our current range of synthetic capabilities to the objective. Such computational experiments are inexpensive, can provide very detailed information, are possible for any structure (whether we can or cannot synthesize it) and will, in general, reduce the "time to market" for the selected product.

Computational experiments let us examine structures quickly and easily, rejecting those which have obvious defects. This kind of examination of the "design space" is impossible with physical experiments today, but is easily done with computational experiments.

Computational experiments also provide more information. For example, molecular dynamics can literally provide information about the position of each individual atom over time, information which would usually be inaccessible in a physical experiment.

Of course, the major advantage of computational experiments over physical experiments in the current context is the simple fact that physical experiments aren't possible for molecular machines that we can't make with today's technology. By using computational models derived from the wealth of experimental data that is available today, we can (within certain accuracy bounds) describe the behavior of proposed systems that we plan to build in the future. If we deliberately design systems that are sufficiently robust that we are confident they will work regardless of the small errors that must be incurred in the modeling process, we can design systems today that we will not be able to build for some years, and yet still have reasonable confidence that they will work.

By fully utilizing the experience that has been developed in the rapid design and development of complex systems we can dramatically reduce the development time for molecular manufacturing systems. It is possible to debate how long it will be before we achieve a robust molecular manufacturing capability. However, it is very clear that we'll get there sooner if we develop and make intelligent use of molecular design tools and computational models. These will let us design and check the blueprints for the new molecular manufacturing technologies that we now see on the horizon, and will let us chart a more rapid and more certain path to their development.

Nanoelectronics

Experts everywhere say that nanotechnology will lead to'smarter, faster, and more efficient electronicsl but they also'admit that researchers face some challenging obstacles along the information superhighway.

Particle contamination is'one of the thorniest problems'facing the electronics and computing industries. Even the tiniest particle can destroy a computer chip and cause other damage. Several University researchers are searching for ways'to detect particle contaminants and prevent their formation.

A team of researchers headed by mechanical engineering professor Peter McMurry is studying'the formation and growth of contaminants in semiconductor processing equipment. Smaller contaminated particles deposit more quickly than larger ones and can destroy a number of memory chips and processors. The team's goal is'to design new processes or tools for producing contaminant-free devices.

"It's important to understand how`to prevent particle deposition, and this`will require an`understanding`of how such particles`are formed and transported," McMurry says.

His team has developed a device called the particle beam mass' spectrometer, the only available instrument for measuring nanoparticles'in low-pressure semiconductor processing equipment.

Electrical engineering professor Steve Campbell is among the researchers who are looking'for ways to'create electronic'devices with greater memory. His studies are aimed at detecting and preventing the formation of particle contaminants'in chemical reactors. Although research in the area is'still relatively new, some early prototypes have been made, says'Campbell.

Campbell's Microtechnology Laboratory team has developed a machine to detect and measure particlesn "Now we're trying to` demonstrate that isolating`these particles`and using them to`our advantage is`feasible," he says, adding that his group is seeking funding to continue its research.

"The importance of smaller and faster semiconductor devices is evident from the trends`we've all seen [toward] faster, more powerful, and less costly computersl" says McMurry. "Work that is` being done to fabricate devices at the nanoscale will ensure that this trend will continue for some time to"come."

The same is true in recording media. Associate Professor Randall Victora and Professor Jack'Judy of the electrical and computer engineering department received grants'two'years ago from the National Storage Industry Consortium and Seagate Corporation to' develop superlattice magnetic recording media.

The focus of their research is magnetic'recording technology for hard drivesl which are vulnerable to thermal fluctuations. These fluctuations can affect the recording process and destroy vital information stored on a disk'in the drive.

"We're preventing "that from happeningl" Victora says. "These superlattices cause the disk to`have a stronger resistance to`these thermal fluctuationsn"

Once developed, the technology would be used primarily by'the computing industry. Companies such as Quantum, IBM, and Seagate already have expressed interest in the group's research, Victora says.

Other University projects also have implications for the electronics industry, including the study of adhesion in computer chip manufacturingl molecular electronics, and the search for an appropriate nonconductor to replace copper, which is'limited in its ability to transport information between resistors.

Nanoelectronics refers to electronics at the sub-micron scale. Many chip components in production already feature sizes at the nanoscale. However, nanoelectronics also encompass what is known as molecular electronics, which uses individual molecules in electronics. Other advances in nanotechnology with applications in electronics include carbon nanotubes that can be used in both chips and displays, and nanomaterials that can be used in films that make smaller, more flexible displays and improved hard disks. Nanoelectronics in Japan and Korea tends to focus on next generation semiconductor devices and single electron devices (SED).

Below is a list of individuals who have been instrumental in advancing the state of the art in the field of nanoelectronics and who are among the world's experts on this next-generation technology. The list is organized according to areas of expertise.

- Dr. Jane Alexander—Dr. Alexander is the initiator of the DARPA ULTRA Program for nanoelectronics research.
- Larry Cooper—Larry Cooper is a long-time advocate and program manager for a broad range of U.S. Navy programs in advanced electronics.
- Dr. Gerry Iafrate—Dr. Iafrate is a visionary program manager and an active research investigator who is widely acknowledged as having been one of the initiators of the U.S. research effort in nanoelectronics during the early 1980s.
- Lt. Col. Gernot Pomrenke—Lt. Col. Pomrenke is the Program Manager of the the DARPA ULTRA Program for nanoelectronics research.
- Dr. William Tolles—Dr. Tolles is the author of two major reports on nanotechnology, including one on Nanotechnology in Europe.

Craig Lent, Wolfgang Porod and Gary Bernstein are on the faculty at the University of Notre Dame, where they are closely associated at the Notre Dame Microelectronics Lab. They are performing among the most important and comprehensive work in the field of pure nanoelectronics. Lent and Porod have proposed and simulated successfully a wireless design for an electronic nanocomputer based upon quantum cellular automata and a two-state nanoelectronic device they term a "quantum dot cell". Bernstein is attempting to fabricate such devices and the logic based upon them. Their quantum cellular automata are a very important new idea that is stimulating important new research into potential designs and architectures for electronic nanocomputers.

- Terry Fountain

  Professor Fountain performs research on computer architecture at the University College London, UK. He is a source of many innovative ideas about how to organize a densely integrated computer system with nanoscale components.

- Brosl Hasslacher and Ronnie Mainieri

  Drs. Hasslacher and Mainieri are on the staff at the Los Alamos National Laboratory. They are leading experts on the limits of nanoscale, low-power electronic devices and the difficult technical issues that must be overcome to build a nanocomputer. They have performed extensive theoretical work and calculations in this area.

- Rolf Landauer

  Dr. Landauer works for IBM where he is a well-known expert on the theory and physics of computation, especially in its nanoscale limits.

- Konstantin Likharev

  Professor Likharev is on the faculty at the State University of New York at Stony Brook. In collaboration with Alexander Korotkov, he helped originate a cellular automaton proposal designed particularly to alleviate some of the weaknesses in the Lent-Porod quantum dot cell approach (which also has been improved). Likharev also is one of the world's preeminent experts on single-electron devices.

- John Storrs-Hall

  Dr. Storrs-Hall is a senior scientist in the Laboratory for Computer Science Research (LCSR) at Rutgers University. He is an expert on the issue of reversibility in nanocomputers. He is also a noted proponent of alternative, nanomechanical approaches for the design and fabrication of nanocomputers.

- Tomasso Toffoli

  Professor Toffoli, of Boston University, is an expert on cellular automaton architectures for nanocomputers and on quantum computation.

- Gary Frazier and Alan Seabaugh

  Drs. Frazier and Seabaugh are on staff at Texas Instruments Corporation (TI). Gary Frazier is the Manager of the Texas Instruments Nanoelectronics Research and Development Group, while Alan Seabaugh is the Technical Leader. TI is among the leaders in the field of nanoelectronics, in large part due to the efforts of Drs. Frazier and Seabaugh, who are involved in many different aspects of the field. Their work in hybrid nanoelectronics—microelectronics technology, as well as their efforts in silicon nanoelectronics research, and in the modeling of nanoelectronic devices are of particular importance. This work could lead to the introduction of the first mass-manufactured nanoelectronics products.

- Federico Capasso

  Capasso works at AT&T where he performed some of the earliest work on "resonance tunneling devices," the class of quantum effect devices that are viewed as among the the more likely candidates for employment as a nanometer-scale transistor.

- Robert Bate

  Bob Bate now is a senior investigator at Texas A&M. He is one of the godfathers of nanoelectronics and an early visionary about the potential of this area. He is also the author of a number of fundamental papers on nanoelectronics. In the early 1980s, Bate started and helped to build the Nanoelectronics Group at Texas Instruments prior to his retirement from TI several years ago.

- Tom McGill

  Professor McGill is on the faculty at the California Institute of Technology, in Pasadena, CA, where he has performed innovative fabrication and experimentation with quantum effect devices.

- Herb Goronkin

  Dr. Goronkin is a senior scientist at the Motorola Corporation. A leading investigator in the area of solid-state quantum effect devices, he is an expert and proponent for using methods of chemical self-assembly for the fabrication of next-generation nanoelectronic devices.

- Professor Yasuaki Masumoto

  Director of the Single Quantum Dot Project in Japan's ERATO Initiative and Professor at the University of Tsukuba in Tsukuba, Japan.

- Professor James Meindl

  Professor Meindl is on the faculty of the Georgia Institute of Technology, where he has done comprehensive work on the constraints that apply in scaling down solid-state devices (i.e., transistors) to nanometer dimensions. He is noted for his extremely clear, comprehensive lectures on this subject, based upon years of research that are summarized in a number of fundamental articles.

- Barry Gilbert

  Gilbert is on the Staff of the Mayo Clinic, where he leads the Mayo Special Purpose Processor Development Group. His research on design and fabrication of solid-state quantum effect devices for signal processing is widely recognized as being among the most advanced in the nanoelectronics field.

- Mark Reed

  Professor Reed is Chairman of the Electrical Engineering Department at Yale University and Director of the Yale Center for Microelectronic Materials and Structures. An acknowledged expert on quantum dots, with much experience fabricating and experimenting with solid-state "dots", Prof. Reed concluded some years ago that they must get much smaller in order to operate at room temperature. Thus, Professor Reed now is performing very sensitive experiments on prototype molecular-scale electronic devices, along with Professor James Tour of the University of South Carolina. They are hoping to produce a molecular-scale quantum dot.

- James Tour

  Tour is a Professor in the Department of Chemistry and Biochemistry at the University of South Carolina, where he is performing pioneering research on molecular electronics by synthesizing the molecules on which Mark Reed of Yale is performing experiments. Recently, Professor Tour and his collaborators successfully fabricated and tested the first functioning molecular wire.

- Ari Aviram

  A long-time proponent of molecular-scale electronic devices, Dr. Aviram is a senior scientist at the IBM Watson Laboratory. He is the author of a series of very influential papers on the subject, dating back to the 1974 classic paper that he co-authored with Professor Mark Ratner. A more recent talk by Dr. Aviram served as the catalyst for the chemical nanofabrication research of Professor James Tour, who has successfully fabricated a conducting molecular wire.

- Mark Ratner

  Professor Ratner, now at Northwestern University in Evanston, Illinois, is one of the originators of the idea of molecular electronics, back in the 1970s. Along with Ari Aviram, Professor Ratner published the seminal technical paper on this topic. He continues to publish innovative research results on the dynamics and modeling of molecular devices, such as those that are being experimented upon by James Tour and Mark Reed.

- Yasuo Wada

  Wada is a senior member of the research technical staff at Hitachi Corp. in Saitama, Japan. He is an expert on nanoprobes. He also has originated an innovative approach for molecular-scale electrical switches.

- Noel MacDonald

  Noel MacDonald is Professor in the School of Electrical Engineering at Cornell University where his conducting research in the Cornell University Nanofabrication Facility Professor MacDonald's research focuses on fabricating an array of scanning tunneling electron microscopes (STMs) on a chip using the techniques for fabricating microelectromechanical systems (MEMS). This work is a groundbreaking engineering achievement and it is potentially very important for a variety of applications in nanofabrication, dense molecular memories, and the exploration of chemical reactions and surface properties. For now, he is focused primarily considering applications of STM arrays to dense memories.

- Calvin Quate

  Quate is Leland T. Edwards Professor of Electrical Engineering and Applied Physics at Stanford University and the inventor of Atomic Force Microscopy (AFM), a primary tool for the manipulation and investigation of nanostructures. More recently, has been focusing his research on using the techniques for fabricating microelectromechanical systems (MEMS) to build an array of a large number of AFM tips on a single silicon "chip." The comments made above for Noel MacDonald apply here, except Professor Quate is focused on using his arrays for nanofabrication.

- Phaedron Avouris

  Avouris is a member of the research staff at IBM. He is an expert on nanoprobes for nanofabrication.

- George Whitesides

  George Whitesides is Mallinckrodt Professor of Chemistry at Harvard University. Professor Whitesides is the one of the world's leading investigators in the area of chemical self-assembly for nanofabrication. He has pioneered in the technique of applying self-assembling monolayers (SAMs) for this purpose. Research in the Whitesides Group covers a wide range of disciplines, including chemistry, biology, physics, and electrical engineering. The work of Professor Whitesides and his collaborators on SAMs and contact printing for nanoelectronic circuitry is an important step toward the fabrication of nanocomputers.

- Steven Chou

  Professor Chou is leading a wide-ranging research program in the Nanostructure Laboratory (NSL) in the Department of Electrical Engineering at the University of Minnesota where, among his other achievements, he has pioneered highly refined techniques for nanoscale "printing." He has applied this technique to fabricate an ultra-dense magnetic information storage structure. He is working on at least a half dozen projects in VLSI and ULSI (Ultra-Large-Scale Intergration).

- Tom Mallouck

  Professor Mallouck is on the faculty of the Chemistry Department at Penn State University, where he has led experimental efforts that resulted in the chemical self-assembly of a single-electron transistor.

- Harold Craighead

Professor Craighead works at Cornell University Nanofabrication Facility and is the head of the Cornell Nanotechnology Lab and an expert on self-assembly.

- James Harris

  Professor of Electrical Engineering at Stanford University and leader of the Harris Research Group there. His group specializes in nanofabrication by Molecular Beam Epitaxy (MBE), as well as in studies of the dynamics of quantum dots.

- James Ellenbogen

  As Lead Scientist of the Nanosystems Group at The MITRE Corporation, Dr. Ellenbogen has been performing research to develop faster and more accurate electron-density-based methods for modeling nanoelectronic devices.

- Kevin Empson

  Program Manager of the U.S. Government's Nanoelectronic Modeling (NEMO) Project.

- David K. Ferry

  Dave Ferry is Professor of Electrical Engineering and Computer Science at Arizona State University and Director of the Nanostructures Research Group at ASU. He is an authority on the physics and modeling of solid-state nanoelectronic devices, having written two text books and many technical articles on the subject.

- William Frensley

  Bill Frensley is Professor and Head of the Department of Electrical Engineering at the University of Texas, Dallas. He has used his expertise and experience in the simulation of solid-state devices and quantum-effect nanoelectronic devices to develop deep insight into which device designs can work and which probably won't, and why. Also, he has developed a clear, unified picture of device designs, their evolution and relationships.

- Harold Grubin

  As President of SRA, Inc., Hal Grubin is an active participant in a diverse range of modeling and simulation activities at the forefront of solid-state nanoelectronics research.

- Gerhard Klimeck

  A software engineer in the Nanoelectronics Research Group at the Texas Instruments Corporation in Dallas, TX, Gerhard is the driving force behind the innovative design of the software for the Nanoelectronic Modeling (NEMO) software.

- Roger Lake

  A scientist working in the Nanoelectronics Research Group at the Texas Instruments Corporation in Dallas, TX, Roger Lake is responsible for the design and development of the unusually fast and accurate algorithms that have been employed in the Nanoelectronic Modeling (NEMO) simulation software for modeling solid-state, nanometer-scale quantum-effect electronic devices.

Nanoscale Electronics

At first there were only a few of them, but recently, their numbers have multiplied wildly. Newspaper headlines, magazine articles, journal papers, even television commercials now are loaded with those big "nano" words: nanometer, nanoscale, nanosecond, and nanotechnology, to name a few. And it seems that every week some organization is announcing yet another "nanoconference." Why all the excitement? Because in recent years, as scientists have begun to get a handle on controlling matter at the nanometer scale, they've recognized that these skills can be used to make new materials with unique and useful properties—perhaps leading to a range of commercial applications in sensing, electronics, and other areas. Impressive laboratory demonstrations of nanoscale dexterity have been widely reported in the scientific and popular press, thereby drawing the attention of more scientists, companies, and technology investors. Nanoelectronics—a developing field in which circuitry is composed of nanometer-sized electronic components—is one topic that's attracting a lot of interest in scientific and nonscientific corners alike. Researchers are driven to explore the field because further miniaturizing today's already small electronic circuits will lead to faster, more sophisticated, and more portable devices. Yet it's widely believed that in a decade or so, silicon-based circuitry will have been shrunk as small as is physically possible. And so the search is on for alternative materials from which nanoscale circuits can be constructed. Carbon nanotubes and nanowires of materials such as gallium arsenide are being studied for just that purpose by several research groups. Other investigators, whose work is often labeled "molecular electronics," focus on the electrical behavior of individual molecules or small numbers of molecules. Scientists who work in these fields aim to design and build new types of computers in which the nanosized entities lie at the heart of logic circuits. Skeptics say that the proposed applications are exaggerated and that reports are full of "hype." But researchers around the globe are exploring and discovering nanometer-scale phenomena, and they are rapidly turning out large numbers of scientific papers. "These are exciting and heady times," says Mark A. Ratner, surveying the combined topics of molecular and nanoelectronics. "There are wonderful experiments being reported these days," he says. "The excitement is justified." A nearly 30-year-old paper by the Northwestern University chemistry professor is often cited as the beginning of modern molecular electronics. In that theoretical study, Ratner and

Arieh Aviram, who was at that time a graduate student, proposed that under certain conditions, individual organic molecules could function as p-n junction diodes. These simple electronic devices typically are formed at the interface between positive charge-carrying (p-type) and negative charge-carrying (n-type) semiconductors and can be used as rectifiers to convert AC current to DC current. Ratner notes that few advances were made in molecular electronics until scanning probe microscopes became available in the late 1980s. The new tools gave the field a much-needed boost by making it possible to measure a whole range of phenomena, including the type Ratner had described in the 1970s. He adds that progress in other areas, for example, in methods for preparing self-assembled monolayers of molecules, was also instrumental in jump-starting nanoscale electronics. "Now the advances are coming thick and fast," he says.

"Thick and fast" aptly describes the flurry of research being carried out on carbon nanotubes. According to Phaedon Avouris, manager of nanoscale science and technology at IBM's T.J. Watson Research Center, Yorktown Heights, N.Y., the strawlike all-carbon structures with nanometer-sized diameters are endowed with unique properties that make them excellent candidates for nanoelectronic applications. Nanotubes can be metals or semiconductors, depending on their chirality, Avouris notes. And because of their strong chemical bonds and satisfied valencies, the materials boast high thermal, mechanical, and chemical stability. In addition, carbon nanotubes can be efficient conductors as a result of their tiny diameters, long lengths, and defect-free structures that make them ideal one-dimensional systems. Some years ago, Avouris' research group and, independently, scientists working with Cees Dekker, a professor of applied physics at Delft University of Technology, in the Netherlands, demonstrated that field-effect transistors (FETs) could be fashioned from carbon nanotubes. FETs are a type of switch in which a semiconducting channel bridges two electrodes designated "source" and "drain." Current flow between these electrodes is controlled by a third electrode known as a "gate." By applying a voltage to the gate, the semiconductor's state can be changed—reversibly—from insulating to conducting, thereby switching the transistor on or off. In conventional FETs, the bridging channel is made of silicon. In nanotube devices, the channel is a single carbon nanotube. Today's sophisticated silicon-based integrated circuits owe much of their success to advances in FET technology. Manufacturers pack tens of millions of the tiny transistors into the postage-stamp-sized computer chips used in modern microprocessors. For that reason, the IBM research group and others have been working on improving the properties of nanotube FETs. Much of the work focuses on understanding and controlling electrical conduction through the tiny tubes. One problem that plagues researchers looking to fashion circuit components from nanotubes is separating metallic tubes from the ones that are semiconducting. Common synthesis procedures produce spaghetti-like mixtures of nanotube ropes that are unusable for semiconductor applications because they contain both types of tubes.

But last year, Avouris and coworkers came up with a way to sort through the tangle. After fashioning electrodes around nanotube bundles via lithography methods, the team applied certain voltages to the gate electrodes to switch off the semiconducting tubes, converting them to insulators. Then, by applying high voltage to the circuit, the IBM group oxidized the metallic tubes, causing them to break down without affecting the semiconducting tubes. The group used the method to prepare FET arrays from single-walled nanotube ropes and to peel apart multiwalled nanotubes shell-by-shell. Just a few months later, the IBM group showed that elementary computing circuits known as logic gates—which typically are constructed from combinations of FETs—can be fashioned from a single nanotube bundle. Shortly thereafter, Delft's Dekker reported similar advances in constructing multi-FET nanotube logic circuits. Complex combinations of AND, OR, and NOT logic gates make up the core of digital processors. To make NOT gates using nanotubes, Avouris and coworkers needed to come up with a procedure for preparing n-type nanotubes. NOT gates require both types of transistors. But the synthesis techniques available at that time, produced only p-type tubes. Hunting for a solution, Avouris and IBM coworkers Vincent Derycke, Richard Martel, and Joerg Appenzeller found that p-type nanotubes can be converted to n-type simply by annealing (heating) in vacuum. Armed with the new preparation trick, the team prepared separate n- and p-type transistors and fabricated a NOT gate. Then they went a step further and fabricated a NOT gate using just one nanotube. For that feat, the team selectively converted a short length of a nanotube to n-type by doping it with potassium through a tiny window in a protective polymer coating while leaving the unexposed portion p-type. The single tube with p- and n-type segments was then used to construct an intramolecular NOT gate. Further advances have come from transistor design modifications. Earlier this year, for example, the IBM group reported that their so-called top-gated nanotube FETs outperform state-of-the-art silicon FETs in terms of switching rate and the amount of current they can carry per width of conductor. One key difference between the latest design and earlier designs is that the silicon wafers that support the FETs do not function as gates. Instead, the gate is fabricated above the nanotube—allowing all FETs in contact with the silicon wafer to be switched independently. In addition, the new FET design benefits from switching voltages that are an order of magnitude lower than those needed to switch older FETs Just recently, the IBM team developed a catalyst-free procedure for preparing single-walled carbon nanotubes. Conventional methods for preparing single-walled tubes, such as discharge and vapor deposition techniques, rely on particles of nickel and cobalt or other catalytic transition metals. A problem with those procedures is that the metal particles left behind in the products disturb the nanotubes' electrical properties, forcing scientists to take complex purification measures.

But now Avouris and coworkers have shown that single-walled nanotubes can be prepared from SiC in the absence of metal catalysts at temperatures above 1500°C.

The method produces nanotubes that are 1.2 to 1.6 nm wide and are aligned along the face of the support. Other researchers have reported techniques for growing vertically aligned products, which they dub nanotube forests. But nanotubes that grow horizontally are amenable to standard vapor deposition methods and may be connected in parallel to lower their electrical resistance Despite the recent advances, Avouris asserts that nanotube FETs remain "far from optimized." Improvements could be made by using thinner insulators with higher dielectric constants, he suggests. "But what's really needed is a better understanding of the mechanism of electrical switching in nanotube FETs." Carbon nanotubes aren't the only game in town. Nanowires made of semiconductors such as silicon, gallium arsenide, and indium phosphide are being investigated as candidate materials for nanoelectronics. The field is advancing rapidly as researchers are making fast progress in synthesis, device fabrication, and testing.

Although Harvard University chemistry professor Charles M. Lieber has published widely on carbon nanotubes, semiconducting nanowires figure prominently into his research program. The tiny wires are versatile building blocks that can be used in a bottom-up approach to constructing nanoelectronic circuits, Lieber notes, because the size, structure, and functional properties of nanowires can be controlled readily via synthesis procedures. In 1998, Lieber and coworkers described a vapor-liquid-solid synthesis method in which laser light is used to ablate nanometer-sized metal clusters that serve as nucleation centers and catalysts for nanowire growth. The Harvard researchers used the technique to prepare uniform single-crystalline nanowires of silicon and germanium with diameters as small as 3 nm and lengths up to 30 mm. Since that time, the procedure has been used to prepare nanowires with even smaller diameters, and it's been extended to a wide variety of materials. Examples include III-V semiconductors such as GaAs and II-VI semiconductors such as ZnSe.

Recently, a number of research groups boosted the complexity of materials that can be prepared by the cluster-nucleation method. The teams prepared modulated structures—nanowires composed of dissimilar segments. The two-tone materials are made by turning the supplies of reactants on and off during synthesis with pulsed lasers or by other methods. These "heterostructured" products open the door to new sophisticated applications, such as terahertz-frequency photon emitters. Lieber, graduate student Mark S. Gudiksen, and coworkers used modulation methods to prepare nanowires with 21 alternating segments of GaAs and GaP. And they prepared Si and InP nanowires with modulated doping, such that the wires were endowed with alternating p- and n-type regions. Using similar methods, Peidong Yang, an assistant chemistry professor at the University of California, Berkeley, prepared Si-SiGe nanowires. And Lars Samuelson of Lund University, in Sweden, synthesized InAs-InP nanowires. To evaluate the usefulness of the tiny wires in nanoscale electronics, the Harvard researchers fashioned the wires into test circuits that were fabricated using lithography methods and then studied the circuits' electrical properties. According to Lieber, Si nanowire FETs, for example, perform remarkably well. The devices exhibit large on/off ratios (>10^5)—a requirement for effective switches—and charge-carrier mobilities that exceed those measured in conventional silicon devices.

In addition to constructing FETs from nanowires, Lieber's team has built and tested photodetectors, biological and chemical sensors, and more complex devices, including light-emitting diodes (LEDs) and logic gates. Most of the papers in which the results are reported were published in just the past 18 months. In the chemical sensing study, Lieber, graduate students Yi Cui and Qingqiao Wei, and Harvard assistant chemistry professor Hongkun Park found that by functionalizing boron-doped Si nanowires, they could prepare efficient sensors. Modifying the wires with an amino-silane compound, for example, produced pH sensors that are linear over a large dynamic range. And they observed that biotin-modified wires can be used to detect picomolar levels of streptavidin. In addition, the Harvard chemists found that the wires could be used to detect proteins reversibly in real time. By crossing an n-type and a p-type InP nanowire and then attaching electrodes to the wires lithographically, Lieber and coworkers made a nanometer-sized junction—at the point of overlap—that behaved as a current rectifier and an LED. Based on the study, Lieber says that more complex devices can be constructed from semiconducting nanowires simply by crossing them and forming tic-tac-toe patterns. But taking advantage of the crossed-nanowire idea requires developing a method for preparing the patterns efficiently and reproducibly. By combining surface patterning techniques and microfluidic alignment methods, the Harvard group developed the needed procedure. Their idea is to flow nanowires from a suspension into tiny parallel channels in a mold, in a layer-by-layer fashion, while rotating the mold orientation—and hence, nanowire flow direction—between layers. With the crossed-nanowire method for making p-n junctions firmly in hand, Lieber and coworkers were well on their way toward making computational logic circuits. Near the end of 2001, the group published a study in Science showing that their procedures could be used to make arrays of nanowire FETs configured as AND, OR, and NOR logic gates. Lieber stresses that in crossed-nanowire structures, such as the Harvard logic gates, the width and length of the FET channels are controlled by synthesis and assembly—not lithography—unlike today's microelectronic components.

These fabrication concepts make it possible "to envision a straightforward path to nanometer-scale electronics of the future," Lieber says. His vision, which is supported by experiments conducted by his group in the past several months, includes a nanoscale logic device known as a decoder that can address individual elements in crossed-wire arrays. Using a handful of molecules—or even just one of them—to make nanoscale switches or other devices is an idea that's gathered momentum in recent times. In 1999, researchers working with chemistry professors James R. Heath and J. Fraser Stoddart of the University of California, Los Angeles, demonstrated that simple circuits—fuses—could be made from a layer of rotaxane molecules. Then a team headed by Rice University chemistry professor James M. Tour and Yale University electrical engineer Mark A. Reed reported success in making reversible switches using benzene thiol molecules. Other groups have also been investigating the possibilities of single-molecule systems. For example, a team at UC Berkeley including Park (now at Harvard), Paul L. McEuen (now at Cornell), and A. Paul Alivisatos, trapped a single C_{60} molecule in a tiny gap between a pair of electrodes to study electronic conduction mechanisms. And just recently, a single molecule of a transition metal-organic complex—containing either one Co atom or two V atoms—was turned into a single-molecule transistor in independent studies by Park and McEuen.

Before molecular devices can be wired up and tested, organic chemists need to synthesize the molecules that drive them. In the UCLA collaboration, Stoddart's group prepares the compounds and Heath's group turns them into circuit components. To make the molecules switchable, Stoddart's group designs them so that one segment of a molecule can move (rotate or translate) relative to another segment. Stoddart notes that, contrary to remarks made by many researchers, the molecules are not difficult to prepare nowadays. But it took some years to build up the necessary expertise in molecular recognition concepts, p-donor/p-acceptor interactions, and other subjects. He adds that his group has synthesized "hundreds, if not thousands" of catenane and rotaxane analogs since 1989. In 2000, the UCLA team demonstrated a reusable switch based on a catenane—a molecule with a pair of interlocked rings. The switching state of the redox-active molecule was shown to change reversibly, depending on an applied potential. Electrostatic repulsion drives rotation of one ring relative to the other between open and closed states. Looking to improve device performance by tailoring the molecules, Jan O. Jeppesen, a visiting graduate student in Stoddart's lab, and postdoctoral associate Hsian-Rong Tseng prepared various rotaxane analogs of the catenane that brought success in 2000. The series of amphiphilic bistable rotaxanes are dumbbell-shaped molecules capped with large stoppers that are threaded through a cyclophane ring. As with the catenanes, the ring's position relative to the other piece of the molecule is controlled by redox interactions. Heath and coworkers constructed circuits with the new molecules using a layer-by-layer deposition method to fabricate tic-tac-toe structures with a few thousand molecules situated at each intersection. The team used this fabrication method to prepare 64-bit random-access memory circuits. And Hewlett-Packard Labs announced earlier this month that R. Stanley Williams, Yong Chen, and coworkers have also succeeded in using the UCLA rotaxane molecules to fabricate a 64-bit memory circuit. Only a few years ago, many scientists sat through molecular electronics presentations thinking that the far-fetched nanocomputing goals would never be reached. But the flurry of demonstration results in just the past two years appears to have decreased the number of nonbelievers. Yet some naysayers remain. Just recently, a California professor was furious about a C&EN story on molecular electronics and wrote to the editor, exclaiming, "In reality, there is no such topic!" The professor has a few surprises in store. In reality, molecular and nanoelectronics are bustling fields. Large numbers of commercial products may not be available in the near future, but as the vibrant research activity reveals, they're coming.

Nanoelectronic Devices

In this chapter we discuss about nanometer-scale, quantum effect alternatives to micron-scale, and bulk effect transistors in digital circuits. The status of R&D and recent important advances are reviewed briefly. For the past forty years, electronic computers have grown more powerful as their basic sub-unit, the transistor, has shrunk. However, the laws of quantum mechanics, plus the limitations of materials and fabrication techniques soon are likely to inhibit further reduction in the minimum size of today's bulk effect semiconductor transistors. Researchers have projected that as the overall size of the bulk-effect, semiconductor transistor is aggressively miniaturized to approximately 0.1 micron (i.e., 100 nanometers) and beyond, the devices may no longer function as well. Thus, in order to continue the miniaturization of integrated circuits well into the next century, it is likely that present day, micron-scale or microelectronic device designs will be replaced with new designs for devices that take advantage of the quantum mechanical effects that dominate on the much smaller, nanometer scale. (Note that 1 nanometer, abbreviated nm, is one billionth of a meter or 10 atomic diameters.)

Here we briefly survey such quantum effect, nanometer-scale alternatives to micron-scale, bulk-effect transistors for use in electronic digital circuits.

The topic of nanoelectronic devices subdivides into two broad areas, as follows:

- Solid-state quantum effect nanoelectronic devices.
- Molecular electronic devices.

Solid-state quantum-effect nanoelectronic devices are the nearer-term alternative for continuing to increase the density and speed of information processing. This technology, which changes the operating principles, but not the solid fabrication medium for integrated circuits, might extend Moore's Law of electronics miniaturization to produce devices down to 25 nm in length, beyond the domain of the bulk effect transistor. Present-day field effect transistors (FETs) on commercial integrated circuits are approximately 1 micron or 1000 nm across, and even the most optimistic proponents of aggressively miniaturized bulk effect FETs predict that they will cease to function effectively when their gate lengths dip below 25 nm, which corresponds to an overall device length of approximately 100 nm. By contrast, quantum effect switching devices tend to function better when they are made smaller. Solid-state quantum-effect nanoelectronic devices might be made as small as approximately 12 to 25 nanometers across and still function effectively if they could be fabricated reliably and uniformly on that scale. Presently, mass fabrication on this small scale does present a set of formidable challenges, no matter what the device design. However, a number of solid-state nanoelectronic switching devices have been fabricated and demonstrated, and prototype solid-state nanoelectronic processors already are operational, as well. Moreover, the drastic decrease in size that could result from the wide-scale introduction of such nanoelectronic devices might produce ultrafast, low power integrated circuits with as many as 100 billion or even 1 trillion switching devices on a single CPU chip, as well as Terabyte nonevanescent memories on a chip. Such great advances would require, however, the reliable, uniform mass fabrication of features only 5 to 10 nanometers wide in solids. This is at least twenty-five times as small as is achievable using UV lithography, the present industrial method of choice. More modest, near term goals do not require such extreme precision, but take advantage of other very desirable properties of solid-state quantum-effect devices, such as low power consumption and high speed.

As is indicated, there are 3 basic categories of solid-state nanoelectronic devices:

(1) Quantum Dots (or "artificial atoms")

(2) Resonant Tunneling Devices

(3) Single Electron Transistors (SETs)

Quantum Dots—A small "island" composed of semiconductor or metal in which electrons may be confined is the essential structural feature that all these quantum-effect, solid-state nanoelectronic devices have in common. The island in a nanoelectronic device assumes a role analogous to that of the channel that forms beneath the gate in a familiar microelectronic field-effect transistor when it is switched on. The composition, shape, and size of the island gives the different types of solid state nanoelectronic devices their distinct properties.

Controlling these factors permits the designer of the device to employ quantum effects in different ways to control the passage of electrons on to and off of the island.

Resonant-tunneling devices—Here, we focus primarily on explaining the operation of resonant tunneling devices, because they employ quantum effects in their simplest form. Presently, these devices usually are fabricated from layers of two different III/V semiconductor alloys, such as the pair GaAs and AlAs. The simplest type of resonant tunneling device is the resonant tunneling diode (RTD). A resonant-tunneling diode is made by placing two insulating barriers in a semiconductor, creating between them an island or potential well where electrons can reside. Resonant tunneling diodes are made with center islands approximately 10 nanometers in width. Whenever electrons are confined between two such closely spaced barriers, quantum mechanics restricts their energies to one of a finite number of discrete "quantized" levels. This energy quantization is the basis for the operation of the resonant-tunneling diode. The only way for electrons to pass through the device is to "tunnel," quantum mechanically, through the two barriers. The probability that the electrons can tunnel is dependent on the energy of the incoming electrons compared to the energy levels on the island of the device. If the energy of the incoming electrons differs from the energy levels allowed inside the potential well on the island, then current does not flow. The device is switched "off." However, when the energy of the incoming electrons aligns with that of one of the internal energy levels, as shown. By adding a small gate electrode over the island of an RTD one may construct a somewhat more complex resonant tunneling device called a resonant tunneling transistor (RTT). In this three-terminal configuration, a small gate voltage can control a large current across the device. Because a very small voltage to the gate can result in a relatively large current and voltage across the device, amplification or "gain" is achieved. Thus, an RTT can perform as both switch and amplifier, just like the conventional bulk effect transistor.

Unlike conventional bulk effect transistors which usually have only two switching states, "on" and "off," resonant tunneling devices like RTDs and RTTs can have several switching states. This occurs because the quantum well on the island may exhibit several possible energy levels.

Thus, as the voltage bias on an RTD is increased from zero, where it is "off," the device initially switches "on" when the first energy level comes in resonance with the incident electrons. Then, it switches off again as the bias is increased further, past resonance. However, if there is a second energy level in the quantum well, then the device can switch on again as the bias voltage of the RTD (or the gate voltage of an RTT) is increased still further. This multistate switching behavior permits each device to "count higher" and represent more logic states.

"Hybrid" Microelectronic—Nanoelectronic Resonant Tunneling Transistors—Purely nanometer-scale RTTs tend to be difficult to fabricate with sufficient uniformity in large quantities because of their relatively complex structure, small size, and the sensitivity of the effects they employ. However, there are also nanoelectronic devices which are "hybrids" of solid-state quantum-effect devices combined with micron-scale transistors. One such hybrid transistor-like device, the RTD-FET, is constructed by building tiny, nanometer-scale quantum-effect RTDs into the drain (or source) of a bulk effect micron-scale FET. A schematic of such a device.

Such a hybrid RTT can exhibit multistate switching behavior of the type described in the preceding section for purely nanometer-scale RTTs. For this reason, the hybrid device can represent more logic states than a pure bulk effect, microelectronic FET with the same "footprint" on the integrated circuit. Thus, the density of the logic can be increased using the multistate switching characteristics of hybrid micro-nanoelectronic RTTs, without appreciably increasing the density of the devices on an integrated circuit. Also, these hybrid RTTs share the advantages of low power and high speed exhibited by the purely nanoelectronic RTTs.

Most important, fabricating circuits with this relatively large, hybrid type of three-terminal RTT is easier than fabricating circuits with the much tinier, complex structures for purely nanoelectronic RTTs. For this reason a number of groups are experimenting with such devices. In recent months, robust prototype circuits based upon such hybrid devices have been demonstrated. Hybrid logic can be viewed as an important, practical engineering step on an evolutionary path toward nanoelectronics. It should accelerate the availability of quantum-effect devices in integrated circuits with very dense functionality.

Ultimately, however, it will be desirable to build ultra dense, low-power nanoelectronic circuits made from purely nanometer-scale switching devices and wires. Molecular electronics—using individual covalently bonded molecules to act as wires and switching devices—is the longer-term alternative for achieving this increase in density and for continuing Moore's Law down to the nanometer scale. Individual molecular switching devices could be as small as 1.5 nanometers across, with densities of approximately 1012 devices per sq. cm.

This decrease in size could result in Terabyte memories on a chip and in excess of one trillion switching-devices on a single CPU chip. A primary advantage of molecular electronics is that molecules are natural nanometer-scale structures that can be made absolutely identical in vast quantities (approximately 10^{23} at one time). Also, synthetic organic chemistry—the chemistry of carbon-based compounds—offers more options for designing and fabricating these intrinsically nanometer-scale devices than the technology presently available for producing solid-state chips with nanometer scale features. It has been shown during the past few years that small organic molecules can conduct and control electricity, that large organic bio-molecules are conductive, and that individual molecules of the newly discovered molecular forms of pure carbon called buckminsterfullerenes ("buckyballs" and "buckytubes") have interesting and useful electrical properties.

Great progress is being made in understanding and harnessing the electrical properties of individual organic molecules. There has been particular experimental progress in demonstrating that individual molecules can conduct electrical current to function as wires and that they also can act as switches to turn this current on and off. No logic circuits using these molecular switching devices have been fabricated yet. However, designs for such circuits have been proposed recently

To some extent, the research and development of molecular electronic switches is recapitulating that for the corresponding solid-state devices, except on a much smaller scale. Thus, it is not surprising, that molecular electronic switching proposals and prototypes may be categorized into molecular analogs of solid-state diodes and analogs for solid-state three-terminal FETs. A molecular analog of the solid state RTD that is discussed above is shown. The hexagonally shaped components are known as benzene "rings." Chains of these rings, such as appear at the right and left ends of the molecule in the figure have been shown to function as conductive "molecular wires". The "CH_2" groups (termed "methylene" groups), on the other hand, act as insulators or "barriers" to electron flow. They can trap electrons on the single benzene ring between them, which forms an island. This molecular sandwich-like structure, with the island in the middle, produces a potential energy well like that sketched at the bottom..

Despite enormous recent progress in the fabrication and demonstration of nanoelectronic devices, many challenges remain. For solid state nanoelectronics, one of the most important challenges is to be able to produce reliably and uniformly in silicon the characteristic nanometer-scale features required for nanoelectronics: nanometer-scale islands, barriers, and "heterojunctions" between islands and barriers. Up to now, solid state nanoelectronic devices largely have been fabricated in III/V semiconductor compounds such as gallium arsenide and aluminum arsenide. It is believed, however, that silicon nanoelectronics would go a long way toward permitting the inexpensive mass manufacture of nanoelectronic devices. For molecular electronics, one of the great challenges is to develop two-terminal and three-terminal devices than can be incorporated in circuits. Then, it must be demonstrated that such molecular switches can be used to make reliable logic, such as has been proposed recently. Using either the solid-state or the molecular electronic approach, in order to fulfill the promise of nanoelectronics it will be necessary to refine greatly both the fabrication techniques and the architectural concepts to permit the useful assembly of small, low-power computing structures that contain trillions of nanoelectronic switching devices.

Nanocomputers & Nanosystems

- "The most talked about technical book of the year." Bob Schwbach, United Press International.
- "With this book, Drexler has`established the field of molecular nanotechnology. The detailed analyses show quantum chemists and synthetic` chemists how`to build upon their knowledge of bonds and

molecules to develop the manufacturing systems of nanotechnlogy, and show physicists and engineers how to scale down their concepts of macroscopic systems to the level of molecules."

- William A. Goddard III, Professor of Chemistry and Applied Physicsl Director Materials and Molecular Simulation Center, California Institute of Technology.
- "Devices enormously smaller than before will remodel engineering, chemistry, medicine, and computer technology. How can we understand machines that are so small? *Nanosystems* covers it all: power and strength, friction and wear, thermal noise and quantum uncertainty. This is *the* book for starting the next century of engineering."
- Marvin Minsky, Professor of Electrical Engineering and Computer Science, Toshiba Professor of Media Arts'and Sciences, Massachusetts'Institute of Technology.
- "What the computer revolution did for manipulating data, the nanotechnology revolution will do for manipulating matterl juggling atoms like bits. This multidisciplinary synthesis opens the door to the new field of molecular manufacturing."
- Ralph C. Merkle, Member of Research Staff, Computational Nanotechnology Project, Xerox Palo Alto'Research Center.
- "This work provides the scientific and technological foundations for the emerging field of molecular systems engineering... It is essential for anyone contemplating research in this area...a milestone in the develpment of the technologies that will underpin the final industrial revolution." John Walker, Cofounder of Autodesk, Inc.
- "It is a scholarly examination of how this technology works, a reference book for the crafters of the future." Byte.
- "Demonstrates not only that nanotechnology is achievable, but shows how it will happen....takes readers from the fundamental physical principles to advanced designs for molecular components and systems." Japan Times | / STRONG>.
- Best Computer Science Book of 1992, Association of American Publishers.
- Over 10,000 copies in print.

Nanosystems was reviewed by James B. Lewis in The Journal of the American Chemical Society (JACSi Vol. 115, No. 24, December 1993, pages 11657-11658:

The goal of Drexler's investigations is "building complex structures with atom-by-atom control", which is`also the ultimate goal of synthetic chemistry. Drexler's approach is`distinguished from conventional chemistry in that complex structures are to be made by using programmable "nanoscale mechanical systems to guide the placement of reactive molecules" to about 0.1-nm precision. The objective of the book is to`present a theoretical foundation for "molecular manufacturing", which Drexler also`calls`"molecular nanotechnology". The objective is`*not* to`present a detailed review`of recent experimental progress in the many disciplines that converge on what is` being increasingly termed "nanotechnology". ....

Several alternative pathways from current technology to'molecular manufacturing are considered, at least briefly, guiding chemists and others toward a plethora of interesting problems'to pursue.

In this'volume, Drexler presents the technical analysis of molecular machinery and manufacturingn...It will probably see use in graduate studies and as'a reference work for many years.

Some quotes from the preface of *Nanosystems*:

Manufactured products are made from atoms, and their properties depend on how'those atoms are arranged. This volume summarizes 15 years of research in molecular manufacturingl the use of nanoscale mechanical systems to guide the placement of reactive molecules, building complex structures'with atom-by-atom control. This degree of control is'a natural goal for technology: Microtechnology strives to build smaller devices;'materials'science strives to make more useful solids{ chemistry strives to'synthesize more complex molecules;'manufacturing'strives to make better productsn Each of these fields' requires'precise, molecular control of complex structures to'reach its natural limit, a goal that has'been termed molecular nanotechnology.

It has become clear that this'degree of control can be achieved. The present volume assembles the conceptual and analytical tools needed to understand molecular machinery and manufacturing, presents an analysis of their core capabilities and explores'how'present laboratory techniques'can be extended, stage by stage, to implement molecular manufacturing systems.

A Debate About Assemblers

The September 2001 issue of *Scientific American* devoted six articles and a great deal of text to various perspectives on nanotechnology. The issue included various attacks on the feasibility of molecular assemblers and the work of K. Eric Drexler and his research associates.

Drexler's textbook *Nanosystems* was published in 1992. It is still being used as a technical reference all over the world, and to date no significant errors have been found. As the reader can well imagine, if there were any significant errors *Scientific American* would have pointed them out. They haven't. The technical claims and conclusions of *Nanosystems* have withstood almost a decade of serious public review.

Besides *Nanosystems*, there is now a very large body of technical articles, books, conferences, newsletters, and technical discussion groups that supports the feasibility of molecular machines in general and molecular assemblers in particular.

Two specific articles in the September *Scientific American* were attempts to cast doubt on the feasibility of nonbiological molecular assemblers.

In "Of Chemistry, Love and Nanobots" Nobelist Richard Smalley stated that: "Self-replicating, mechanical nanobots are simply not possible in our world". For an in depth analysis of where his technical argument falls short, see the article: "On Physics, Fundamentals, and Nanorobots: A Rebuttal to Smalley's Assertion that Self-Replicating Mechanical Nanorobots Are Simply Not Possible" at http://www.imm.org/SciAmDebate2/smalley.html.

George Whitesides, in "The Once and Future Nanomachine," expresses concerns about many issues that have been previously addressed in the literature. He stated: "Fabrication based on the assembler is not, in my opinion, a workable strategy and thus not a concern." For commentary and references, see the article: "Many Future Nanomachines: A Rebuttal to Whiteside's Assertion That Mechanical Molecular Assemblers Are Not Workable and Not A Concern" at http://www.imm.org/SciAmDebate2/whitesides.html.

While there are quite a few questionable statements in the rest of that issue, nowhere else is there a serious attempt to advance a technical argument against the feasibility of molecular nanotechnology.

How is it possible that an otherwise respectable publication would publish these attacks? None of their technical criticisms of molecular assemblers has withstood scrutiny — all have fallen by the wayside when it became obvious that they were incorrect. Some of the reasons are reviewed in "That's impossible! How good scientists reach bad conclusions"

Nanocomputer Technology Behind the Logo

In the magnifying glass on the logo for The Nanoelectronics and Nanocomputing Home Page we see a vision of nanoelectronics spreading throughout the world. Pervasive use of nanoelectronics is likely to transform human society in the next thirty years as much as have microelectronics over the last thirty. We have represented this vision by a "magnified" portion of a schematic diagram of a nanoelectronic full adder.

Such quantum dot cells have been proposed by Professors Craig Lent and Wolfgang Porod of the University of Notre Dame as a basis for future nanoelectronic computers.

Lent's and Porod's proposal for the use of quantum dot cells as a basis for nanoelectronic technology not only is highly original, but it is described in considerable detail in a series of technical articles that they have written. Professor Gary Bernstein, Director of the and his collaborators are based upon these quantum-effect nanoelectronic devices.

An icon and as a visual place marker throughout THE Nanoelectronics and Nanocomputing World-Wide Web site. For the same reasons, we have adopted a diagram of the Lent-Porod wireless logic as part of our logo.

Wireless Electronic Logic

On Tuesday, 16 May 1995, I attended a talk at MIT by Professor Craig Lent of Notre Dame. He spoke of a possible architecture for computer logic based on quantum dots. A quantum dot is a box that holds a discrete number of electrons. This number can be changed by adjusting electric fields in the neighborhood of the dot, for example by applying a voltage to a nearby metal gate. In the following, I will refer to quantum dots that have either zero or one electron in them. Since quantum dots are fabricated in solids, not in vacuum, of course there are many electrons in them. However, almost all of these are tightly bound to atoms in the solid. The few electrons that I will speak of are extra ones beyond those that are tightly bound. These extra electrons could roam free in a solid were they not confined in a quantum dot.

We arrange that two electrons reside in each cell. They may hop (tunnel) from dot to dot within the cell to find a favorable, low-energy configuration. Of course, because electrons are charged, they repel each other, so the two electrons will not both choose to sit in the same dot within the 4-dot cell. In fact, they will choose to occupy two opposite corners of the cell, since this gives them their maximum possible separation.

This is nice, because it gives us two possible "polarization" states for a cell, which we can associate with a binary zero and one. We can use a voltage on an external gate to force a cell into one of its two a priori equally good alternative states. This is a signal, analogous to a high or low voltage at a point within a conventional integrated circuit. A conventional integrated circuit uses two tools to transmit a voltage signal over long distances: an aluminum or silicon wire (to carry signals from place to place) and a transistor used as an amplifier (to refresh weakened signals so that they may travel farther without corruption). In the quantum dot circuits proposed by Lent, both of these tasks are accomplished simply by arranging as many cells as necessary in a row. If two cells are placed next to each other, and the polarization of first is fixed, the second will match its own polarization.

This, extended to a row of many cells, is the task normally carried out by a wire. In fact, even if the polarization of the first dot is between zero and one (the electrons are not fully localized on one diagonal), as more dots are added to the chain, the polarization of later dots will rapidly approach a perfect zero or one. This is the task of amplification or refreshing signals, the trademark of digital circuitry. Although I will not illustrate them, one can also build a corner, fan-out, or inverter (some of the building blocks of digital circuits). "Wires" carrying signals can even cross each other in the plane. So far, we could make a simple translation from objects in standard integrated circuits to objects in quantum dot circuits. However, the cornerstone of digital circuitry, logic gates, are not so simply translated into this new architecture. A standard logic gate has two inputs and an output determined by the inputs. For example, an AND gate puts out a high output only if both input. Here, inputs 1 and 2 vote together and hence determine the middle cell, which in turn determines the output. One can build any ordinary logic using these gates (most clumsily, one can make an OR gate by fixing input 3 to have polarization 1, an AND gate by forcing it to have polarization 0). More impressively, if the center-to-center distance between dots within a cell in 20 nm (extremely aggressive though not impossible with today's electron-beam lithography), a single bit full adder will fit in an area of 1 micron^2. By contrast, the semiconductor industry projects that in 2010 the maximum packing density for transistors will be approximately 1 micron^2. Forty transistors would be needed to build an adder! This dramatic difference in density is explained by two facts:

1. Much of the space in a conventional integrated circuit is taken up by wiring, which is unnecessary here.

2. The minimum feature size required to pack 1 transistor/ micron^2 would be 70 nm, and relative alignment between features produced in different lithographic steps generally needs to be good to 10% of this minimum feature size, or 7 nm. Only one stage of quantum dot manufacture need involve small features, so no sensitive alignment is required. This means that the minimum feature size could probably be made smaller than 70 nm even abandoning electron beams in favor of optical techniques favored by industry for their high throughput. In addition, the diameter of a single cell is only a few times the minimum feature size, as compared to 1 micron/70 nm which is approximately 14 times. In short, for given lithographic capabilities, quantum dot cells can be packed far more densely than can transistors.

Switching

Lent's quantum dot cells can be switched from one state to another adiabatically (reversibly). This is accomplished by lowering the barriers between dots within each cell, and removing the global inputs to the circuit, hence relaxing the polarization of each cell, then applying new global inputs and raising the barriers again. This produces very little heat, an important quality in densely integrated circuits (a DEC Alpha already has a fan mounted on top of it, continually blowing cold air on it so that it doesn't melt).

Readout

Readout could be accomplished by passing a current through a very narrow constriction near a corner of a cell. An electron in that corner of the cell could shut off current. This was demonstrated by Field et al.; PRL 70, 1311 ('93).

Drawbacks

This whole discussion has assumed that when new boundary conditions (inputs) are imposed, the system rapidly and reliably finds its ground (or lowest energy) state. This would not be true if the ambient temperature were comparable to the difference in energy between a "correct" and an "incorrect" polarization of a cell. For the quoted 20 nm dot-to-dot distance, this energy associated with an error in one cell's polarization would be 1 millielectron volt, or one twentieth of thermal energies (kT) at room temperature, so this is a major worry. Even if the error energy could be made many times larger, which could be accomplished by making the individual dots smaller and closer together, entropy would limit the size of an array of cells to about 20 thousand at error energy = 10 kT. Finally, no one knows how long an array of cells would take to reach its ground state, though Lent estimates 30 picoseconds per cell in a "wire".

Stray charges within 1 cell's length of a "wire" would lock a nearby cell permanently into one polarization state, stymieing computation. Charges are always sprinkled liberally on surfaces of semiconductors, so this would seem to be a major barrier to dense integration using this architecture. Perhaps most seriously, an attendee at the talk pointed out that the ground state of a large array may not be the obvious one determined by propagating signals "correctly" from inputs to outputs (though Lent has showed by modeling that his adder would not suffer from this problem).

Potential Nanoelectronic: Two-State Devices

Making much smaller, nanometer-scale electronic digital computers requires making nanometer-scale two-state devices—i.e., nanoswitches or nanotransistors with the two states ON and OFF or 1 and 0. These devices will be used to record and manipulate the bits (1s and 0s) on the nanometer scale. On this page are organized information and links that describe some of the technologies for nanoelectronic devices and mechanisms that have been proposed and investigated for that purpose.

Types of Nanometer-Scale 2-State Devices: Descriptions and Definitions

- Quantum Dot
- Quantum-Dot Cell
- Single-electron Transistors
- Molecular Quantum Dot (and Molecular-Scale Electronics)
- Resonance Tunneling Device
- "Hybrid" Microelectronic-Nanoelectronic Devices
- Atom Relay
- Refined Atom Relay
- Review of Conventional, *Micro*-scale Two-State Devices

Nanocomputers, Nanoelectronics and Nanosensors

In the broadest sense, nanodevices are the critical enablers that will allow mankind to exploit the ultimate technological capabilities of electronic, magnetic, mechanical, and biological systems. While the best examples of nanodevices at present are clearly associated with the information technology industry, the potential for such devices is much broader. Nanodevices will ultimately have an enormous impact on our ability to enhance energy conversion, control pollution, produce food, and improve human health and longevity.

In the past decade, our ability to manipulate matter from the top down, combined with advances and in some cases unexpected discoveries in the synthesis and assembly of nanometer-scale structures, has resulted in advances in a number of areas. Particularly striking examples include the following:

Current Scientific Advances: The unexpected discovery and subsequently more controlled preparation of carbon nanotubes and the use of proximal probe and lithographic schemes to fabricate individual electronic devices from these materials:

- The ability in only the last one or two years to begin to place carefully engineered individual molecules onto appropriate electrical contacts and measure transport through the molecules.
- The explosion in the availability of proximal probe techniques and their use to manipulate matter and thereby fabricate nanostructures.
- The development of chemical synthetic methods to prepare nanocrystals, and methods to further assemble these nanocrystals into a variety of larger organized structures.
- The introduction of biomolecules and supermolecular structures into the field of nanodevices.

- The isolation of biological motors, and their incorporation into nonbiological environments.

Current Technological Advances: A number of examples of devices in the microelectronics and telecommunications industries rely on nanometer-scale phenomena for their operation. These devices are, in a sense, "one-dimensional" nanotechnologies, because they are micrometer-scale objects that have thin film layers with thicknesses in the nanometer range. These kinds of systems are widely referred to in the physics and electronics literature as two-dimensional systems, because they have two classical or "normal" dimensions and one quantum or nanoscale dimension. In this scheme, nanowires are referred to as one-dimensional objects and quantum dots as zero-dimensional. In this document, and at the risk of introducing some confusion, we have chosen to categorize nanodevices by their main feature nanodimensions rather than by their large-scale dimensions. Thus, two dimensional systems such as two-dimensional electron gases and quantum wells in our notation are one-dimensional nanotechnologies, nanowires are two-dimensional nanotechnologies, and quantum dots are three-dimensional nanotechnologies. Examples include high electron mobility transistors, heterojunction bipolar transistors, resonant tunneling diodes, and quantum well optoelectronic devices such as lasers and detectors. The most recent success story in this category is that of giant magnetoresistance (GMR) structures. These structures can act as extremely sensitive magnetic field sensors. GMR structures used for this purpose consist of layers of magnetic and nonmagnetic metal films. The critical layers in this structure have thicknesses in the nanometer range. The transport of spin-polarized electrons that occurs between the magnetic layers on the nanometer length scale is responsible for the ability of the structure to sense magnetic fields such as the magnetic bits stored on computer disks. GMR structures are currently revolutionizing the hard disk drive magnetic storage industry worth $30-40 billion/year. Our ability to control materials in one dimension to build nanometer-scale structures with atomic scale precision comes from a decade of basic and applied research on thin film growth, surfaces, and interfaces. The extension from one nanodimension to two or three is not straightforward, but the payoffs can be enormous. Breakthroughs in attempting to produce three-dimensional nanodevices include the following:

- Demonstration of Coulomb blockade, quantum effect, and single electron memory and logic elements operating at room temperature.
- Integration of scanning probe tips into sizeable arrays for lithographic and mechanical information storage applications.
- Fabrication of photonic band-gap structures.
- Integration of nanoparticles into sensitive gas sensors.

In order to exploit nanometer-scale phenomena in devices, we must have a better understanding of the electronic, magnetic, and photonic interactions that occur on and are unique to this size scale. This will be achieved through experiment, theory, and modeling over the next decade. In addition, new methods to image and analyze devices and device components will be developed. These might include three-dimensional electron microscopies and improved atomic scale spectroscopic techniques. Over the same time period, we believe that it will become possible to integrate semiconductor, magnetic, and photonic nanodevices as well as molecular nanodevices into functional circuits and chips. The techniques now being developed in biotechnology will merge with those from nanoelectronics and nanodevices. Nanodevices will have biological components. Biological systems will be probed, measured, and controlled efficiently with nanoelectronic devices and nanoprobes and sensors. There will be significant progress in nanomechanical and nanobiomechanical systems, which will exhibit properties that are fundamentally different from their macroscopic counterparts.

There are important applications for instruments that will fly into space: nanocomponents are needed to achieve overall instrument sizes in the micron or millimeter range. Some of the same issues apply to battlefield sensors for situational awareness. Finally, a significant goal is the development of nanometer-scale objects that manipulate and perform work on other nanometer-scale objects, efficiently and economically achieving the same things we currently rely on scanning tunneling microscopy (STM) or atomic force microscopy (AFM) to carry out. A first step towards this goal might be the integration of nanometer-scale control electronics onto micromachines. In the information technology arena, nanodevices will both enable and require fundamentally new information processing architectures. Early examples of possible architectural paradigm shifts are quantum computation, quantum dot cellular automata, molecular electronics, and computation using DNA strands.

Such architectures will fundamentally change the types of information technology problems that can be attacked. Effective implementation of these types of architecture will require nanodevices. Other paradigm shifts include the emergence of quantized magnetic disks; single photonic systems that will allow efficient optical communication; nanomechanical systems; a broad class of structures and devices that merge biological and non-biological objects into interacting systems; and use of nanocomponents in the shrinking conventional circuit architectures. Research on nanodevices using nanoscale wiring and molecular logic, as well as new principles for devices such as spin electronics, have made significant inroads in the past year or two. The exploration and fabrication of nanodevices requires access to sophisticated and sometimes expensive tools. More and better access to such equipment as well as rapid prototyping facilities is needed. Of equal importance is the recognition that success in nanodevices will draw upon expertise from a broad range of traditional disciplines. Therefore, it is imperative that programs be established that facilitate and strengthen cross-fertilization among diverse disciplines and that allow rapid adoption of new methods across field boundaries. Nanodevices are in some ways the most complicated nanotechnological systems. They require the understanding of fundamental phenomena, the synthesis of appropriate materials, the use of those materials to fabricate functioning devices, and the integration of these devices into working systems. For this reason, success will require a substantial funding level over a long period of time. There is strong sentiment for single investigator funding as well as for structured support of interdisciplinary teams.

Organic Nanostructures: The Electrical Conductivity of a Single Molecule—By combining chemical self-assembly with a mechanical device that allows them to break a thin gold wire with nanometer scale control, researchers have succeeded in creating a "wire" consisting of a single molecule that can connect two gold leads. Using this structure, they have been able to begin to measure and study the electrical conductivity of a single molecule.

Molecular Electronics—If the reduction in size of electronic devices continues at its present exponential pace, the size of entire devices will approach that of molecules within a few decades. However, well before this happens, both the physics upon which electronic devices are based and the manufacturing procedures used to produce them will have to change dramatically. This is because current electronics are based primarily on classical mechanics, but at the scale of molecules, electrons are quantum mechanical objects. Also, the cost of building the factories for fabricating electronic devices, or fabs, is increasing at a rate that is much larger than the market for electronics; therefore, much less expensive manufacturing process will need to be invented.

Thus, an extremely important area of research is molecular electronics, for which molecules that are quantum electronic devices are designed and synthesized using the batch processes of chemistry and then assembled into useful circuits through the processes of self-organization and self-alignment. If molecular electronics achieves the ultimate goal of using individual molecules as switches and carbon nanotubes as the wires in circuits, we can anticipate nonvolatile memories with one million times the bit area density of today's DRAMs and power efficiency one billion times better than conventional CMOS circuitry. Such memories would be so large and power-efficient that they could change the way in which computation is performed from using processors to calculate on the fly to simply looking up the answer in huge tables. A major limitation of any such process is that chemically fabricated and assembled systems will necessarily contain defective components and connections. By describing a silicon-based computer that was designed to operate perfectly in the presence of huge numbers of manufacturing defects, researchers from Hewlett-Packard (HP) and the University of California–Los Angeles (UCLA) presented an architectural solution to the problem of defects in molecular electronics, as described. In 1999, researchers from HP Labs and UCLA experimentally demonstrated the most crucial aspect for such a system, an electronically addressable molecular switch that operates in a totally "dry" environment. Logic gates were fabricated from an array of configurable molecular switches, each consisting of a monolayer of electrochemically active rotaxane molecules sandwiched between metal electrodes. The operation of the switches. In the "closed" state, current flow is dominated by resonant tunneling through the electronic states of the molecules. The switches are irreversibly opened by applying an oxidizing voltage across the device. In this case, since the memory of the molecules is not volatile, only one set of wires is needed to set and read the state of the molecules, and in principle, one molecule can replace seven transistors in a conventional silicon circuit. In the demonstration, several devices were configured together to produce AND and OR logic gates. The high/low current levels of those gates were separated by factors of 15 and 30, respectively, which is a significant enhancement over that for conventional wired-logic gates.

Molecular Logic: Electron transport studies in molecular-scale systems have recently become possible with the utilization of advanced microfabrication and self-assembly techniques. Investigations are now possible of the electronic conduction through conjugated molecules that are end-bound onto surfaces; these have been demonstrated with a scanning tunneling microscope, with micromachined silicon nanopores, and with proximal probes. Work on the proximal probes demonstrated that 0.1 microamp of current can be transported through a single molecule. However, in all of the past embodiments, the electronic properties exhibit simple diodic behavior that is unsuitable for potential circuit applications. Researchers recently observed the first large and useful reversible switching behavior in an electronic device that utilizes molecules as the active component. The essential feature of the fabrication process is the employment of nanoscale device area that gives rise to a small number of self-assembled molecules (ca. 1,000), which eliminates pinhole and other defect mechanisms that hamper through-monolayer electronic transport measurements. This technique has demonstrated good control over the device area and intrinsic contact stability and produces a large number of devices with acceptable yield so that statistically significant results can be produced The active electronic component was made from an organic compound upon exposure to Au. The I-V is fully reversible upon change in bias sweep direction. This is the first observation of robust and large negative differential resistance (NDR) in a device where molecules form the active region with peak-to-valley-ratios (PVRs); and the PVRs here are >1000:1. The performance exceeds that observed in typical solid state quantum well resonant tunneling heterostructures. Therefore, in addition to the obvious size advantages for scaling, the intrinsic device characteristics (i.e., valley current shutoff) may be superior to solid state embodiments; present silicon devices rarely exceed PVRs of 100:1.

A Field-Effect Transistor Made from a Single-Wall Carbon Nanotube: Several research groups around the world have succeeded in fabricating electrical switches such as the field-effect transistor from single-walled carbon nanotubes. A single-walled carbon nanotube 1.6 nm in diameter was manipulated into place using an atomic force microscope. Once placed on the metal contacts, the semiconducting tube behaved like the channel in a field-effect transistor, turning on or off depending on the applied gate voltage. Nanotubes hold great promise as electronic elements for a variety of different nanostructures. Researchers are just beginning to understand how they conduct electricity and how to place them into appropriate device structures. It is interesting to note that both the atomic force microscope used to fabricate this structure and the carbon nanotubes that form the critical element were developed only in the past decade.

A Commercial IBM Giant Magnetoresistance Read Head: When certain kinds of materials systems are exposed to a magnetic field, their electrical resistance changes. This effect, called the magnetoresistive effect, is useful for sensing magnetic fields such as those in the magnetic bits of data stored on a computer hard drive. In 1988, the giant magnetoresistance effect was discovered in specially prepared layers of nanometer-thick magnetic and nonmagnetic films. By 1991, work at the IBM Almaden Research Center demonstrated that the GMR effect could be observed in easily made samples and that a special kind of GMR structure, a spin valve, could sense very small magnetic fields. This opened the door to the use of GMR in the read heads for magnetic disk drives. IBM first announced a commercial product based on this design in December 1997.

Nanoelectronics offers a broad set of opportunities by focusing on quantum devices and addressing their potential for high performance through increases in density (factors of 5 to 100), speed (factors of 10 to 100), and reduced power (factors of more than 50). Resonant tunneling devices are being explored with demonstrated successes in multivalued logic and various logic circuits and memory circuits. SET logic and memory concepts are being explored with focus on memory applications. Molecular electronics and self-assembly approaches have shown a path towards manufacturing alternatives and device options for regimes beyond traditional scaling. Spin devices in the form of nanomagnetics using the magnetoresistive effect in magnetic multilayers have demonstrated their use for nonvolatile, radiation-hard memory. Quantum cellular automata and coupled quantum dot technology are being explored and their potential assessed for transistorless computing. By exploring Si-based heterojunctions, bandgap engineering, vertical device structures, and quantum devices, inroads are being made into extending CMOS capabilities. Potential applications are in digital radar, electronic support measures (ESM) receivers, ATM data stream processing, wide bandwidth communications, digital image processing, waveform generation, and the broad area of analog to digital (A/D) applications. Demonstrations have shown the efficacy of resonant tunneling devices in various network environments. The long-term vision for nanoelectronics sees the use of quantum devices in other high performance systems especially in telecommunications for signal processors and electronics for A/D converters in detectors.

After more than three decades of exploring space, the National Aeronautics and Space Administration (NASA) has completed an initial reconnaissance of our solar system. The next missions will involve sending spacecraft to destinations that are much more difficult to travel to, like the Sun or Pluto. Also, spacecraft will be required to perform more difficult tasks, such as landing on a celestial body, collecting a sample of its material, and returning it to Earth. To carry out such technically challenging missions at an affordable cost, NASA has created the Deep Space Systems Technology Program, known as X2000. Every two to three years starting in the year 2000, the program will develop and deliver advanced spacecraft systems and body structures to missions bound for different areas of the solar system and beyond. In order to achieve reduction in the size of spacecraft, the avionics systems of the spacecraft are being reduced in size with each delivery of X2000, in part by means of integrating nanotechnology with microtechnology. The forecasts of the mass, volume, and power of future avionics systems of spacecraft. The leftmost column shows the Mars Pathfinder spacecraft, which represents the current state of the art. The first delivery for X2000 is an integrated avionics system that subsumes the functionalities of command and data handling, attitude control, power management and distribution, and science payload interface. Advanced packaging technologies as well as advanced design automation techniques are used to define a highly integrated, modular, building-block architecture for highly reliable and long-term survivable deep-space planetary missions. Advanced low-power techniques and architectures will drastically reduce overall power consumption compared to currently available flight hardware. "System On A Chip" (SOAC) will prototype single chip and multichip module solutions that lead towards an avionics system on a chip. This chip will integrate the avionics system that is being developed for the X2000 avionics deliverable. That is, the chip will include power management, sensor technology, and telecommunications modules, together with CPU and storage technology. To accomplish this, nanotechnology will be needed to miniaturize and integrate the different subsystems.

The goal for the year 2020 is to establish and maintain a world-class program to research revolutionary computing technologies (RCT) that will not only take us beyond the limits of semiconductor technology scaling but also will enable the vision of a "thinking spacecraft." A thinking spacecraft would be a totally autonomous, highly integrated, extremely capable spacecraft that operates at ultralow power. To achieve this goal, without a doubt, we need to employ nanoscience. In spite of the phenomenal advances in digital computing in recent years and those expected in the near future, even future supercomputers cannot compete with biological systems in performing certain ill-defined tasks such as pattern recognition, sensor fusion, fault-tolerant control, and adaptation to the environment.

— *Quantum computing*, that is, a joint venture between computer science and quantum physics. Although, the concept of a quantum computer is simple, its realization is not. Two issues motivate quantum computing:

- Quantum mechanical concepts must be applied to solve intractable (NP-complete) computing problems.
- From a computer miniaturization point of view, the size limit of a bit of information is important. Recently, this issue has attracted increased attention, due to the current development of nanotechnology and the design problems of semiconductor and metal devices that are approaching the quantum size limit. Consequently, the idea of quantum computing, in which the elements that carry the information are atoms, has attracted the attention of many scientists.

— *Biomimetics*, that is, systems or technologies inspired by architectures, functions, mechanisms, and principles found in biological systems, for example:

- One gram of DNA could possibly store all the data in the Library of Congress.
- The human brain contains about 1014 interconnects and operates at 1016 operations per second, using ultra low power and imprecise computing elements.
- Humans are endowed with an immune system that provides recovery from illness—a "self-repair system".

As devices become smaller, lighter, and consume less power, NASA will be able to design and fly space probes on missions that are not currently possible.

A Biological Nanodevice for Drug Delivery: The nanobiological anticancer agent PK1 exploits the enhanced permeability and retention (EPR) effect associated with disease tissues with low integrity vasculature in order to deliver cytotoxin (doxorubicin) to tumors. The synthetic backbone of PKI (N-2-(hydroxypropyl) methacrylimide or HPMA) gives the complex a size (diameter in the mid-nanometer range) that makes it unable to extravasate efficiently into healthy tissues with normal vasculature. Tumor vasculature is abnormally permeable, allowing preferential accumulation of PK1 in tumor tissue. HPMA-bound doxorubicin is non-toxic, limiting toxicity to healthy tissue, and active doxorubicin is released from the complex preferentially in tumor tissues. The labile peptidic linker tethering doxorubicin to HPMA was selected because it is the substrate for a protease known to be over-expressed in the target tumor types. PK1 increases the tolerated doxorubicin dose by more than an order of magnitude by virtue of EPR-based targeting and its engineered tumor-preferred doxorubicin release properties. It is in human clinical trial in Europe. Contemplated embellishments to this and similar polymer therapeutics include use of monodisperse nanopolymers (dendritic polymers) to enhance control of EPR properties, incorporation of protein docking domains that recognize tumor associated antigens to tether the complex following its delivery to the tumor, and incorporation of additional antitumor agents thought to have synergistic effects with cytotoxins, that is, angiostatic agents, among others.

Nanotechnology on a Chip: A New Paradigm for Total Chemical Analysis Systems, the ability to make chemical and biological information much cheaper and easier to obtain is expected to fundamentally change healthcare, food safety, law enforcement, national security, and many other areas of direct interest to the American public. The vision of broadly available chemical analysis is fueling an international effort to develop "mChemLabTM-on-a-chip" technology. Micro-total analysis systems (m-TAS, as they are often referred to) are distinguished from simple sensors because they conduct a complete analysis; a raw mixture of chemicals goes in and an answer comes out. Sandia National Laboratories is developing a hand-held mChemLabTM demonstrator that will analyze for air-born chemical warfare agents and liquid-based explosives agents. The mChemLabTM development project brings together an interdisciplinary team of about 50 staff members from throughout the laboratory in areas of expertise including microfabrication, chemical sensing, microfluidics, and information sciences. Although nanotechnology plays an important role in current mTAS efforts, most mTAS approaches use miniaturized versions of conventional architecture and components to achieve system tasks. Small valves, pipes, pumps, separation columns, etc. are patterned after their macroscopic counterparts. Even though we are finding that these miniaturized components can work as well as (and sometimes better than) their macroscopic analogs, they simply will not allow for the vision of chemical laboratories in a grain of sand. Nanotechnology will enable a completely new architecture, or nano-TAS. The ability to build materials with switchable molecular functions could provide completely new approaches to valves, pumps, chemical separations, and detection. For example, fluid streams could be directed by controlling surface energy without the need for a predetermined architecture of physical channels. Switchable molecular membranes and the like could replace mechanical valves. By eliminating the need for complex fluidic networks and micro-scale components used in current m-TAS efforts, nano-TAS is a fundamentally new approach to allow greater function in much smaller, lower power total chemical analysis systems.

The Development of Useful Nanotech Robotic Systems: It is potentially feasible to manufacture nanorobots that are capable of sophisticated symmetric behaviors, either through independent function or by assembling themselves into collective units. Imagine, for example, high-resolution video screens that can repair themselves simply by having a microscopic robot at each screen element. These "pixelbots" would be capable of producing light, but also be smart enough to remove themselves from the video array should they ever fail. Other pixelbots would sense the vacancy left by any defective device and reorganize themselves to fill the hole. Another example is the incorporation of autonomous "nurse" robots into the human body that are chemically benign but are capable enough to remove cancer cells at the source. Having the ability to discriminate between healthy and cancerous cells, the "nurse-bots" would function independently to continuously heal tissue in ways beyond the current ability of the human body. The same notion can be implemented in self-optimizing silicon memories or processors, where a blown transistor would mean one just had to wait for the computer to heal itself.

One key to establishing such capabilities is research into autonomous self-assembled systems. Researchers at Los Alamos National Laboratory are exploring these systems by creating very inexpensive macro-scale robots. These sense and adapt to their environment, including assimilating other robots to execute such tasks as searching for and marking the location of unexploded land mines. The capabilities of these intelligent cellular systems are readily scaled, providing untapped possibilities for large numbers of inexpensive nano-machines to become microscopic building blocks for heretofore unimaginable functions—a form of "nano-Lego" for the new millennium with novel, untapped market potential.

Integrated Nanotechnology in Microsystems: Advances in nanotechnology will have a profound effect on the future of integrated microsystems. The integration of microelectronic, microelectromechanical, optical, and chemical microsensors into "systems on a chip" is an area that may involve mechanical, optical, and/or chemical functions as well. These advances will make possible miniaturized systems that sense, think, talk (communicate), and act. However, these microscale systems will only become a reality if enabled by the control of performance at the nanoscale. Thus, for example, advances in microelectromechanical systems (MEMS) and photonics shown in the figure depend on discoveries in nanoscience and nanoscale fabrication.

Economic Analysis of Nanoelectronics

The prospective affordability of any future nanotechnology is a key consideration in attempting to understand its practicality. Thus, one task in the MITRE Nanosystems Modeling and Nanoelectronic Computers research project has been an effort to initiate a prospective economic analysis of nanoelectronics. The initial objective of the Economic Analysis Task was to develop and to explain an approach to a prospective cost-benefit analysis (CBA) for nanoelectronics. As a basis for this effort, the members of the MITRE Nanosystems Group began to assess the past and current expenditures/

costs for nanoelectronics research and a development (R&D) in order to make projections of anticipated future costs. While an actual CBA has not yet been conducted, several methods and approaches to such an analysis were identified. In addition to approaches to conducting a CBA, methods for estimation of R&D costs of advanced technologies such as nanoelectronics, were identified. They include:

- Evaluation of R&D investments in electronics industries.
- Use the Cost Estimation Relationships developed at RAND.
- Extend two different cost curves for microelectronics (developed by MITRE and RAND)
- Evaluate cost, benefits, and possibilities for next generation parallel computing hardware.
- Modify cost estimation technique for state-of-the-art technologies.

The project team determined that the first two of these were most applicable to assessing the potential costs of nanoelectronics. Task Leader Michael D. Smith has continued the research for this economic analysis of nanoelectronics in his Masters' Thesis, "Estimation of Future Manufacturing Costs for Nanoelectronics," which he completed in May 1996 in the Department of Industrial Engineering at the Virginia Polytechnic Institute and State University in Blacksburg, VA. Michael D. Smith's thesis has been made available on the World-Wide Web by the Virginia Polytechnic Institute.

We firmly believe that the converging fields of nanotechnology, evolutionary computing, and pervasive networking together represent both the greatest opportunity and threat for our universe. We think that the safest and best way forward as these fields merge is to provide a virtual environment for self-replicating machines running evolving software to be tested, evaluated and even farmed. This is no trivial task. If we are to avoid the so called 'gray goo' problem, and at the same time harness the power of natural selection, we must find ways of containing self-replicators while the possibility of their 'going postal' exists. To this end, we will be deploying a massively parallel supercomputer based on the "generic workers around a shared jobs bag" pattern. It provides a very simple structure for the distributed comutation of all manner of scenarios. We seek the following intersectable sets of collaborators: To register your interest, please provide your email address and indicate the nature of your interest using the checkboxes below.

- Helpers—People willing to run services of the distributed computing platform on their computers for some, if not all day. You should have installed Java1.2 or better. Mac Users note Java1.2 will not be available until the release of MacOS X. We will make available a a suite of Jini Services as a single installer and simple launch interface.

- Developers—Java programmers familiar with CVS and other Open Source tools for distributed development who are keen to write simulation scenarios, simulation components and various utilities, visualisation tools, high level editors and user interfaces. We will provide a simple upload utility for adding new simulations to the network.
- Gardeners—Bringing up healthy, usefull nanotechology simulation is a lot like gardening. The gardens will need constant weeding, and the more people willing to keep an occasional eye on a crop of networked nanobots the better. We will provide simple browser utilities enabling you to provide critical feedback to active simulations.
- Writers—Like any community, we want to be social, and we want to make sure that everyone who is interested can get the most out of the efforts of the community. We want commentators to comment, critics to critique, and writers to write. By imagining the future, we can help ward off many disasters without even having to simulate them. Speculative fiction is simulation.
- Visual Artists—Visual representations of possible scenarios, "an artist's impression", if you can draw, paint or 3d render we need your help. First up we need a logo which simply illustrates both the collective and the various aspects of the gRobots project.

gRobots Project

We are 4 private individuals who have come together to kick start the gRobots project. It is our intention to establish a not-for-profit company structure along the lines of the Foresight Institute. In the meantime we are not a legally incorporated body, but an ensemble of impassioned professionals. We are not soliciting funds of any kind.

- Dave Sag

  Dave has been writing and programming on the themes of Artificial Life and Nanotechnology for almost 20 years. He is a Senior Associate of the Foresight Institute and Director/Equity partner in a diverse range of commercial and non-commercial online projects. He is internationally regarded as an artist, programmer, business person and portable whole.

- David (DayV) Parry.

  In 1984 DayV owned the only copy of Mandelbrot's "the fractal geometry of nature" in Australia. He has been obsessed with self replicating forms, evolutionary comupting and nanotechnolgy almost as a consequence of his earlier obsessions with electronic music and mathematics. He is most recently the author of a handy tutorial on XSP Logic sheets. He is a member of the Eurpoean Technology Forum, and God Emperor King of the virtual nation of Suran.

- Dr Phillip Blythe

  Phil is an interdisciplinary scientist, with fingers in many different research pies. Originally an aeronautical engineer, He has since conducted research in adaptive computation, control theory, cognitive psychology, and economics. There have been three central themes that have remained with him through each of these various research projects; evolution, dynamic systems and decision making. He was recently a visiting professor to the Centre for Adaptive Behaviour at the Max Planck Institute for Human Development.

- Anthony Aldridge

  Tony is a musician, inventor, programmer and all round chaos junkie. He's worked on virtual interfaces for the blind, recorded servral albums and for a while ran the UK's largest music technology department at University of London. He is also a specialist software security expert and quite a dab hand at opening a beer bottle with a cigarette lighter.

Links of relevance

- Google's Nanotechnology Directory - http://directory.google.com/Top/Science/Technology/Nanotechnology/
- Why the future doesn't need us by Bill Joy - http://www.wired.com/wired/archive/8.04/joy_pr.html
- Why the future needs Bill Joy - http://www.atoma.f2s.com/BillJoyWhyCrit.htm
- Jini(tm) Pervasive Networking - http://www.jini.org/ and http://www.sun.com/jini/
- nanoCAD in Java - http://world.std.com/~wware/ncad.html
- Nanodot - http://www.nanodot.org/
- Atoma - http://www.atoma.f2s.com/index.html
- The Foresight Institute - http://www.foresight.org/
- Nanodot - http://nanodot.org/
- Nanotechnology and the Commons - http://www.cm.ksc.co.th/~bruns/opennan2.htm
- Open Source - http://www.opensource.org/
- Zyvex - http://www.zyvex.com/

- Colin's guide to Evolutionary Computing - http://www.cs.bris.ac.uk/~colin/evollect1/evollect0/index.htm
- The Genetic Algotithms Archive, Dissertations on Evolutionary Computing - http://www.aic.nrl.navy.mil/galist/dissert.html
- The GA Achive, source code collection (java) - http://www.aic.nrl.navy.mil/galist/src/#java and of course the GA Archive - http://www.aic.nrl.navy.mil/galist
- Some Limits to Global Ecophagy by Biovorous Nanoreplicators, with Public Policy Recommendations

Regarding the possible ecological risks of nanotech, the first quantitative technical analysis of Drexler's "gray goo" scenario, in part as an answer to Bill Joy's recent concerns.

Nanodot: Nanotechnology Weblog

"In the next five to 10 years, mobile phone users will be able to detect changes in the facial expressions and even in the smell of the person they are talking to, according to Jeong Kim, president of Bell Labs, the research arm of the U.S. firm Lucent Technololgies.

"As part of a five-day business trip here, Mr. Kim met with reporters in southern Seoul yesterday to introduce cutting-edge future technologies and offer predictions on the world's information-technology industry.

"Elaborating on the new cell phone technology developed by the laboratory, Mr. Kim said that smell-transmitting sensors, lenses that follow the movement of eyeballs and microphones as narrow as a human hair already exist, and would be on sale within a decade.

"Mr. Kim said nanotechnology — techniques used to create structures as small as one-millionth of a millimeter — had played a key role in the development of the new technologies.

"Mr. Kim predicted that nanotechnology could bring huge changes to the way humans live, citing the example of a new computer that will enable simultaneous translation of telephone conversations.

" 'If nanotechnology maintains its current pace of development, it will give birth to a computer that has the information processing capacity equivalent to every human brain combined by 2060,' he said.

"Mr. Kim said that while communication technologies have so far mostly focused on speed, future developments will look to improve their convenience. Eventually, he added, phones will no longer need to be touched or even spoken to, but will instead respond to mental commands."

REFERENCES

Barber, Benjamin. 1996. *Jihad vs. McWorld: How Globalism and Tribalism are Reshaping the World* (New York: Ballantine Books).

Bijker, W. E. *Of Bicycles, Bakelites, and Bulbs: Toward a Theory of Sociotechnical Change.* Cambridge, MA: MIT Press, 1995.

Blumenthal, D.M., M. Gluck, K.S. Louis, M. Stoto, and D. Wise. 1986. "University-Industry Research Relationships in Biotechnology: Implications for the University," *Science* 232: pp. 1361-1366 (June 13).

Brave, Ralph. 2000. "Genome Hell is Revealed in Many Forms." *Baltimore Sun*, July 2, p. 1C.

Brown, J. S. and Duguid, P. Don't Count Society Out: A Response to Bill Joy. Paper prepared for the Societal Implications of Nanotechnology Conference, 2000.

Bruchez, M.; Moronne, M.; Gin, P.; Weiss, S.; Alivisatos, A.P. 1998. "Semiconductor nanocrystals as fluorescent biological labels", *Science*, 281, 2013-2016.

Casey, Jr., H.C., and M.B. Panish. 1978. *Heterostructure Lasers, Part A: Fundamental Principles*. (Academic Press. New York). pp. 1-9.

Cerf, Christopher, and Victor Navasky. 1984. *The Experts Speak*. New York: Pantheon Books.

Christensen, Clayton M. *The Innovator's Dilemma: When New Technologies Cause Great Firms to Fail*. New York: Harperbusiness, 2000.

Cipra, Barry A. 2000. The best of the 20th century: editors name top 10 algorithms. *SIAM News*. vol. 33(4).

Cook, T. K. and Campbell, D. T. *Quasi-Experimentation*. Rand-McNally, 1979 Fischer, C. S. *America Calling: A Social History of the Telephone to 1940*. Berkeley: U. of California, 1992.

Csicsery-Ronay, I. Jr.: 1991, 'The SF of Theory: Baudrillard and Haraway', *Science Fiction Studies*, 18, 387-404.

David, Paul. 1991. "Computer and Dynamo: The Modern Productivity Paradox in a Not-too-Distant Mirror," *Technology and Productivity: The Challenge for Economic Policy* (Paris: OECD).

DeSimone, J.M., E.T. Samulski, et al. 2000. Critical micelle density for the self-assembly of block copolymer surfactants in supercritical carbon dioxide. *Langmuir*. Vol.16. 416-421.

Di Paolo, E. A., *Artificial Life Bibliography of On-line Publications*, June 28, 2000.

Doering, Robert and Yoshio Nishi. 2000. "Limits of Integrated-Circuit Manufacturing." *Proceedings of the IEEE*. September.

Doi, M. and S.F. Edwards. 1986. *The Theory of Polymer Dynamics*. Oxford University Press (Clarendon), London-New York.

Donald, A.M. and A.H. Windle. 1992. Liquid crystalline polymers. *Cambridge Solid State Science Series*. Cambridge University Press.

Drell, S. D., A. D. Sofaaer, and G. D. Wilson, Hoover Digest 2000, No. 1, *The Present Threat*.

Dym, H. and H.P. McKean,. 1972. *Fourier Series and Integrals.* Academic Press.

Elkins, C.: 1979, 'Science Fiction versus Futurology: Dramatic Versus Rational Models', *Science Fiction Studies*, 6, 20-31.

Ellul, J. 1964. *The Technological Society*. New York: Alfred Knopf. (First published 1954).

Empedocles, S.; Bawendi, M. 1999. "Spectroscopy of single CdSe nanocrystallites," *Accounts of Chemical Research*, 32, 389-396.

Etzkowitz, H., M. Gulbrandsen and J. Levitt. 2000. *Public Venture Capital: Government Funding Sources for Technology Entrepreneurs*. New York: Harcourt.

Evans, J.H.: 2002, *Playing God? Human Genetic Engineering and the Rationalization of Public Bioethical Debate*, Chicago University Press, Chicago.

Fantel, Hans. 1987. "Portable CD Players Advance." *New York Times*, May 17, Section 2, p. 33, col. 1.

Fermi, E., J. Pasta, and S. Ulam. 1974. Studies of nonlinear problems, I. *Los Alamos Report*. LA1940. 1955.

Feynman, R.P. 1961. "There is plenty of room at the bottom." In *Miniaturization*. New York: Reinhold.

Fisher, D. E. and Fisher, M. J. *Tube: The Invention of Television*. Harcourt Brace, 1997.

FitzGerald, Frances. 2000. *Way Out There in the Blue: Reagan, Star Wars, and the End of the Cold War*. New York: Simon & Schuster.

Fogelberg, H.: 2003, '"Science" and "Technology" as Knowledge Cultures', in: H. Fogelberg, H. Glimell, *Bringing Visibility to the Invisible: Towards a Social Understanding of Nanotechnology*, Göteborg University, Göteborg, pp. 77-85.

Fogelberg, H.; Glimell, H.: 2003, *Bringing Visibility to the Invisible: Towards a Social Understanding of Nanotechnology*, Göteborg University, Göteborg.

Forest, G. 2000. Comment at Conference on Societal Implications of Nanoscience and Nanotechnology, September 29, 2000, NSF, Arlington, VA.

Forest, M.G., Q. Wang, and H. Zhou. 2000b. Homogeneous pattern selection and director instabilities of nematic liquid crystal polymers induced by elongational flows. *Physics of Fluids*. Vol. 12(3). 490-498.

Forum Proceedings of Sigma Xi, the Scientific Research Society, *Ethics, Values, and the Promise of Science*, Feb. 25-26, 1993.

Foucault, M. 1977. *Power/Knowledge: Selected Interviews and Other Writings 1972-1977*. New York, Pantheon Books.

Foucault, M.: 1992, *The Archaeology of Knowledge*, Routledge, London.

Fourier, J. 1878. *The Analytical Theory of Heat*. translated by A. Freeman. Cambridge University Press. London and New York.

Franklin, N.R.; Dai, H.J. 2000. "An enhanced CVD approach to extensive nanotube networks with directionality", *Advanced Materials*, 12, 890-894.

Frenken, J.W.M. 1998. "Scanning Tunneling Microscopy", section 5.2, A. ten Wolde (ed.), *Nanotechnology: Towards a molecular construction kit*. STT Report #60, The Hague, 289-299.

Gates, B.; Park, S.H.; Xia, Y.N. 2000. "Tuning the photonic bandgap properties of crystalline arrays of polystyrene beads by annealing at elevated temperatures", *Advanced Materials*, 12, 653-656.

Geneva Convention, *Protocol for the Prohibition of the Use in War of Asphyxiating, Poisonous or Other Gases, and of Bacteriological Methods of Warfare*, signed at Geneva on June 17,1925.

Gergen, K. J. Social psychology as history. *Journal of Personality and Social Psychology*, 1973, 26, 309- 20.

Gerlach, N.; Hamilton, S.: 2000, 'Telling the Future, Managing the Present: Business Restructuring Literature as SF', *Science Fiction Studies*, 27, 461-477.

Gieryn, T.: 1999, *Cultural Boundaries of Science*, Univ. of Chicago Press, Chicago.

Goldbeck-Wood, G. and A.H. Windle. 1999. Lattice modeling of nematodynamics. *Rheol. Acta*. Vol. 38. 548-561.

Graham, P.: 2002, 'Hypercapitalism: Language, New Media and Social Perceptions of Value', *Discourse and Society*, 13(2), 227-249.

Grosberg, A.Y. and A.R. Khokhlov. 1994. *Statistical Physics of Macromolecules*, AIP Series in Polymers and Complex Materials, AIP Press, New York.

Gubrud, M. A., *Nanotechnology and International Security*, Fifth Foresight Conference on Molecular Nanotechnology, November 5-8, 1997. Ref: http://www.foresight.org/Conferences/MNT05/Papers/Gubrud/.

Gurley, Bill. 2000. Digital music: the real law is Moore's law. *Fortune*. 2 October. page 268. Joy, Bill. 2000. Why the future doesn't need us. *Wired*. April. pp. 238 - 262.

Hayes, B., "The Square Root of NOT," *American Scientist*, July-August 1995, pp. 304-308.

Hayward, R.C.; Saville, D. A.; Aksay, I.A. 2000. "Electrophoretic assembly of colloidal crystals with optically tunable micropatterns", *Nature*, 404, 56-59.

Hendrickson, C.T., A. Horvath, S. Joshi, and L.B. Lave. 1998. Economic input-output models for environmental life-cycle assessment. *Environmental Science & Technology*. p. 32.

Hughes, P. M., *Global Threats and Challenges: The Decades Ahead*, Lt. Gen. Patrick M. Hughes, Director of the Defense Intelligence Agency, in Statement for the Senate Committee on Intelligence, January 28, 1998. Ref:http://www.fas.org/irp/congress/1998_hr/s980128h.htm.

James, E.: 1994, *Science Fiction in the 20th Century*, Oxford University Press, Oxford.

Jameson, F.: 1982, 'Progress Versus Utopia; or, Can We Imagine the Future', *Science Fiction Studies*, 9, 147-158.

Janet Raloff, "Nano Hazards: Exposure to minute particles harms lungs, circulatory system," Science News Online, Week of March 19, 2005; Vol. 167, No. 12.

Johnson, D.G. and H. Nissenbaum (eds). 1995. *Computers, Ethics and Social Values*. Prentice Hall:Englewood Cliffs, NJ. pp. 262-393.

Johnson, P.C.: 2003, 'Implications of the Continuum of Bioinformatics', in: M.C. Roco; W.S. Bainbridge (eds.), *Converging Technologies for Improving Human Performance*, Kluwer, Dordrecht, pp. 207-212.

Kalman B., F.D. Lublin. 1999. "The Genetics of Multiple Sclerosis. A Review." *Biomedicine and Pharmacotherapy*, Sep; 53 (8): pp. 358-370.

Kay, L.: 2000, *Who Wrote the Book of Life? A History of the Genetic Code*, Stanford University Press, Stanford.

Kruskal, M., and N. Zabusky. 1965. Interaction of solitons in a collisionless plasma and the recurrence of initial states, *Phys. Rev. Lett.* Vol. 15. 240-243.

Kupferman, R., M. Kawaguchi, and M.M. Denn. 2000. Emergence of structure in models of liquid crystalline polymers with elastic coupling. *J. Non-Newtonian Fluid Mech.* Vol. 91. 255-271.

Kuusi, O. 1999b. *Expertise in the future use of generic technologies.* VATT Research Reports #59, Helsinki.

Kuusi, O. and M. Meyer. 2001. "Technology Generalizations and Leitbilds – The Anticipation of Technological Opportunities." Manuscript submitted to *Technological Forecasting and Social Change.*

Kuusi, O., 1999. "Epistemic value analysis – a tool to evaluate technological options." Personal communication.

Laibinis, P.E.; Hickman, J.J.; Wrighton, M.S.; Whitesides, G.M. 1989. "Orthogonal Self-Assembled Monolayers - Alkanethiols On Gold and Alkane Carboxylic-Acids On Alumina", *Science*, 245, 845- 847.

Lambright, W. Henry. 1995. *Powering Apollo: James E. Webb of NASA.* Baltimore: Johns Hopkins University Press.

Latour, B. & Woolgar, S.: 1986, *Laboratory Life: The Social Construction of Scientific Facts*, 2nd edn., Princeton University Press, Princeton.

Latour, B.: 1986, 'Visualisation and Cognition: Thinking With Eyes and Hands', *Knowledge and Society*, 6, 1-40.

Lave, L.B., E. Cobas-Flores, C.T. Hendrickson, and F.C. McMichael. 1995a. Using input-output analysis to estimate economy wide discharges. *Environmental Science & Technology*, 29(9).

Lax, Peter D. 1989. The flowering of applied mathematics in America. in *A Century of Mathematics in America-Part II.* edited by Peter Duren et al. American Mathematical Society. 455-466.

Leah Eisenberg, "Medicating Death Row Inmates So They Qualify for Execution," AMA Case in Health Law, Vol. 6, No. 9, September 2004.

Ledley, Fred D. 1995. "Nonviral Gene Therapy: The promise of Genes as Pharmaceutical Products," *Human Gene Therapy*, Vol. 6, Sep, pp 1129-1144.

Lipowsky, R. 1991. The conformation of membranes. *Nature.* Vol. 349. 475.

Lipson, H. and J. B. Pollack, Nature, 406, 974-978, (2000). *Automatic design and manufacture of robotic life forms.* See, also, several additional articles on this subject in contemporary issues of Nature.

Mahmood U., C.H. Tung, A. Bogdanov Jr., R. Weissleder. 1999. "Near-Infrared Optical Imaging of Protease Activity for Tumor Detection." *Radiology*, Dec; 213 (3): pp. 866-870.

Malinow, R., Z.F. Mainen, and Y. Hayashi. 2000. LTP mechanisms: from silence to four-lane traffic. *Curr. Opin. Neurobiol.* 10(3): p. 352-7.

Mark, H., Statement of The Honorable Hans Mark, Director, Defense Research and Engineering, before the House Armed Service Committee, October 20, 1999.

McConnell, S.A., ed. 1998. *Pharmaceuticals.* Dun and Bradstreet Industry Reference Handbooks, Gale, Detroit, pp. 30-34.

McHale, B.: 1987, *Postmodern Fiction*, Methuen, New York & London.

Meadows, D.L., et al. 1972. *The Limits to Growth*, New York: University.

Merz, J.L. 1986. "The Optoelectronics Joint Research Laboratory: Light Shed on Cooperative Research in Japan." *Scientific Bulletin* (ONR Far East Office). 11 (4), 1-30 (Oct.-Dec.).

Meyer, M. and O. Persson. 1998. "Nanotechnology - interdisciplinarity, patterns of collaboration and differences in application," *Scientometrics*, XXXXII (2), 195-205.

Milburn, C.: 2002 'Nanotechnology in the Age of Posthuman Engineering: Science Fiction as Science', *Configurations*, 10, 261-295.

Mnyusiwalla, A.; Daar, A.S.; Singer, P.A.: 2003, '"Mind the Gap": Science and Ethics in Nanotechnology, *Nanotechnology*, 14, R9-R13.

Nardi, B., O'Day, V. 1999. *Information Ecologies: Using Technology with Heart*. MIT Press.

National Science and Technology Council (NSTC). 2000. *National Nanotechnology Initiative: Leading to the Next Industrial Revolution* (Supplement to the President's FY 2001 Budget) (Washington, DC: February; available at http://www.nano.gov).

National Science and Technology Council (NSTC). 2000. *National Nanotechnology Initiative: Leading to the Next Industrial Revolution*. February. (http://www.nano.gov/nni.pdf).

Parikh, A.N.; Schivley, M.A.; Koo, E.; Seshadri, K.; Aurentz, D.; Mueller, K.; Allara, D.L. 1997. "nalkylsiloxanes: From single monolayers to layered crystals. The formation of crystalline polymers from the hydrolysis of n- octadecyltrichlorosilane", *Journal of the American Chemical Society*, 119, 3135-3143.

Philip Ball, "Synthetic Biology: Starting from Scratch," Nature, 431, pp. 624-626, 7 October 2004.

Philipse, A.P. 1998. "Colloidal Dispersions," section 3.4, A. ten Wolde (ed.), *Nanotechnology: Towards a molecular construction kit*. STT Report #60, The Hague, 171-178.

Pierce, N.A. and M.B. Giles. 2000. Adjoint reconstruction of superconvergent functionals from PDE approximations. *SIAM Rev.* Vol. 42(2). 247-264.

Piveteau, Laurent-Dominique, Anthe S. Zandvliet and Robert Langer. 2001. "Nitroxide and Galactose Grafted Dendrimer: A Specifically Targeted Contrast Agent for MRI and EPR Imaging of the Liver," *in preparation.*

Polanyi, Karl. 1944. *The Great Transformation: The Political and Economic Origins of Our Time* (Boston: Beacon Press, 1957; orig. ed. 1944).

Pritchard, M.S. 1996. "Conflicts of Interest: Conceptual and Normative Issues," *Academic Medicine*, 71:12, December, pp. 1305-1313.

Putnam, D., Gentry, C.A., Pack, D.W., Langer, R. 2001. "Polymer-based Gene Delivery with Low Cytotoxicity by a Unique Balance of Side-chain Termini." *Proceedings of the National Academy of Sciences*, U.S.A., Volume 98, Number 3, pages 1200-1205.

Ramos, L.; Lubensky, T.C.; Dan, N.; Nelson, P.; Weitz, D.A. 1999. "Surfactant-mediated two-dimensional crystallization of colloidal crystals", *Science*, 286, 2325-2328.

Reed, Mark A. and James M. Tour. 2000. "Computing with Molecules." *Scientific American*. June..
SIA (Semiconductor Industry Association). 1999. "1999 International Technology Roadmap for Semiconductors."

Rinzler, A.G.; Liu, J.; Dai, H.; Nikolaev, P.; Huffman, C.B.; Rodriguez-Macias, F.J.; Boul, P.J.; Lu, A.H.; Heymann, D.; Colbert, D.T.; Lee, R.S.; Fischer, J.E.; Rao, A.M.; Eklund, P.C.; Smalley, R.E. 1998.

Roco, M. C., R. S. Williams, and P. Alivisatos, *Nanotechnology Research Directions: Vision for Nanotechnology in the Next Decade*, Kluwer Academic Publishers (2000).

Roco, M.C. & Bainbridge, W.S., (eds.): 2001, *Societal Implications of Nanoscience and Nanotechnology*, National Science Foundation.

Roco, M.C.: 2003b, 'Coherence and Divergence in Megatrends in Science and Engineering', in: M.C. Roco, W.S. Bainbridge (eds.), *Converging Technologies for Improving Human Performance*, Kluwer, Dordrecht, pp. 79-96.

Roco, M.C.: 2003c, 'Fundamentally New Manufacturing Processes and Products', in: Roco, M.C. & Bainbridge, W.S., (eds.), *Converging Technologies for Improving Human Performance*, Kluwer, Dordrecht, pp. 300-302.

Roco, M.C.: 2004, 'The Emergence and Policy Implications of Converging Technologies' [www.nsf.gov/home/crssprgm/nano/nbic_roco_04_0422_@aaas_57sl.pdf, accessed May 2004].

Rodney Brooks, "The Merger of Flesh and Machines," The Next Fifty Years: Science in the First Half of the Twenty-First Century, ed. by John Brockman, 2002, p. 191.

Roland Pease, "'Living' robots powered by muscle," BBC News, January 17, 2005.

Schummer, J.: 2004, 'Interdisciplinary Issues in Nanoscale Research', in: D. Baird, A. Nordmann, J. Schummer (eds.), *Discovering the Nanoscale*, IOS Press, Amsterdam, pp. 9-20.

Schumpeter, Joseph Alois. 1942. *Capitalism, Socialism, and Democracy*. New York: Harper.

Senturia, S., N. Aluru, and J. White. 1997. Simulating the behavior of MEMS devices: computational methods and needs. *IEEE Computational Science and Engineering*. Vol. 4(1). 30-43.

Shor, P., *Proc. 35th Ann. Symp. Foundations of Computer Science*, 1994.

Shultz, W.: 2000, 'Nanotechnology: The Next Big Thing', *Chemical and Engineering News*, 78(18), 41-47.

Snider, G.L.; Orlov, A.O.; Amlani, I.; Zuo, X.; Bernstein, G.H.; Lent, C.S.; Merz, J.L.; Porod, W. 1999. "Quantum-dot cellular automata: Review and recent experiments (invited)", *Journal of Applied Physics*, 85, 4283-4285.

Soong, R.K.; Bachand, G.D.; Neves, H.P.; Olkhovets, A.G.; Craighead, H.G.; Montemagno, C.D. 2000. "Powering an inorganic nanodevice with a biomolecular motor", *Science*, 290, 1555-1558.

Steelman, John R. 1947. *Science and Public Policy* (Washington, DC: US Government Printing Office). Stephenson, Neal. 1995. *The Diamond Age, or, Young Lady's Illustrated Primer* (New York: Bantam Books).

Stix, G. 1996. Trends in nanotechnology: waiting for breakthroughs. *Sci. Am.* April.

Sun, S.H.; Murray, C.B.; Weller, D.; Folks, L.; Moser, A. 2000. "Monodisperse FePt nanoparticles and ferromagnetic FePt nanocrystal superlattices", *Science*, 287, 1989-1992.

Suvin, D.: 1979, *Metamorphoses of Science Fiction*, Yale University Press, New Haven.

Tilton, John E. (ed). 1991. *World Metal Demand*, Washington, DC: Resources for the Future.

Tobio, M., R. Gref, A. Sanchez, R. Langer and M.J. Alonso. 1998. "Stealth PLA-PEG Nanoparticles as Protein Carriers for Nasal Administration", *Pharmaceutical Research*, Vol. 15, No 2, pp 270-275.

Tramontin, A.D. and E.A. Brenowitz. 2000. Seasonal plasticity in the adult brain. *Trends Neurosci*. 23(6): p. 251-8.

Vaia, R., D. Tomlin, M. Schulte, and T. Bunning. 2000. Two-phase nanoscale morphology of polymer/LC composites. *Polymer*. In press.

Vale, R.D.; Milligan, R.A. 2000. "The way things move: Looking under the hood of molecular motor proteins", *Science*, 288, 88-95.

Valenti. Plaza y Valdes, S.A. de C.V. Instituto de Investigaciones Sociales. Universidad Nacional Autonoma de Mexico. Universidad Autonoma Metropolitana, pp.81-93.

Van Maanen, J. *Tales of the Field*. Chicago: U. Chicago, 1988.

Vettiger, P.; Brugger, J.; Despont, M.; Drechsler, U.; Durig, U.; Haberle, W.; Lutwyche, M.; Rothuizen, H.; Stutz, R.; Widmer, R.; Binnig, G. 1999. "Ultrahigh density, high-data-rate NEMS-based AFM data storage system", *Microelectronic Engineering*, 46, 11-17.

Voter, A.F. 1997. Hyperdynamics: accelerated molecular dynamics of infrequent events. *Phys. Rev. Lett.* Vol. 78. 3908.

Warner, M. and E. M. Terentjev. 1996. Nematic elastomers: a new state of matter? *Progress in Polymer Science*. Vol. 21(5). 853.

Warner, M., E. M. Terentjev, R. B. Meyer, and Y. Mao. 2000. Untwisting of a cholesteric elastomer by a mechanical field. *Phys. Rev. Lett.* Vol. 85(11). 2320.

Webb, E. J., Campbell, D. T., Schwartz, R. D., Sechrest, L., and Grove, J. B. *Unobtrusive Measures: Nonreactive Research in the social Sciences* (2nd ed.). Boston: Houghton Mifflin, 1981.

Webster, A. and H. Etzkowitz. 1991. "Academic-industry Relations: The Second Academic Revolution?" Science Policy Support Group, London, 1991.

Weil, V. 1988. "Afterword," *Biotechnology: Professional Issues and Social Concerns*. (AAAS Publication) co-edited with Paul DeForest, Mark Frankel, and Jeanne Poindexter.

Weiss, S. 1999. "Fluorescence spectroscopy of single biomolecules", *Science*, 283, 1676-1683.

White, J.G. 1986. *Philos. Trans. R. Soc. Lond. B Biol. Sci.* 314: pp. 1-340.

Whitesides, G.M.; Mathias, J.P.; Seto, C.T. 1991. "Molecular Self-Assembly and Nanochemistry - a Chemical Strategy For the Synthesis of Nanostructures", *Science*, 254, 1312-1319.

Wilbur, J.L.; Whitesides, G.M. 1999. *Self-Assembly and Self-Assembled Monolayers in Micro- and Nanofabrication*; Timp, G., Ed.; Springer-Verlag New York, Inc.: New York, pp 331-370.

William-Jones, B.; Corrigan, O.: 2003, 'Rhetoric and Hype: Where's the Ethics in Pharmacogenomics?', *American Journal of Pharmacogenomics*, 3(6), 375-383.

Appendices

APPENDIX - I

NANOCOMPUTERS, NANOBIOTECHNOLOGY AND NANOTECH INFORMATION RESOURCES

Nanolinks

Nanoelectronics Planet

Nanoelectronics Planet provides news and events for the nanotechnology business communities of interest: business development, investment,technology transfer, and government.

NanoTechnology Magazine

Excellent all-around source for news and information about nanotechnology. Good for beginners as well as seasoned veterans.

Ralph C. Merkle's Nanotechnology Web Site

Good introduction to nanotechnology with lots of links to additional information. The site is maintained by Ralph C Merkle, a scientist at Xerox PARC.

CSC Scientists Discover Ways to Build Chips From the Atom Up

This article from the Computer Sciences Corporation details how they reduced the size of existing chips but by building them up from individual molecules.

Feynman's 1959 talk

Nobel Laureate Richard P. Feynman's 1959 talk to the American Physical Society, in which he discusses minituarization at the molecular level. It is widely viewed as the seminal speech that launched nanotechnology as an independent field of research.

The Nanoelectronics and Nanocomputers Home Page

Focuses on the electronics and computer applications of nanotechnology. An excellent source for top-down information.

Books

These and other books can be ordered from *The Foresight Institute's book store.* The best technical introduction to this area is:

- *Nanosystems: molecular machinery, manufacturing, and computation* by K. Eric Drexler (Wiley 1992).

A technical introduction to medical applications of nanotechnology:

- *Nanomedicine*, currently being written by Robert A. Freitas, is a technical introduction to medical applications of nanotechnology. Volume I is available. A web page on *Nanomedicine* has an overview. The full text is also available.

Further reading:

- *Engines of Creation*(full text in html) by K. Eric Drexler (Anchor 1986) discusses both the technology and its possible applications and consequences.
- *Unbounding the Future*, by K. Eric Drexler, Chris Peterson and Gayle Pergamit (Quill 1991) provides a non-technical discussion of what nanotechnology should let us do, using technically feasible scenarios to clearly illustrate the possibilities.
- *Nano!* by Ed Regis (Little, Brown 1995) is an engaging and entertaining book that describes the researchers involved in this area, particularly Drexler, and the reactions of different members of the scientific community to the concept.

Journals, publications and newsgroups

- The Foresight Update is a newsletter published by the Foresight Institute and is an excellent way to keep abreast of developments and events in this rapidly moving area.
- *Foresight lists a variety of resources about nanotechnology*.
- *sci.nanotech* is a net news discussion group that covers nanotechnology and related areas.
- The *journal Nanotechnology* covers nanotechnology both in the specific sense used here and in the broader sense. It has had a special issue for each of the Foresight Conferences on Molecular Nanotechnology and is well worth reading. Ask your library to subscribe! *Nanotechnology* is published by the *Institute of Physics Publishing*.

General Information & Policy

- Future Trends in Microelectronics Device Simulation (JPL) (May 1999)
- *International Comparative Study on Applying Molecular and Mat erials*

Modelling (World Technology Division (WTEC), *International Technology Research Institute (ITRI)*) (March 2000)

- *CAD Framework initiative* standards for CAD tools and systems.
- *DOE Initiative in Computational Materials Science* (May 1998)
- *DOE Strategic Simulation Plan: Basic Science Component* (October 1998)
- *IDA MEMS* ("identifying transition opportunities for MEMS technology into defence systems") (2000)
- *Future & Emerging Technologies (FET) Proactive Initiative: Nanotechnology Information Devices (NID)* (European Commission, Information Society Technologies (IST))
- *PHANTOMS*—Nanotechnology for Information Processing and Storage (European Commission, Information Society Technologies (IST)) *http://www.phantomsnet.com*
- *Technology Roadmap for Nanoelectronics* (MELARI NANO, ed. 1999)
- *U.S. National Nanotechnology Initiative* (July 2000)
- *Nanotechnology Research Directions: Vision for Nanotechnology R&D in the Next Decade* (NSTC IWGN Workshop Report, Sept. 1999)
- *NSF National Nanotechnology Initiative* (| Crosscutting | NANO) (2000)
- *Notes on Funding of Nanotechnology in Japan* (1999)
- *WTEC Panel Report on Nanostructure Science & Technology* (August 1999)
- *Introduction to Nanotechnology* (from Zyvex)
- *Molecular Simulation and Nanotechnology*
- *Nanoelectronic Modelling* (JPL) (November 1998)

Associations

Directories of Associations

- *Professional Societies and Associations in Metals and Materials Engineering* listed at the University of British Columbia Library:

International

- *IEEE* — Institute of Electrical and Electronic Engineers
- *Semiconductor Equipment and Materials International*
- *International Society for Molecular Electronics & BioComputing (ISMEBC)*
- *Materials Research Society (MRS)*

- *Microelectricalmechanical Systems (MEMS) Clearinghouse*
- *Applied Computational Research Society (ACRS)*
- *Foresight Institute (FI)* (non-profit organization devoted to nanotechnology)
- *Institute for Molecular Manufacturing (IMM)*
- *Institute of Nanotechnology*

Regional / National

- *CORDIS* Community Research and Development Information Service The European Commision's Research home page
- *IST* The European Commision's fifth framework Information Society Technologies Program
- *FET* Future and Emerging Technologies; a key action within the IST program
- *FET Initiative Quantum Information Processing and Communication*
- *Psi-k* (or *try here*). Psi-k is an EU network dealing with quantum chemical calculations of solids and materials for the semiconductor industry
- *ATOMCAD* An EU network, the objective of which is to integrate new atomistic TCAD tools with existing conventional packages with the aim of introducing atomic scale modelling into the microelectronics industry
- *EMRS* The European Materials Research Society
- *NEXUS User-Supplier Club (USC) on CAD for Microsystems* (European Microsystems Technology On-Line (EMSTO))
- *National Microelectronics Application Centre* (product development, design, information technology)
- *IEE* Institute of Electrical Engineers (UK)
- *Institut fuer Nanotechnologie*. Forschungszentrum Karlsruhe
- *DARPA* Defence Advanced Research Projects Agency (USA)
- *DARPA Microsystems Technology Office*, quantum computing. Involves theory and technology demonstration
- Use of the spin degree of freedom for new devices, *SPINS*, including quantum information processing
- *NSF* National Science Foundation (USA)
- *Electronics, Photonics and Device Technologies* Program run by the NSF
- *DesCartES*, Distributed Center for Electronic Simulation, is a program run by the NSF in the field of atomic/quantum scale simulation in electronics devices down to the nanoscale

- *NIST Office of Microelectronics Programs* (USA)
- *Computational Material Science Network (CMSN)* (USA)
- *DoD Computational Electronics & Nanoelectronics (CEN)* (USA)
- *MITI* The Ministry of Trade and Industry (Japan)
- *Taiwan Semiconductor Industry Association*
- *Laboratory of Semiconductor Materials science*. Institute of semiconductors, Chinese academy of sciences
- *Institute of Software*, Chinese Academy of Sciences
- *Center for Nanoscale Science and Technology* (Rice University, USA))
- *Center for Simulating Dynamic Response of Materials* (USA, Caltech)
- *Institute for Nanotechnology* (Northwestern University, USA)
- *Interagency Working Group on Nano Science, Engineering and Technology* (USA)
- *Metallurgy Division* of the U.S. National Institute of Standards (NIST) ("developing measurement and standards infrastructure for nanotechnology") (USA)
- *National Nanofabrication Users Network (NNUN)* ("provides users with access to some of the most sophisticated nanofabrication technologies in the world with facilities open to all users from academia, government, and industry") (USA)
- *Japan Society for Simulation Technology on NACSIS* (Japan)
- *Atom Technology Group, National Institute for Advanced Interdisciplinary Research (NAIR)* (Japan)

Companies

- *Alcatel Microelectronics* (Belgium)
- *Infineon Technologies AG* (Germany)
- *Philips Semiconductors* (Holland)
- *STMicroelectronics* (France)
- *TDK Semiconductor Europe*
- *Advanced Micro Devices Inc.* (USA)
- *Analog Devices Inc.* (USA)
- *CMP Cientmfica* (Spain)
- *Dallas Semiconductor* (USA)

- *International Business Machines (IBM) Corporation* (USA)
- *Intel Corporation* (USA)
- *Lucent Technologies Microelectronics Group — Agere Systems* (USA)
- *MEMX, Inc.* Offering turn-key MEMS and Nanotechnology Design and Product realization capabilities
- *Motorola Semiconductor Products Sector* (USA)
- *Semiconductor Research Corp.* (USA)
- *SRI International* (USA)
- *Texas Instruments* (USA)
- *Fujitsu* (Japan)
- *FECIT* — Fujitsu European Centre for Information Technology
- *Hitachi* (Japan)
- *NEC Global* (Japan)
- *Sony Semiconductor* (Japan)
- *Toshiba Corporation* (Japan)
- *Hyundai Heavy Industries* (Korea)
- *Samsung Semiconductor* (Korea)
- *California Molecular Electronics*
- *HP Labs*
- *Innovations for High Performance (IHP) Microelectronics*
- *List of Company Links* (from Nanotechnology Industries)
- *List of Company Links* (from IDA MEMS, DARPA)
- *List of Organizations* (from Mitre)
- *Molecular Manufacturing Enterprises, Inc. (MMEI)* (a seed capital firm)
- *Nanochip* ("Develops mass storage devices, based on molecular scale technology")
- *NanoMagnetics, Ltd.*
- *Nanomat* ("manufacturing nanomaterials and nanotechnology for structural, non-structural, microelectronic, and biomedical applications")
- *NanoWorld Projects*
- *SciCo* ("innovation for materials design — data, simulation, analysis")
- *Zyvex* ("The First Molecular Nanotechnology Company")

Academic Institutes and Groups

- *NMRC* at *University College Cork* Ireland
- *Computational Modelling* at the NMRC.
- *IMEC* Belgium
- *DIMES* Delft Institute for Microelectronics and Sub-Micron Technology at the technical university of Delft, Holland
- *Institute for Microelectronics* at the Technical University of Vienna
- *Nanoscale Science Laboratory* at the Cambridge University Engineering Department
- *Silicon Technology Research at the University of Edinburgh*
- *Scottish Microelectronics Centre* at the *department of electronic and electrical engineering*, university of Edinburgh, Scotland
- *TCAD* Research at the University of Stanford
- *TCAD Training and Research* at Louisiana Tech University
- *Microsystem Technology laboratory at MIT*. Includes Microsystems TCAD
- *Software and Analysis of Advanced Materials Processing Center* in the college of engineering at the university of Florida.
- *NASA Semiconductor Device Modelling*
- *NASA Nanoelectronic modelling*
- *Electronic Engineering at University of California, Berkeley*
- *University of Texas at Austin Microelectronics Research Center*
- *S. Dunham's research group at Washington* Atomistic simulation of deep sub-micron fabrication

Constants and Conversion Factors

- *Constants / Conversion Factors*

Databases

- *Database of materials studied using CRYSTAL.* From the theoretical chemistry group at Torino.
- *NSF Nanotechnology Database*
- *U. Idaho's VLSI Database*

Software Links

- *Silvaco*
- *Avant! Software* Formerly Technology Modelling Associates

- *Integrated Systems Engineering AG*
- *Microelectronics Software* (from Institute for Microelectronics)
- *Siborg System Inc.* MicroTec: 2D process and devices simulator for the PC
- *Los Alamos Grid Toolbox* Grid generation and optimisation software for device modelling
- *Purdue University Network Computing Hubs (PUNCH) Online Computing for Engineering & Science* (Purdue Simulation Hub: Computational Electronics, Computer Architecture, Parallel Programming, VLSI Design)
- *BIPSIM Inc.* BIPOLE3: Quasi 3D device simulation
- *PDF Solutions Inc.*
- *Coventor* formerly MEMCAD
- *Domain Software Solutions Inc.* Statistical Software for Process Simulation
- *Celestry* formerly BTA Technolgy Inc.
- *The Computer Physics Communications* software library at Queen's University Belfast
- *GAMESS* a free quantum chemical code
- *GAMESS-UK* a quantum chemical code
- *Gaussian Inc*
- *Accelrys.* Formerly Molecular Simulations Inc
- *Q-Chem Inc*
- *Q-Chem Inc — ab initio and DFT molecular modeling*
- *Schroedinger Inc*
- *TURBOMOLE*
- *SPARTAN* available from Wavefunction Inc.
- *FHI96MD* from the Fritz Haber Institut, Berlin
- *Nanotechnology Software links* (from Nanotechnology Industries)
- *Nanoelectronics Modelling (NEMO)*

Comprehensive Sites

- *Harris Lexicon of semiconductors*
- *Semiconductor Subway* at MIT is a comprehensive resource providing links to information related to microelectronics and microsystems technology.
- The *Semiconductor Manufacturing Technology* consortium of semiconductor manufacturing companies in the US and, with international SEMATECH, the world.

- The *International Technology Roadmap for Semiconductors* home page
- *MEMS Virtual Learning Cybercenter* (by Abdelkader Tayebi; "a distance-learning educational web page")
- *NANOMAT*
- *NANONET*
- *About.com's Nanotechnology category* (articles, list of centers, etc.)
- *NanoPhiles* (extremely wide-ranging nanotechnology site — even includes a section on careers)
- *Nanotechnology Industries*
- *THE Nanoelectronics & Nanocomputing Home Page* (by Mitre's Nanosystems Group; Internet gateway to nanoelectronics research & development information and resources from around the world)
- *Computational Chemistry List (CCL)*

Journals

Technical Journals

IEEE Publications. Some of the more pertinent journals include:

- TCAD Journal of Technology Computer Aided Design, an electronic journal covering Technology Computer Aided Design
- IEEE Transactions on Computer Aided Design of Circuits and Systems
- IEEE Electron Device Letters
- IEEE Journal of Quantum Electronics
- IEEE Transactions on Semiconductor Manufacturing
- Elsevier Science or ScienceDirect a gateway direct to the Journals published by Elsevier Science
- Microelectronic Engineering
- Microelectronics Journal
- Materials Science in Semiconductor Processing
- Solid State Electronics
- Computer Physics Communications
- Online Journal Publication Service from the American Institute of Physics
- Applied Physics Letters
- Journal of Applied Physics
- Journal of Chemical Physics

Electronic Journals, Articles, etc.

- EE Times.
- Nanotech Bulletin.
- Semiconductor Magazine
- Computational Methods for Atomistic Simulations of Materials
- Small Times Daily news, mostly in the area of MEMS
- Yahoo! Semiconductor news
- Wired Daily News
- Integrated System Design Magazine
- VLSI Design: An International Journal of Custom-Chip Design, Simulation, and Testing
- Archive: Nanotechnology Papers, sci.nanotech
- Year 2067.com (Emerging Technologies E-Magazine)
- List of Relevant Electronic Journals (from Sean Morgan's Nanotechnology Pages)
- Computational Science Education Project (for >= advanced undergrads)
- Daily Diffs Nanotechnology Folder
- Yahoo! Nanotechnology News (Full Coverage)
- Journal of Nanoparticle Research
- NanoTechnology Magazine

Electronic Lists

- CCP5 Collaborative Computational Project; Computer simulation of condensed matter.

Upon subscribing, one can receive mailings regarding job and studentship postings and upcoming conference announcements

- List of Nanotechnology Mailing Lists (from Sean Morgan's Nanotechnology Pages)
- Nanotechnology Conference/Discussion (Council of Chemical Research's Net Web Board)

Lists of Links

- NanoLink ("Key Nanotechnology Sites on the Web")
- Webring for Nanotechnology (you can add your site to the webring)

Related Keywords

Microelectronics

- nanoelectronics, molecular electronics, molectronics
- molecular electronic devices, molecular nanoelectronic devices, molecular scale devices, nanoscale electronic devices, single-electron devices
- molecular engineering, nanotechnology, microsystems
- nanoscience, nanophysics
- VLSI circuits, nanoscale integrated circuits
- semiconductor physics, solid-state physics, device physics

Design

- computational materials science, computational electronics, computational nanoelectronics, computational nanoscience, computational nanotechnology
- modelling, modelling, simulation

Conferences and events

- See the Foresight web page listing of events.

The Feynman Prizes

- *The Foresight Institute has a web page which gives information on the prizes they sponsor*, most notably the Feynman prizes in nanotechnology.

Some articles on the web

- *There's plenty of room at the bottom*, by Richard P. Feynman, is a classic 1959 article which discusses the limits of miniaturization and forecast the ability to "...arrange the atoms the way we want; the very atoms, all the way down!"
- *Molecular engineering: an approach to the development of general capabilities for molecular manipulation*, by K. Eric Drexler. The first journal article on molecular nanotechnology.
- A summary of *Advanced automation for space missions*, a 1980 NASA study which provides a good introduction to self replicating systems.
- *Atomistic design and simulations of nanoscale machines and assembly..*
- *That's impossible: how good scientists reach bad conclusions*
- *Nanotechnology: what will it mean?*, IEEE Spectrum, January 2001
- *Nanotechnology is coming*, Frankfurter Allgemeine Zeitung, September 11 2000

- *Nanotechnology: Designs for the Future*
- Several papers on nano design and related issues (including several mpeg movies of simulated nanostructures) and a paper discussing NASA applications of molecular nanotechnology from the computational nanotechnology project at NASA Ames.
- *A proposed "metabolism" for a hydrocarbon assembler.*
- *Overview of self replication.*
- *Self replicating systems and molecular manufacturing.*
- *Self replicating systems and low cost manufacturing.*
- *Molecular manufacturing: adding positional control to chemical synthesis.*
- *It's a small, small, small, small world*, published in *MIT's Technology Review*, provides a general introduction to nanotechnology.
- *Nanotechnology and the next 50 years*, by Richard Smalley.
- *A new family of six degree of freedom positional devices* discusses the Stewart platform, a simple robotic arm, and a new proposal: the double tripod. It then analyzes and compares their positional accuracy in the face of thermal noise at room temperature.
- *Steps towards molecular manufacturing* discusses the design of molecular building blocks that could be used in conjunction with positional assembly in solution (no vacuum) to build a useful range of non-diamondoid molecular structures, including early assemblers.
- *Computational nanotechnology* discusses the idea of using computer simulation to speed the development of this new technology.
- *Theoretical studies of a hydrogen abstraction tool for nanotechnology* is an ab initio study of a proposed molecular tool.
- *A proof about molecular bearings.*
- *Design considerations for an assembler* discusses the design of a "simple" diamondoid assembler.
- *Convergent assembly* can make meter scale or larger products starting with nanometer scale parts.
- *Nanotechnology and medicine* discusses some of the possible medical applications of nanotechnology.

Drexler and Smalley debate feasibility of molecular nanotechnology in Chemical & Engineering News cover story.

- Foresight issues *press release*. "[Smalley] offers vehement opinions and colorful metaphors but no relevant, defensible scientific arguments..."

- Kurzweil analyzes the issues. "Smalley's position, which denies both the promise and the peril of molecular assembly, will ultimately backfire"
- Howard Lovey's nano blog covers *Clash of the nanotech titans.* "...I've covered local and national government enough to confidently question the motives of those who side with the Smalley camp."
- The Center for Responsible Nanotechnology (CRN) issued a press release. "If Smalley's goal is to demonstrate that machine-phase chemistry is fundamentally flawed, he has not been effective..."
- The *New York Times* :"The debate has caught widespread attention among nanotechnology researchers..."
- A bibliography on mechanosynthesis and proposal for further research. Computational chemistry can validate the feasibility of mechanosynthesis, what's needed is funding.
- Lawrence Lessig in Wired says: "Should science tell the truth? You'd think that question would need no answer. But in the vortex known as Washington, DC, the obvious too often gets bent."

Sites with many links

- The Foresight Institute
- KurzweilAI.net
- The National Nanotechnology Initiative
- Nanotechnology Industries
- UCLA's chemistry page has many links to chemistry-related topics.
- The NanoLink list of nanotechnology web sites.

Some groups focused on nanotechnology

- The Foresight Institute. Motto: *Preparing for future technologies.* A nonprofit organization, the Foresight Institute has played a pivotal role in educating both the general public and the research community about the potential impact of nanotechnology. address: Foresight Institute, Box 61058, Palo Alto CA 94306 USA; phone: 415-324-2490; fax: 415-324-2497; e-mail: inform@foresight.org; WWW: http://www.foresight.org.
- The Institute for Molecular Manufacturing, a nonprofit foundation formed to carry out research aimed at developing molecular manufacturing.
- The National Nanotechnology Initiative
- The Center for Responsible Nanotechnology, focuses on nano policy research

- Molecular Manufacturing Enterprises, Incorporated (MMEI) was founded to help accelerate advancements in the field of nanotechnology. They provide seed capital and other support to those developing key advances.
- The Numerical Aerodynamic Simulation Systems Division (NAS) at NASA Ames Research Center, in partnership with the Ames computational chemistry branch and others, has pursued • substantial research in computational molecular nanotechnology, and funded a grant program in the field.
- The Center for Nanoscale Science and Technology at Rice University is devoted to nurturing science and technology at the nanometer scale.
- The Molecular Manufacturing Shortcut Group (MMSG) is a chapter of the National Space Society (NSS). MMSG's motto: *promote the development of nanotechnology as a means to facilitate the settlement of space.* NSS has a position paper on molecular nanotechnology

Other pages

• The House Science Committee, Subcommittee on Basic Research, held hearings on nanotechnology on June 22nd, 1999. Testimony was heard from Eugene Wong (NSF), Paul McWhorter (Sandia), Richard Smalley (Rice), and Ralph Merkle.

- NSF is funding research in nanotechnology. Neal Lane, the Director of NSF, said: "If I were asked for an area of science and engineering that will most likely produce the breakthroughs of tomorrow, I would point to nanoscale science and engineering, often called simply "nanotechnology"."
- James Gimzewski (formerly at IBM Zurich) made the world's smallest abacus as well as positioned individual molecules at room temperature.
- The Rice University Nanotechnology Initiative
- The Laboratory for Molecular Robotics at USC is run by Aristides Requicha and is investigating the precise manipulation of atoms and molecules.
- The NASA Institute for Advanced Concepts is interested in revolutionary new ideas that "leap-frog" the evolution of current aerospace systems in a 10-40 year time horizon.
- Wilson Ho and his group show their atomically resolved and precise work in pictures.
- Charles Lieber's group at Harvard.
- Scanning tunneling microscopy at IBM Almaden includes images of several structures built by positioning individual atoms.
- The Materials and Process Simulation Center at Caltech, run by Bill

Goddard, has computationally modeled a broad range of structures, including those relevant to the development of nanotechnology. For example, Charles Musgrave and Jason Perry, then with Goddard's group, used ab initio quantum chemistry to analyze a molecular tool which should be useful in the synthesis of diamondoid structures (*Theoretical studies of a hydrogen abstraction tool for nanotechnology*, Musgrave et. al., *Nanotechnology* 2 (1991) pages 187-195).

- NRL (Naval Research Laboratory) has several groups pursuing various aspects of nanotechnology. The Chemistry Division (among others) pursues research in nanostructures and nanofabrication.
- Ned Seeman's lab is working on nanotechnological applications of DNA, including (for example) a truncated octahedron. The *Stewart platform*, a well known positional device, is basically an octahedron six of whose struts can be adjusted in length. While DNA is not as stiff as might be desired for molecular robotics applications, the ability to synthesize an octahedral structure suggests that the self assembly of a simple positional device is possible.
- Links to information about diamond CVD (Chemical Vapor Deposition).
- An Alpha release of Carol Shaw's Molecular Assembly Sequence Software (MASS) for the Macintosh.
- Ralph C. Merkle's talk on the need for continued nanotechnology research at the Stanford • Spiritual Robots Symposium.
- Ralph C. Merkle's brief video introduction to nanotechnology (from his appearance on • Big Thinkers).
- Some constants, conversion factors, etc. that are useful in nanotechnology.
- Geoff Leach's nano directory with information on Crystal Clear, a crystal editor with a graphical user interface.
- University of North Carolina at Chapel Hill's Virtual Reality Nanomanipulator Project.
- A group at Oak Ridge National Lab (ORNL) is modeling molecular components.
- Some reactions to nanotechnology from the technical community.
- RAND has issued a report on *The Potential of Nanotechnology for Molecular Manufacturing*
- Nanotechnology in manufacturing by John Walker, part of a talk he gave in 1990 at the Autodesk technology forum.

- NIST has an interest in nanomanufacturing of atom-based standards.
- A macroscopic modular reconfigurable robot has been designed modeled and a prototype built at Stanford.
- HotWired has a page of scenarios about the future, including some speculative scenarios about nanotechnology.
- A new version of the planetary gear illustrated in *Nanosystems* on pages 311 and 312.
- MITRÈ has a web page on nanoelectronics and nanocomputing.
- Reversible computing is also an important issue if we are to continue improving computer performance. Molecular manufacturing will let us put a very large number of logic elements into a very small volume, so if we are to avoid creating a *great* deal of heat we'll need to keep the energy dissipation per logic operation *very* low indeed!
- Visual images of some proposed molecular machines.
- The slides for some talks on nanotechnology are available.

Site Listing of Nanotechnology

- Nanotechnology Now—offers a resource portal for nano science and nano tech news with event information, interviews, directories, glossary, and a tutorial on the basics.
- *NanotechNews.com*—news for nanotechnologists.
- *NanoComputer Dream Team*—desires to directly influence the design and development of a nanometer scale computer.
- *Nanomedicine*—analyzes developments in molecular machine systems to address medical problems.
- *Scientific American: Nanotechnology*—features current coverage, highlights, and article archives.
- *A to Z of Nanotechnology*—offering nanotechnology information, news, new products, suppliers, and expert directory.
- *Nanotech 2005: 2005 NSTI Nanotechnology Conference and Trace Show*—May 8-12, 2005; Anaheim, California, U.S.A.
- *Nanotechnology Gallery*—images, presentations, reports, and webcasts from NASA's Center for Nanotechnology.
- *NanoTechWire.com*—provides news and information on nanotechnology resources, research, patents, materials, investments, industry events, and optics.

- *Nanotech 2003: NanoTechnology Conference & Trade Show*—February 23-27, 2003; San Francisco, CA.
- *ANTS: Automomous NanoTechnology Swarm*—NASA mission architecture and AI paradigm for space exploration based on large numbers of autonomous specialized spacecraft working together as inspired by social insect colonies.
- *Nanoword.net*—online distributor of publications, with a focus on nano-science, technology, and education. Includes the Encyclopedia Nanotech.
- *Nanotechnology in Australia*—information for nanotechnology capability companies in Australia.
- *Nanotechnology Engineering*—collection of articles presented by the Institute of Atomic-Scale Engineering.
- *Societal Implications of Nanoscience and Nanotechnology*—final report from the September 2000 workshop held at the National Science Foundation.
- *Foresight Institute vs Scientific American: Debate on Nanotechnology*
- *Exploring the Nanoworld*—images, K-12 teaching material, and general information about nanotechnology.
- *Nanodot*—news and discussion of emerging technologies.
- Nanotechnology & The Motley Fool—Download this free report from The Motley Fool and discover a handful of rocket stocks with spectacular profit potential. Don't miss out on the next round of market-busting growth stocks. www.fool.com
- *Nanotechnology Consulting*—Nanotech Plus is a nanotechnology consulting firm providing information on nanotechnology products, markets and applications with a realistic viewpoint. www.nanotechplus.net
- *Subscribe—Forbes / Wolfe Nanotech Report*—Intelligent nanotechnology research based on a sound understanding of science. Get 1? issues of the Forbes/Wolfe Nanotech Report for $195—a 67% savings—plus a free report. Click here. www.forbesnanotech.com

Open Directory—Science Technology & Nanotechnology

- *The Foresight Institute*—Non-profit institute focused on nanotechnology, the coming ability to build materials and products with atomic precision, and systems to aid knowledge exchange and critical discussion, thus improving public and private policy decisions.
- *Nanotechnology Now*—Comprehensive and informative nanotechnology portal. Provides introduction to nanotechnology, general information, images, interviews, news, events, research, books, glossary and links.

- *Applied Computational Research Society*—Nonprofit organization fostering interdisciplinary approaches to modeling and simulation in the advancement of computational science and high technology. Focused on nanoscience and MEMS applications.
- *The ASME Nanotechnology Institute*—American Society of Mechanical Engineers: nanotechnology resources, events, programs, activities, online courses, webcasts, news and links.
- *CMP Cientifica*—News, networks, conferences and nanotechnology resources in Europe
- *Euspen*—European Society for Precision Engineering and Nanotechnology—contains society news, conference information, discussion forums and expertise search. Euspen is a not-for-profit company based at Cranfield University in the UK, with members around the world.
- *Exploring the Nanoworld*—Movies of nano-structured materials: ferrofluids, memory metals, amorphous metals, LEDs, re-entrant foams, self assembly, DNA, Magnetic Resonance Imaging, atomix imaging, Lego models, Giant Magneto Resistance, silicon, carbon nanotubes, polymers, and semiconductor devices. National Science Foundation supported Materials Research Science and Engineering Center on Nanostructured Materials and Interfaces at the University of Wisconsin-Madison.
- *The gRobots Project*—An open source project to build and run a globally distributed supercomputer for the simulation of evolvable nanotechnology.
- *How Stuff Works: How Nanotechnology Will Work*—Animated narrative shows how Nanotechnology has the potential to totally change manufacturing, health care and many other areas.
- *IBM Almaden STM Molecular Art*—Some of the famous images of atoms and molecules made with IBM's scanning tunneling microscope.
- *Institute for Atomic-Scale Engineering*—Personal page of Forrest Bishop: published and unpublished concept articles.
- *Institute of Nanotechnology (UK)*—The Institute of Nanotechnology has been created to foster, develop and promote all aspects of science and technology in those domains where dimensions and tolerances in the range of 0.1 nm to 100nm play a critical role.
- *Iran Nanotechnology Policy Studies Committee*—A committee for studying nanotechnology trends in Iran and the world.
- *Minatec*—Centre for innovation in micro and nanotechnology. Teaching, research, and industrial development.

- *Minatec*—Centre for Innovation in Micro and Nanotechnology in Grenoble. Teaching, research, and industrial development.
- *MITRE Corp. Nanosystems Group*—Reviews current nanotechnology research and people behind it, downloadable copies of several widely-used articles. Nanoelectronics focus.
- *Molecular Manufacturing Shortcut Group*—Promotes developing nanotechnology as a way to facilitate space exploration and settlement.
- *Moletronics and Nanotechnology references*—Links to sites with information mainly on molecular electronics.
- *Nano Science & Technology Institute*—Events, publications and news in nanotechnology, microtechnology and biotechnology.
- *Nano Space*—Nano technology as it applies now and in the future to Space Exploration and Studies.
- *NanoApex*—Nanotechnology portal.
- *Nanobase*—Loyola College, Maryland. National Science Foundation sponsored site presenting up-to-date sources of information on nanotechnology in the areas of major research centers, funding agencies, major reports and books.
- *NanoComputer Dream Team*—Multidisciplinary project to make Earth's first nanometer supercomputer via Internet.
- *Nanodot*—News and Discussion of Coming Technologies: Weblog devoted to nanotechnology-related news stories, with attached discussion forum. (based on Slashdot software)
- *Nanoforum.org: European Nanotechnology Gateway*—Offers background information, news and developments in industry and research and a selection of publications.
- *nanogloss*—Online dictionary of nanotechnology.
- *Nanoguys*—Nanotechnology Career Consultants. Recruiting and placement of staff in nanotechnolgy related positions such as Organic, Inorganic, Biological, Project Management, Research Scientist, Engineer, and Lab Technician.
- *Nanomagazine*—Interviews with people in the Nanotechnology field.
- *NanoManipulator: 3rdTech*—Commercial version of the NanoManipulator system originally from University of North Carolina, Chapel Hill.
- *NanoManipulator: University of North Carolina*—The nanoManipulator provides an improved, natural interface to SPMs (STMs and ATMs) by

coupling the microscope to a virtual-reality interface giving a virtual telepresence on the surface, scaled by a factor of about a million to one.

- *Nanomedicine*—Devoted to the medical applications and implications of molecular nanotechnology. Nanomedicine may be defined as the monitoring, repair, construction and control of human biological systems at the molecular level, using engineered nanodevices and nanostructures. Includes the Nanomedicine Art Gallery. (From the Foresight Institute.)
- *Nanoscale Science and Engineering*—National Science Foundation. Activities, Information & Education, Research & Development, Connections, and NSF & NNI (National Nanotechnology Initiative) Reports.
- *NanoScout*—Portal with forums, and links sorted by topic and popularity.
- *NanoSpace*—The Center for NanoSpace Technologies is a Texas-based nonprofit scientific research and education foundation chartered to conceive, establish, and conduct cutting-edge technology, research, and development in the areas of aerospace, education, energy, life sciences, and shipping & transportation.
- *NanotechNews*—News for nanotechnologists and investors: regular updates, many links to other nanotechnology websites, archives, search function, newswire.
- *Nanotechnology*—Institute of Physics quarterly journal
- *Nanotechnology*—Institute of Physics monthly journal for aspects of nanoscale science and technology
- *The NanoTechnology Group*—A consortium of nano companies, universities and organizations developing a nano science curriculum for K-12.
- *Nanotechnology in Manufacturing*—What Next? The Coming Revolution In Manufacturing: Autodesk Technology Forum Presentation by John Walker, May 10th, 1990. Somewhat dated but well worth reading.
- *Nanotechnology Journals Database*—References, and links to, papers about nanotechnology, from selected scientific journals (eg PRB, PRL, JACS, JAP, JPCB).
- *Nanotechweb.org*—A portal for nanoscience and nanotechnology online resources for academics, industrialists and investors, as well as for laymen interested in nanotechnnology.
- *NanoTechWire.com*—Provides information for nanotechnology and research.
- *Nanotek*—Nanotechnology: articles online, news, pictures, cvs
- *nanoTEN*—Nanotechnology consulting firm. Services include nanotechnology

matchmaking, assessment of trends, feasibility studies, materials and products analysis, and presentation assistance.

- *nanoTITAN*—Nanotechnology Software, Data & Services: nanoTITAN offers Java libraries and applications, a nanodevice database, the nanoML specification, custom simulation and visualization to the nanotechnology and general scientific communities.
- *Nanotube Patent Search*—Results from a search of nanotube or nanotube related patents at the United States Patent & Trademark Office
- *The Nanotube Site*—Michigan State University's Library of Links for the Nanotube Research Community
- *NanoWave*—An MIT startup, Nanowave offers SPPE (Scanning Probe Position Encoder) technology for picometer-order (subnanometer) resolution over ranges greater than several inches.
- *National Science Foundation*—Partnership in Nanotechnology (US). Recent technical and policy reports, funding opportunities, profiles of projects currently supported, and links to other nanoscience/technology sites.
- *Phantoms*—European Union sponsored nano electronics network. Contains comprehensive information about European nanotechnology, and links to groups and events worldwide.
- *Polymer Simulation*—Computer simulation of a polymer sticking to a surface.
- *Scanning Tunneling Microscope (STM)*—Describes the invention of the topografiner, a precursor instrument, between 1965 and 1971, and also tells of the STM's development.
- *Scientific American*—Nanotechnology articles, some free and some archived.
- *Self Replicating Systems*—NASA and Self-Replicating Systems: Implications for Nanotechnology.
- *Small Times*—Daily articles covering MEMS, nanotechnology, and microsystems, with a business angle.
- *Stony Brook Buckyballs*—A virtual tour of fullerenes in Laszlo Mihaly's laboratory at the Physics Department at SUNY, Stony Brook.
- *STT: Netherlands Study Center for Technology Trends*—Somewhere in this confusing site is good material in English, though it is often labeled in Dutch, and Dutch material is often labeled in English. STT hopes to bring their project to the attention of a wide audience, thereby contributing to the development of nanotechnology.

- *Technology Review: Nanotechnology and Materials*—Articles, discussion and services for nanotech built on MIT's award-winning monthly magazine.
- *Thermodynamics Research Laboratory*—Classical, Quantum, Nanoscale & Statistical Thermodynamics & Mechanics data and property calculation sites.
- *Virtual Journal of Nanoscale Science & Technology*—A weekly multijournal compilation of the latest research on nanoscale systems. Published by the American Institute of Physics and the American Physical Society.
- *VISION Online*—Virtual Institute supported by the EC, committed to promotion and training in the precision engineering and nanotechnologies. Contains discussion forums, training programmes and patent library.
- *Xerox/Zyvex Nanotechnology*—Former Xerox Palo Alto Research Center Nanotechnology page: brief introduction to core concepts of molecular nanotechnology (MNT), and links for further reading.
- *Yahoo Groups: Nanotechnology*—Active nanotechnology discussion group.
- *Yashnanotech*—Provides marketing and consultancy services for products developed by nanotechnology. Promotes nanotech awareness through training, educational publications, seminars, workshops and conferences.

Nanoword Feature Articles

Interview with Rocky Rawstern

We've heard plenty about the potential of nanotechnology from scientists, engineers, capitalists and entrepreneuers, but what does the unbiased public want and expect from nanotechnology? Rocky Rawstern addresses public expectations, media spin and 'the singularity'.

Trends in NanoTechnology (TNT) 2001

The TNT 2001 conference took place September 3-7, 2001 in Segovia, Spain. Some of the more trendy aspects of nanotechnology were: Electronics, Photonics, Nanotubes, Mechanical Devices, Theoretical Models, Self-Assembly, Networks and Funding.

Molecular Electronics

With our increasing understanding of electron transfers within and between individual molecules, it may only be a matter of time before a lucky researcher discovers the right parameters to cheaply integrate moles of addressable molecular circuits.

Interview With Tim Harper

This interview with Tim Harper, CEO of CMP Cientifica discusses what makes a product 'nano', revolutionary products and the potential of nanotechnology.

Alchemy, The Next Generation

Nanotechnology can be qualitatively understood as an approach to alchemy that is based on the current model of matter. Only time will tell whether its dreams will be realized or face the same fate as the philosopher's stone and the elixir of life.

Electrons: from Microscopy to Lithography

The electron is a most convenient particle (or wave) for microscopy and lithography. Whether they are being focused via e-beams or tunneled through STM tips, without the electron there would be no nanotech.

Mechanical VLSI

The miniaturization of mechanical devices (MicroElectroMechanical Systems—MEMS) is gaining increasing attention due to numerous commercial applications. Integration of basic MEMS components is bridging the gap between micro- and nanotechnology.

Frontiers in Optical Lithography

Several methods are available to the chip designer who wishes to use light to carve nanoscale features. The diffraction barrier can be broken in various ways and novel photosensitive materials promise a bright future for photolithography.

Nanotech Education

Which subjects should a student learn in preparation for nanotechnology? Biology, chemistry, physics, engineering and computer science each provide a unique perspective of the nanoscale. Various combinations of these fields are where the most progress is being made, thus resulting in interdisciplinary nanoscience.

Surface Wetting

Understanding surface wetting has had important implications for preventing wear, for medicine and for self-cleaning products. A model for surface tension based on a two-dimensional frozen film is proposed.

Nanoscale Chemistry

While chemistry deals with molecules in a statistical sense, nanotechnology deals with them as discrete entities, each requiring special attention. For instance, in order to understand and fabricate molecular assembly lines or carry out single molecule reactions in vessicles it is useful to tweak some fundamental units such as temperature.

Quantum Biology

At a time when numerous physicists are racing to construct quantum computers, molecular biologists may unknowingly be racing to dismantle them.

Biomolecular Self-Assembly

Living systems have a vast array of molecular components that are specially designed for self-assembly. Why build your own components when you can borrow DNA, protein and lipids from nature?

Seeing Things Smaller Than Light

Scanning Probe Microscopy (SPM) is a family of techniques that allows one to observe and create features far smaller than the wavelength of visible light. STM, SFM (AFM), SNOM (NSOM), MFM and SCM are a few of the variations.

Quantum Dots

Quantum dots have zero dimensional electronic properties and could be used as the qubits in quantum computers. Quantum dots are nothing new to biological systems, which use them for everything from photosynthesis to the electron transport chain.

DNA Mediated Energy Transfer

The ability of DNA to transfer electrons through the one-dimensional double helix has been experimentally observed. As biologists figure out what this means for medicine, nanoscientists are using DNA to assemble nanoelectronic devices.

Ethical & Social Issues in Nanotechnology

Bonsor, Kevin. "How Nanotechnology Will Work." *(From www.howstuffworks.com).*

At some point in the near future, nanomachines will produce consumer goods, rather than the bulky machines that are used today. NT works "...by piecing together one atom or molecule at a time..." For nanotechnology (NT) to work, small devices called assemblers must be created in order to combine atoms that will produce consumer goods. Replicators will also have to be made to produce enough assemblers that will be required to create goods.

Of the many positive features of NT, nanomachines will produce: stronger products than those produced by traditional methods; food and water will be able to be replicated, thus, eliminating hunger worldwide; computers could become dramatically more powerful without any increase in size; nanosurgeons could undertake delicate operations much more precise than current surgery is able to; and nanorobots could be used to alter one's physical features such as ears, nose, eye colour, etc.

Nanotechnology could also have many positive effects on the environment, including: reconstruction of the ozone layer; quickly cleaning up oil spills; purifying water; and eliminating the use of non-renewable resources (which could be made by nanomachines).

Brown, Doug "Nano Litterbugs? Experts See Potential Pollution Problems." *(From www.smalltimes.com).*

The U.S. Environmental Protection Agency (EPA) has begun research into the possible negative impacts associated with NT. Even as some products using NT have begun to be widely distributed, the environmental impact is still unknown.

A concern for Vicki Colvin, who is director of The Center for Biological and Environmental Nanotechnology, is that no research is being conducted into how to control nanomaterial if it was discovered to be harmful to humans or the environment.

Based on preliminary research on animals, it is known that nanomaterials do accumulate within the body. Also, nanomaterials can be overtaken by bacteria, which could mean nanomaterials could infiltrate the food chain. Bacteria enhanced by nanomaterials could produce more potent bacteria. While NT promises to have numerous benefits for society, many of the potential risks remain uninvestigated.

Joy, Bill "Why the future doesn't need us." (*In* Wired *magazine*. April, 2000).

Joy's concern over NT is amplified, due to the fact that engineered organisms can self-replicate. Such replication could lead to situations where things could quickly get out of hand. "A bomb is blown up only once—but one bot can become many, and quickly get out of control." An additional worry for Joy is, unlike weapons of mass destruction (WMD) – which require hard-to-get materials and highly specialized knowledge – genetics, nanotechnology, and robotics (GNR) are available to a wide range of people, thus making them all the more dangerous. While WMD are strictly controlled by the military, GNR's are corporate sponsored. Such a wide dispersion of NT increases the risk. Joy emphasizes prudence in our development of NT, because if we proceed too quickly, we could cause our own extinction. After all, we are still unable to control the spread of viruses and other undesirable components of life.

Joy draws a parallel between NT and the atomic bomb. The creation of the atomic bomb led to the development of an arms race that lasted nearly half a century and had many detrimental effects. Atomic and nuclear weapons have the ability to destroy the world many times over, as does NT. We should not repeat the same mistakes with NT that we did with WMD.

"The only realistic alternative I see is relinquishment: to limit development of the technologies that are too dangerous, by limiting our pursuit of certain kinds of knowledge." Limiting access to critical information involving NT must be enforced because it contains such a destructive force to humanity (e.g. exterminating the entire race). People will inevitably object to the infringement on their right to privacy and pursuit of intellectual property, but this is a necessary step if we are to avoid the dangers NT poses. Additionally, scientists will have to comply with strict ethical codes to ensure compliance with relinquishment rules.

While humanity's dream of immortality will likely continue forever, certain limits to the means creating this end must be imposed due to the inherent danger.

Mehta, Michael D. "On Nano-Panopticism: A Sociological Perspective."

This article deals with privacy issues associated with surveillance, and how surveillance will be changed with the development of NT.

It has been scientifically documented that observation of a subject will change the regular behaviour of that subject. For example, prisoners who are held in prison cells that are in open view of a prison guard behave better than those prisoners who are afforded more privacy. Therefore, if this concept is applied to society as a whole, one can see the ramifications increased surveillance might have on public behaviour. Increased surveillance with the use of NT may have many damaging effects that may express themselves through a decrease in public trust, less involvement in public life, and may result ultimately in an Orwellian state.

Mehta offers several suggestions on how to deal with the dangers related to nano-panopticism. They are: develop an independent agency to monitor and regulate progress in NT; introduce tough laws to ensure that privacy is protected; a review of a corporation's code of conducts to ensure nano-panopticism does not become a problem; public consultation of the appropriate uses of NT; and finally, increase the awareness of scientists so that they are better able to understand the impact new technologies have on society.

Mnyusiwalla, A. Abdallah S. Daar, & Peter A. Singer "'Mind the gap': science and ethics in nanotechnology." *(From* Nanotechnology, *February 13, 2003).*

As NT quickly develops, the ethical evaluation of such a development has yet to begin. Research into NT's impact on ethical, environmental, economic, legal, and social implications (NE^3LS) must try to keep pace with the technological progress that has been made. Otherwise, the technological progress will slow down.

K. Eric Drexler, author of *Engines of Creation*, and currently working for the Foresight Institute, has begun to develop guidelines for the use of NT, particularly concerning self-replication, but also issues such as wealth distribution and environmental protection.

While there is a call for increased research into the effects of NT on society, the environment, etc, and furthermore, that the funds for such research are available, very little research has been done. For example, The National Nanotechnology Initiative (NNI) spent less than half of its budget on studying the impacts NT will have on society. In addition, the National Science Foundation (NSF) did not fund any research into the societal implications of NT due to lack of research grant proposals.

The ethical issues associated with NT fall into a variety of categories including:

1. *Equity*: NT does not stand to help developed countries only, but also (and perhaps mainly) developing countries. For example, third world countries suffer most from things that can be improved upon from advancements made in NT. For instance, providing cleaner water, developing cheaper energy, and also the enormous health benefits to be reaped from NT are all aspects of NT that could have a dramatic impact on third world countries.
2. *Privacy and security*: While NT could dramatically improve surveillance systems and would undoubtedly have numerous military applications, some are left wondering how personal privacy would be affected. Questions concerning the regulation of this new technology are arising without many answers being offered.
3. *Environment*: The effects of NT materials on the environment are unknown. The EPA has increased funding to study the effects of NT on the environment.
4. *Human or machine?* How far are humans willing to go with replacement of human parts with replacement robot parts?

Earlier lessons from genomics and biotechnology (recommendations):

- A percentage of the research and development funds should go to study the societal impacts of NT. In the *Human Genome Project*, 3-5% of the total budget was dedicated to studying the societal impacts.
- Large-scale interdisciplinary research platforms should be avoided.
- The capacity for research should be increased. This would include research grants, career awards, increased funding, etc.
- There should be a cross-section of groups working on the implications of NT in order to have a variety of views expressed.
- A global opinion-leaders network for social and ethical implications ought to be established so that third world countries may be involved.
- Public engagement is crucial if NT is to have the impact it potentially holds. The public needs to have accurate information concerning the social

and ethical implications of NT. Science museums could include exhibits on NT; as well, schools could discuss the issue in depth.

Moor, James & John Weckert "Nanoethics: Assessing the Nanoscale from an Ethical Point of View."

Weckert and Moor argue that nanoethics cannot develop fully or effectively until the technology develops further and its consequences become known. Weckert and Moor do acknowledge the potentially enormous impact NT will have on society, but are hesitant to develop strategies to deal with problems that do not yet exist. They recommend continued monitoring of NT.

Pagán, Sylvia "DNA nanoballs boost gene therapy." *(In* New Scientist*, May, 2002).*

NT is now beginning to enhance older technologies used to treat patients with cystic fibrosis. Nanoparticles made up of a single DNA molecule are much smaller, and therefore much better able to reach the nucleus of a cell, than were previous methods involving modified viruses. NT shows promising signs of contributing to the advancement of the cure for cystic fibrosis.

Phoenix, Chris & Mike Treder "Applying the Precautionary Principle to Nanotechnology." *(From* The Center for Responsible Nanotechnology*, January, 2003).*

There are two forms of the precautionary principle: (1) the strict form; and (2) the active form.

Strict form: "...requires inaction when action might pose a risk."

Active form: "...calls for choosing less risky alternatives when they are available, and for taking responsibility for potential risks."

One shortcoming of the strict form of the Precautionary Principle is that most actions carry some sort of risk. If we follow the strict form, much of the scientific research currently underway would have to be halted. Second, sometimes inaction can be more harmful than action. Sometimes the benefits to be gained by scientific research outweigh the minimal risks involved.

The Center for Responsible Nanotechnology (CRN) believes that a total ban on development of NT would not be practical; enforcement of such a ban would be nearly impossible. Not only is such a ban not practical, it may not be desired. There are many benefits that could be brought about by NT, including increased health, less environmental damage, cheap and efficient production of goods, etc. These factors must be considered when determining the fate of NT.

The CRN believes that the strict form of the Precautionary Principle is inadequate for dealing with NT. This is so because inaction carries with it certain risks:

1. No other solution may be found for certain pressing problems.
2. Inaction on the part of responsible people could simply lead to the development and use of MNT by less responsible people.
3. Lack of understanding of the technology will leave the world ill-equipped to deal with irresponsible use.

The CRN does, however, believe that the active form of the Precautionary

Principle is adequate in dealing with research into NT. Because the active form seeks to develop the least risky solution to existing problems, this is more desirable than the strict form.

The final recommendation of the CRN is to create "...one–*and only one*–molecular nanotechnology program, [which would permit] the widespread but restricted use of the resulting manufacturing capability.

Phoenix, Chris & Mike Treder "Safe Utilization of Advanced Nanotechnology." *(From* The Center for Responsible Nanotechnology, *January, 2003).*

There are many risks associated with NT. For instance, Drexler's "gray goo" problem–where self-replicating nanoassemblers multiply out of control; NT falling into the hands of rogue states; and decreased privacy due to the sizing-down of surveillance equipment, to name a few. Given these risks, it would appear that some regulation of NT is in order. If NT is regulated too strictly this could lead to the development of a black market where irresponsible users could do a great deal of damage. Phoenix and Treder propose a two-dimensional approach to the restriction of NT which will reduce risks associated with NT, yet allow the technology to further develop.

First, products that use NT do not necessarily pose any extraordinary risks, they are simply products that have been enhanced in some way by the use of NT; they will not be able to self-replicate whatsoever. However, the factories used to produce NT products could quite easily be very dangerous. NT factories, if controlled by the wrong people, could hold great danger for humankind with the potential to develop destructive weapons much greater than are available today. Phoenix and Treder stress that "...research leading to advanced nanotechnology will have to be carefully monitored and controlled. However, the same *is not true of product research and development*."

If NT factories are to be safe, certain precautions must be taken. First, assemblers need not ever leave the factory, they can easily be fastened to the factory to avoid them escaping into the environment and getting out of control. Second, factories can be programmed to produce only specified products that are known to be safe. Third, one could go so far as to build in a tracking device to ensure that NT products were being used safely and for their intended purpose. Furthermore, nanofactories could be made tamper-proof so that they could shut down if attempt at alteration was made. Finally, a nanofactory could be connected to a central controller which would then determine if the desired product was safe. If the central controller determined the product to be unsafe, the controller could disable the factory. Additional advantages of this scenario would be that the controller could automatically provide updates to the nanofactories and also relay the location of the factory.

Rotman, David "Measuring the Risks of Nanotechnology." *(In* Technology Review*, April, 2003).*

Vicki Colvin, Director of The Center for Biological and Environmental Nanotechnology at Rice University, states that the possible dangers associated with NT are largely unknown at this point. Despite the fact that nanomaterials have been put to use in products such as sunscreen, the potential risks of these materials is unknown. It is believed that some nanoparticles can be transmitted from the blood stream to brain material. Colvin believes that the benefits of NT–especially its medical applications–far outweigh any risks that have been hypothesized.

Groups such as Greenpeace have begun to investigate NT for any risks it may pose.

"Handle Nano-Technology with Care," (In African Business. *March, 2003). [not available on-line]*

The action group on Erosion, Technology and Concentration (ETC) is worried that developments in NT are going unnoticed both by the public and government regulatory agencies. This is of great concern given that NT will have such a profound impact on society. One problem with regulating NT is that it has such a wide variety of applications and is therefore difficult to control under one regulatory agency. Furthermore, because many of the products that have incorporated NT merely use the same compounds that were previously used but on a lower scale, many people do not recognize any associated risks whatsoever. ETC is calling for a worldwide evaluation of the potential impacts of NT, and until such a process has begun, production of nanomaterials ought to cease.

Career Links

- FEI Company

  http://www.careerexchange.com/cejobs/templatefei.asp
- Career Resource Center for Materials Science & Engineering

http://www.crc4mse.org/

- tinytechjobs

  http://www.tinytechjobs.com/

Electron Microscopy Links (General)

- History of the Microscope

  http://inventors.about.com/library/inventors/blmicroscope.htm

- Electron Microscope Web Course

  http://em-outreach.ucsd.edu/web-course/toc.html

- Electron Microscopy

  http://www.biologie.uni-hamburg.de/b-online/e03/03e.htm

- MicroElectronics—Atomic Scale Design

  http://www.atomicscaledesign.net/microelectronics/links/software/index.shtml

Industry Organizations

- American Society for Cell Biology

  http://www.ascb.org/

- American Society for Materials International

  http://www.asminternational.org/

- Cientifica

  http://www.cientifica.com/

- Electronic Device Failure Analysis Society/ISTFA

  http://www.asminternational.org/MSTemplate.cfm?Site=Electronic_Device_Failure_Analysis_Society

- European Microscopy Society

  http://www.eurmicsoc.org/

- IDEMA

  http://www.idema.org/

- International Federation of Societies for Microscopy

  http://www.ifsm.umn.edu/members.html

- Japanese Society of Microscopy

  http://wwwsoc.nii.ac.jp/jsm/index.html

- Materials Research Society

http://www.mrs.org/

- NanoBusiness Alliance
  http://www.nanobusiness.org/
- SEMI
  http://www.semi.org/

Nanotechnology Links

- The Center for Nanotechnology at the University of Washington
  http://www.nano.washington.edu/index.asp
- nano tech 2006
  http://www.ics-inc.co.jp/nanotech/index_e.html
- The Nanotechnology Site
  http://inventors.about.com/library/inventors/blmicroscope.htm
- Nanotechnology and Cryonics
  http://www.futurescience.com/nanocryo.html
- Nanotechnology Now
  http://www.nanotech-now.com/
- National Nanotechnology Initiative
  http://www.nano.gov/
- Open Encyclopedia Project: Nanotechnology
  http://open-site.org/Science/Technology/Nanotechnology/
- TNTlog: Global Nanotechnology Blog
  http://www.cientifica.com/archives/000031.html

Publications

- Advanced Materials & Processing
  http://www.asminternational.org/
- European Semiconductor
  http://www.eurosemi.eu.com/
- Forbes/Wolfe Nanotech Report
  http://www.forbesinc.com/newsletters/nanotech/
- Materials Today
  http://www.materialstoday.com/

- Microscopy & Analysis
  http://www.microscopy-analysis.com/
- Microscopy Today
  http://www.microscopy-today.com/
- Micro
  http://www.micromagazine.com/
- MRS Bulletin
  http://www.mrs.org/publications/bulletin/
- News.Nano.Apex
  http://news.nanoapex.com/
- R&D Magazine
  http://www.mrs.org/publications/bulletin/
- Scanning
  http://www.scanning.org/
- Semicondcutor Manufacturing
  http://www.semimfg.com/
- Semiconductor International
  http://www.semiconductor.net/
- Small Times
  http://www.smalltimes.com/
- Solid State Technology
  http://www.solid-state.com/

Research Organizations

- Center for Advanced Electron Microscopy
  http://www.bnl.gov/tem/
- Imaging Technology Group
  http://www.itg.uiuc.edu/ms/equipment/microscopes/tem/
- Nano Science and Technology Institute
  http://www.nsti.org/Nanotech2005
- SEM—EDS Laboratory
  http://www2.arnes.si/guest/sgszmera1

APPENDIX - II

NANOBIOTECHNOLOGY AND NANOTECHNOLOGY REPORTS

1. Small Wonders, Endless Frontiers: A Review of the National Nanotechnology Initiative.

The chapter on history has a table indicating planned goals until 2007. Stupp, S.I., *Small Wonders, Endless Frontiers: A Review of the National Nanotechnology Initiative*. 2002, National Academy Press: Washington, D.C.,2002.

2. Nanotechnology-Size Matters.

Researched by 3i, Economist Intelligence Unit and The Institute of Nanotechnology, this report examines input from the leading experts in the field of nano-science and technology around the world and summarizes the key pointers that help understand the dynamics of the field as a whole. 3i. "Nanotechnology- Size Matters", *Building a Successful Nanotechnology Company*, http://www.3i.com/, July 2002

3. Nanostructure Science and Technology: A Worldwide Study.

This report reviews the status of research and development in nanoparticles, nanostructured materials, and nanodevices worldwide, with particular focus on comparisons between the United States and other leading industrialized countries. Topics covered include particle synthesis and assembly, dispersions and coatings of nanoparticles, high surface area materials, functional nanoscale devices, bulk behavior of nanostructured materials, and biological methods and applications. The final chapter is a review of related government funding programs around the world. Siegel, R.W., E. Hu, and M.C. Roco, eds., *Nanostructure Science and Technology: A Worldwide Study*., NSTC/CT/IWGN, 1999

4. Nanotech: the Tiny Revolution.

This white paper is a preview of The Nanotechnology Opportunity Report™ which provides a thorough analysis of the global nanotechnology market and of the key technologies coming to market now and in the near future. It also includes an extensive guide to the 455 public and private companies, 95 investors, and 271 academic institutions, and government entities that are involved in the near-term applications of the technology worldwide. Analysis is provided on both markets & technologies, at a price of $1995. Hollister, P., *Nanotechnology- the Tiny Revolution*., July 2002, CMP cientifica: www.cientifica.com.

5. Economic Perspectives of Nanotechnology: Enormous Markets for Tiny Particles.

Growth forecast of the world market of nanomaterials from the stand point of

BASF. Being one of the world leaders in chemical manufacturing, BASF's point of view may be valuable in assessing the market for nanomaterials. Ebenau, A., *Economic Perspectives of Nanotechnology: Enormous Markets for Tiny Particles*, BASF Future Business GmbH, Ludwigshafen: Mannheim, October 2002.

6. CORDIS

This web site provides almost all required information on the EU's efforts and achievements in nanotechnology and science and technology in general. http://www.cordis.lu/nanotechnology/.

7. Sci-Tech Focus Report

Concise discussion of the growth of nanotechnology in Korea. "Survey of Korea's Nanotechnology", *Sci-Tech Focus*; 2002, http://nr.stic.gov.tw/ejournal/SciTechFocus/SciTechFocus_e.htm. p. 5.

8. Asia Pacific Nanotech Weekly

Publishes weekly reports, commentary and analyses on nanotechnology activities in Asia Pacific. The reports are in PDF format and freely accessible. Liu, L., Asia Pacific Nanotech Weekly, http://www.nanoworld.jp/apnw/.

9. Nanoscale Chemicals and Materials—An Overview on Technology, Products and Applications.

Compiled by SRI Consulting, a subsidiary of SRI international, this by far is the most informative report particularly on Asia; it provides data on current and future budget plans of Asian and European countries, along with the core emphasis technologies. Fink, U., et al., *Nanoscale Chemicals and Materials-An Overview on Technology, Products and Applications*. December 2002, http://scup.sric.sri.com/Enframe/Report.html?report=NANOT000&show=Navigaton.html

10. Nanotechnology Market and Company Report 2003.

The definition of the term "nanotechnology" was discussed with an international advisory board. The nanotechnology world market is predicted for specific product categories in each of the four nanotechnology segments. The company profiles are identified via various databases, conferences and internet researches. These profiles include information such as founding year, revenue, number of staff and short descriptions of key business activities with respect to nanotechnology. For an analysis of the present status and future visions of nanotechnology, interviews with 48 leading experts are carried out. The experts' responses on the future visions and future products serve as an indicator of future developments from the present point of view. Stark, D., *Finding Hidden Pearls: Nanotechnology Market and Company Report 2003*. 2003, http://www.nanoreport.de/home.html.

11. Current Medical Technologies, Applications & Market Opportunities in Nanotechnology & MEMS, 2002-2012.

While much of the enormous potential in nanotechnology and micro-electro-mechanical systems (MEMS) is at least a few years from beginning to materialize, the existence of substantial current revenue, current profits and a wide array of current activity demands scrutiny now by any entities seeking to truly capitalize on this market. This report on nanotechnology and MEMS is a detailed market and technology assessment and forecast of the products and technologies involved in the medical application of MEMS and nanotechnology. The Report details the current and emerging products, technologies and markets in the medical use of MEMS and nanotechnology. Specifically, the report comprehensively details the clinical applications, the status of products & technologies under development, the current/forecast market for each major application, the current or likely competitors and their positions in the market, and the opportunities for current or hopeful competitors in this field. Driscoll, P., *Current Medical Technologies, Applications & Market Opportunities in Nanotechnology & MEMS, 2002-2012*. 2003: http://www.mediligence.com;rpt601.htm/.

12. Implications of Emerging Micro- and Nanotechnologies.

An evaluation of the current trends in micro and nanotechnology for the Air Force. Increased information capabilities, miniaturization, new materials and increased functionality and autonomy emerged as the four main themes for emerging technologies. Brueck, S.R.J., *Implications of Emerging Micro-and Nanotechnologies*. 2002: Washington D.C.

13. Societal Implications of Nanoscience and Nanotechnology.

This report was created right before the commencement of the NNI in 2001. Current status is documented in section I.2.2.5. of this report. Roco, M.C. and W.S. Bainbridge, eds. *Societal Implications of Nanoscience and Nanotechnology*. NSET Workshop Report, NSET: Arlington, Virginia, March 2001.

14. The National Nanotechnology Initiative: The Initiative and Its Implementation Plan.

The purpose of the initiative was to support long-term nanoscale research and development leading to potential breakthroughs in areas such as materials and manufacturing, nanoelectronics, medicine and healthcare, environment, energy, chemicals, biotechnology, agriculture, information technology, and national security. The effect of nanotechnology on the health, wealth, and lives of people could be at least as significant as the combined influences of microelectronics, medical imaging, computer-aided engineering, and man-made polymers developed in this century.

Downey, M.L., ed. *National Nanotechnology Initiative: The Initiative and Its Implementation Plan*. NSTS/CT/NSET: Washington D.C. 144. 2000.

15. The National Nanotechnology Initiative FY2004 Budget Request.

NNI FY2004 Budget, in http://www.nano.gov/fy2004_budget_ostp03_0204.pdf.

16. National Nanotechnology Initiative: From Vision to Commercialization.

This meeting was designed to update attendees on the most promising nanotech advances. The meeting would feature status reports by the participating U.S. Government Departments and Agencies and the Nanoscale Science and Engineering Centers addressing:

- The main focus areas of nanotech research for FY2002 and FY2003
- The primary research objectives and associated timelines
- Highlights of research to-date and examples of the most promising developments
- Important challenges that need to be overcome
- The potential for near-term commercial applications and their estimated time-frames
- Other commercial applications that could be derived from the research and their estimated time-frames
- Efforts to transition such developments into the private sector
- Solicitations, proposals, and grants

National Nanotechnology Initiative. From Vision to Commercialization, April 2003, http://www.ccst.us/www.infocastinc.com/NNI/home.asp

17. Nanotechnology's Power Brokers.

The team at Forbes/Wolfe Nanotech Report surveyed leading investors, scientists, corporate executives and high-ranking government officials providing a jump on who the top movers and shakers are in nanotech. Survey responses were combined with quantitative criteria to arrive at the final rankings. Wolfe, J., "Nanotechnology's Power Brokers," *Nanotech Report*. March 2003, p. 1-8, http://www.forbesnanotech.com/

18. U.S. Nanotechnology 2002: Technologies, Application Development, M&A, Patent Disputes, Markets and Business Opportunity.

Gives an insightful overview of nanotechnology. The report analyses how this technology works and how it will apply to the consumer market in the near future.

The report also details the activities of private and government innovators involved in the highly budgeted nanotechnology R&D arena. This technology, which uses the most miniscule of building-blocks as a base for technological innovations will soon revolutionize the commercial world. MRG, U.S. Nanotechnology 2002: *Technologies, Application Development, M&A, Patent Disputes, Markets and Business Opportunity*, 2002, http://www.mrgco.com/TOC_Nanotechnology_2002.html.

19. 21st Century Nanotechnology Research and Development Act

This legislation, signed on 12/3/2003, puts into law programs and activities supported by the NNI. The authroization bill calls for $3.68 Billion for nanotechnology R&D for FY 2005—2008. http://www.nano.gov/html/news/PresSignsNanoBill.htm.

20. Preparing for the Next Silicon Valley: Opportunities and Choices.

The Next Silicon Valley Initiative is working to shape both a framework for understanding and communicating what is happening in the Valley economy, and a process for engaging leaders in a regional discussion of the opportunities and choices for the next wave of innovation. This paper identifies the economic opportunities and risks associated with the evolving convergence of biotechnology, nanotechnology and information technology. The purpose of this paper is to stimulate discussion and action in preparing for the next wave of social and technological innovation. Henton, D., et al., *Preparing for the Next Silicon Valley: Opportunities and Choices*, Joint Venture: June 2002, http://ww.jointventure.org/

21. State Technology and Science Index: Comparing and Contrasting California.

Clusters of existing technologies expand and emerging science-based technologies formed will be critical factors in determining economic winners and losers in the first half of the 21st century. As economic activity is based more on intangible assets, those states with vibrant technology clusters will experience superior economic growth. It is imperative for state and local development officials and business leaders to promote high-tech expansion and cluster formation. Although high tech is not the only development strategy to pursue, it will be the key distinguishing feature of regional vitality in the 21st century. States that recognize these changes and alter course quickly will be ahead in the economic development game. DeVol, R.C., R. Koepp, and F. Fogelbach, State Technology and Science Index: Comparing and Contrasting California. Milken Institute: September 2002,

http://www.milkeninstitute.org/publicactions/publicaltions.taf?function=detail&ID=163&cat=ResRep

22. Nanotechnology Yellow Pages.

Generated by Larta, this is a somewhat out of date description of some of the research being carried out in academic and commercial setups in the Southern California region. This report portrays the most prominent themes of California's endeavors in the field of nanotechnology. It does not highlight the diverse scientific developments, restricted primarily to academic research laboratories, that gives the southern California region its paramount position in the global nanotechnology map at these early stages. Foster, L., *Nanotechnology Yellow Pages*. Larta: 2001, http://www.larta.org/.

Worldwide Studies

23. Promoting Japanese-Style Nanotechnology Enterprise.

An analysis of Japan's strategy in developing nanotechnology. The presentation emphasizes that strategic alliances across national boarders may help Japan acquire the leading role in the global market. It gives a useful comparison of key technologies owned by the US and Japan. KAMEI, S.-i., Promoting Japanese-style Nanotechnology Enterprises (The Need for Strategic International Alliances). 2002: http://www.intv.net/ftmrw/DrKamei022602/pdf.

24. Proceedings of EPA Nanotechnology and the Environment: Applications and Implications (STAR Progress Review Workshop)

Collection of papers presented in the EPA conference addressing the impact of the growth and development of nanomaterials and nanotechnology from EPA's standpoint. Karn, B. and N. Savage, *EPA Nanotechnology and the Environment: Applications and Implications STAR Progress Review Workshop*, The Office of Research and Development's National Center for Environmental Research, 2002.

25. Nanotechnology Innovation for Chemical, Biological, Radiological, and Explosive (CBRE): Detection and Protection.

A workshop on May 2-3, 2002, was organized by the AVS and coordinated with a meeting of the AVS Science and Technology Society held in Monterey, California on May 1 and 2, 2002. The workshop was supported in part by the NNCO. This report summarizes the workshop's conclusions concerning the opportunities and challenges for nanoscience and technology research as applied to the NNI Grand Challenge on Chemical, Biological, Radiological, and Explosive (CBRE) Detection and Protection. Baker, J., et al., *Nanotechnology Innovation for Chemical, Biological, Radiological, and Explosive (CBRE): Detection and Protection*, November 2002, p. 32.

26. Nanoscale Science, Engineering and Technology in DOE's Office of Basic Energy Sciences. Research Directions and Nanoscale Science Research Centers.

This brochure briefly discusses the challenges of science at the nanoscale and DOE's role in addressing them. It includes a brief description of the Basic Energy

Sciences (BES) research program, and the new Nanoscale Science Research Centers are introduced. These user facilities will provide the Nation's research community with world-class resources for the synthesis, processing, fabrication, and analysis of materials at the nanoscale. BES, D., *Nanoscale Science, Engineering and Technology in DOE's Office of Basic Energy Sciences: Research directions and nanoscale science research centers*, 2003, p. 20.

27. Nanobusiness 2003.

The NanoBusiness Conference brings together leaders from business, government, academia and the financial community, providing attendees with all the tools and information required to push nanotechnology research and application development toward commercialization. 2003, N., The official conference of the Nanobusiness Alliance:

http://www.nanobusiness2003.com/index.shtml

28. Molecular Manufacturing: Societal Implications of Advanced Nanotechnology.

In this U.S. House of representatives committee on science hearing, more research into the societal impacts and ethical responsibilities of molecular manufacturing was urged. Witnesses praised H.R. 766, the Nanotechnology Research and Development Act of 2003, sponsored by Committee Chairman Sherwood Boehlert (R-NY) and Rep. Mike Honda (D-CA), as an important step toward achieving that goal. The full Committee hearing is available at [http://www.house.gov/science/hearings/full03/index.html] Peterson, April 9, 2003, 2003; Tringe, 2003 #24;, April 9, 2003, 2003

29. Nano Republic

As in 2002, the conference will be held on July 10, 2003 in Pasadena, California, and will be chaired by Dr. Jim Heath of Caltech. The conference is produced by LARTA, a prominent think tank for technology businesses, in collaboration with Caltech, the California NanoSystems Institute, Rockwell Scientific Company, UCSB, UCLA, USC, and UCI. The Nano Republic Conference will discuss recent developments in creating actual products and services based on nanotechnologies. The program features presentations and discussion by world leaders from industry and academia on topics such as materials, design and instrumentation, components (simple devices), and systems (complex devices). LARTA, Nano Republic. 2003: http://www.larta.org/nanorepublic/index.htm.

30. California NanoSystems Institute(CNSI)

The vision of the CNSI is to establish a coherent and distinctive organization that serves California and national purposes and that is embedded on the UCLA and UCSB campuses. The CNSI will be a world-class intellectual and physical environment that supports collaboration among California's university, industry and national laboratory scientists. UCLA and UCSB, *California NanoSystems Institute*, http://www.cnsi.ucla.edu/mainpage.html.

31. Center for Nanoscale Science and Engineering (CNSE)

UC Riverside in its current phase of strong growth is building a pre-eminent program in Nanotechnology through the establishment of the CNSE. Nanomedicine, where nanomaterials and nanodevices are brought to bear on biological processes and medical ailments is CNSE's thrust area. The effort that UCR is mounting in nanotechnology and its outreach in the Inland Empire will start to catalyze the location of high-tech industry in the Inland Empire.

32. Center for Nanoscience Innovation for Defense (CNID)

In addition to the campus center, UCR joined UCLA and UCSB in July 2002 to form the Center for Nanoscience Innovation for Defense (CNID), an alliance created to facilitate a rapid transition of research innovation in the nanosciences into applications for the defense sector. The three UC institutions will equally share U.S. government allocations of about $20 million. The Defense Advanced Research Project Agency (DARPA) and Defense MicroElectronics Activity (DMEA) sponsor the three-campus CNID. The center aims at the control and understanding of nanoscale materials, with applications in information and communications technology.

33. Northern California Nanotechnology Initiative

The NCNano Northern California Nanotechnology Initiative is a regional economic development program committed to building the world's leading Nanotechnology Cluster in Northern California. Their major organizational goals are to bring $6 billion in Nanotechnology investment and grant money into the Northern California Region and to create 150,000 new local jobs. Through creation of the Northern California Nanotechnology Institute NCNano will provide the unifying fabric integrating Universities, Research Labs, Businesses, Capital, Local and Regional Governments and Entrepreneurs. The challenge is fostering the creation of a dynamic environment where new ventures, spinouts and established companies can mutually prosper in the new, nanotechnology-driven, global technology economy.

Initiative, T.N.C.N., NC nano. 2003: http://www.ncnano.org/index.php.

Jr, R.P., *House Approves Boehlert-Honda $2.36 Billion Nanotechnology Legislation Bill to Boost Silicon Valley Economy*. 2003, May 7: http://www.ncnano.org/index.php?module=ContentExpress&func=display&ceid=28

34. Bay Area Nanotechnology Initiative (BANI)

BANI was initiated in April by the San Francisco Center for Economic Development in conjunction with leaders from industry and academia in the Bay Area and Silicon Valley. BANI is currently undertaking a regional assets assessment to assist the region to retain its pre-eminent position as the leader in research and development of nanoscience and nanotechnology. BANI has been building partnerships with industry, academia, research laboratories, venture capitalists and existing nanotechnology start ups in the San Francisco Bay Area and Silicon Valley. Piasente, C., R. Achtenberg, and T. Ewing, Bay Area Nanotech Initiative Receives State Funding For Regional Collaboration to Capitalize on Emerging Industry, 2003, May 12,

http://www.sfchamber.com/nanotech_initiative.htm

35. Bay Area Economic Forum

The Bay Area Economic Forum conducts projects and initiatives which mobilize leaders from the public and private sectors, higher education, labor and the community to work together to strengthen the region's economic climate and address its major challenges. With its sponsors, the Bay Area Council and the Association of Bay Area Governments, and partner organizations representing constituencies throughout the region, the Forum addresses issues of overarching concern to the Bay Area and its economic future. The Bay Area Science Innovation Consortium (BASIC) is in the process of producing a Bay Area regional nanotechnology futures report, highlighting and demonstrating the importance and competitiveness of the region's R&D infrastructure in the field. Forum, B.A.E., BASIC,

http://www.bayeconfor.org/baefdesc3.htm.

Research Programs on Nanotechnology in the World

Scientific breakthroughs combined with recent research programs in the United States, Japan, and Europe, and various initiatives in Australia, Canada, China, Korea, Singapore, and Taiwan highlight the international interest in nanoscale science and technology. Definitions of nanotechnology vary somewhat from country to country. Nanotechnology as defined for the projects reviewed in this chapter arises from the exploitation of the novel and improved physical, chemical, mechanical, and biological properties, phenomena, and processes of systems that are intermediate in size between isolated atoms/molecules and bulk materials, where phenomena length and time scales become comparable to those of the structure. It implies the ability to generate and utilize structures, components, and devices with a size range from about 0.1 nm (atomic and molecular scale) to about 100 nm (or larger in some situations) by control at atomic, molecular, and macromolecular levels. Novel properties occur compared to bulk behavior because of the small structure size and short time scale of various processes. Nanotechnology's size range and particularly its new phenomena set it apart from the technologies referred to as microelectromechanical systems (MEMS) in the United States or microsystems technologies (MST) in Europe.

It is estimated that nanotechnology is presently at a level of development similar to that of computer/information technology in the 1950s. As indicated in the preceding chapters and as evidenced by the WTEC panel's research and observations during the course of this study, the development of nanoscale science and technology is expected by most scientists working in the field to have a broad and fundamental effect on many other technologies. This helps to explain the phenomenal levels of R&D activity worldwide. This chapter presents an overview of most of the significant nanotechnology research programs in the world. Where possible, a general picture is given of the funding levels of the programs, based on site interviews and publications.

TheUnited States

Various U.S. public and private funding agencies; large companies in chemical, computer, pharmaceutical, and other areas; as well as small and medium-size enterprises provide support for precompetitive research programs on nanotechnology. Most of the supported programs are evolving out of disciplinary research programs, and only some are identified as primarily dealing with nanotechnology. U.S. government agencies sponsored basic research in this area at a level estimated at about $116 million in 1997 (Siegel et al. 1998), as shown in Table 8.1. The National Science Foundation (NSF) has the largest share of the U.S. government investment, with an expenditure of about $65 million per year, or about 2.4% of its overall research investment in 1997. In 1998 it expanded its research support to functional nanostructures with an initiative in excess of $13 million.

NSF activities in nanotechnology include research supported by the Advanced Materials and Processing Program; the Ultrafine Particle Engineering initiative dedicated to new concepts and fundamental research to generate nanoparticles at high rates; the National Nanofabrication User Network (NNUN); and Instrument Development for Nano-Science and Engineering (NANO-95) to advance atomic-scale measurements of molecules, clusters, nanoparticles, and nanostructured materials. A current activity is the initiative, Synthesis, Processing, and Utilization of Functional Nanostructures (NSF 98-20 1997).

In the United States, a number of large multinational corporations, small enterprises, and consortia are pursuing nanotechnology-related research and development activities. Dow, DuPont, Eastman Kodak, Hewlett-Packard (HP), Hughes Electronics, Lucent, Motorola, Texas Instruments, Xerox, and other multinationals have established specialized groups in their long-term research laboratories, where the total research expenditure for nanotechnology research is estimated to be comparable to the U.S. government funding. Computer and electronics companies allocate up to half of their long-term research resources to nanotechnology programs. HP spends 50% of long-term (over 5 years) research on nanotechnology (Williams 1998). Small business enterprises, such as Aerochem Research Laboratory, Nanodyne, Michigan Molecular Institute, and Particle Technology, Inc., have generated an innovative competitive environment in various technological areas, including dispersions, coatings, structural materials, filtration, nanoparticle manufacturing processes, and functional nanostructures (sensors, electronic devices, etc.). Small niches in the market as well as support from several U.S. government agencies through the Small Business for Innovative Research (SBIR) program have provided the nuclei for high-tech enterprises. The university-small business technology transfer (STTR) program at NSF is dedicated to nanotechnology in fiscal year 1999. Two semiconductor processing consortia, the Semiconductor Manufacturing and Technology Institute (Sematech) and the Semiconductor Research Corporation (SRC), are developing significant research activities on functional nanostructures on inorganic surfaces. A series of interdisciplinary centers with nanotechnology activities has been established in the last few years at many U.S. universities, creating a growing public research and education infrastructure for this field. Examples of such centers are

- Brown University, Material Research Science and Engineering Center
- Rice University, Richard Smalley's Center for Nanoscale Science and Technology (CNST)
- University of California–Berkeley, nanoelectronics facilities
- University of Illinois at Urbana, the Engineering Research Center on Microelectronics in collaboration with the Beckman Institute, a private foundation
- University of North Carolina
- University of Texas–Austin
- Rensselaer Polytechnic Institute
- University of Washington (focus on nanobiotechnology)
- University of Wisconsin at Madison (focus on nanostructured materials)

NNUN, mentioned above, is an interuniversity effort supported by NSF at five universities: Cornell, Stanford, University of California–Santa Barbara (UCSB), Penn State, and Howard. It has focused on nanoelectronics, optoelectronics, electromechanical systems, and biotechnology. The Center for Quantized Electronic Structures (QUEST) at UCSB is a national facility developing expertise on underlying physics and chemistry aspects. Hundreds of graduate students have completed their education in connection with these centers in the last few years.

Current interest in nanotechnology in the United States is broad-based and generally spread into small groups. The research themes receiving the most attention include

1. metallic and ceramic nanostructured materials with engineered properties
2. molecular manipulation of polymeric macromolecules
3. chemistry self-assembling techniques of "soft" nanostructures
4. thermal spray processing and chemistry-based techniques for nanostructured coatings
5. nanofabrication of electronic products and sensors
6. nanostructured materials for energy-related processes such as catalysts and soft magnets
7. nanomachining
8. miniaturization of spacecraft systems

In addition, neural communication and chip technologies are being investigated for biochemical applications; metrology has been developed for thermal and mechanical properties, magnetism, micromagnetic modeling, and thermodynamics of nanostructures; modeling at the atomistic level has been established as a computational tool; and nanoprobes have been constructed to study material structures and devices with nanometer length scale accuracy and picosecond time resolution. While generation of nanostructures under controlled conditions by building up from atoms and molecules is the most promising approach, materials restructuring and scaling-down approaches will continue. Exploratory research includes tools of quantum control and atom manipulation, computer design of hierarchically structured materials (e.g., Olson 1997), artificially structured molecules, combination of organic and inorganic nanostructures, biomimetics, nanoscale robotics, encoding and utilization of information by biological structures, DNA computing, interacting textiles, and chemical and bioagent detectors.

Commercially viable technologies are already in place in the United States for some ceramic, metallic, and polymeric nanoparticles, nanostructured alloys, colorants and cosmetics, electronic components such as those for media recording, and hard-disk reading, to name a few. The time interval from discovery to technological application varies greatly. For instance, it took several years from the basic research discovery of the giant magnetoresistance (GMR) phenomenon in nanocrystalline materials (Berkowitz et al. 1992) to industry domination by the corresponding technology by 1997. GMR technology has now completely replaced the old technologies for computer disk heads, the critical components in hard disk drives, for which there is a $20+ billion market (Williams 1998). All disk heads currently manufactured by

IBM and HP are based on this discovery. In another example, nanolayers with selective optical barriers are used at Kodak in more than 90% of graphics black and white film (Mendel 1997) and for various optical and infrared filters, which constitute a multibilliondollar business. Other current applications of nanotechnology are hard coatings, chemical and biodetectors, drug delivery systems via nanoparticles, chemical-mechanical polishing with nanoparticle slurries in the electronics industry, and advanced laser technology. Several nanoparticle synthesis processes developed their scientific bases decades ago, but most processes are still developing their scientific bases (Roco 1998). Most of the technology base development for nanoparticle work is in an embryonic phase, and industry alone cannot sustain the research effort required for establishing the scientific and technological infrastructure. This is the role of government (e.g., NSF and NIH) and private agency (e.g., Beckman Institute) support for fundamental research.

Nanotechnology research in the United States has been developed in open competition with other research topics within various disciplines. This is one of the reasons that the U.S. research efforts in nanotechnology are relatively fragmented and partially overlapping among disciplines, areas of relevance, and sources of funding. This situation has advantages in establishing competitive paths in the emerging nanotechnology field and in promoting innovative ideas; it also has some disadvantages for developing system applications. An interagency coordinating "Group on Nanotechnology" targets some improvement of the current situation. The group was established in 1997 with participants from twelve government funding/research agencies to enhance communication and develop partnerships among practicing nanoscience professionals.

Canada

Canada's National Research Council supports nanotechnology through the Institute for Microstructural Science, which has the mission to interact with industry and universities to develop the infrastructure for information technology. The main project, the Semiconductor Nanostructure Project, was initiated in 1990. It provides support for fundamental research at a series of universities, including Queen's, Carleton, and Ottawa Universities.

Japan

The term "nanotechnology" is frequently used in Japan specifically to describe the construction of nanostructures on semiconductors/inorganic substrates for future electronic and computer technologies, and to describe the development of equipment for measurement at nanometer level (Sienko 1998). There are, however, Japanese programs in a number of other areas related to nanotechnology in the broader definition used in this report.

Government agencies and large corporations are the main sources of funding for nanotechnology in Japan; small and medium-size companies play only a minor role. Research activities are generally grouped in relatively large industrial, government, and academic laboratories. The three main government organizations sponsoring nanotechnology in Japan are the Ministry of International Trade and Industry (MITI), the Science and Technology Agency (STA), and Monbusho (the Ministry of Education, Science, Sports, and Culture). Funding for nanotechnology research should be viewed in the context of an overall increased level of support for basic research in Japan since 1995 as a result of Japan's Science and Technology Basic Law No. 130 (effective November 15, 1995), even if the law has not been fully implemented. The data presented below are based on information received from Japanese colleagues during the WTEC visit in July 1997. All budgets are for the fiscal year 1996 (1 April 1996 to 31 March 1997) and assume an exchange rate of ¥115 = $1, unless otherwise stated. The first five-year program on ultrafine particles started in 1981 under the Exploratory Research for Advanced Technologies (ERATO) program; an overview of the results of that program was published in 1991 (Uyeda 1991).

It is estimated that the Agency of Industrial Science and Technology (AIST) within MITI had a budget of approximately $60 million per year for nanotechnology in 1996/97 (roughly 2.2% of the AIST budget). The National Institute for Advancement of Interdisciplinary Research (NAIR) hosts three AIST projects:

1. Joint Research Center for Atom Technology (JRCAT), with a ten-year budget of about $220 million for 1992-2001 ($25 million per year in 1996)
2. Research on Cluster Science program, with about $10 million for the interval 1992-1997
3. Research on Bionic Design program, with $10 million for 1992-1997, about half on nanotechnology

Other efforts supported to various degrees by MITI include the following:

- the Electrotechnical Laboratory in Tsukuba, which allocates about 17% (or $17 million per year) of its efforts on advanced nanotechnology projects
- the Quantum Functional Devices Program, funded at about $64 million for 1991-2001 (about $6.4 million in 1996)
- the Osaka National Research Institute and the National Industrial Research Institute of Nagoya, which each spend in the range of $2.5-3 million per year for nanotechnology
- the Association of Super-Advanced Electronics Technologies (ASET), a relatively new MITI-sponsored consortium with partial interest in

nanotechnology; it has similarities with the U.S. Ultra Electronics program of DARPA

It is estimated that STA investment in nanotechnology research was about $35 million in 1996, mainly within five organizations:

1. Institute of Physical and Chemical Research (RIKEN), where nanotechnology is included in the Frontier Materials Research initiative
2. National Research Institute for Metals (NRIM)
3. National Institute for Research in Inorganic Materials (NIRIM)
4. Japan Science and Technology Corporation (JST—formerly called JRDC), which manages the ERATO program, including four nanotechnology-related projects, each with total budgets of $13-18 million for five years:
   - Quantum Wave Project (1988-1993)
   - Atomcraft Project (1989-1994)
   - Electron Wavefront Project (1989-1994)
   - Quantum Fluctuation Project (1993-1998)

Monbusho supports nanotechnology programs at universities and national research institutes, as well as via the Japan Society for Promotion of Science (JSPS). The most active programs are those at Tokyo University, Kyoto University, Tokyo Institute of Technology, Tohoku University, and Osaka University. The Institute of Molecular Science and the Exploratory Research on Novel Artificial Materials and Substances program promote new research ideas for next-generation industries (5-year university-industry research projects). The "Research for the Future" initiative sponsored by JSPS has a program on "nanostructurally controlled spin-dependent quantum effects" (1996-2001) at Tohoku University. Monbusho's funding contribution to nanotechnology programs is estimated at ~ $25 million.

In total, MITI, STA, and Monbusho allocated ~ $120 million for nanotechnology in 1996.

Large companies also drive nanotechnology research in Japan. Important research efforts are at six institutions: Hitachi (Central R&D Laboratories, where nanotechnology is ~ 25% of long-term research)—Hitachi has ~ $70 billion per year in sales; NEC (Fundamental Research Laboratories, where nanotechnology is estimated to be ~ 50% of the precompetitive research)—NEC has ~ $40 billion per year in sales; NTT (Atsugi Lab); Fujitsu (Quantum Electron Devices Lab); Sony; and Fuji Photo Film Co. An allocation of 10% of sales for research and development is customary in these companies, with ~ 10% of this for long-term research. Some Japanese nanostructured products already have considerable market impact. Nihon Shinku Gijutsu (ULVAC) produces over $4 million per year in sales of particles for electronics, optics, and arts. Also, there are in Japan, at the United States, private consortia making an increased contribution to nanotechnology R&D:

- The Semiconductor Industry Research Institute of Japan (SIRI), established in 1994, focuses on long-term research with partial government funding
- Semiconductor Leading Edge Technologies, Inc. (SELETE), established by ten large Japanese semiconductor companies in 1996, focuses on applied research and development with an estimated budget of $60 million in 1997
- Semiconductor Technology Academic Research Center (STARC) promotes industry-university interactions

Strengthening of the nanotechnology research infrastructure in the last years has been fueled by both the overall increase of government funding for basic research and by larger numbers of academic and industry researchers choosing nanotechnology as their primary field of research. Potential industrial applications provide a strong stimulus. A systems approach has been adopted in most laboratory projects, including multiple characterization methods and processing techniques. A special Japanese research strength is instrumentation development. The university-industry interaction is stimulated by the new MITI projects awarded to universities in the last few years that encourage temporary hiring of research personnel from industry. Other issues currently being addressed are more extensive use of peer review, promoting personnel mobility and intellectual independence, rewarding researchers for patents, promoting interdisciplinary and international interactions, and better use of the physical infrastructure.

China

Nanoscience and nanotechnology have received increased attention in China since the mid-1980s. Approximately 3,000 researchers there now contribute to this field (Bai 1996). The ten-year "Climbing Project on Nanometer Science" (1990-1999) and a series of advanced materials research projects are the core activities. The Chinese Academy of Sciences sponsors relatively large groups, while the China National Science Foundation (CNSF) provides support mainly for individual research projects. Areas of strength are development of nanoprobes and manufacturing processes using nanotubes. The Chinese Physics Society and the Chinese Society of Particuology are societies involved in the dissemination of nanotechnology research.

India

India's main research activities are on nanostructured materials and electronic devices (Sikka 1995). These involve a combination of research institutions (the Central Electronics Engineering Research Institute in Pilani, the Space Application

Center in Ahmedabad, and others), funding organizations (the Centre for Development of Materials in Pune, the Indian Institute of Science in Bangalore, and others), and industry.

Germany

The Federal Ministry of Education, Science, Research, and Technology (BMBF) in Germany provides substantial national support for nanotechnology. The Fraunhofer Institutes, Max Planck Institutes, and several universities have formed centers of excellence in the field. It is estimated that in 1997 BMBF supported programs on nanotechnology with a budget of approximately $50 million per year. Two of the largest upcoming projects are "CESAR," a $50 million science center in Bonn equally sponsored by the state and federal governments with about one-third of its research dedicated to nanoscience, and a new institute for carbon-reinforced materials near Karlsruhe ($4 million over 3 years, 1998-2001). BMBF is establishing five "centers of competence in nanotechnology" in Germany starting in 1998, with topics ranging from molecular architecture to ultraprecision manufacturing.

Taiwan

Taiwan's major nanotechnology research effort is conducted in the area of miniaturization of electronic circuits. The research is conducted in academic institutions and at the Industrial Technology Research Institute. Government funds for fundamental research are channeled via the National Science Council.

South Korea

A national research focus on nanotechnology was established in Korea in 1995. The Electronics and Telecommunications Research Institute (ETRI) in Taejon, Korea's science city, targets advanced technologies for information and computer infrastructures, with a focus on nanotechnology (ATIP 1998). The emphasis is on nanoscale semiconductor devices and particularly on semiconductor quantum nanostructures and device applications (lasers, modulators, switches and logical devices, resonant tunneling devices, self-assembled nanosize dots, single-electron transistors, and quantum wires).

Singapore

Nanotechnology research received a considerable boost in Singapore by the initiation of a national program in this area in 1995.

Australia

The National Research Council (NRC) of Australia has sponsored R&D in nanotechnology since 1993 (ASTC 1993). Research groups work on synthesis of nanoparticles for membranes and catalysts (University of New South Wales), nanofiltration (UNESCO Center for Membrane Science and Technology), and use of nanoparticles in processing minerals for special products (the Advanced Mineral Products Research Center at the University of Melbourne). AWA Electronics in Homebush has the largest industrial research facility for nanoelectronics in Australia.

U.K.

A network program (LINK Nanotechnology Programme) was launched in the United Kingdom in 1988 with an annual budget of about $2 million per year. The Engineering and Physical Sciences Research Council (EPSRC) is funding materials science projects related to nanotechnology with a total value of about $7 million for a five-year interval (1994-1999). About $1 million is specifically earmarked for nanoparticle research. The National Physical Laboratory established a forum called the National Initiative on Nanotechnology (NION) for promoting nanotechnology in universities, industry, and government laboratories.

European Community (EC)

The term "nanotechnology" is frequently defined in Europe as "the direct control of atoms and molecules" for materials and devices. A more specific definition from H. Rohrer (1997) is a "one-to-one relationship between a nano-object or nano-part of an object and another nano-, micro- or bulk object." The nanotechnology field as defined in this WTEC report includes these aspects, with the clarification that only the specific, distinctive properties and phenomena manifesting at length scales between individual atoms/molecules and bulk behavior are considered.

There are a combination of national programs, collaborative European (mostly EC) networks, and large corporations that fund nanotechnology research in Europe. Multinational European programs include the following:

1. The ESPRIT Advanced Research Initiative in Microelectronics and the BRITE/EURAM projects on materials science in the EC are partially dedicated to nanotechnology.
2. The PHANTOMS (Physics and Technology of Mesoscale Systems) program is a network created in 1992 with about 40 members to stimulate nanoelectronics, nanofabrication, optoelectronics, and electronic switching. Its coordinating center is at the IMEC Center for Microelectronics in Leuven, Belgium.
3. The European Science Foundation has sponsored a network since 1995 for Vapor-phase Synthesis and Processing of Nanoparticle Materials (NANO) in order to promote bridges between the aerosol and materials science communities working on nanoparticles. The NANO network includes 18 research centers and is codirected by Duisburg University and Delft University of Technology.

4. The European Consortium on NanoMaterials (ECNM) was formed in 1996, with its coordinating center in Lausanne, Switzerland. This group aims at fundamental research to solve technological problems for nanomaterials and at improved communication between researchers and industry.
5. NEOME (Network for Excellence on Organic Materials for Electronics) has had some programs related to nanotechnology since 1992.
6. The European Society for Precision Engineering and Nanotechnology (EUSPEN) was designed in 1997 with participation from industry and universities from six EC countries.
7. The Joint Research Center Nanostructured Materials Network, established in 1996, has its center in Ispra, Italy.

It is expected that the European Framework V will introduce additional programs on nanotechnology, particularly by adding a new dimension in nanobiology in the next four-year plan.

France

The Centre National de la Récherche Scientifique (CNRS) has developed research programs on nanoparticles and nanostructured materials at about 40 physics laboratories and 20 chemistry laboratories in France. Synthesis methods include molecular beam and cluster deposition, lithography, electrochemistry, soft chemistry, and biosynthesis. Nanotechnology activity has grown within a wide variety of research groups, including ones focused on molecular electronics, large gap semiconductors and nanomagnetism, catalysts, nanofilters, therapy problems, agrochemistry, and even cements for ductile nanoconcretes. It is estimated that CNRS spends about 2% of its budget and dedicates 500 researchers in 60 laboratories (or about $40 million per year) on projects related to nanoscience and nanotechnology. Companies collaborating to research and produce nanomaterials include Thompson, St. Gobain, Rhône Poulenc, Air Liquide, and IEMN. Also, there is the "French Club Nanotechnologie," aimed at promoting interactions in this field in France.

Sweden

The estimated total expenditure for research on nanotechnology in Sweden is ~ $10 million per year. There are four materials research consortia involved in this field: 1. Ångström Consortium in Uppsala, with a budget of ~ $0.8 million per year in 1998 for surface nanocoatings 2. Nanometer Structures Consortium in Lund with a budget of ~ $3.5 million per year partially supported by ESPRIT (~ $1 million per year) 3. Cluster-based and Ultrafine Particle Materials in the University of Uppsala and Royal Institute of Technology with a budget of ~ $0.4 million per year in 1998 4. Brinell Center at the Royal Institute of Technology

Switzerland

There is a Swiss national program on nanotechnology with a special strength in instrumentation. The most advanced research centers are focused on nanoprobes and molecule manipulation on surfaces (IBM Research Laboratory in Zürich), devices and sensors (Paul Scherrer Institute), nanoelectronics (ETH Zürich), and self-assembling on surfaces in patterns determined by the substrate or template (L'École Polytechnique Fédérale de Lausanne). See the site reports on all of these institutions.

The Netherlands

The most active research centers in the Netherlands are the DIMES institute at Delft University of Technology, which receives one-third support from industry, and the Philips Research Institute in Eindhoven, which researches self-assembling monolayers and patterning on metallic and silicon surfaces. The SST Netherlands Study Center for Technology Trends is completing a study on nanotechnology and aims at promoting increased funding and research networking in the Netherlands (ten Wolte 1997).

Finland

The Academy of Finland and the Finnish Technology Development Center began a three-year nanotechnology program in 1997. The program involves sixteen projects with funding of \$9 million for a three-year period (1997-1999) for nanobiology, functional nanostructures, nanoelectronics, and other areas. Research on actuators and sensors is the Finnish area of strength.

Belgium and Spain

Since about 1993 both Belgium and Spain have established nanotechnology programs, centers of excellence, and university-industry interactions.

Multinational Efforts

Large multinational companies with significant nanotechnology research activities in Europe include IBM (Zürich), Philips, Siemens, Bayer, and Hitachi. Degussa Co., with headquarters in Germany, is a commercial supplier since 1940 of microparticles and, now, nanoparticles.

Western Europe has a variety of approaches to funding research on nanotechnology. These are discussed in detail in other studies. IPTS (the Science and Technology Forecast Institute) has conducted a study on nanotechnology research in the EC (Malsh 1997). Other European studies published recently include those by VDI (1996), UNIDO (1997), the U.K. Parliamentary Office of Science and Technology (1997), and NANO network (Fissan and Schoonman 1997). The overall expenditure for nanotechnology research within the EC was estimated in 1997 to be over \$128 million per year.

Russia and Other FSU Countries

Support for generation of nanoparticles and nanostructured materials has a tradition in Russia and other countries of the former Soviet Union (FSU) dating back to the mid-1970s; before 1990 an important part of this support was connected to defense research. The first public paper concerning the special properties of nanostructures was published in Russia in 1976. In 1979 the Council of the Academy of Sciences created a section on "Ultra- Dispersed Systems." Research strengths are in the areas of preparation processes of nanostructured materials and in several basic scientific aspects. Metallurgical research for special metals, including those with nanocrystalline structures, has received particular attention; research for nanodevices has been relatively less developed. Due to funding limitations, characterization and utilization of nanoparticles and nanostructured materials requiring costly equipment are less advanced than processing.

Russian government funds are allocated mainly for research personnel and less for infrastructure. Funding for nanotechnology is channeled via the Ministry of Science and Technology, the Russian Foundation for Fundamental Research, the Academy of Sciences, the Ministry of Higher Education, and other ministries with specific targets. The Ministry of Higher Education has relatively little research funding. Overall, 2.8% of the civilian budget in Russia in 1997 was planned for allocation to science. There is no centralized program on nanotechnology; however, there are components in specific institutional programs. Currently, about 20% of science research in Russia is funded via international organizations. The significant level of interest in the FSU can be identified by the relatively large participation at a series of Russian conferences on nanotechnology, the first in 1984 (First USSR Conference on Physics and Chemistry of Ultradispersed Systems), a second in 1989, and a third in 1993.

The Ministry of Science and Technology contributes to nanotechnology through several of its specific programs related to solid-state physics, surface science, fullerenes and nanostructures, and particularly "electronic and optical properties of nanostructures." This last program involves a network of scientific centers: the Ioffe Institute in St. Petersburg, Lebedev Institute in Moscow, Moscow State University, Novgograd Institute of Microstructures, Novosibirsk Institute of Semiconductor Physics, and others. This research network has an annual meeting on nanostructures, physics, and technology, and has developed interactions with the PHANTOMS network in the EC. The U.S. Civilian Research and Development Foundation has provided research funds in the FSU for several projects related to nanotechnology, including "Highly Non-Equilibrium States and Processes in Nanomaterials" at the Ioffe Institute (1996-1998).

Russian government and international organizations are the primary research sponsors for nanotechnology in Russia. However, laboratories and companies privatized in the last few years, such as the Delta Research Institute in Moscow, are under development. With a relatively lower base in characterization and advanced computing, the research focus is on advanced processing and continuum modeling. Research strengths are in the fields of physico-chemistry, nanostructured materials, nanoparticle generation and processing methods, and applications for hard materials, purification, and the oil industry, and biologically active systems (Siegel et al. n.d.). There are related programs in Ukraine, Belarus, and Georgia, mostly under the direction of the respective academies of sciences in these countries, that are dedicated to crystalline nanostructures and advanced structural and nanoelectronic materials. Several innovative processes, such as diamond powder production by detonation synthesis at SINTA in Belarus, are not well known abroad.

Nanotechnology in the United States, Japan, and Western Europe is making progress in developing a suitable research infrastructure. The promise of nanotechnology is being realized through the confluence of advances in two fields: (1) scientific discovery that has enabled the atomic, molecular, and supramolecular control of material building blocks, and (2) manufacturing that provides the means to assemble and utilize these tailored building blocks for new processes and devices in a wide variety of applications. Technology programs cannot be developed without strong supporting science programs because of the scale and complexity of the nanosystems. The overlapping of discipline-oriented research with nanotechnology-targeted programs seems appropriate at this point in time. Highly interdisciplinary and multiapplication nanotechnology provides generic approaches that enable advances in other technologies, from dispersions, catalysts, and electronics to biomedicine. Essential trends include the following:

- learning from nature (including templating, self-assembly, multifunctionality)
- building up functional nanostructures from molecules
- convergence of miniaturization and assembly techniques
- novel materials by design
- use of hierarchical/adaptive simulations

A characteristic of discovery in nanotechnology is the potential for revolutionary steps. The question "what if?" is progressively replaced by "at what cost?" The road from basic research to applications may vary from a few months to decades. Research and development is expensive, and the field needs support from related areas. The R&D environment should favor multiapplication and international partnerships. Based on the data for 1996 and 1997 collected during this WTEC study, 1997 government expenditures for nanotechnology research were at similar absolute levels in the United States, Japan, and Western Europe. (Estimated OECD data for 1997 indicated GDPs of $4.49 billion for Japan, $7.76 billion for the United States, and $7.00 billion for Western Europe.) The largest funding opportunities for nanotechnology are provided by NSF in the United States (approximately $65 million per year for fundamental research), by MITI in Japan (approximately $50 million per year for fundamental research and development), and by BMBF in Germany (approximately $50 million per year for fundamental and applied research). Large companies in areas such as dispersions, electronics, multimedia, and bioengineering contribute to research to a larger extent in Japan and the United States than in Europe.

While multinational companies are pursuing nanotechnology research activities in almost all developed countries, the presence of an active group of small and medium-size companies introducing new processes to the market is limited to the United States. In the United States, individual and small-group researchers as well as industrial and national laboratories for specialized topics have established a strong position in synthesis and assembly of nanoscale building blocks and catalysts, and in polymeric and biological approaches to nanostructured materials. The Japanese large-group research institutes, and more recently academic laboratories, have made particular advances in nanodevices and nano-instrumentation. The European "mosaic" provides a diverse combination of university research, networks, and national laboratories with special performance in dispersion and coatings, nanobiotechnology, and nanoprobes.

With a relatively lower base in characterization and computing infrastructure, the research focus in Russia is on physico-chemistry phenomena, advanced processing, and continuum modeling. Interest and economic support, particularly for device-related research, is growing in China, Australia, India, Taiwan, Korea, and Singapore.

The pace of revolutionary discoveries that we are witnessing now in nanotechnology is expected to accelerate in the next decade worldwide. This will have a profound impact on existing and emerging technologies in almost all industry sectors, in conservation of materials and energy, in biomedicine, and in environmental sustainability.

APPENDIX - III

RESEARCH CENTERS OF NANOTECHNOLOGY

- Institute for Molecular Manufacturing - nonprofit foundation carrying out research aimed at developing molecular manufacturing (molecular nanotechnology).
- Rice University - Center for Nanoscale Science and Technology - devoted to nurturing science and technology at the nanometer scale.
- Cornell NanoScale Science & Technology Facility (CNF) - subjects of research encompass physical sciences, life sciences, and engineering, particularly with inter-disciplinary emphasis.
- Cornell University - Nanobiotechnology Center (NBTC) - devoted to studying the convergence of nano-microfabrication and biosystems.
- University of Washington - Center for Nanotechnology University of Birmingham (United Kingdom) - Nanoscale Physics Research Laboratory - advancing the frontiers of the physics, chemistry, and technology of nanometre-scale structures, devices, and processes.
- University of Newcastle upon Tyne - Centre for Nanoscale Science and Technology - multidisciplinary research centre developing micro- and nano-devices for biomedical applications.
- University of California, Santa Barbara Nanotech - offers expertise in compound semiconductor-based device fabrication providing a full range of processes to the scientific and research communities.
- Center for Nanoscience and Nanotechnology - Georgia Institute of Technology - working to improve the human condition by providing fundamental and applicable knowledge to nanotechnology and its related fields of science.
- University of Michigan - Center for Biologic Nanotechnology - dedicated to the application of nano-molecular architecture to medicine.
- University of Notre Dame Nanofabrication Facility (NDNF) - provides information on the nanoelectronics fabrication facility.
- Arizona State University - Graduate Research Training Program in Biomolecular Nanotechnology - offers training in biomolecular nanotechnology, molecular electronics, and molecular devices.
- University of Nebraska-Lincoln - Center for Electro-Optics - specializes in optical/electromagnetic measurement and remote sensing technologies research.

- Schubert-Group: Macromolecular Chemistry and Nanoscience - Eindhoven University of Technology - devoted to the combinatorial materials research efforts.
- California Nanosystems Institute (CNSI) - R&D institute working on nanotechnologies and its commercial applications. Jointly established by University of California, Los Angeles, and University of California, Santa Barbara.
- Center for Nanotechnology - NASA Ames Research Center - focuses on experimental research and development in nano and bio technologies as well as computational nanotechnology, nanoelectronics, and optoelectronics.
- Institute for Soldier Nanotechnologies - intent to create a University Affiliated Research Center (UARC), with industry partners, to develop nanometer-scale science and technology solutions for the soldier.
- National Institute of Standards and Technology - Nanometer-Scale Metrology - research projects and measurement services in nanometer scale metrology

Glossary

Artificial Intelligence (AI): A field of research that aims to understand and build intelligent machines; this term may also refer to an intelligent machine itself.

Basal body: Short cylindrical array of microtubules plus their associated proteins found at the base of a eucaryotic cell cilium or flagellum. Serves as a nucleation site for the growth of the axoneme. Closely similar in structure to a centriole.

Binding: The process by which a molecule (or ligand) becomes bound, that is, confined in position (and often orientation) with respect to a receptor. Confinement occurs because structural features of the receptor create a potential well for the ligand; van der Waals and electrostatic interactions commonly contribute.

Biomaterials: Synthetic or natural materials that can replace or augment tissues, organs or body functions.

Biomotors: Driven by energy sources such as *adenosine triphosphate (ATP)* for chemical transduction and other processes. These biomotors are considered to be biomolecular and are discussed in the body of this report, but strictly speaking they do not conform to the panel's definition of self- assembly.

Biorobotics: Our research focuses on the role of sensing and mechanical design in motor control, in both robots and humans. This work draws upon diverse disciplines, including biomechanics, systems analysis, and neurophysiology. The main approach is experimental, although analysis and simulation play important parts. In conjunction with industrial partners, we are developing applications of this research in biomedical instrumentation, teleoperated robots, and intelligent sensors.

Biosensor: The term "biosensor" is a general designation that denotes either a sensor to detect a biological substance or a sensor which incorporates the use of biological molecules such as antibodies or enzymes. Biosensors are a subcategory of chemical sensors.

Bose-Einstein Condensates [BEC's]: Bose-Einstein Condensates "...aren't like the solids, liquids and gases that we learned about in school. They are not vaporous, not hard, not fluid. Indeed, there are no ordinary words to describe them because they come from another world — the world of quantum mechanics."

Bottom Up: Building larger objects from smaller building blocks. Nanotechnology seeks to use atoms and molecules as those building blocks. The advantage of bottom-up design is that the covalent bonds holding together a single molecule are far stronger than the weak. Mostly done by chemists, attempting to create structure by connecting molecules.

Breakdown: Failure of a material resulting from an electrical overload. The resulting damage may be in the form of thermal damage (melting or burning) or electrical damage (loss of polarization in piezoelectric materials). The failing of a physical principle or unit of measurement as the scale is changed.

Brownian Assembly: Brownian motion in a fluid brings molecules together in various position and orientations. If molecules have suitable complementary surfaces, they can bind, assembling to form a specific structure. Brownian assembly is a less paradoxical name for self-assembly (how can a structure assemble itself, or do anything, when it does not yet exist?).

Brownian Motion: Motion of a particle in a fluid owing to thermal agitation, observed in 1827 by Robert Brown. (Originally thought to be caused by vital force, Brownian motion in fact plays a vital role in the assembly and activity of the molecular structures of life).

Buckyball: Round (convex) fullerenes ranging in size from 20 to over 500 carbon atoms.

Bush Robot: A concept for robots of ultimate dexterity, they utilize fractal branching to create ever-shrinking "branches," eventually ending in nanoscale "fingers." Developed by Hans Moravec.

Cantilever: A lever beam held down at one end, with some support near the middle and which supports a load on the other end. Diving boards and drawbridges are cantilevers.

Cobots: Collaborative robots designed to work alongside human operators. Prototype cobots are being used on automobile assembly lines to help guide heavy components like seats and dashboards into cars so they don't damage auto body parts as workers install them.

Combinatorial materials design: Uses computing power (sometimes together with massive parallel experimentation) to screen many different materials possibilities to optimize properties for specific applications (e.g., catalysts, drugs, optical materials).

Communicyte: In medical nanorobotics, a theorized mobile, mass-storage (nanorobotic) device that can be used for information transport throughout the human body.

Compliance: The reciprocal of stiffness; in a linear elastic system, displacement equals force times compliance.

Composites: Combinations of metals, ceramics, polymers, and biological materials that allow multi- functional behavior. One common practice is reinforcing polymers or ceramics with ceramic fibers to increase strength while retaining light weight and avoiding the brittleness of the monolithic ceramic. Materials used in the body often combine biological and structural functions (e.g., the encapsulation of drugs).

Computational Nanotechnology: Permits the modeling and simulation of complex nanometer-scale structures. The predictive and analytical power of computation is critical to success in nanotechnology: nature required several hundred million years to evolve a functional "wet" nanotechnology; the insight provided by computation should allow us to reduce the development time of a working "dry" nanotechnology to a few decades, and it will have a major impact on the "wet" side as well. [Rice University]

Conformation: The shape of a molecule. A molecular geometry that differs from other geometries chiefly by rotation about single or triple bonds; distinct conformations (termed con formers) are associated with distinct potential wells. Typical biomolecules and products of organic synthesis can interconvert among many conformations; typical diamondoid structures are locked into a single potential well, and thus lack conformational flexibility.

Copolymer: A polymer that consists of two or more dissimilar monomer units in combination in its molecular chains. Also a polymer formed from the polymerization of more than one type of monomer.

Corrosion: Deteriorative loss of a metal as a result of dissolution environmental reactions.

Covalent bond: A bond formed by sharing a pair of electrons between two atoms. A primary interatomic bond that is formed by the sharing of electrons between neighboring atoms. An attachment between two atoms resulting from the sharing of a pair of electrons

Covalent radius: Given a set of *N* elements that can form covalent single bonds in molecules, with $N(N - 1)$ possible elemental pairings, it has proved possible to define a covalent radius for each element such that the actual bond length between any two elements that form a covalent single bond is roughly equal to the sums of their covalent radii.

CPU: The central processing unit of a computer, responsible for executing instructions to process information.

Crosslinked polymer: A polymer in which adjacent linear molecular chains are joined at various positions by covalent bonds.

Cross-sensitivity: The influence of one measurand on the sensitivity of a sensor, another measurand.

Crystal structure: For crystalline materials, the manner in which atoms or ions are arrayed in space. It is defined in terms of the unit cell geometry and the atom positions within the unit cell.

Crystallescence: In medical nanorobotics, the crystallization of solid solute that is offloaded by nanorobot sorting rotors at a concentration that exceeds the solvation capacity of the surrounding solvent.

Cyclotron: A type of particle accelerator in which an ion introduced at the center is accelerated in an expanding spiral path by use of alternating electrical fields in the presence of a magnetic field.

Cytocarriage: In medical nanorobotics, the commandeering of a natural motile cell, by a medical nanorobot, for the purposes of in vivo transport (of the nanorobot), or to perform a herding function (of the affected cell), or for other purposes.

Debye Shielding: The Debye length in front of a sensing electrode depends on the ionic strength of the electrolyte used. In a 0.001N NaCl the Debye length measures 96.5 Å, while for a 1.0 N solution it is reduced to 3.0 Å. An adsorbed protein can stick out from the surface for as much as 50 to 100 Å. As a result, the charges which could contribute to the surface potential will be shielded in a 1.0 N solution. To make more sensitive measurements a solution of low ionic strength should be used.

Denaturation: The breaking down of the three-dimensional structure of a protein resulting in the loss of its function.

Dendrimer: A dendrimer is a spherical, highly branched polymer molecule. Dendrimers are made from two different monomers – a reactive amine and an acrylic acid – and are assembled in discrete steps, which allow them to be constructed with an exact size that depends on the number of enlargement steps. This picture shows a dendrimer that has undergone three "generations" of enlargements. Dendrimers are of particular interest for cancer applications because of their defined and reproducible size, but more importantly, because it is easy to add a variety of other molecules to the surface of a dendrimer. Such molecules could include tumor-targeting agents (including but not restricted to monoclonal antibodies), imaging contrast agents to pinpoint tumors, drug molecules for delivery to a tumor, and reporter molecules that might detect if an anticancer drug is working. (2) A dendrimer is a tree-like highly branched polymer molecule (Greek *dendra* = *tree*). Dendrimers are synthesized from monomers with new branches added in discrete steps ("generation") to form a tree-like architecture. A high level of synthetic control is achieved through step-wise reactions and purifications at each step to control the size, architecture, functionality and monodispersity. Several different kinds of dendrimers have been synthesized utilizing different monomers and some are commercially available. This picture shows a "3rd generation" polyamidoamine (PAMAM) dendrimer. Dendrimers are of particular interest for cancer applications because of their defined and reproducible size, but more importantly, because it is easy to attach a variety of other molecules to the surface of a dendrimer. Such molecules could include tumor-targeting agents (including but not restricted to monoclonal antibodies), imaging contrast agents to pinpoint tumors, drug molecules for delivery to a tumor, and reporter molecules that might detect if an anticancer drug is working.

Dendrite: Extension of a nerve cell, typically branched and relatively short, that receives stimuli from other nerve cells

Desmosome: Specialized cell-cell junction, usually formed between two epithelial cells, characterized by dense plaques of protein into which intermediate filaments in the two adjoining cells insert.

Detergent: Type of small amphipathic molecule that tends to coalesce in water, with its hydrophobic tails buried and its hydrophilic heads exposed; widely used to solubilize membrane proteins.

Determination: Commitment by an embryonic cell to a particular specialized path of development; it reflects a change in the internal character of the cell.

Dielectric: Any material that is electrically insulating.

Electric field [V/m]: In simplest form, the potential difference between two points divided by the distance between the two.

Electrical Bistability: A phenomenon in which an object exhibits two states of different conductivity at the same applied voltage.

Electrical breakdown: Condition in which, particularly with high electric field, a nominal insulator becomes electrically conducting.

Electrochemical gradient: Driving force that causes an ion to move across a membrane due to the combined influence of a difference in its concentration on the two sides of the membrane and the electrical charge difference across the membrane.

Electroluminescence: In electrical engineering: the emission of visible light by a p-n junction across which a forward-biased voltage is applied. In electrochemistry: emission of light by a molecule which is being reduced or oxidized on a biased electrode. If the exciting cause is a photon, rather than an electron, the process is called photoluminescence.

Electrolyte/Insulator/Silicon (EIS): Structures at the heart of a broad family of potentiometric silicon sensors. The best-known member of the family is the ion-sensitive field effect transistor, known as the ISFET or CHEMFET and the light-addressable potentiometric sensor LAPS . The principle of operation of devices using such structures is as follows. A potential with respect to a reference electrode is generated at the interface between the liquid solution and the insulator. The surface potential ($ø_0$) is determined by that ionic species which has the fastest exchange rate (i_o) with the membrane covering the insulator. If no intentional membrane is deposited on an oxide covered insulator that species will be H^+. Surface potential changes in turn change the Si flat-band voltage V_{FB}. The flat-band voltage is the potential one needs to apply to the Si in order to have the bands flat throughout the semiconductor. The flat band voltage of an EIS structure has been shown to be given by: $V_{FB} = E_{REF} - Ö^{Si}/q - ø_0 - Q_{ins}/C_{inss}$ where V_{FB} stands for the flat-band voltage of the structure, E_{REF} for the reference electrode potential, $Ö^{Si}$ for the work function of silicon, $ø_0$ for the surface potential at the insulator/electrolyte interface, Q_{ins} for the charge at the insulator/silicon interface and C_{ins} for the insulator capacitance. At least two terms in the above equation are not known with a precision greater than a few hundred millivolts. This is true for E_{REF} as well as for Q_{ins}/C_{ins} which can vary from device to device by several hundred millivolts. For a given EIS sensor, these inaccurately known quantities are constant, and variations in flat-band voltage can be equated to variations of the surface potential.

Electrolyte: A solution through which an electric current may be carried by the motion of ions.

Electromotive force (emf) series: A series of chemical elements arranged in order of their electromotive force. The electromotive force is the greatest potential difference that can be generated by a particular source of electric current. In practice this potential may be observable only when the source is not supplying current, because of its internal resistance.

Electron acceptor: Atom or molecule that takes up electrons readily, thereby gaining an electron and becoming reduced.

Electron Beam Lithography (EBL): A method of fabricating sub-micron and nanoscale features by exposing electrically sensitive surfaces to an electron beam.

Electron beam: A stream of electrons moving in the same direction at the same speed.

Electron donor: Molecule that easily gives up an electron, becoming oxidized in the process.

Electron: Electrons are negatively charged elementary particles with a mass of $9.1093897 \times 10^{-31}$ kg, a charge of $-1.60217733 \times 10^{-19}$ C, and spin 1/2. They cannot be divided into smaller particles. What is the radius of an electron? There is not an easy answer to this question. In an atom, the wavefunction of an electron has a width of about 10^{-10} meters. The wavefunction for an electron in a metal or travelling through vacuum can be much larger; it can be meters in width. Elementary negative particle whose charge is 1.602×10^{-19} coulombs.

Electron state (level): One of a set of discrete, quantized energies that are allowed for electrons. In the atomic case each state is specified by 4 quantum numbers.

Electron Transport Chain: Biomolecular machinery present in prokaryotic membranes and eukaryotic mitochnodria that couples the flow of electrons to proton pumps in order to convert energy from sugar to ATP.

Embryogenesis: Development of an embryo from a fertilized egg, or zygote.

Exponential assembly: A manufacturing architecture starting with a single tiny robotic arm on a surface. This first robotic arm makes a second robotic arm on a facing surface by picking up miniature parts ó carefully laid out in advance in exactly the right locations so the tiny robotic arm can find them ó and assembling them. The two robotic arms then make two more robotic arms, one on each of the two facing surfaces. These four robotic arms, two on each surface, then make four more robotic arms. This process continues with the number of robotic arms steadily increasing in the pattern 1, 2, 4, 8, 16, 32, 64, etc. until some manufacturing limit is reached (both surfaces are completely covered with tiny robotic arms, for example). This is an exponential growth rate, hence the name exponential assembly.

Femtosecond: Femtosecond is one quadrillionth of a second, and is to a second what a second is to 32,700,000 years. At 186,000 miles per second, in one femtosecond light travels only far enough to traverse about 1,000 silicon atoms. When used to time a laser pulse, it allows for ultra-precise micromachining, with virtually no damage to surrounding material.

Ferroelectric material: A dielectric material such as Rochelle salt and barium titanate with a domain structure containing dipoles (asymmetric distributions of electrical charge) which spontaneously align. Their domain structure makes them analogous to ferromagnetic materials. They exhibit hysteresis and usually the piezoelectric effect.

Free-energy change (DG): Change in the free energy during a reaction: the free energy of the product molecules minus the free energy of the starting molecules. A large negative value of DG indicates that the reaction has a strong tendency to occur.

G2 phase: Gap 2 phase of the eucaryotic cell-division cycle, between the end of DNA synthesis and the beginning of mitosis.

Glass transition temperature (T_g): The temperature at which, upon cooling, a noncrystalline ceramic or polymer transforms from a supercooled liquid to a rigid glass.

Haploid: Having only one set of chromosomes, as in a sperm cell or a bacterium, as distinct from diploid (having two sets of chromosomes).

Hardness: The measure of a material's resistance to deformation by surface indentation or by abrasion. There are various scales in use to express hardness. The Mohs scale is qualitative and somewhat arbitrary and ranges from 1 on the soft end for talc to 10 for diamond. Quantitative scales are the Rockwell (HR), Brinell (indicated by HB), Knoop (HK) and Vickers (HV). Knoop and Vickers are referred to as microhardness testing methods on the basis of load and indenter size.

Harmonic oscillator: A system in which a mass is subject to a linear restoring force, like an ideal spring. A harmonic oscillator vibrates at a fixed frequency, independent of amplitude.

The major protein in red blood cells that associates with O_2 in the lungs by means of a bound heme group.

Hemopoiesis (hematopoiesis): Generation of blood cells, mainly in the bone marrow.

Heterozygote: Diploid cell or individual having two different alleles of a specified gene.

Heuristics: Rules of thumb used to guide one in the direction of probable solutions to a problem.

Highest Occupied Molecular Orbital (HOMO): The highest energy molecular orbital of an atom or molecule that contains an electron.

Homogeneous and Heterogeneous Assays: A homogeneous assay does not require a separation step to remove free antigen from bound antigen and relies upon the fact that the function of the label is modified upon binding, leading to a change in signal intensity. Because of high background signal a heterogeneous approach incorporating a separation step of bound and unbound makes the detection limit lower, approaching the values obtained by RIA. The homogeneous assay is less technically demanding.

Hypsithermal limit: The maximum amount of energy that may be released at Earth's surface, as a result of human technological activities, without significantly altering the natural global energy balance; estimated as 10^13-10^15 watts.

IMP: Electronic implant, especially in the brain. [Ron Hale Evans]

Ion: An atom or molecule with a net charge. **(2)** An atom with more or fewer electrons than those needed to cancel the electronic charge of the nucleus. An ion is an atom with a net electric charge.

Isotropic: Having identical values of a property in all crystallographic directions.

Ketone: Organic molecule containing a carbonyl group linked to two alkyl groups.

Kevlar (TM): A synthetic fiber made by E. I. du Pont de Nemours & Co., Inc. Stronger than most steels, Kevlar is among the strongest commercially available materials and is used in aerospace construction, bulletproof vests, and other applications requiring a high strength-to-weight ratio.

Label: Chemical group or radioactive atom added to a molecule in order to follow its progress through a biochemical reaction or to locate it spatially. Also, as a verb, to add such a group or atom to a cell or molecule.

Langmuir-Blodgett (LB) Film: A film of organic material (often surfactant molecules) assembled at the liquid-gas interface and subsequently transferred onto a solid substrate.

LCD (Liquid Crystal Display): LCD is the predominant technology used in flat panel displays. The principle that makes the display work is this: A crystalís alignment can be altered with an electric current. If the crystal is lined up one way ñ it will allow the light waves to pass through a polarized filter, but if the electric current alters the crystalís alignment, it will guide light so that the polarized filter blocks the light. By densely packing red, blue and green light emitting crystals next to each other on a sheet (ìcalled a substrateî), one can create a full color display. The great thing about LCD is that the crystals can be packed together closely, allowing for a higher-resolution, finer-detail display. The con is that LCDs are somewhat fragile, require a lot of power and are relatively less bright. Liquid Crystal Display — display device employing light source and electrically alterable optically active thin film.

Machine-phase chemistry: The chemistry of systems in which all potentially reactive moieties follow controlled trajectories (e.g., guided by molecular machines working in vacuum).

Macroscale: Larger than nanoscale; often implies a design that humans can directly interact with; too large to be built by a single assembler (one cubic micron of diamond contains 176 billion atoms).

Macrosensing: In medical nanorobotics, the detection of global somatic states (inside the human body) and extrasomatic states (sensory data originating outside of the human body) by in vivo nanorobots.

Mechatronics: The study of the melding of AI and electromechanical machines to make machines that are greater than the sum of their parts. The synergistic combination of precision mechanical engineering with electronic control.

Megabyte (MB): 2^{20} (= 1,048,576, or about one million) bytes of information.

Megahertz (Mhz): One million cycles per second

Micelles: Micelles are small, spherical structures composed of molecules that attract one another to reduce surface tension. The head of the molecule is hydrophilic, meaning it likes water, while the interior portion is hydrophobic, meaning it avoids water.

Micro-Electromechanical Systems (MEMS): "The fabrication or micro-machining of materials to make stationary and moving structures, devices and systems of a nominal size scale from a few centimeters to a few micrometers."

Molecular Recognition: A chemical term referring to processes in which molecules adhere in a highly specific way, forming a larger structure; an enabling technology for nanotechnology.

Molecular robotics: Ralph Merkle, A New Family of Six Degree of Freedom Positional Devices, Zyvex.

Molecular self-assembly: The spontaneous formation of molecules into covalently bonded, well- defined, stable structures - is a very important concept in biological systems and has increasingly become a focus of non- biological research.

Molecular sorting rotor: A class of nanomechanical device capable of selectively binding (or releasing) molecules from (or to) solution, and of transporting these bound molecules against significant concentration gradients.

Nanobarcode: SurroMed's Nanobarcode™ technology uses cylindrically-shaped colloidal metal nanoparticles, in which the metal composition can be alternated along the length and the size of each metal segment can be controlled. Intrinsic differences in reflectivity between the metal segments allow individual particles to be identified by conventional optical microscopy.

Nanobeads: Polymer beads with diameters of between 0.1 to 10 micrometers. Also called nanodots, nanocrystals and quantum beads. *Impregnating fluorescent crystal chips into these beads allows simultaneous measurement of thousands of biological interactions, a stepping stone for breakthroughs in the diagnosis and treatment of disease. ... with the potential to accelerate drug discovery and clinical diagnostics."*

Nanochip: In Friday's issue [Aug. 1, 2001] of the journal *Science,* physicists from IBM's Thomas J. Watson Research Center [Philip G. Collins, Michael S.

Arnold and Phaedon Avouris] announce their fabrication of the world's first array of transistors made from carbon nanotube. We are approaching the limits of standard microchip technology; thus, the "nanochip" — a next-smaller microchip. [ed] They are also a next-gen device for mass storage, of significantly higher density, with greater speed, and much lower cost.

Nanochronometer: In medical nanorobotics, a proposed clock or timing mechanism constructed of nanoscale components.

Nanocomputer: A computer made from components (mechanical, electronic, or otherwise) built at the nanometer scale. These computers could be many orders-of-magnititude faster than today's, which enables software to take proportional leaps. (2) A computer whose fundamental components measure only a few nanometers in size. State of the art current computer components are no smaller than about 350 nm. [Mnemosyne Mnews 21 (3) January 2001 " The Nanotechnology Initiative and Future Electronics" Presentation by Gail J. Brown, Air Force Research Laboratory, Wright- Patterson Air Force Base, November 16, 2000] (3) A computer with parts built on a molecular scale.

Nanocones: Nonplanar graphitic structures. Carbon-based structures with five-fold symmetry that form due to disclination defects in two-dimensional graphene sheets. They have been observed as nanotube caps and as freestanding structures. [North Carolina State University].

Nanocontainers: "Micellar nanocontainers" or "Micelles," these are nanoscale polymeric containers that could be used to selectively deliver hydrophobic drugs to specific sites within individual cells.

Nanocrit (Nct): In medical nanorobotics, volume-fraction or bloodstream concentration of medical nanorobots, expressed as a percentage.

Nanocrystals: A nanocrystal typically has a diameter of between 1 and 10 nm and may contain as few as a hundred or as many as tens of thousands of atoms. Many fundamental properties of nanocrystals depend strongly on their size in smooth and predictable ways. Examples include the external field required to switch a magnetized particle of great importance in magnetotactic bacteria and in hard disk drives and the color of light emission from a semiconductor used for the fluorescent *labeling* of cells and in lasers. This facile tuning of properties by size variation is one reason why nanocrystals are widely viewed as promising components for new artificial optical and electrical materials. Also known as nanoscale semiconductor crystals. "Nanocrystals are aggregates of anywhere from a few hundred to tens of thousands of atoms that combine into a crystalline form of matter known as a "cluster." Typically around ten nanometers in diameter, nanocrystals are larger than molecules but smaller than bulk solids and therefore frequently exhibit physical and chemical properties somewhere in between. Given that a nanocrystal is virtually all surface and no interior, its properties can vary considerably as the crystal grows in size." The first atomic-scale images of nanocrystals that help reduce pollution show a surprising triangular, rather than hexagonal, shape. The new information should help researchers improve the chemical process. *"Nanocrystals might be used to make super-strong and long-lasting metal parts. The crystals also might be added to plastics and other metals to make new types of composite structures for everything from cars to electronics."* See Discovery could bring widespread uses for 'nanocrystals'. Single atoms caged inside nanocrystals gives you a "quantum confined atom", or QCA, *"with potential uses ranging from clear-glass sunglasses to bio-sensors to optical computing and just about anything optical in between."* Single-electron transistor (SET) is a three terminal device, where single electron current between a source and a drain through a nanocrystal is controlled by a gate. The nanocrystals are the tiny light specs.

Nanodefenses: Any of the "good" goo's, such a Blue Goo. Protectors against Grey Goo, destructive nanoswarms, and the like.

Nanoelectronics: Electronics on a nanometer scale, whether made by current techniques or nanotechnology; includes both molecular electronics and nanoscale devices resembling today's semiconductor devices. [NTN]

Nanoengineering: We use chemistry to construct *nanostructures* and their composites, then focus our attention on the electronic, optical, and transport properties of these nanostructures and the macroscopic films and materials that can be constructed from them. This research lies at the common frontier of chemistry, condensed matter physics, optics, and bioengineering.

Nanophase Carbon Materials (carbon nanotubes, nanodiamond, nanocomposite]: A form of matter in which small clusters of atoms form the building blocks of a larger structure. These structures differ from those of naturally occurring crystals, in which individual atoms arrange themselves into a lattice.

Nanosystem: A eutactic set of nanoscale components working together to serve a set of purposes; complex nanosystems can be of macroscopic size.

Nanotech: Slang for nanotechnology.

National Nanotechnology Initiative: US federal government agencies participating include the National Science Foundation, the Department of Defense, the National Institute of Health, NASA, and NIST. [National Nanotechnology Initiative website] http://www.nano.gov/

Nucleotide: A monomer of the nucleic acids composed of a five-carbon sugar, a nitrogen-containing base, and phosphoric acid. A small molecule composed of three parts: a nitrogen base (a purine or pyrimidine), a sugar (ribose or deoxyribose), and phosphate. Nucleotides serve as the building blocks of nucleic acids (DNA and RNA).

Pathogen (adjective pathogenic): An organism or other agent that causes diseases.

Poisson's ratio: A bar of an isotropic, elastic material ordinarily shrinks laterally when it is stretched longitudinally. The lateral contracting strain divided by the applied tensile strain is Poisson's ratio, which varies from material to material.

Quantum Mirage: A nanoscale property that may allow information to be transfered through use of the wave property of electrons. Thus, quantum computers might not require wires as we know them. A nanoscale property that may allow information to be transfered through use of the wave property of electrons.

Ras protein: One of a large family of GTP-binding proteins that help relay signals from cell-surface receptors to the nucleus. Named for tne *ras* gene, first identified in viruses that cause rat sarcomas.

Regenerative medicine: A field of medicine concerned with developing and using strategies aimed at repair or replacement of damaged, diseased, or metabolically deficient organs, tissues, and cells via TISSUE ENGINEERING; CELL TRANSPLANTATION; and ARTIFICIAL ORGANS and BIOARTIFICIAL ORGANS and tissues. MeSH 2004

Sealed Assembler Laboratory: A work space, containing assemblers, encapsulated in a way that allows information to flow in and out but does not allow the escape of assemblers or their products.

Semiconductor: A pure semiconductor is a poor electrical conductor but when certain impurities are added, the conductivity can increase by orders of magnitude. Common semiconductors are silicon, germanium, and gallium-arsenide. Computer chips are usually made from thin wafers cut from large single crystals of silicon. The silicon is a badly conducting matrix in which better conducting regions are defined by adding impurity atoms (often called dopants). The conductivity of a semiconductor can be described by the formula ó = *ne*ì, where ó is the conductivity measured in units of Ohm^{-1} m^{-1}, *n* is the density of free charge carriers measured in m^{-3}, *e* is the electron charge -1.6022×10^{-19} C, and ì is the mobility of the semiconductor measured in m^2 V^{-1} s^{-1}. In a doped semiconductor, the density of free charge carriers is typically equal to the density of dopant atoms that have been added. Thus, the conductivity depends on the number of dopant atoms. Each dopant atom contributes one charge carrier. Silicon is the second most common element in the earth's crust (the first most common is oxygen). Silicon is commonly found in sand and stone in the form of silicon-dioxide. A substance or object with conductive properties between those of a conductor and a insulator. Material whose conductivity, due to charges of both signs, is normally in the range between that of metals and insulators and in which the electric charge carrier density can be changed by external means. [IUPAC Compendium] Nonmetallic material, such as silicon, whose electrical conductivity is moderate and alterable by doping.

Single bond: A sigma bond having no associated pi bonds.

Tetrahymena: Genus of ciliated protozoa used in studies of ciliary axonemes, self-splicing RNA, and telomere reproduction.

Tight junction: Cell-cell junction that seals adjacent epithelial cells together, preventing the passage of most dissolved molecules from one side of the epithelial sheet to the other.

Tight-receptor structures: A receptor structure in which a bound ligand of a particular kind is confined on all sides by repulsive interactions (note that favorable binding energies are compatible with repulsive forces). A tight-receptor structure discriminates strongly against all molecules larger than the target.

Triple bond: A double bond is formed when a pi bond is superimposed on a single bond; adding a second pi bond results in a triple bond. The two pi bonds have perpendicular nodal planes, and their sum has roughly cylindrical symmetry, permitting rotation in much the same manner as a single bond.

Vitamins (engineering): In machine replication theory, vitamin parts are components of a self-replicating machine which the machine is incapable of producing itself, therefore these vital parts must be supplied from an external source.

Weber: Unit of magnetic flux. One weber is a magnetic flux that, linking a circuit of 1 turn, would produce in it an electromotive force of 1 volt if it were reduced to zero at a uniform rate in 1 second.

Bibliography

Averback, R.S., J. Bernholc, and D.L. Nelson. 1991. *MRS Symposium Proceedings* Vol. 206.

Baird, D.; Nordmann, A. & Schummer, J. (eds.): 2004, *Discovering the Nanoscale*, Amsterdam: IOS Press.

Baker, R.T.K. Synthesis, properties and applications of graphite nanofibers. In *R&D status and trends*, ed. Siegel et al.

Bate, R., Frazier, G., Frensley, W., Reed., M., "An Overview of Nanoelectronics," *Texas Instruments Technical Journal*, July-August 1989, pp. 13-20.

Beck, J.S., J.C. Vartuli, W.J. Roth, M.E. Leonowicz, C.T. Kresge, K.D. Schmitt, C.T.-W. Chu, D.H. Olsen, E.W. Shepard, S.B. McCullen, J.B. Higgins, and J.L. Schlenker. 1992. *J. Am. Chem. Soc.* 114:10834.

Bensaude-Vincent, B.: 2001, 'The Construction of a Discipline: Materials Science in the United States', *Historical Studies in the Physical and Biological Sciences*, 31, 223-248.

Bensaude-Vincent, B.: 2004, 'Two Cultures of Nanotechnology?', *Hyle: International Journal for Philosophy of Chemistry*, 10(2), 65-82.

Berube, D.M.: 2004, 'The Rhetoric of Nanotechnology', in: D. Baird, A. Nordmann & J. Schummer (eds.), *Discovering the Nanoscale*, Amsterdam: IOS Press, pp. 173-192.

Bowes, C.L., A. Malek, and G.A. Ozin. 1996. *Chem. Vap. Deposition* 2:97.

Braun, P.V., P. Osenar, and S.I. Stupp. 1996. *Nature*. 368: 2.

Braun, T.; Schubert, A. & Zsindely, S.: 1997, 'Nanoscience and nanotechnology on the balance', *Scientometrics*, 38, 321-325.

Brinker, C.J. 1996. *Curr. Opin. Solid State Mater. Sci.* 1:798.

Brown, N.: 2004, 'Needle on the Real: Technoscience and Poetry at the Limits of Fabrication', in: N.K. Hayles (ed.), *Nanoculture: Implications of the New Technoscience*, Bristol, UK: Intellect Books, pp. 173-190.

Bueno, O.: 2004, 'The Drexler-Smalley Debated on Nanotechnology: Incommensurability at Work?', *Hyle: International Journal for Philosophy of Chemistry*, 10(2), 83-98.

Bueno, O.: 2004, 'Von Neumann, Self-Reproduction and the Constitution of Nanophenomena', in: D. Baird, A. Nordmann & J. Schummer (eds.), *Discovering the Nanoscale*, Amsterdam: IOS Press, pp. 101-115.

Carroll, J.S.: 2001, 'Social Science Research Methods for Assessing Societal Implications of Nanotechnology', in: M.C. Roco and W.S. Bainbridge (eds.), *Societal Implications of Nanoscience and Nanotechnology*, Dordrecht: Kluwer, pp. 188-192.

Chen, C-Y., S.L. Burkett, H.-X. Li, and M.E. Davis. 1993. *Microporous Mater.* 2:27.

Chianelli, R.R. 1998. Synthesis, fundamental properties and applications of nanocrystals, sheets, and fullerenes based on layered transition metal chalcogenides. In *R&D status and trends,* ed. Siegel et al.

Chianelli, R.R., M. Daage, and M.J. Ledoux. 1994. *Advances in Catalysis* 40:177.

Claeson, T., and Likharev, K.," Single Electronics," *Scientific American,* June 1992, pp. 80-85.

Coenen, C.: 2004, 'Nanofuturismus: Anmerkungen zu seiner Relevanz, Analyse und Bewertung', *Technikfolgenabschätzung ' Theorie und Praxis*, 13 (2), 78-85.

Crandall, B.C. and Lewis, J., *Nanotechnology: Research and Perspectives*, MIT Press, Cambridge, 1992.

Crow, M. & Sarewitz, D.: 2001, 'Nanotechnology and Societal Transformation', in: M.C. Roco and W.S. Bainbridge (eds.), *Societal Implications of Nanoscience and Nanotechnology*, Dordrecht: Kluwer, pp. 45-54.

de Souza e Silva, A.: 2004, 'The Invisible Imaginary: Museum Spaces, Hybrid Reality and Nanotechnology', in: N.K. Hayles (ed.), *Nanoculture: Implications of the New Technoscience*, Bristol, UK: Intellect Books, pp. 27-82.

Decker, M.; Fiedeler, U.; Fleischer, Th.: 2004, 'Ich sehe was, was Du nicht siehst... zur Definition von Nanotechnologie', *Technikfolgenabschätzung ' Theorie und Praxis*, 13 (2), 10-16.

Dresselhaus, M., and G. Dresselhaus. 1995. *Ann. Rev. Mat. Sci.* 25:487.

Dresselhaus, M.S. 1998. Carbon-based nanostructures. In *R&D status and trends*, ed. Siegel et al.

Dresselhaus, M.S., G. Dresselhaus, and P. Eklund. 1996. *Science of fullerenes and carbon nanotubes.* San Diego: Academic Press.

Drexler, K.E.: 2004, 'Nanotechnology: From Feynman to Funding', *Bulletin of Science, Technology & Society*, 24, 21-27.

Dupuy, J.-P.: 2004, 'Complexity and Uncertainty: A Prudential Approach To Nanotechnology', in: European Commission (Community Health and Consumer Protection): *Nanotechnologies: A Preliminary Risk Analysis on the Basis of a Workshop, Brussels, 1-2 March 2004*, pp. 71-93 (www.europa.eu.int/comm/health/ ph_risk/documents/ ev_20040301_en.pdf).

Dupuy, J.-P.: 2004, 'Pour une évaluation normative du programme nanotechnologique', *Annales des Mines*, (February 2004), 27-32.

Einsiedel, E.F.; Goldenberg, L.: 2004, 'Dwarfing the Social? Nanotechnology Lessons from the Biotechnology Front', *Bulletin of Science, Technology & Society*, 24, 28-33.

ETC: 2003a, *The Big Down: Atom Tech ' Technologies Converging at the Atomic Scale*. Winnipeg, Canada: Action Group on Erosion, Technology and Concentration [www.etcgroup.org/documents/TheBigDown.pdf].

ETC: 2003b, 'No Small Matter II: The Case for a Global Moratorium ' Size Matters!' *Occasional Paper Series* 7(1) [www.etcgroup.org/documents/Occ.Paper_Nanosafety.pdf].

Etzkowitz, H., 2001, 'Nano-Science and Society: Finding a Social Basis for Science Policy', in: M.C. Roco and W.S. Bainbridge (eds.), *Societal Implications of Nanoscience and Nanotechnology*, Dordrecht: Kluwer, pp. 121-128.

European Comission: *European Workshop on Social and Economic Research on Nanotechnologies and Nanosciences, Brussels, 14-15 April 2004* [www.stage-research.net/STAGE/PAGES/Nano.html].

European Commission (Community Health and Consumer Protection): 2004, *Nanotechnologies: A Preliminary Risk Analysis on theBasis of a Workshop, Brussels, 1-2 March 2004* [www.europa.eu.int/comm/health/ ph_risk/documents/ev_20040301_en.pdf].

European Commission: 2004, *Converging Technologies: Shaping the Future of European Societies (Report of the High Level Expert Group "Foresighting the New Technology Wave")*, Brussels: European Commission Research [http://europa.eu.int/comm/research/conferences/2004/ntw/index_en.html].

F. Buot, "Mesoscopic Physics and Nanoelectronics: Nanoscience and Nanotechnology," *Physics Reports*, pp.73-174, 1993.

F. Capasso and S. Datta, "Quantum Electron Devices," *Physics Today*, pp.74-82, February 1990.

Feynman, R., "There's Plenty of Room at the Bottom: An invitation to Enter a New Field of Physics," Talk at the Annual Meeting of the American Physical Society, 29 December 1959. Reprinted in Appendix B of Crandall and Lewis. See citation above.

Fielder, F.A.; Reynolds, G.H.: 1994, 'Legal Problems of Nanotechnology: An Overview', *Southern California Interdisciplinary Law Journal*, 3, 593-629.

Fleischer, Th.; Decker, M. & Fiedeler, U. (eds.): 2004, *Große Aufmerksamkeit für kleine Welten ' Nanotechnologie und ihre Folgen*, special issue of *Technikfolgenabschätzung ' Theorie und Praxis*, 13 (2), 5-85 [www.itas.fzk.de/tatup/042/inhalt.htm].

Fogelberg, H. & Glimell, H.: 2003, 'Molecular Matters: In Search of the Real Stuff', in: H.

Fogelberg & H. Glimell, *Bringing Visibility to the Invisible: Towards A Social Understanding of Nanotechnology*, Göteborg: Göteborg University, pp. 5-32 [www.sts.gu.se/publications/STS_report_6.pdf].

Fogelberg, H. & Glimell, H.: 2003, *Bringing Visibility to the Invisible: Towards A Social Understanding of Nanotechnology*, Göteborg: Göteborg University [www.sts.gu.se/publications/STS_report_6.pdf].

Fogelberg, H.: 2003, 'The Grand Politics of Technoscience: Contextualizing Nanotechnology', in: H. Fogelberg & H. Glimell, *Bringing Visibility to the Invisible: Towards A Social Understanding of Nanotechnology*, Göteborg: Göteborg University, pp. 33-54 [www.sts.gu.se/publications/STS_report_6.pdf].

Fogelberg, H.: 2003, 'The Material Culture of Nanotechnology', in: H. Fogelberg & H. Glimell, *Bringing Visibility to the Invisible: Towards A Social Understanding of Nanotechnology*, Göteborg: Göteborg University, pp. 99-114.

Frazier, G., "An Ideology For Nanoelectronics," in *Concurrent Computations: Algorithms, Architecture, and Technology*, Plenum Press, New York, 1988.

Glimell, H.: 2001, 'Challenging Limits ' Excerpts from an Emerging Ethnography of Nano Physicists', in: H. Glimell & O. Johlin (eds.), *The Social Production of Technology: On the Everyday Life with Things*, Göteburg, SE: BAS Publisher, chapter 7, pp. 111-131 (reprinted in: H. Fogelberg & H. Glimell, *Bringing Visibility to the Invisible: Towards A Social Understanding of Nanotechnology*, Göteborg: Göteborg University, pp. 115-139.

Glimell, H.: 2001, 'Dynamics of the Emerging Field of Nanoscience', in: M.C. Roco and W.S. Bainbridge (eds.), *Societal Implications of Nanoscience and Nanotechnology*, Dordrecht: Kluwer, pp. 156-160.

Glimell, H.: 2003, 'A Nano Narrative: The Mircopolitics of a New Generic Enabling Technology', in: H. Fogelberg & H. Glimell, *Bringing Visibility to the Invisible: Towards A Social Understanding of Nanotechnology*, Göteborg: Göteborg University, pp. 55-77 [www.sts.gu.se/publications/STS_report_6.pdf].

Glimell, H.: 2003, 'Dynamics of the Emerging Field of Nanoscience', in: H. Fogelberg & H. Glimell, *Bringing Visibility to the Invisible: Towards A Social Understanding of Nanotechnology*, Göteborg: Göteborg University, pp. 79-85 [www.sts.gu.se/publications/STS_report_6.pdf].

Glimell, H.: 2004, 'Grand Visions and Lilliput Politics: Staging the Exploration of the 'Endless Frontier", in: D. Baird, A. Nordmann & J. Schummer (eds.), *Discovering the Nanoscale*, Amsterdam: IOS Press, pp. 231-246.

Goldhaber-Gordon, D., Montemerlo, M.S., Love, J.C., Opiteck, G.J., and Ellenbogen, J.C., "Overview of Nanoelectronic Devices," submitted to the *Proceedings of the IEEE*, February 1997. For more information, please send e-mail to nanotech@mitre.org.

Gorman, M.E.; Groves, J.F. & Shrager, J.: 2004, 'Societal Dimensions of Nanotechnology as a Trading Zone: Results from a Pilot Project', in: D. Baird, A. Nordmann & J. Schummer (eds.), *Discovering the Nanoscale*, Amsterdam: IOS Press, pp. 63-73.

Grinbaum, A. & Dupuy, J.-P.: 2004, 'Living with Uncertainty: Toward the Ongoing Normative Assessment of Nanotechnology', *Techne: Research in Philosophy and Technology*, 8(3) (forthcoming).

Grinbaum, A.: 2004, 'La condition de l'homme moderne et les nanotechnologies', in: G. Nivat (ed.), *Les limites de l'humain. 39èmes Rencontres Internationales de Genève*, L'Age d'Homme, Genève, p. 141.

Grunwald, A.: 2004, 'Ethische Aspekte der Nanotechnologie. Eine Felderkundung', *Technikfolgenabschätzung ' Theorie und Praxis*, 13 (2), 71-78.

Gupta, V.K. & Pangannaya, N.B.: 2000, 'Carbon nanotubes: bibliometric analysis of patents', *World Patent Information*, 22, 185-189.

Hansson, S.O.: 2004, 'Great Uncertainty about Small Things', *Techne: Research in Philosophy and Technology*, 8(3) (forthcoming).

Haruta, M. 1997. *Catalyst surveys of Japan* 1:61 and references therein.

Hennig, J.: 2004, 'Changes in the Design of Scanning Tunneling Microscopic Images from 1980 to 1990', *Techne: Research in Philosophy and Technology*, 8(3) (forthcoming).

Hessenbruch, A.: 2004, 'Nanotechnology and the Negotiation of Novelty', in: D. Baird, A. Nordmann & J. Schummer (eds.), *Discovering the Nanoscale*, Amsterdam: IOS Press, pp. 135-144.

Hullmann, A. & Meyer, M.: 2003, 'Publications and Patents in Nanotechnology. An overview of previous studies and the state of the art', *Scientometrics*, 58 (3) 507-527.

Huo, Q., D.I. Margolese, U. Ciesla, P. Feng, T.E. Gier, P. Sieger, R. Leon, P.M. Petroff, F. Schuth, and G.D. Stucky. 1994. *Nature* 368:317.

Jena, P., S.N. Khanna, and B.K. Rao. 1996. In *Science and technology of atomically engineered materials*, ed. P. Jena. River Edge, NJ: World Scientific.

Johansson, M.: 2003, 'Plenty of room at the bottom: Towards an anthropology of nanoscience', *Anthropology Today*, 19 (No. 6), 3-6.

Johnson, A.: 2004, 'The End of Pure Science: Science Policy from Bayh-Dole to the NNI', in: D. Baird, A. Nordmann & J. Schummer (eds.), *Discovering the Nanoscale*, Amsterdam: IOS Press, pp. 217-230.

Jounet, C., W.K. Maser, P. Bernier, A. Loiseau, M. Lamy de la Chapelle, S. Lefrant, P. Deniard, R. Lee, and J.E. Fischer. 1997. *Nature* 388:756.

K.E. Drexler, *Nanosystems: Molecular Machinery, Manufacturing, and Computation*, Wiley, New York, 1992.

Karger, J., and D.M. Ruthven. 1992. *Diffusion in zeolites*. New York: J. Wiley.

Keiper, A.: 2003, 'The Nanotechnology Revolution', *The New Atlantis*, 2, 17-34.

Khushf, G.: 2004, 'A Hierarchical Architecture for Nano-scale Science and Technology: Taking Stock of the Claims About Science Made By Advocates of NBIC Convergence', in: D. Baird, A. Nordmann & J. Schummer (eds.), *Discovering the Nanoscale*, Amsterdam: IOS Press, pp. 21-33.

Khushf, G.: 2004, 'Systems Theory and the Ethics of Human Enhancement: A Framework for NBIC Convergence', *Annals of the New York Academy of Sciences*, 1013, 124-149.

Krätschmer, W., L.D. Lamb, K. Fostiropoulos, and D.R. Huffman. 1990. *Nature* 347:354.

Kresge, C.T., M.E. Leonowicz, W.J. Roth, J.C. Vartuli, and J.S. Beck. 1992. *Nature* 359:710.

Kupperman, A., S. Nadimi, S. Oliver, G. Ozin, J. Garcés, and M. Olken. 1993. *Nature* 365:239.

Kuusi, O.; Meyer, M.: 2002, 'Technological generalizations and leitbilder ' the anticipation of technological opportunities', *Technological Forecasting & Social Change*, 69, 625-639.

Landon, B.: 2004, 'Less is More: Much Less is Much More: The Insistent Allure of Nanotechnology Narratives in Science Fiction', in: N.K. Hayles (ed.), *Nanoculture: Implications of the New Technoscience*, Bristol, UK: Intellect Books, pp. 131-146.

Laszlo, P.: 2004, 'Is There Life After Partington?', *Hyle: International Journal for Philosophy of Chemistry*, 10(2), 169-178.

Lenhard, J.: 2004, 'Nanoscience and the Janus-Faced Character of Simulations', in: D. Baird, A. Nordmann & J. Schummer (eds.), *Discovering the Nanoscale*, Amsterdam: IOS Press, pp. 93-100.

Lent, C.S., Tougaw, P.D., Porod, W., Bernstein, G.H., "Quantum Cellular Automata," *Nanotechnology*, Vol. 4, p. 49, 1993.

Lewak, S.E.: 2004, 'What's the Buzz? Tell Me What's A-Happening: Wonder, Nanotechnology, and Alice's Adventures in Wonderland', in: N.K. Hayles (ed.), *Nanoculture: Implications of the New Technoscience*, Bristol, UK: Intellect Books, pp. 201-.

Lide, D.R., ed. 1993-1994. *CRC Handbook of Chemistry and Physics*, 74th ed.

Lin-Easton, P.C.: 2001, 'It's Time for Environmentalists to Think Small ' Real Small: A Call for the Involvement of Environmental Lawyers in Developing Precautionary Policies Molecular Nanotechnology', *Georgetown International Law Review*, 14, 106-134.

López, J.: 2004, 'Bridging the Gaps: Science Fiction in Nanotechnology', *Hyle: International Journal for Philosophy of Chemistry*, 10(2), 129-152.

Lösch, A.: 2004, 'Nanomedicine and Space: Discursive Orders of Mediating Innovations', in: D. Baird, A. Nordmann & J. Schummer (eds.), *Discovering the Nanoscale*, Amsterdam: IOS Press, pp. 193-202.

Marshall, K.: 2004, 'Atomizing the Risk Technology', in: N.K. Hayles (ed.), *Nanoculture: Implications of the New Technoscience*, Bristol, UK: Intellect Books, pp. 147-160.

Martin, T.P., N. Malinowski, U. Zimmerman, U. Naher, and H. Schaber. 1993. *J. Chem. Phys*. 99:4210.

Martin, T.P., U. Naher, H. Schaber, U. Zimmerman. 1993. *Phys. Rev. Lett.* 70:3079.

Mayer, S.: 2002, 'From genetic modification to nanotechnology: the dangers of 'sound science", in: T. Gilland (ed.), *Science: Can We Trust the Experts?*, London: Hodder and Stoughton, pp. 1-15.

Mehta, M.D.: 2002, 'Nanoscience and Nanotechnology: Assessing the Nature of Innovation in These Fields', *Bulletin of Science, Technology & Society*, 22(4), 269-273.

Mehta, M.D.: 2004, 'From Biotechnology to Nanotechnology: What Can We Learn from Earlier Technologies?, *Bulletin of Science, Technology & Society*, 24, 34-39.

Meyer, M. & Kuusi, O.: 2004, 'Nanotechnology: Generalizations in an Interdisciplinary Field of Science and Technology', *Hyle: International Journal for Philosophy of Chemistry*, 10(2), 153-168.

Meyer, M.: 2000a, 'Does science push technology? Patents citing scientific literature', *Research Policy*, 29, 409-434.

Meyer, M.: 2000b, 'Patent citations in a novel field of technology: What can they tell about interactions of emerging communities of science and technology?', *Scientometrics*, 48, 151-178.

Meyer, M.: 2001a, 'Patent citations in a novel field of technology: An exploration of nano-science and nano-technology', *Scientometrics*, 51, 163-183.

Meyer, M.: 2001b, 'Socio-economic Research on Nanoscale Science and Technology: A European Overview and Illustration', in: M.C. Roco and W.S. Bainbridge (eds.), *Societal Implications of Nanoscience and Nanotechnology*, Dordrecht: Kluwer, pp. 217-241.

Meyer, M.; Persson, O.: 1998, 'Nanotechnology' interdisciplinarity, patterns of collaboration and differences in application', *Scientometrics*, 47, 195'205.

Milburn, C.: 2002, 'Nanotechnology in the age of post-human engineering: science fiction as science', *Configurations*, 10, 261-295 [reprinted in: N.K. Hayles (ed.), *Nanoculture: Implications of the New Technoscience*, Bristol, UK: Intellect Books, 2004, pp. 109-130].

Milburn, C.: 2004, 'Nano/Splatter: Disintegrating the Postbiological Body', *New Literary History*, 35 (in print).

Mnyusiwalla, A.; Abdallah, S.D.; Singer, P.A.: 2003, 'Mind the gap: science and ethics in nanotechnology', *Nanotechnology*, 14, R9-R13.

Mody, C.C.M.: 2004, 'How Probe Microscopists Became Nanotechnologists', in: D. Baird, A. Nordmann & J. Schummer (eds.), *Discovering the Nanoscale*, Amsterdam: IOS Press, pp. 119-133.

Mody, C.C.M.: 2004, 'Instruments in Training: The Growth of American Probe Microscopy in the 1980s', in: D. Kaiser (ed.), *Pedagogy and the Practice of Science: Producing Physical Scientists, 1800-2000*, Cambridge, MA: MIT Press (forthcoming).

Mody, C.C.M.: 2004, 'Small, but Determined: Technological Determinism in Nanoscience', *Hyle: International Journal for Philosophy of Chemistry*, 10(2), 99-128.

Mody, C.C.M.: 2004, *Crafting the Tools of Knowledge: The Invention, Spread, and Commercialization of Probe Microscopy, 1960-2000*, Ph.D. dissertation, Cornell University.

Montemerlo, M.S., Love, J.C., Opiteck, G.J., Goldhaber, D. J., and Ellenbogen, J.C., "Technologies and Designs for Electronic Nanocomputers," MITRE Technical Report 96W0000044, The MITRE Corporation, McLean, VA, July 1996. For more information, send e-mail to nanotech@mitre.org.

Moor, J.H. & Weckert, J.: 2004, 'Nanoethics: Assessing the Nanoscale From an Ethical Point of View', in: D. Baird, A. Nordmann & J. Schummer (eds.), *Discovering the Nanoscale*, Amsterdam: IOS Press, pp. 301-310.

Munn Sanchez, E.: 2004, 'The Expert's Role in Nanoscience and Technology', in: D. Baird, A. Nordmann & J. Schummer (eds.), *Discovering the Nanoscale*, Amsterdam: IOS Press, pp. 257-266.

Nordmann, A.: 2003, 'Shaping the World Atom by Atom: Eine nanowissenschaftliche WeltBildanalyse', in: A. Grunwald (ed.), *Technikgestaltung zwischen Wunsch und Wirklichkeit*, Berlin: Springer, pp. 191-199.

Nordmann, A.: 2004, 'Molecular Disjunctions: Staking Claims at the Nanoscale', in: D. Baird, A. Nordmann & J. Schummer (eds.), *Discovering the Nanoscale*, Amsterdam: IOS Press, pp. 51-62.

Nordmann, A.: 2004, 'Nanotechnology: Convergence and Integration', Presentation at *EuroNanoForum, Trieste, December 10, 2003* (Proceedings in preparation).

Nordmann, A.: 2004, 'Nanotechnology's WorldView: New Space for Old Cosmologies', *IEEE Technology and Society Magazine*, 23.

Nordmann, A.: 2004, 'Social Imagination for Nanotechnology', in: European Commission (Community Health and Consumer Protection): *Nanotechnologies: A Preliminary Risk Analysis on the Basis of a Workshop, Brussels, 1-2 March 2004*, pp. 111-113 [www.europa.eu.int/comm/health/ph_risk/documents/ev_20040301_en.pdf].

Nordmann, A.: 2004, 'Was ist TechnoWissenschaft? ' Zum Wandel der Wissenschaftskultur am Beispiel von Nanoforschung und Bionik', in: T. Rossmann & C. Tropea (eds.), *Bionik ' Neue Forschungsergebnisse aus Natur-, Ingenieur- und Geisteswissenschaften*, Berlin: Springer, 2004 (forthcoming)

Paschen, H.; Coenen, C.; Fleischer, T.; Grünwald, R.; Oertel, D. & Revermann, C.: 2004, *Nanotechnologie: Forschung, Entwicklung, Anwendung*, Berlin: Springer (*Nanotechnologie, TAB-Arbeitsbericht 92*, Berlin: Büro für Technikfolgen-Abschätzung beim Deutschen Bundestag).

Pitt, J.C.: 2004, 'The Epistemology of the Very Small', in: D. Baird, A. Nordmann & J. Schummer (eds.), *Discovering the Nanoscale*, Amsterdam: IOS Press, pp. 157-163.

Pressman, J.: 2004, 'Nano Narrative: A Parable from Electronic Literature', in: N.K. Hayles (ed.), *Nanoculture: Implications of the New Technoscience*, Bristol, UK: Intellect Books, pp. 191-200.

Prigogine, I., and S. Rice. 1988. *Advances in chemical physics*, Vol. 70, Parts 1 & 2. New York: J. Wiley.

Rao, M.B., and S. Sircar. 1993. *Gas Separation and Purification* 7:279.

Reed, M.A., "Quantum Dots," *Scientific American*, January 1993, pp. 118-123.

Roberts, J.A.: 2004, 'Deciding the Future of Nanotechnologies: Legal Perspectives on Issues of Democracy and Technology', in: D. Baird, A. Nordmann & J. Schummer (eds.), *Discovering the Nanoscale*, Amsterdam: IOS Press, pp. 247-255.

Robinson, C.: 2004, 'Images in NanoScience/Technology', in: D. Baird, A. Nordmann & J. Schummer (eds.), *Discovering the Nanoscale*, Amsterdam: IOS Press, pp. 165-169.

Robison, W.L.: 2004, 'Nano-Ethics', in: D. Baird, A. Nordmann & J. Schummer (eds.), *Discovering the Nanoscale*, Amsterdam: IOS Press, pp. 285-300.

Roco, M.C. & Bainbridge, W.S. (eds.): 2001, *Societal implications of nanoscience and nanotechnology*, (Proceedings of a workshop organized by the National Science Foundation, September 28-29, 2000), Kluwer: Dordrecht [available online at http://itri.loyola.edu/nano/societalimpact/nanosi.pdf]

Roco, M.C. & Tomellini, R. (eds.): 2002, *Nanotechnology: Revolutionary Opportunities and Societal Implications, Workshop, Lecce (Italy), 31 January - 1 February 2002*, Luxemburg: Office for Official Publications of the European Communities, [200 pp.]

Roco, M.C.; Bainbridge, W.S. (eds.): 2002, *Converging Technologies for Improving Human Performance: Nanotechnology, Biotechnology, Information Technology and the Cognitive Science*, Arlington, VA: National Science Foundation.

Roher, H. 1993. *Jpn. J. Appl. Phys*. 32:1335.

Rohlfing, E.A., D.M. Cox, and A. Kaldor. 1984. *J. Chem. Phys*. 81:3846.

Rosen, A. 1998. A periodic table in three dimensions: A sightseeing tour in the nanometer world. In *Advances in quantum chemistry*. In press.

Ruthven, D.M., S. Farooq, K.S. Knaebel. 1994. *Pressure swing adsorption*. New York: VCH Publishers.

Sarewitz, D.; Woodhouse, E.: 2003, 'Small is Powerful', in: A. Lightman, D. Sarewitz & Chr. Desser, (eds.), *Living with the Genie: Essays on Technology and the Quest for Human Mastery*, Washington, DC: Island Press, pp. 63-83.

Schiemann, G.: 2004, 'Dissolution of the Nature-Technology Dichotomy? Perspectives on Nanotechnology from an Everyday Understanding of Nature', in: D. Baird, A. Nordmann & J. Schummer (eds.), *Discovering the Nanoscale*, Amsterdam: IOS Press, pp. 209-213.

Schmidt, J.C.: 2004, 'Unbounded Technologies: Working Through Technological Reductionism of Nanotechnology', in: D. Baird, A. Nordmann & J. Schummer (eds.), *Discovering the Nanoscale*, Amsterdam: IOS Press, pp. 35-50.

Schuler, E.: 2004, 'Perception of Risks and Nanotechnology', in: D. Baird, A. Nordmann & J. Schummer (eds.), *Discovering the Nanoscale*, Amsterdam: IOS Press, pp. 279-284.

Schummer, J.: 2001, 'Ethics of Chemical Synthesis', *Hyle: International Journal for Philosophy of Chemistry*, 7, 103-124 [online: www.hyle.org/journal/issues/7/schummer.htm].

Schummer, J.: 2003, 'Aesthetics of Chemical Products: Materials, Molecules, and Molecular Models', *Hyle: International Journal for Philosophy of Chemistry*, 9, 73-104 [online: www.hyle.org/journal/issues/9-1/schummer.htm].

Schummer, J.: 2003, 'The Notion of Nature in Chemistry', *Studies in History and Philosophy of Science*, 34 (2003), 705-736.

Schummer, J.: 2004, 'Interdisciplinary Issues in Nanoscale Research', in: D. Baird, A. Nordmann & J. Schummer (eds.), *Discovering the Nanoscale*, Amsterdam: IOS Press, pp. 9-20.

Schummer, J.: 2004, 'Multidisciplinarity, Interdisciplinarity, and Patterns of Research Collaboration in Nanoscience and Nanotechnology', *Scientometrics*, 59, 425-465.

Schummer, J.: 2004, 'Naturverhältnisse in der modernen Wirkstoff-Forschung', in: K. Kornwachs (ed.), *Technik ' System ' Verantwortung*, Münster: LIT, pp. 629-638.

Schummer, J.: 2004, 'Why do Chemists Perform Experiments?', in: D. Sobczynska, P. Zeidler, E. Zielonacka-Lis (eds.), *Chemistry in the Philosophical Melting Pot*, Peter Lang (Frankfurt/M.), 2004, pp. 395-410.

Schummer, J.: 2005, 'Reading Nano: The Public Interest in Nanotechnology as Reflected in Book Purchase Patterns", *Public Understanding of Science*, 14 (2) (forthcoming).

Schummer, J.; Baird, D. (eds.): 2004-5, *Nanotech Challenges*, joint special issue of *Hyle: International Journal for Philosophy of Chemistry & Techne: Research in Philosophy and Technology* (forthcoming).

Schwarz, A.E.: 2004, 'Shrinking the 'Ecological Footprint' with NanoTechnoScience?', in: D. Baird, A. Nordmann & J. Schummer (eds.), *Discovering the Nanoscale*, Amsterdam: IOS Press, pp. 203-208.

Schwarz, R.B. 1998. Storage of hydrogen in powders with nanosized crystalline domains. In *R&D status and trends*, ed. Siegel et al.

Siegel, R.W., E. Hu, and M.C. Roco, eds. 1998. *R&D status and trends in nanoparticles, nanostructured materials, and nanodevices in the United States*. Baltimore: Loyola College, International Technology Research Institute. NTIS #PB98-117914.

Stix Gary., "Toward 'Point One'," *Scientific American*, February 1995, pp. 90-95.

Stuckless, J.T, D.E. Starr, D.J. Bald, C.T. Campbell. 1997. *J. Chem. Phys*. 107:5547.

Suchman, M.: 2001, 'Envisioning Life on the Nano-Frontier', in: M.C. Roco and W.S. Bainbridge (eds.), *Societal Implications of Nanoscience and Nanotechnology*, Dordrecht: Kluwer, pp. 211-216.

Suchman, M.: 2002, 'Social Science and Nanotechnologies', M. Roco & R. Tomellini (eds.), *Nanotechnology ' Revolutionary Opportunities and Societal Implications*, Luxembourg: European Communities, pp. 95-99.

Sweeney, A.E.; Seal, S. & Vaidyanathan, P.: 2003, 'The promises and perils of nanoscience and nanotechnology: Exploring emerging social and ethical issues', *Bulletin of Science, Technology & Society*, 23 (4), 236-245.

Swiss Re: 2004, *Nanotechnology: Small Matter, Many Unknowns*, Zurich: Swiss Re [www.swissre.com].

Index

S

T

U

V

W

Y